The American West and the Nazi East

The American West and the Nazi East

A Comparative and Interpretive Perspective

Carroll P. Kakel III

Research Historian and Lecturer, Johns Hopkins University Center for Liberal Arts

First published 2011
First published in paperback 2013 by
PALGRAVE MACMILLAN

Palgrave Macmillan in the UK is an imprint of Macmillan Publishers Limited, registered in England, company number 785998, of Houndmills, Basingstoke, Hampshire RG21 6XS.

Palgrave Macmillan in the US is a division of St Martin's Press LLC, 175 Fifth Avenue, New York, NY 10010.

Palgrave Macmillan is the global academic imprint of the above companies and has companies and representatives throughout the world.

Palgrave® and Macmillan® are registered trademarks in the United States, the United Kingdom, Europe and other countries.

ISBN 978–0–230–27515–7 hardback
ISBN 978–1–137–35273–6 paperback

A catalogue record for this book is available from the British Library.

A catalog record for this book is available from the Library of Congress.

Transferred to Digital Printing in 2013

To the memory of my father and mother, with love

If the jigsaw puzzle does not work out, the reason may be not that some pieces are missing but that we have set it up wrongly.

Geoffrey Barraclough

Remaining faithful to the complexities and contingencies of the past need not entail abandoning the search for patterns and logics.

A. Dirk Moses

Contents

List of Illustrations and Maps

Illustrations

1 Covered wagons headed 'west'. A 'wagon train' of American 'settlers' heads 'west' across the northern plains to seek their individual 'manifest destinies' in America's 'western empire'.

2 Covered wagons headed 'east'. A covered 'waggon convoy' of German 'settlers' stops to rest before resuming their journey to a new life in the Nazi 'eastern empire'.

3 Pioneers in the 'American West'. A family of 'homesteaders' on the northern plains pose for a photo in front of their new home (called a 'sod house') in Custer County, Nebraska.

4 Pioneers in the 'Nazi East'. In the *Reichsgau Wartheland* (areas of western Poland annexed by Nazi Germany), a 'settler' family is visited by a nurse from the National Socialist Volunteers (NSV).

5 Forced 'removal' in the 'American West'. US Army troops oversee a group of Navajo Indians who have been forcibly 'removed' from their homes and 'force-marched' to a military reservation at Fort Sumner, New Mexico.

6 Forced 'removal' in the 'Nazi East'. German police and SS personnel oversee the forced 'removal' and forced 'resettlement' of Poles from their homes in Sol, Katowice, Poland, to an internment camp.

7 Attrition in the 'American West'. Indians line up to receive their often inadequate food rations on 'ration day' at the Pine Ridge Agency Reservation in South Dakota.

8 Attrition in the 'Nazi East'. Jews in the Lodz Ghetto (Poland) wait outside Kitchen #452 to receive their meagre food rations.

9 Mass shooting in the 'American West'. Sioux Indian civilians shot by the US Army Seventh Cavalry during the 1890 Wounded Knee massacre in South Dakota are buried in a mass grave.

Maps

Note: 'USHMM' is an abbreviation for the United States Holocaust
Memorial Museum. The views and opinions expressed in this book and
the context in which the images are used do not necessarily reflect
the views or policy of, nor imply approval or endorsement by, the US
Holocaust Memorial Museum.

Preface

Like most first scholarly books, this book had its origins in research undertaken for a doctoral degree. Unlike most first books, however, it had an unusually long gestation period, spanning almost 40 years. This book is about historical questions framed by more than four decades of engagement with the histories and historiographies of Early America and Nazi Germany, an engagement recently focused on their respective national expansionist projects in the 'American West' and the 'Nazi East'. It is also informed by the emerging field of genocide studies (an offspring of the longer-standing discipline of Holocaust studies), a field that encourages us to ask new questions about supposedly familiar historical events and periods.

As a lifelong learner, I am indebted to inspiring teachers from some 40 years ago who instilled in me a love for history and historical inquiry: Robert Kragalott of Ohio Wesleyan University and Norman Rich of Brown University. When I decided to 'go back to school', a new generation of scholars gave me a window onto new trends, themes, and debates in the historiography (as well as the benefits of interdisciplinary studies) and provided me with invaluable support and critical guidance during my postgraduate studies: Ron Walters and Paul Kramer of The Johns Hopkins University; and Dan Stone and Robert Eaglestone of Royal Holloway, University of London.

My primary academic debt is, of course, to my PhD thesis supervisor, Dan Stone, for agreeing to sponsor my doctoral project, for his support of my topic and proposed research methodology, for his constructive feedback and unceasing encouragement, and, most of all, for his example as a model scholar, teacher, and mentor. Along the way, talks with fellow junior and senior colleagues helped me discover the book I happened to be writing as I was researching and writing my PhD thesis in modern history. My PhD thesis examiners, Jürgen Zimmerer and Gail MacLeitch, offered useful suggestions that ultimately helped in the transformation of my manuscript from a thesis to a book. The publishing professionals at Palgrave Macmillan provided a warm and enthusiastic welcome, for a first-time author, to the world of academic publishing. In addition, two anonymous readers gave a careful and thoughtful reading to my manuscript and supplied me with insightful comments, which led to important revisions and, in the end, a much better book.

Thanks to the following institutions for providing opportunities for me to test (and shape) my thesis and book arguments in front of a critical audience: Postgraduate Research Forum, Department of History, Royal Holloway, University of London; Workshop on Genocide and Colonialism, Department of German, Royal Holloway, University of London and the Imperial War Museum (London); the 12th Annual Postgraduate Students' Conference, German Historical Institute (London); and the First International Graduate Students' Conference on Holocaust and Genocide Studies, Clark University, Strassler Family Center for Holocaust and Genocide Studies (USA). Thanks also to numerous scholars who willingly and enthusiastically provided me with articles, papers, book chapters, or books in advance of publication. And thanks to the following libraries where I conducted the majority of my research: University of London Library (Senate House), The Wiener Library, The Library of Congress, and the Sheridan Libraries of The Johns Hopkins University.

On the home front, thanks to my former employer, Marsh USA Inc., for granting me a sabbatical to read, think, and write about a 'non-business pursuit' and for allowing me numerous liberal leaves of absence, over five years, to 'do history'. Above all, special thanks to my family – especially my wife, Lois – for supporting my obsession with history's 'unyielding questions' (in spite of the many sacrifices it entailed) and without whose support this project would have remained a distant and unfulfilled dream. And thanks to my grandchildren for providing me welcome and entertaining distractions from the mostly solitary undertakings of researching and writing a PhD thesis, and then of transforming the thesis into a book. Hopefully, there will be some lovers of history among them.

Introduction

In private conversations during the Second World War, German leader Adolf Hitler frequently compared the German war for *Lebensraum* (living space) in 'the East' to the colonial wars waged by the nineteenth century's Euro-American great powers. The Slavic world, he believed, had to be conquered and colonized and its population vanquished. Completion of this 'colonizing mission' inevitably demanded the destruction of the 'natives', as a result of methods similar to those used in the conquest of the 'American West'. In a monologue to his close associates, Hitler declared, 'There is only one duty: to Germanize ["the East"] by the immigration of Germans, and to look upon the natives as Redskins.' He also compared the quelling of partisan resistance in the 'Wild East' to 'the struggle in North America against the Red Indians'.[1] According to his understanding, the American 'Nordics' had colonized 'the West' after they had 'shot down the millions of redskins to a few hundred thousand'.[2] 'Here in the [E]ast', Hitler predicted, 'a similar process will repeat itself for a second time as in the conquest of America.'[3]

These (and other) scattered references have allowed numerous scholars to suggest that Hitler modelled his concept of *Lebensraum* and colonial expansion in the 'Nazi East', as well as his treatment of indigenous Slavs and Jews, on American westward expansion and US Indian policy. For instance, Norman Rich, a historian of Nazi Germany, has argued that '[the] United States policy of westward expansion, in the course of which the white men ruthlessly thrust aside the "inferior" indigenous population, served as the model for Hitler's entire concept of *Lebensraum*'.[4] 'Hitler modeled his conquest of the East', political scientist Norman Finkelstein notes, 'on the American conquest of the West.'[5] Native American scholar-activist Ward Churchill argues that Hitler 'explicitly anchor[ed] his concept of *Lebensraumpolitik* ("politics

1

of living space") directly upon U.S. practice against American Indians'.[6] And genocide scholar Robert Cribb more broadly asserts that there is a 'clear parallel' between the 'actions of [colonizing] Western settlers in the lands of indigenous peoples and the policies of Nazi Germany in eastern Europe'.[7]

Yet despite the highly suggestive nature of Hitler's references, as well as scholarly claims based on these references, there exists no sustained comparison of the 'American West' and the 'Nazi East' in the scholarly literature. This book was written to fill that 'gap'.

This project was motivated by a number of specific questions: Was the American campaign of violence against Native American communities equivalent in ideology and/or practice to the Nazi genocides? Or were they similar enough in other dimensions to prompt more comparative research? Can we make valid comparisons between these two cases of extreme political violence? Is there, in fact, more to it than the above scattered references by Hitler? Was the Nazi conquest of 'the East' a consequence of conscious imitation of the American model? Or were these separate efforts to resolve very similar problems? In Hitler's vision, were 'the Jews' and/or 'the Slavs' to become Europe's 'Indians'?

In the search for answers, this book will explore the conceptual and historical relations between the Early American dispossession and destruction of Native American communities in the 'American West' and the Nazi genocide of European Jews and Slavs in the 'Nazi East'. These two cases of extreme political violence, moreover, will be investigated within the broader contexts of the Early American and Nazi-German national projects of territorial expansion, racial cleansing, and settler colonization in their respective 'western' and 'eastern' empires.

Some readers, no doubt, may have difficulty with the notion of any comparison between Early America and Nazi Germany, between the actions and policies of a democratic society and a totalitarian regime. As genocide scholar Robert Melson observes, however, the comparison of two or more cases of mass violence 'do[es] not imply that they are identical or even similar'.[8] 'Comparison', he reminds us, 'does not imply equivalence.'[9] Other readers, adhering to a belief in the Holocaust's 'uniqueness', may reject the idea that the Holocaust can or should be compared to other cases of mass political violence. Nonetheless, one of the 'founding fathers' of Holocaust studies, Israeli historian Yehuda Bauer, rightly argues that 'a deeper understanding of the Holocaust obligates us to make comparisons'.[10] For if the Holocaust is not compared to past and contemporary instances of genocide, its message and significance will wither and fade.[11]

This book targets a wide audience. Consistent with this broad audience, it seeks to offer meaningful benefits to each category of readers. Undergraduate students, for instance, will find that this book places the national histories of Early America and Nazi Germany in a new and, hopefully, enlightening context. Postgraduate history students will find arguments that challenge those of many specialist historians of the respective national periods, as well as counterfactual glimpses that undermine overdetermined historical narratives and return contingency to history. Through a comparative approach, specialists in the history of the Early American Republic or in the history of Nazi Germany will discover underlying empirical patterns and insights that a single country analysis often obscures, minimizes, or ignores completely. Students and researchers in the field of Holocaust and genocide studies will find a comparative look at two distinct (but linked) cases of extreme political violence, at parallel histories that shed light on the intimate relations between the larger historical phenomena of imperialism, colonialism, and genocide, as well as on the genocide and colonialism nexus. General readers and 'history buffs' will discover an alternative explanatory and interpretive framework for events previously presented as 'American western expansion' or 'the Second World War'.

In these pages, the reader will find a fresh approach to familiar events, including new ways to read, compare, and connect these two historical experiences. By its comparative approach, moreover, the reader will gain important insights into the respective national histories. Rather than an exception to imperialism, colonialism, and genocide, as most historians contend, Early American western expansion and the resulting campaign of extreme political violence against Native American communities are very much a central part of these histories. Violence and American expansion progressed hand in hand across the North American continent. Far from being an inexplicable anomaly, as some Holocaust scholars argue, much Nazi genocidal violence and many of the events we have come to call the Holocaust were a radicalized blend of several forms of mass political violence whose patterns, logics, and pathologies[12] can be located in the Early American project, a project which provides a unique window onto the colonial origins, context, and content of Nazi genocide (including the Holocaust). And finally, the analogue of the 'American West' and the 'Nazi East' became, in fact, an obsession for Hitler and other Nazi 'true believers', an obsession which, as we shall see, exerted a strong influence on planned and actualized Nazi policies and practices in the 'Wild East'.

Both the 'American West' and the 'Nazi East' were important regions in the respective histories of the Early American Republic and Nazi Germany, regions where major events decisively impacted the historical development of these nation-states, as well as the future of peoples living within and near their borders. In both cases, these regions were the object of obsessive ideological visions held by expansionist political elites who sought to use agricultural settlement to 'obtain' new 'living space' and to achieve enhanced national security. In practice, as political leaders acted on their ideological obsessions, they became the sites of violent national projects of territorial expansion, racial cleansing, and settler colonization – projects with deadly consequences for ethnic and racial 'out-groups'[13] in both metropolitan and colonized 'living space'.

Throughout the first 100 years of American history, America's 'frontiers' were 'transitory Wests'.[14] At different periods in American history, moreover, 'the West' has been differently located. Indeed, every part of the United States 'was once a frontier, every region was once a West'.[15] In the popular and cultural imagination, as well as in some early historical representations, the 'American West' is a triumphalist narrative of heroic American pioneers heading westward to find their individual manifest destinies, in support of the collective national Manifest Destiny. In historical terms, the 'American West', during the early years of the young American Republic, was largely a colonial construct referring to Indian lands (and eventually Hispanic lands in northern Mexico) on the constantly moving western 'frontiers' of 'white' American 'settlement'. These indigenous lands were the object of 'acquisition' by the US government for agricultural settlement by its 'white' settler pioneers and for the establishment of a coast-to-coast empire whose 'destiny', it was claimed, had been made 'manifest' by Providence. The 'American West' was, however, also a series of Indian ancestral homelands, as well as a series of Anglo-American 'frontiers' and 'borderlands'.[16]

As frontier myth, the 'German East' was the European equivalent to the nineteenth-century notion of Manifest Destiny in the 'American West'.[17] In twentieth-century history and memory, the 'Nazi East' was the scene of brutal fighting between the German Army and Soviet military and partisan forces, as well as the site of the Nazi killing centres where Jewish men, women, and children were gassed as part of the 'final solution to the Jewish question'. Within Nazi discourse, 'the East' was an ideologically loaded term[18] used to denote the site of long-held German imperialist designs and Hitler's proposed drive for *Lebensraum* (living space). Like its American counterpart, the 'Nazi East' was also a colonial construct which, for the purposes of this investigation, refers to the eastern border provinces of Germany itself, Poland, the Baltic States, Ukraine, and Russia. During the Nazi era, these lands were the objects of Hitler's *Lebensraumpolitik*, a 'politics' that aimed at 'acquiring' an eastern land-based empire stretching from Germany's eastern borderlands to Russia's Ural Mountains (and beyond). Ideologically driven German National Socialists also referred to the 'Nazi East' as 'the German East', 'the East', or the 'Wild East'.

As subfields of larger fields of historical inquiry, the 'American West' and the 'Nazi East' have been (and are) the subject of massive and rapidly growing historiographies. While 'the West' has attracted the attention of a wide range of political, military, economic, and social historians, 'the East' – as the location of the Second World War's Eastern front in the European theatre and the site of most Nazi genocidal violence – has been largely the purview of historians of military history and the Holocaust. Despite this huge amount of historical attention, however, there remains, in both cases, continuing gaps in our knowledge and understanding about the events that took place in the 'American West' and the 'Nazi East'.

Within the historiography of 'the West', the violence towards Indian peoples that accompanied the 'settlement' of the North American continent 'is at once the most familiar and overlooked subject in American history', a 'violent encounter with the indigenous inhabitants' whose true magnitude 'remains unacknowledged even today'.[19] Historian Ned Blackhawk is correct when he asserts that '[d]espite an outpouring of work over the past decades, those investigating American Indian history and U.S. history more generally have failed to reckon with the violence upon which the continent was built'.[20] Regrettably, the history of the North American 'West', its events and incidents, 'have too seldom been examined in the context of comparative genocide studies'.[21]

Today, almost 60 years on from the events themselves, we still know much more about *how* the Holocaust happened than we do about *why* it happened; among specialists in the field, moreover, there is widespread (and often heated) argument about what 'caused' the Holocaust, as well as general disagreement as to its origins and nature. In addition, too many studies of the Holocaust and Nazi genocide have been done in isolation, with little or no reference to, or consideration of, long-term world historical patterns and processes (although this is happily changing). And finally, many Holocaust historians have resisted studying the Nazi Judeocide within the context of the broader field of genocide studies, insistent on maintaining a distinction between 'the Holocaust' and 'genocide'.

Accordingly, this book has eagerly embraced a new 'optics', using the theoretical and methodological tools and insights from the emerging and increasingly interdisciplinary subfields of transnational colonialism and comparative genocide studies and then applying them to the two cases under investigation. Explicitly rejecting an approach of simply adding 'more facts', this book purposefully sets the 'jigsaw puzzle' up differently, with a combination of empirical and theoretical inquiry dedicated to the 'search for patterns and logics'.

Broadly speaking, this book asks new questions of supposedly familiar historical events and periods. It proceeds from the notion that large historical processes – in this case, imperialism, colonialism, and genocide – can be traced through space and time (that is, in different historical contexts), interacting but not necessarily determining one another. It suggests that historians can productively study world-historical patterns and processes, without losing sight of the local and contingent. It proposes that it is possible for historians to tie discrete events and national histories to transnational and international processes.

Specifically, this is a book about the conceptual and historical relations between the nineteenth-century Early American and twentieth-century Nazi-German national projects of territorial expansion, racial cleansing, and settler colonization, along with their associated campaigns of extreme political violence. This study is explicitly comparative in the sense that both historical experiences are placed side by side for the purposes of investigation. As a work of comparative history, this book seeks to preserve the specificity of the individual cases while, at the same time, demonstrating the value of comparative analysis. As one historian has recently suggested, a serious scholarly comparative study of the 'American West' and the 'German East' should address both 'provocative parallels' and 'contrasts',[22] and this book will follow that judicious advice.

This comparative study proceeds from the analogue of the 'American West' and the 'Nazi East', a point of relation which, as we shall see, provided an historical model – in Hitler's spatial and racial fantasies – for Nazi expansion and racial engineering. As implied by its title, this investigation is both comparative and interpretive in nature. It does not aim (or claim) to be a comprehensive history or a complete historical narrative of the two respective national experiences; instead, it filters specific eras of these national histories through the lenses of imperialism, colonialism, and genocide. This book looks at the expansionist ideologies, actions, and policies of two nation-states: Early America and

Nazi Germany. Its main chronological focus is on Early America from the beginning of its national independence until the closing of the American 'western frontier' (1783–1890) and on Nazi Germany from Hitler's rise to power until its military defeat ended the Second World War in the European theatre (1933–45). Earlier periods in both national histories, however, will be touched on where historical antecedents provide important continuities or legacies to the later historical eras under examination.

Drawing primarily upon the findings of recent scholarship, this study aims to illuminate both the specific national histories of the 'American West' and the 'Nazi East', as well as the intimate relations between the larger historical phenomena of imperialism, colonialism, and genocide. Like all comparative history,[23] it is concerned with similarities and differences between the two cases (giving equal attention to each), and it is characterized by a keen interest in causation (in this case, with the causation of extreme political violence against ethnic and racial 'out-groups'). It aims to offer insights into each case that may have remained unrevealed, marginalized, or undervalued had the study of these two histories continued in isolation.

By changing the angle of vision, and by employing the new 'optics' of transnational colonialism and comparative genocide studies, this book helps us recognize the unexpected and unsettling connections between the 'American West' and the 'Nazi East', linking histories previously thought of by most readers as totally unrelated. Challenging established explanatory and interpretive frameworks within both national historiographies, it offers a fresh empirically and theoretically based alternative reading of these distinct (but linked) histories. On one level, the book provides empirical data about the patterns, logics, and pathologies that link these two national projects, and it gives us fresh ways to read, compare, and connect these two national histories. On another level, it offers overarching explanatory frameworks while, at the same time, respecting the individual characteristics and specificities of each case, as well as the complexities and contingencies of the past.

It is the central argument of this book that the Early American and Nazi-German national projects of territorial expansion, racial cleansing, and settler colonization – despite obvious differences in time and place – were strikingly similar projects of 'space' and 'race', with lethal consequences for 'alien' 'out-groups' in the metropole and for 'unwanted' indigenous peoples in the new colonial 'living space'. The following chapters will show that there are strong continuities and similarities, as well as important differences and crucial links – in both ideology and practice – between the Early American national project in 'the West' and the Nazi-German national project in 'the East'.

In the 'Nazi East', as we shall see, we find echoes, glimpses, and traces of the 'American West'.

This book consists of three parts. Together, these parts contain the six thematically linked chapters; in addition, there is an introductory note to each part, offering a theoretical grounding for the reader on the analytical tools that provide the book's explanatory and interpretive framework. The book's chapters are similarly structured: that is, each chapter sets up a side-by-side examination of the Early American and Nazi German cases, with a focus on the similarities and differences between the two cases under investigation, as well as their historical links to one another. In the book's concluding section, I sum up the two historical experiences, I offer reasons behind the similarities and differences between the two cases (making clear where the similarities end), and I reaffirm the surprising links between the two historical experiences.

Part I, 'Continental Imperialism', looks at two key ideological developments in the Early American Republic and the Nazi Third Reich: the growth of a national ideology of territorial expansion linked to notions of alleged racial superiority, and the evolution of 'race thinking' within the political culture of the nation-state and the broader popular culture. This part uses political theorist Hannah Arendt's notion of 'continental imperialism' as an analytical tool to help conceptualize and explain the comparable ideological underpinnings for proposed territorial expansion in the 'American West' and the 'Nazi East'.

Part II of the book, 'Settler Colonialism', looks at the process and practice of settler colonization, as intended, planned, and actually carried out by the two nation-states in their respective 'western' and 'eastern' empires. In this part, I employ the concept of settler colonialism – as formulated by Patrick Wolfe and other scholars of transnational colonialism – as an analytical tool to help conceptualize and explain a method of conquest and expansion, as well as policies and practices towards indigenous peoples in the new 'living space' of the 'Wild West' and the 'Wild East'.

Part III, 'Frontier Genocide', looks at how 'continental imperialism' and 'settler colonialism' manifested as 'genocide' in the 'American West' and the 'Nazi East'. This part utilizes historical sociologist Martin Shaw's notion of 'genocidal war'[24] to conceptualize and explain how and why distinctive genocidal explosions took place on the 'frontier' colonial peripheries of Early America's 'western empire' and Nazi Germany's 'eastern empire'.

My goal in the pages that follow is not simply to narrate the underlying patterns of empirical similarity that led to extreme political violence in the 'Wild West' and the 'Wild East'. It is, rather, to provide fresh insights into familiar events and to suggest a new way to read, interpret, and understand these events. I hope that, in the end, this book – with its explicitly comparative approach – will lead readers towards a deep revisioning of the 'American West' and the 'Nazi East', based on a balanced and appropriately nuanced understanding of their similarities, differences, and historical links to one another.

Part I

Continental Imperialism

Introductory note

In the classic sense, an 'empire' is a form of political organization which expands its control by conquest or coercion in a premeditated, sustained imperial project, a project featuring a territorial agenda as well as the domination or subjugation of other peoples (who may be subordinated or eliminated).[1] As a transnational structure which rules over territories outside its borders (either remote and overseas or spatially contiguous to the core territory), it often depends on aggressive, coercive, expansionist, hierarchical, and racist forms of power (as well as on the maintenance of social differentiation) and is typically established and maintained by violence (sometimes extreme violence). In the context of 'empire', 'imperialism' is generally used to mean the actions and attitudes that create or uphold formal empires. It can also refer to an attitude or policy advocating territorial expansion, or it can be used as a descriptive term for an expansionist and aggressive foreign policy.[2] As a distinct set of ideas, it refers primarily to a political system based on colonies governed from an imperial metropolitan centre for its own direct or indirect economic benefit. In the modern period, imperialism often involves wars of colonial expansion, focused on extending the sovereignty of nation-states beyond their current boundaries.[3]

In the modern world, imperialism became the organizing principle of world politics. It also became closely linked to 'race' and racial thinking, to a process of racial 'othering'. The process of racial 'othering' is a form of what anthropologist Alexander Laban Hinton has called 'manufacturing difference'.[4] 'Difference, it cannot be stressed enough, is not simply given. It is,' as historian Patrick Wolfe notes, 'the outcome of differentiation, which is an intensely conflictional process.'⁵ In the modern era, 'race' and racial 'othering' provided the categorical boundaries that led to the construction of hierarchical typologies of human difference, based on a racial scale marked by shades of 'inferiority' and 'superiority'.⁶ 'Race' emerged as a socially constructed category of 'difference'. As a social and cultural invention, race became a *'set of beliefs and attitudes about human differences'*, as well as a systematic set of coherent beliefs that conveniently served the needs and desires of their creators.⁷

As a result of this process of racial 'othering', certain categories of people became de-humanized 'out-groups', who constituted an intolerable presence and who, in the majority view, must be – and, indeed, deserved to be – 'removed'. In many historical contexts, this racial 'otherness' came to be bound up with imperialism, providing a convenient legitimizing rationale for policies of expansion, conquest, slavery, removal, and, ultimately, genocide. Within a settler-colonial context, racial 'othering' often became an 'eliminationist' discourse, deprecating and disparaging targeted 'out-groups'. In imperial and colonial contexts, there were two principal ways in which dominant groups constructed an understanding of racial difference: dehumanization and demonization. The dehumanization of 'others' asserted that 'other people inherently lack qualities fundamental to being human in the sense of deserving moral respect, rights, and protection'; lacking certain human capacities, therefore, they 'do not need to be treated as human beings'. By contrast, demonization held that these 'others' are 'literally or figuratively, demonic [and] morally evil'.⁸ In our two cases, as we shall see, an 'eliminationist' logic implied (and, indeed, demanded) an 'eliminationist' solution.

In her seminal book, *The Origins of Totalitarianism* (1951), the German émigré philosopher and political theorist Hannah Arendt posited the notion of 'continental imperialism' as territorial expansion in 'close geographic continuity' to the metropole. As distinguished from overseas imperialism, continental imperialism, she observed, 'does not allow any geographic distance between the methods and institutions of colony and nation'. 'Continental imperialism', she wrote, 'truly begins at home.' While overseas imperialism was premised on racial superiority and on a national 'civilizing' mission, continental imperialism started with 'absolute claims to choseness'. 'Continental imperialism', Arendt asserted, 'therefore, started with a much closer affinity to race concepts, enthusiastically absorbed the tradition of race-thinking, and relied very little on specific experiences.' Its race concepts, moreover, were 'completely ideological in basis and developed much more quickly into a convenient political weapon than similar theories expressed by overseas imperialists which could always claim a certain basis in authentic experience'. As a result, race hatred became 'its central and centralizing issue' and 'an enlarged tribal consciousness' its 'emotional motor'.[9] Arendt's chapter on 'continental imperialism', however, is a Euro-centric analysis, dealing solely with European colonial imperialism. While Arendt ignored the precedent and model of Anglo-American continental imperialism, Hitler and other so-called 'blood and soil' Nazis would place it centre stage, using it as a conscious historical model for Nazi territorial expansion and racial engineering.

Like-minded imperialists and expansionists in Early America and Nazi Germany viewed 'the West' and 'the East', respectively, as the source of new 'living space' for colonization and settlement. In specific historical contexts, both the Early American national project in 'the West' and the Nazi-German national project in 'the East' would become characterized by an explicit imperialism and by an exclusionary nationalism, a convenient fusion of expansionism and racism. Both the Early American and Nazi-German projects of 'space' and 'race' in the 'American West' and the 'Nazi East', respectively, were national projects: that is, they were led by the nation-state, they were widely supported by the national political elites (as well as by many 'ordinary' citizens), and they required vast institutional and material resources.

In the next two chapters, I examine two key ideological developments in the Early American Republic and the Nazi Third Reich: the growth of a national ideology of territorial expansion linked to notions of alleged racial superiority, and the evolution of 'race thinking' within the political culture of the nation-state and the broader popular culture. In both cases, these developments provide the crucial ideological underpinning to aggressive policies of continental expansion and brutal treatment of indigenous peoples in the new settler 'living space'.

Chapter 1, 'Empire', looks at the respective continental expansionist ideological discourses of both nation-states: Manifest Destiny in the Early American Republic and *Lebensraum* in pre-Nazi and Nazi Germany. It sketches the antecedents of both these discourses in earlier historical eras and shows how, in both cases, these pre-histories shaped and influenced the resultant continental imperialist discourse. It examines the main components, ideas, and elements of these ideological discourses and discusses the leading proponents of continental expansionism and empire, as well as those who helped popularize their views. And it discusses individuals and institutions who would serve as 'agents of empire' to carry out political elite expansionist visions in the 'American West' and the 'Nazi East'.

Chapter 2, 'Racial "Othering"', looks at how 'race thinking' became operationalized in the Early American and Nazi-German political and popular cultures. It sketches the antecedents of racial 'otherness' which formed a background for later racial categories and processes of manufacturing 'difference', and it examines how early racial prejudices hardened at crucial moments in their national histories. It describes how, in both cases, these notions of 'difference' and 'otherness' further hardened into newly constructed racial ideologies which served as convenient justifications for policies of expansion, conquest, and racial exclusion. And it shows how specific historical circumstances brought about a radicalization of racial 'othering', as political leaders elected to pursue even more aggressive policies of territorial expansion.

1
Empire: National Projects of 'Space' and 'Race'

Lacking the insatiable appetite for overseas expansion, Early America and Nazi Germany both preferred, instead, to establish a contiguous, land-based continental empire, aimed at finding new land for agrarian settlement, providing food for a growing population, and securing the future of the nation-state. As envisioned by their creators, both projects of empire, moreover, entailed internal national consolidation, as well as the external conquest of indigenous peoples. Both the Early American and Nazi-German expansionist ideologies and projects were informed by the notion of the need for additional 'living space' in concrete, specific geographical areas of expansion and by agreed, general ideological beliefs shared by expansionist political leaders and propagandists.

In the Early American and Nazi-German cases, political leaders were strongly influenced by imperialist discourses, discourses founded on strikingly similar notions of 'space' and 'race'. The declared ideological goal of Early American political leaders and expansionists was to 'acquire' 'living space' in the 'American West' for 'white' agricultural settlement and to 'cleanse' the new 'living space' for 'white' settlers by the displacement of Native Americans. The declared ideological goal of Hitler and radical Nazis was to 'acquire' *Lebensraum* (living space) in 'the East' for 'Aryan' agricultural settlement and to 'cleanse' the new 'living space' for 'Aryan' settlers by the displacement of Jews and Slavs. In both cases, these ideological discourses reflected strongly held political and intellectual elite preoccupations and obsessions with territorial expansion, racial prejudice/division, and an agrarian idealism. Backed by an agrarian state ideology, a commitment to national expansion and notions of racial superiority would serve to reinforce 'eliminationist' thinking in both the 'American West' and the 'Nazi East'.

Throughout its colonial, Revolutionary, and early national periods, many leading American political leaders and opinion-makers eagerly promoted visions of a land-based, continent-wide American empire. For many of these continental visionaries, the notion of a land empire stretching from the Atlantic Ocean to the Pacific Ocean was based on a national 'destiny' made 'manifest' by 'Providence'. In addition, there were strong ideological and racial motivations behind American continental expansion. Along with enhanced security, empire was, in fact, the chief motivation for the creation of a union of states. Right up to the eve of the American Civil War, an expansionist consensus unified the American nation and supplied an ultimate rationale for its existence.[1] In Early American empire-building, 'acquisition' of indigenous lands and 'white' settlement on the American continental landmass were 'the right and left hands of the same imperial organism'.[2]

Nazi Germany's declared mission, as voiced by Hitler and other Nazi 'true believers', was racial empire-building in 'the East'. In Germany, the idea of territorial expansion was focused eastward, on lands adjacent to the German nation-state – especially in Poland and the Baltic States – in what was viewed historically as Germany's 'frontier' territories.[3] During the Nazi era, a consensus formed within German society, backing territorial expansion into the 'eastern lands'. Broad segments of German society, moreover, supported and promoted the national project to transform 'the East' into 'Aryan' German 'living space'.[4] In the eyes of Nazi expansionists, 'the East' was Germany's 'manifest destiny'. Under their leadership, Eastern Europe would become Nazi Germany's 'Wild East', a vast expanse – similar to the 'wide open spaces' of the 'American West' – to be transformed by massacre, racial 'cleansing', and colonial 'settlement'.

Antecedents

In both cases, these expansionist ideologies had inherited legacies that would ultimately influence and shape the resultant continental imperialist discourse. In the American case, the development of British colonial North America provided ideas of providential destiny, as well as strong expansionist impulses, which caused the ruling colonial elite to seek independence from the British metropole in order to build an empire of their own on a continental scale. While the early colonial experience produced the idea of a providential 'right' and 'destiny' of western expansion, the American Revolution provided both the vision and the ideology supporting a continent-wide 'western empire'. In the German case, *Lebensraum* eastern territorial expansion won out over an alternative vision of a maritime-based colonial and commercial empire. In Germany, a prehistory of nationalist, imperialist, and racialist ideas anticipated much of what would become the Nazi worldview, ideas that Hitler would integrate and radicalize into a lethal ideology combining 'racial purification' and territorial expansion. Interestingly, one of *Lebensraum*'s early theorists was part of a transatlantic dialogue with the leading American proponent of the 'frontier thesis' of American history, providing evidence of a shared genealogy between the two expansionist discourses.

Early America

British North America was colonized through conquest, with an expansionist justification built on ideas of providential 'destiny', 'mission', and 'chosenness' to carry out God's will. In the early seventeenth century, the New England Puritans considered themselves the 'chosen' founders of a 'New Israel' in the North American wilderness. Indeed, the powerful Puritan theology of 'chosenness' proved decisive for the course of continental expansion.[5] As economic development propelled the first settlements outward, colonial expansionism found a waiting justification in the Puritan theology/ideology. So strong was their notion of providential and historical 'destiny' that New England's settlers saw the 'clearing' of Native American communities by disease as evidence that God 'intended' the colonists to possess Indian lands. In addition to religious belief, early settlers created self-serving myths as a rationalization for the invasion and conquest of indigenous peoples. The so-called conquest myth, for instance, proclaimed that America was 'virgin land', a 'pristine wilderness', inhabited by 'non-peoples' called 'savages' who were 'incapable of civilization'. Accordingly, European explorers and settlers were commanded by divine sanction or by the necessity of 'progress' to conquer the 'wilderness' and make it a 'garden': to bring 'civilization' to the 'savage wilderness'.

In the early nineteenth century, Manifest Destiny would become a catchphrase for the idea of a providentially or historically sanctioned right to continental expansionism. When it was coined in the 1840s, the notion of America's 'manifest destiny', however, was anything but new. It can be traced back to the earliest moments of English colonization in North America. Already, in 1616, an early agent of British colonization wrote of the colonists as a 'peculiar people marked and chose by the finger of God to possess' the 'vacant' lands of North America.[6] Puritans envisioned that American settlement would be a providential 'city upon a hill'. American ideas of 'empire' date, then, from the first English settlements in Virginia and Massachusetts. 'The early colonies were no sooner established in the seventeenth century', writes historian Richard Van Alstyne, 'than expansionist impulses began to register in each of them. Imperial patterns took shape', he notes, 'and before the middle of the eighteenth century the concept of an empire that would take in the whole continent was fully formed.'[7]

Over time, moreover, many in the ruling colonial elite became convinced that they wanted to rule those territories and indigenous peoples themselves, instead of acting as agents for Great Britain. In the Declaration of Independence, one of the leading Virginian expansionists and land speculators, Thomas Jefferson, charged King George III – among other things – with blocking 'new appropriation of [Indian] lands' by the colonists. Not surprisingly, many of Virginia's most prominent Revolutionary leaders were also major speculators in 'western' lands. Angered by the direction of British colonial policy, they wanted to break away from the British metropole in order to establish their own empire. As leaders of the newly independent American nation, these men would shape the destiny of the new nation. Indeed, there were no more self-assured imperialists than America's 'founding fathers', unbridled imperialists reaching out for 'empire' on a continental scale.[8]

Inherited from the seventeenth century was the notion that the entire North American continent belonged, as of right, to the Anglo-American colonists on the Atlantic coast. Besides a war for political independence, the rebellion against British rule was also a continuation of the fight over Indian land and who was to get it. The new American Republic was, thus, created and fought under the spell of an imperial idea. The same American Revolutionary leaders 'who fought for freedom from the British Empire in the East also fought to create an empire of their own in the West'.[9] The end of the Revolutionary War opened the way for a renewed assault on 'native' lands by backcountry settlers and sent former American soldiers westward, eager to seize the lush Indian lands promised in return for their service to the new nation. The white settlers would pursue their 'happiness' by the 'acquisition' of Indian lands and by dispossessing the 'natives'. In the post-Revolutionary period, the struggle for Indian lands on the 'frontier' became a crucial part of the American national identity.[10]

In a dual struggle, then, American revolutionaries fought for an empire in 'the West' as well as for their own freedom in 'the East' – an empire-building project explicitly based on the invasion, conquest, and dispossession of Native American peoples. For Americans, their successful revolution was a powerful, clear sign that Providence had indeed marked them for greatness. In the end, the American Revolution furnished the vision, the ideology, and the methodology for the new nation to construct its own 'western empire'.[11] Political independence from Britain, then, only strengthened the notion of a continental destiny for Early America's 'white' settler colonists. After achieving its independence, the new American Republic eagerly looked 'west' to build an empire of its own in 'Indian country'. In the American historical experience, independence 'was, simultaneously, both the engine and the product of [western] expansion'.[12]

Nazi Germany

During the years 1890–1914, there were two main Wilhelmine ideologies of German imperialism: *Weltpolitik* (world politics) and *Lebensraum* (living space).[13] German expansionists used the slogan '*Weltpolitik*' to evoke their demand for a colonial and commercial empire to be built largely on German sea power. Alongside *Weltpolitik* grew ideas of territorial expansion in Eastern Europe, taking territory from the 'inferior' Slavs, and gaining *Lebensraum* for the German nation. Germany would thus become both a continental and a world power. These ideologues recognized that a major war was a precondition of *Lebensraum* and saw large-scale annexations in 'the East' as one of the desired outcomes of a general European war. In 1911, the main focus of German foreign policy shifted from *Weltpolitik* to *Kontinentalpolitik* (continental politics), from a policy favouring naval armaments and overseas colonies to one favouring landward expansionism supported by the army. This continental policy of eastward expansionism was based on territorial conquests, new 'living space', colonial settlement policies, and the creation of what was called a 'frontier peasantry'. By 1914, *Lebensraum* imperialism was firmly planted in German political culture.

The new twentieth century, German expansionists argued, should be a 'German century'. Rapid population growth, they claimed, had left Germany a 'people without space'. Furthermore, as a great and expanding power, Germany needed and deserved an empire, and their own 'place in the sun'. In their view, Germany would attain greatness and its rightful place in the world only through expansion and conquest, based on its alleged racial and cultural 'superiority'. These nationalist, imperialist, and racist ideas were quickly taken up by nationalist pressure groups in Wilhelmine Germany. One of these groups, the Pan-German

League (*Alldeutscher Verband*) became the most important organization in the construction of the *Lebensraum* imperialist ideology.

The Pan-German League considered *Lebensraum* as its central programmatic element. The League advocated a radical nationalism, supported a sturdy German frontier peasantry, promoted the supremacy of the 'German race' in world politics, and sought to eliminate the Reich's 'internal enemies' (including socialists and Jews).[14] Inspired by radical and social Darwinist ideas, the League aimed to mobilize all those of the German 'race' in Europe with a Germanism 'cleansed' of internal enemies. It advocated dictatorship and the conquest of *Lebensraum* in 'the East', it opposed international finance capitalism (with its supposed Jewish influence), and it sought to revoke the citizenship of Jews. To the Pan-Germanists, the demand for 'living space' was the key to combating the Jews and the Poles.[15] According to the Pan-Germanists, the individual 'settler-farmer' was the ideal foundation upon which to build a 'new' German national character. In their view, the settlement experience would transform the farmer's innate spirit of independence into an ethics of self-reliance and ethnic superiority – all modelled on the contemporary experience of the 'American frontier'.[16]

Lebensraum became an important element of Wilhelmine politics due largely to the influence of Friedrich Ratzel. A well-known geographer, Ratzel invented the term '*Lebensraum*' in the context of his own biological theories (or what he called 'bio-geography'). He had been one of the founders of the Pan-German League, was instrumental in formulating the demand that Germany acquire new 'living space' (or, as he liked to put it, 'elbow room'), and was a leading advocate of *Lebensraum* imperialism. Ratzel's concept of *Lebensraum* became a powerful intellectual construct supporting German imperialism, racial struggle, and the extermination of 'primitive peoples'. In his 1901 book, *Lebensraum*, Ratzel applied the Darwinian struggle for existence to humans, noting the extermination of the American Indians and other 'less civilized' peoples by Euro-American conquerors. Rather than projects of trade or exploitation of 'native' labour, he favoured settler colonization as the most effective way to find new 'living space' for an expanding population, as well as wars of conquest, which 'quickly and completely displace the inhabitants, for which North America, southern Brazil, Tasmania, and New Zealand provide the best examples'. In his broader work, Ratzel set out to explore the relationship between a state's political history and its relevant geographical conditions, laying the foundation for what would later be called 'geopolitics'. Ratzel suggested that *Raum* (space) – or, as he called it, *Lebensraum* – was essential to the growing state. He offered a wide-ranging theory of historical progress in which 'space' was the primary factor. Heavily influenced by social Darwinism, Ratzel interpreted Darwin's concept of the 'struggle for survival' as primarily a 'struggle for space' (*Kampf um Raum*).[17] His major work, *Politische Geographie (Political Geography)* was published in 1897, in 1903, and, again, in 1923. For his part, Ratzel brought geopolitical ideas from the realm of academia to broader awareness, helping to shape popular notions about *Lebensraum*.

Interestingly, at the turn of the twentieth century, Ratzel was part of a growing transatlantic dialogue about the connection between politics and geography – a dialogue that included American historians Frederick Jackson Turner and Alfred Thayer Mahan, the geographer Halford Mackinder in Great Britain, and a number of European social scientists (most notably Rudolf Kjellén in Sweden).[18] For his part, Ratzel had complimentary things to say about Turner's recently formulated 'frontier thesis' of American history, a thesis which celebrated the irresistible march of 'white' Anglo-Saxon civilization across the North American continent, the 'colonization' of America's 'Great West', and the 'frontier' as the incubator for 'Americanness'. In his 'frontier thesis', Ratzel enthusiastically pointed out, Turner had 'contrasted the dynamic borders of American westward expansion ... to static European borders situated amidst densely populated peoples'.[19] Indeed, Turner's thesis and arguments resonated with many contemporary German intellectuals, some of whom explicitly or implicitly compared the 'German East' and the 'American West' in their writings.[20] Crucially, this transatlantic dialogue between Turner and Ratzel confirmed a shared genealogy between the classic American 'frontier thesis' and later Nazi-German ideas about *Lebensraum*.[21]

Ideology of empire

In both Early America and Nazi Germany, many political leaders possessed a powerful commitment to territorial expansion. These expansionists aspired to expand the domain of 'Anglo-Saxon' and 'Aryan' 'civilization', respectively, at the expense of the 'native' and allegedly 'inferior' indigenous inhabitants. To justify, explain, and legitimate these desires, both nation-states constructed formal ideologies of empire – that is, American Manifest Destiny and Nazi-German *Lebensraum* – ideologies which, as we shall see, were formulated on markedly similar notions of 'space' and 'race'. The construction of the Manifest Destiny and *Lebensraum* ideologies of empire, moreover, developed in their own specific historical settings and became deeply embedded in the respective political cultures. Both ideologies were used by their creators and advocates to justify and legitimate aggressive pro-grammes of continental territorial expansion. In the American case, some actual westward expansion preceded the formal creation of the Manifest Destiny ideology, while, in the German case, the Nazis refor-mulated earlier ideas of *Lebensraum* – in harshly racist terms – into an aggressive racial imperialism.

Early America

In the 1840s, a group of politicians, journalists, and intellectuals con-structed a formal ideology of American expansionism, based on the young republic's self-proclaimed providential destiny to 'overspread' the entire North American continent.[22] Manifest Destiny, as the ideology came to be called, was not a deeply held American folk belief, as some historians have portrayed it; it was, rather, the self-conscious creation of these political propagandists.[23] The expansionists of the 1840s, like their predecessors, relied on self-serving myths to explain and justify continental expansionism. Above all, they subscribed to the myth of an 'empty' continent, an uninhabited 'wilderness', which God's 'chosen people' would transform from 'savagery' to 'civilization' during their 'predestined' march from the Atlantic to the Pacific. In the Jacksonian era (which both preceded and followed Andrew Jackson's presidential years), these expansionists conducted a sustained campaign to 'obtain' more land for the American people. John O'Sullivan, editor of the *New York Morning News* and a propagandist for the Democratic Party, composed two of the most famous phrases in American history when he wrote, in 1845, of America's 'manifest destiny to overspread the conti-nent' and described American abundance as a revelation of 'the manifest design of providence'.[24]

The idea of 'manifest destiny' centred on the early American Republic's presumed providentially sanctioned right to continental expansionism. More broadly stated, Manifest Destiny was a convic-tion that God intended America to be under the control of the 'white' Americans. It was, in many ways, an early projection of Anglo-Saxon supremacy, with a distinctly racist element to it. There was also, how-ever, an idealist element to it that reflected the new American nation's belief in democratic institutions and self-government. The ideology of Manifest Destiny, then, was a fusion of expansion with democratic mis-sion. It was, in part, an expression of a genuine ideal on the part of Americans, but it was also a justification or excuse for taking land from indigenous peoples.[25] It provided both retrospective and prospective justification for territorial expansion. The idea of westward expansion also contained another important element. As one scholar has recently pointed out, in a gendered notion of expansion, the 'masculine frontiersman' was to be the 'empire builder', dispossessing and destroying the 'feminine savages'. 'By feminizing Native Americans', writes historian Amy Greenberg, 'white Americans could prove themselves to be the legitimate possessors of American land. This gender dynamic', she notes, 'would help propel American expansion westward.'[26]

Permeated by the assumption of white supremacy, 'manifest destiny' functioned as both a label and a justification for policies of American racial imperialism. As noted above, racism became a key component of the early American Republic's notion of Manifest Destiny, implying (as it did) a conscious rejection of non-American, non-Anglo-Saxon peoples. Within the settlement culture, 'native' indigenous peoples were defined as 'non-persons'. The American territorial expansionist ideology, therefore, was no benign expansionism: one race was destined to lead, others to serve – one race was to flourish, others to die or 'disappear'.[27] The expansionists' frequent maligning of non-white peoples and their repeated predictions of their demise and extinction were essential components of Manifest Destiny.[28] Between 1815 and the mid-1850s, a distinctly American Anglo-Saxon ideology was used internally to sustain the power, as well as protect the privileged status, of the 'white' population and was also used externally to justify aggressive American territorial and economic expansion.[29] Many American expansionists were preoccupied with the new American nation attaining racial homogeneity, and they looked forward to the day when 'non-white' peoples – that is, Indians, Mexicans, and free blacks – would 'disappear' from the entire North American continent and 'whites' would, as 'destined' by Providence, take sole possession.

Manifest Destiny was a composite of ideas and emotions that provided an intricate justification for both the 'nation' and the 'empire'. Its central assumption was that the American nation and its transcontinental territorial empire were 'divinely ordained'. Overall, no specific policy followed from this discourse of expansionism as such. Although certainly conducive to expansionism, the idea of Manifest Destiny was not a strategic doctrine. It was, however, of decisive importance in the way in which the United States came to understand itself – an understanding with determinate effects (as we shall see). Like all ideological power, Manifest Destiny worked in convenient ways and was always institutionally embedded in American political culture.

It also fostered a strong sense of national place and direction in a variety of specific – and different – historical settings, carrying the notion of an agreed trajectory of spatial aims made 'manifest' by providential 'destiny'.[30]

In the mid-nineteenth century, the expansionist agenda was adopted by popular periodicals, by the press, and by many American politicians. As a political force, however, it was by no means a clearly defined movement, or one that enjoyed wide, bipartisan support. The proponents of Manifest Destiny were at best a varied collection of interest groups, motivated by a number of differing – and sometimes contradictory – objectives, and expressing a broad range of distinctively American concerns. Echoing the political philosophy of Thomas Jefferson, they viewed an abundance of land as the mainstay of a prosperous republic, providing unlimited economic opportunities for future generations of 'white' Americans. The idea of Manifest Destiny was central to the thinking of many Americans during the mid-nineteenth century.[31] Indeed, the whole nation seemed consumed by the emotional appeal of Manifest Destiny – the notion that the expansion of the American Republic and its institutions in the western lands of the North American continent was undeniably 'divinely ordained'.

Nazi Germany

Since the 1890s, the notion of *Lebensraum* had been a prominent strand of the German imperialist ideology. The concept of 'living space', therefore, was not a Nazi invention. It was simply the German version of a commonplace of European culture at the high tide of imperialism. In Germany, it inspired a policy of conquest and was invoked to justify the stated goals of Pan-Germanism. The actual expression *Lebensraum* was coined by geographer Friedrich Ratzel in 1901 and became part of the vocabulary of German nationalism well before the advent of Nazism. It resulted from the fusion of social Darwinism and imperialist geopolitics, and it stemmed from a vision of the non-European world as a 'space' to be colonized by allegedly 'superior' groups. Under Adolf Hitler, the idea of *Lebensraum* would be revoiced, radicalized, and reformulated into a violent racial imperialism.

Like most European imperialist ideologies, *Lebensraum* imperialism drew heavily from nationalism, from the identification of national survival as the primary foreign policy goal and the major source of legitimation for the proposals advanced by *Lebensraum* ideologues. German nationalism became what one historian of Imperial Germany has called a 'huge secular religion', often radical and warlike.[32] Racist and *völkisch* ideas, then widely held on the German Right, influenced Wilhelmine notions of *Lebensraum* (especially in social Darwinist presentations), but they did not become central features of *Lebensraum* ideology until the 1920s. Until the appearance of the Nazis, in fact, antisemitism had relatively little impact on the *Lebensraum* ideology. While leading advocates of *Lebensraum* might be personally antisemitic, they usually avoided overt antisemitism in their ideological pronouncements.[33]

The idea of territorial annexation in Eastern Europe became the central focus of the *Lebensraum* imperialist ideology. This element focused on the need to acquire lands adjacent to Germany, especially in Poland and the Baltic area – lands, which it was claimed, were 'historically' part of Germany's 'frontier' territories – and to place agricultural settlement colonies on these lands. Another important constituent was a popular, peasant-centred romantic agrarianism, which promoted the virtues of the 'frontier' farmer and a romantic image of the small peasant farm. Unlike advocates of economic imperialism who supported the idea of overseas trading colonies, *Lebensraum* imperialists advocated colonial expansion and the establishment of settlement colonies. Indeed, the notion of settler colonialism provided the key element of the *Lebensraum* imperialist ideology. *Lebensraum* advocates identified various geographies for German settlement colonies: overseas settlement colonies in Africa or South America, so-called 'internal' colonies in eastern Germany, and/or settlement colonies in Eastern Europe. The settler farmer became, in their eyes, the idyllic foundation for a 'new' German national character. Modelled on the myth of the American frontier, these settler farmers would convert the small farmer's spirit of independence into an ethos of self-reliance and would form communities bound together by genuine feelings of racial and cultural affinity.[34]

The imperialist and geopolitical ideas that became *Lebensraum* were common currency on the *völkisch* Right in post-First World War Weimar Germany. They were strongly represented, moreover, in the Pan-German League and supported by the publications of press baron Alfred Hugenberg. Most Weimar political leaders were not interested in continental expansion, but they did consider overseas colonies necessary to Germany's resumption of its proper role as an economic world power. On the German radical Right, however, the focus was on territorial expansion in Eastern Europe (on what has been recently called '*Lebensraum* imperialism'), not on overseas colonies.[35] The idea of *Lebensraum* was further popularized by Hans Grimm's best-selling novel

Volk ohne Raum (*People without Space*), which sold over 315,000 copies between 1926 and 1935.

In Nazi Germany, the three words *der deutsche Osten* (the German East) became a magic formula charged with passion and longing.[36] Richard Walther Darré, head of National Socialist agricultural policy, a member of the SS, and a close adviser to SS chief, Heinrich Himmler, wrote that 'our [German] people must prepare for the struggle and also for this, that in that battle [in "the East"] there can be only one outcome for us: absolute victory! The idea of blood and soil', he continued, 'gives us the moral right to take back as much eastern land *as is necessary to achieve harmony between the body of our people and geopolitical space.*'[37] 'The German east is our nostalgia and fulfillment', Nazi propaganda minister Josef Goebbels told Germany's young people. By the end of the 1930s, the idea of 'living space' had become, said the German émigré Hans Weigert, 'the national obsession of the German people'. By 1941, on the eve of the Nazi invasion of the Soviet Union, the urge to conquer *Lebensraum* in 'the East' was firmly embedded in the mainstream of German political culture. In Nazi Germany, *Lebensraum* imperialism became a frequent topic of political rhetoric as well as a focus of military consideration. For many influential and for many 'ordinary' Germans, its objectives informed their thinking and encouraged their actions.[38] Despite a whole range of views and images of a 'German East' among the political elites, Hitler's vision of 'the East' – as an imperium of 'living space' for large-scale German 'settlement' strictly run according to the dictates of Nazi racial ideology – would form the driving force of Nazi *Lebensraumpolitik*.

Ideologists of empire

Political theorists, politicians, and propagandists, in both Early America and Nazi Germany, disseminated their expansionist ideas, theories, and visions in political speeches, newspaper articles, and other writings. Within their specific historical contexts, Thomas Jefferson and Adolf Hitler, respectively, became the leading proponents of continental expansionism. While Jefferson constructed his own notion of an 'empire of liberty', many of Hitler's ideas of 'living space' and a German empire in 'the East' were 'borrowed' from Karl Haushofer, the foremost German geopolitician of the pre-Nazi and Nazi eras. Both Jefferson and Hitler needed others to popularize their ideas, with the further objectives of building a broad, popular consensus for their individual expansionist visions and agendas, as well as for attracting willing agents of empire to carry out their expansionist policies. Crucially for the purposes of this investigation, based on Hitler's own writings and private conversations, it is abundantly clear that the so-called 'North American precedent' influenced Adolf Hitler's notions of *Lebensraum* in the 'Nazi East' and that the United States – what Hitler called the 'American Union' – became for him and other leading Nazis a model for future German expansion.

Early America

While the precise term 'manifest destiny' would not be coined for another generation, America's continental 'destiny' was surely 'manifest' to Thomas Jefferson, Early America's foremost political philosopher/statesman and the leading proponent of western territorial expansion. Jefferson cherished and nurtured an imperial and expansionist vision for the new American nation. His vision of vigorous and rapid westward expansion took form in his mind about the time of the American Revolution. For him, the new American 'empire' spreading across the continent had been the whole purpose of the American Revolution. Jefferson insisted that the United States was indeed a 'chosen country'. This 'rising nation', he noted in 1805, was already 'advancing rapidly to destinies beyond the reach of the mortal eye'.[39] Ultimately, Jefferson's dream of agrarian settlement across the continent meant conveniently ignoring the prior land claims of Native Americans and Hispanics.

Thomas Jefferson was not alone in his vision of a new 'American empire' in 'the West'. In his popular 1792 textbook, *American Geography*, clergyman and geographer Jedediah Morse declared that 'the American Empire' would become 'the largest empire that ever existed' and would, in the near future, 'comprehend millions of souls west of the Mississippi'.[40] America's first president, George Washington, also envisaged the new nation as a 'rising empire'. Based on his experiences as a surveyor and land speculator in the pre-Revolutionary 'West', Washington's vision was to build a new, stable 'imperial order' in the trans-Appalachian West by an 'orderly' expansion of farming settlements. James Madison, a 'founding father', 'the father of the US Constitution', and fellow Jeffersonian, called Early America 'one great, respectable, and growing empire'.[41] Andrew Jackson, another Jeffersonian, nourished a vision of a populist/nationalist empire with 'ordinary', 'white' settlers in the vanguard of American continental expansion.

Jefferson's geopolitical vision was of a republican empire: that is, an empire without a metropolis and without an aristocratic ruling class, an agrarian empire of virtuous ('white') yeomen farmers, an 'empire of liberty' (in Jefferson's phrase) that would continuously expand westward. In proposing continuous westward expansion, Jefferson headed a popular cause. His expansionist vision, moreover, imagined an ocean-to-ocean American empire, as well as the possible annexation of Canada and Cuba. Jefferson's 'empire of liberty' was a contiguous landward empire, which would grow as Americans took 'possession' of Indian lands on the 'vacant' continent. There were almost no limits to his dreams of expansion, which saw America, he wrote in 1786, as 'the nest from which all [the] America[n] [continent], North and South is to be peopled'. He looked forward to 'distant times' when the nation's 'rapid multiplication' would 'cover the whole northern, if not the southern, continent'.[42] Throughout his political career and, indeed, into his retirement, Jefferson's vision of an America empire continued to expand. Less than a decade before his death, he noted that his hope for America's future was 'built much on the enlargement of the resources of life going hand-in-hand with the enlargement of [our] territory'.[43]

Jefferson's worldview was founded on the notion of an agrarian republic. He believed in the virtues of the independent farmer and in the need for an agrarian-based expansionism, leading to a land-based continental empire. In his *Notes on the State of Virginia* (1784), a promotional tract for westward expansion, Jefferson declared that 'those who labor in the earth are the chosen people of God'.[44] He singled out the 'white' yeomen farmer – his agrarian noblemen, the toilers in the American earth – as the appropriate social foundation for a United States of America. To Jefferson, the yeoman farmer was an heroic, poetic figure, and agriculture was the most 'natural' and worthy of occupations. In the aftermath of the victorious American Revolution, in a letter to American statesman and diplomat John Jay, dated 23 August 1785, Jefferson wrote that the new nation 'now have lands enough to employ an infinite number of people in their cultivation'. 'Cultivators of the earth', he declared 'are [its] most valuable citizens. They are the most vigorous, the most independent, the most virtuous', he continued, 'and they are tied to their country, and wedded to its liberty and interests, by the most lasting bonds.'[45] Taking up Jefferson's vision, in 1792 the *Town and Country Almanac* addressed the 'Yeoman of the United States' as 'Ye honest Sons of the earth', declaring them to be 'the basis of the Western Empire!'[46]

As a political leader and later as president, Thomas Jefferson would make certain that there would always be 'vacant lands' for his 'white' yeomen farmers. In his first Inauguration Address, on 4 March 1801, Jefferson already saw 'a rising nation, spread over a wise and fruitful land...advancing rapidly to destinies beyond the reach of mortal eye'. The newly born American Republic, he told his audience, was 'a chosen country, with room enough for our descendants to the hundredth and thousandth generation'.[47] Crucially, Jefferson handed down to his political heirs and fellow Virginians – James Madison and James Monroe – a 'blueprint for a republican political economy of westward expansion promoted by the activist agrarian state'.[48] Like many early expansionists, Jefferson held the view that the new American Republic's stability depended on steady expansion of the increasing population into new 'living space'. For him, the land was clearly a regenerative force. The key to the continued independence and righteous virtue of Americans, he believed, would be ever more land and, thus, the need for a growing landed empire. America would remain virtuous, he thought, 'as long as there shall be vacant lands in any part of America' and as long as people were not 'piled up on one another in large cities, as in Europe'.[49] In a now-famous phrase, America would be, as Jefferson wrote to James Madison following his return to private life in 1809, an 'empire for liberty', a nation based on 'extensive empire & self government'.[50]

Taken together, Jefferson's notions of an 'agrarian republic' and an 'empire of liberty' became the guiding ideology for the new United States. The future growth of his agrarian republic, he realized, would require an infinite supply of new lands – that is, Indian lands – for settlement and farming; a geographic and demographic reality that obliged the federal government to make more land available for western settlement, allowed Jefferson to rationalize an infinitely expansive America, and encouraged him to aggressively pursue a national policy of expansionism (most evident in the west and south). Beset by fears of an overcrowded, urbanized, and industrialized 'East', he looked forward to a nation one day extending from ocean to ocean. In Jefferson's view, more territory meant a safer nation and a more stable political entity, as well as heightened economic opportunity for 'white' Americans to 'pursue their happiness' (as he had promised in the Declaration of Independence).

Jefferson and his followers became early advocates of the notion of an American continental empire extending from the Atlantic Ocean to the Pacific Ocean. Thanks largely to presidents Jefferson, Madison, and Monroe – collectively known as the Jeffersonians – the idea of Manifest Destiny was, even if not in name, certainly a driving force of Early American government policy during the first two decades following

American independence. The Jeffersonians philosophically supported an early notion of Manifest Destiny and purposefully tried to realize it. In their beliefs, policies, and actions, we see the early impulses and the first whisperings of Manifest Destiny.

Following their lead, in the early years of the republic, many of their fellow Americans accepted continental expansion as both 'natural' and 'inevitable'. While Thomas Jefferson spoke of an 'empire for liberty', Andrew Jackson spoke of 'extending the area for freedom', viewing western settlers as guarantors of American national existence and the decisive source of American democracy. In the 1830s and 1840s, the Jacksonian expansionists – Andrew Jackson, James Polk, and Sam Houston – followed in the footsteps of their Jeffersonian predecessors. The Jacksonians accepted the basic tenets of Jeffersonian agrarianism, including ever-westward expansion by ('white') independent, yeoman farmers, and they hoped that, through aggressive territorial expansion in 'the West', American democratic government and institutions would ultimately spread across the continent.

In the 1830s and 1840s, there were, in fact, two rival versions of American imperialism: one, an aggressive version (supported by the Jacksonian Democrats) of expansion through violence, conquest, and war; and the other, a more restrained version (supported by the Whigs) of economic and cultural imperialism through commerce and missionary activity. Given the growing political dominance of the Jacksonian Democrats, as well as their strength in the south and west, the more aggressive version of American imperialism would prevail. As the primary driving force behind American history between 1815 and 1848, America's imperialist programme of western expansion would be built on the preservation and extension of African American slavery, the dispossession of Native Americans, and the expropriation of Mexicans.[51]

Better than anyone else, John O'Sullivan espoused the ideology of Jacksonian expansionism. A propagandist for the Democratic Party, he was editor of the *New York Morning News*, one of the dozens of cheap newspapers – the so-called 'penny press' – which helped to spread political views to 'ordinary' citizens. After consulting with Jackson himself, O'Sullivan founded a journal, the *Democratic Review*, to give an intellectual and political voice to the Jacksonian movement, including its ideology of settler-imperial territorial expansionism. Certain that God was on the American side, O'Sullivan claimed that 'American fecundity amounted to nothing less than a revelation of "the manifest design of providence" '.[52] The United States would not, he asserted, repeat the mistakes of other past empires. In the new American empire, he wrote, 'the population will be homogeneous', providing an 'element of power and stability'. In his article coining the phrase 'manifest destiny', O'Sullivan boldly asserted a unique American model for empire-building, predicated on what he called 'peaceful' pioneer settlement in 'frontier' regions, formation of their own territorial governments, and, finally, annexation by the United States. Above all, he argued, the United States must acquire more and more land by this 'population dispersion' for 'the free development' of its 'yearly multiplying millions'.[53] O'Sullivan argued that 'acquisitions of territory in America, even if accomplished by force of arms, are not to be viewed in the same light as the invasions and conquests of the States of the old world. Our way lies', he wrote, 'not over trampled nations, but through desert wastes.'[54] Unfortunately, O'Sullivan's model of Early American empire-building bore little (if any) relationship to reality for America's indigenous native peoples and their Mexican neighbours to the south.

O'Sullivan and the other expansionists of the 1840s provided Americans (then and since) with a convenient and useful legitimizing myth of American empire. As we shall see in this book, in reality, the American empire (*contra* O'Sullivan) was based on patently false notions of American exceptionalism. But by joining the concepts of exceptionalism and empire, the expansionists of the 1840s 'found a [convenient] rationale for denying to all other nations and peoples...any right to any portion of the entire North American continent'.[55] Far from being exceptions to the American past, war, empire, and imperial ambitions were, central to the Early American Republic.[56] In many ways, America's history would be an imperial one, with the 'settlement' of the country a classic example of imperial hubris.[57]

Nazi Germany

Widespread German support for *Lebensraum* imperialism was due, in large part, to the work and influence of Karl Haushofer, a geography professor at Munich Polytechnic University (where Friedrich Ratzel was a colleague of his father, Max). A First World War veteran and academic mandarin, Haushofer – building on Ratzel's work and arguments – reconfigured Ratzel's ideas about geography and history into a new, formalized system of political thought, namely geopolitics. Haushofer spread a message of Germany's mass claustrophobia.[58] For him, the nation-state had the right and duty to provide sufficient 'living space' for its people. In order to 'acquire' adequate *Lebensraum*, the state, according to Haushofer, could resort to empire, peaceful expansion, or it could opt for what he called 'just wars'. In his view, 'borders' were temporary political boundaries, living organisms, battle zones in the 'struggle for space'. 'Everywhere,' he wrote, 'we encounter the frontier as battlefield.' Haushofer openly called for fluid, dynamic, and ever-changing 'border regions', seeing borders as 'breathing spells' on the state's eventual march to expansion and conquest.[59] His concept of fluid and dynamic 'frontiers' led him to favour the construction of a Greater German empire that included all ethnic Germans.

As the prophet of the new geopolitics, Haushofer envisaged 'geopolitics' as the study of *Raum* (space) for the German nation-state. At the University of Munich, one of his devoted students was Rudolf Hess, an early convert to the fledgling Nazi Party who had become party leader Adolf Hitler's private secretary. Through Hess, Haushofer was introduced to Hitler. In 1924, Haushofer visited Hitler and Hess in Landsberg prison numerous times to 'educate' (Haushofer's word) them in the theories of geopolitics and *Lebensraum*.[60] Privately (via Hess), he fed the Nazi leader his ideas about 'living space' and 'just wars' of expansion and conquest. In turn, many of Haushofer's ideas found their way into a new book titled *Mein Kampf* (*My Struggle*), which Hitler was dictating to Hess while the Nazi leaders were serving time for their participation in the failed Beer Hall Putsch of November 1923 (a Nazi attempt to topple the pre-Nazi Weimar Republic).

After 1933, Karl Haushofer was at the service of Hitler's 'New Order', preaching the gospel of geopolitics in countless newspaper articles and radio broadcasts. He provided Nazi slogans and popularized them under the guise of 'scientific research', and he was hailed by the Nazis as the 'educator of the [German] *Volk*'.[61] The Nazis, for their part, got much of their terminology and language of expansionism from Haushofer. In addition, they found his ideas useful in offering up ready-made justifications for an aggressive foreign policy as well as in promoting so-called '*Raum* consciousness' among the German public.[62] For both *Lebensraum* ideology propagandists and practitioners, his geopolitical ideas lent a pseudo-scientific character to outright greed and territorial conquest in 'the East'. Under the Nazis, Haushofer saw many of his theoretical geopolitical constructs being translated into reality, a reality (it should be noted) not always to his liking. Razel's leading disciple in the 1920s, Haushofer published a selection of his teacher's selected works during the Third Reich, claiming that Ratzel's ideas were crucial to the formation of National Socialist ideology.[63]

For his part, Haushofer made Nazi imperialism and expansionism acceptable to the broad German public, providing a strong endorsement of its course of expansion and conquest.[64] In addition, he laid much of the intellectual framework that underpinned the Nazis' concept of *Lebensraum*. In the hands of the Nazi regime, these ideas became a justification for brutal policies of 'race' and 'space'. Haushofer also played an important role in popularizing and transmitting ideas of which the Nazis made ready use. The ideas he represented, moreover, were among those factors that did most to justify and legitimate Nazi rule in the popular mind. On the Eastern front, as well as on the home front, 'ordinary' Germans made repeated use of Haushofer's geopolitical terms and ideas – particularly the idea of *Lebensraum* – to justify state policy in which they were witnesses, supporters, and/or active participants.[65] In a March 1936 article, Haushofer reminded the German people of their 'duty to race and *Volk*', and he told them to 'trust the *Führer*' and to aspire to *Lebensraum* 'by way of the *Führer*'.[66]

In Weimar Germany, *Lebensraum*'s most forceful advocate was Adolf Hitler, leader of the small but growing National Socialist German Workers' Party (NSDAP). Born in Austria, the failed artist and social dropout left Vienna for Munich where he joined the German Army when Germany declared war in August 1914. In the First World War, Hitler, a conscientious soldier, was wounded on the Western front and received an Iron Cross, First Class. Returning to Munich after the war, the war veteran and staunch Pan-Germanist quickly became active in local radical right-wing politics as a beer hall agitator and effective political speaker for the newly formed NSDAP. In his speeches and writings during the 1920s and early 1930s, Hitler ridiculed as a *Grenzpolitiker* (border politician) anyone who merely sought to undo the hated Treaty of Versailles; by contrast, he was a self-described *Raumpolitiker* (space politician) who, as leader of a new German Reich, intended to conquer enormous areas in 'the East' and thereby gain much needed 'living space' for the German nation.[67]

The views expressed in the first and second volumes of *Mein Kampf (My Struggle)*, as well as in the unpublished *Hitlers zweites Buch (Hitler's Second Book)*, formed the ideological guidelines for National Socialist foreign, expansionist, and racial policies. The overarching goal of German policy, Hitler wrote, was the *'strengthening of our continental power by gaining new soil in Europe'*. Invoking God and Providence, Hitler called for a 'sacrifice of blood . . . to secure for the German people the land and soil to which they are entitled on this earth'.[68] In his view, the *Lebensraum* policy would gain 'living space' for the German Reich for generations to come and it would, at the same time, provide the underpinning for Germany's renewed position as a world power. In Adolf Hitler's hands,

Lebensraum became a convenient tool to explain Germany's past failure in the Great War of 1914–18, its perilous present situation, and its future possibilities.[69]

Hitler's *Lebensraum* doctrine was based on a perceived economic need for population expansion and colonial settlement in new territory – new 'living space' that would allow Germany to achieve the strength and vitality of a great colonial power and to secure its long-term future. The primary goal of his proposed *Ostpolitik* (Eastern policy), Hitler wrote in *Mein Kampf*, was '*acquiring the necessary soil for our German people*'. The coming National Socialist regime, he declared, would '*turn our [colonial] gaze toward the land in the east*' (Hitler's italics). Under his leadership, the Nazis would finally close the politics of (overseas) colonialism and trade and go over to the 'soil policy of the future'. Captured in the slogan *Blut und Boden* (Blood and Soil), the Nazis, he told his readers, aimed to reclaim a pristine agrarian past of 'the Teutonic knights of old' and to 'obtain by the German sword sod for the German plow and daily bread for the nation'. As Germany's future political leader, Hitler looked to a German history which profited from '*the soil which our ancestors acquired by the sword and settled with German peasants*'.[70] In his unpublished *Second Book*, he defined foreign policy as 'the art of securing for the people the necessary quantity and quality of *Lebensraum*', and he announced his intention to secure additional 'living space' in 'the one and only place possible: space in the East'.[71]

In *Mein Kampf*, Hitler invoked the American conquest of 'the West' as a model for Nazi continental territorial expansion in 'the East'. In his view, the Nazis must lead the German people 'from its present restricted living space to new land and soil'; this was necessary to 'free [Germany] from danger of vanishing from the earth or of serving others as a slave nation'. As an example, Hitler looked to 'the American Union which possesses its own [land] base in its own continent'; from this continental land base, he continued, 'comes the immense inner strength of this state'. As the 'Aryans' of the American continent cleared the 'wild soil' and made a 'stand against the natives', he noted, 'more and more [white] settlements sprang up in the land'. Germans should look to this historical experience for 'proof', since its population of 'largely Germanic elements mixed little with lower colored peoples'. Because they had remained 'racially pure and unmixed', Hitler argued, the 'Germanic inhabitants' of North America 'rose to be master of the continent'.[72]

Like Jefferson's 'western empire', Hitler's 'eastern empire' would be built around an essentially agrarian ideology. The German settlers and 'frontier' farmers in 'the East', the Nazis proclaimed, were to be the source for national renewal and the rejuvenation of German society. For his part, Hitler called the German farmer 'the most important participant' in the National Socialist revolution; in his view, 'a healthy peasant class' would be the 'foundation for a whole nation'.[73] He saw the hardy settler type as 'sturdy stock' that would prevent the German nation from sinking into 'softness'.[74] The 'pioneer spirit' of earlier German settlers in the twelfth-century colonization of 'the East' became a 'staple of Nazi party organizations, disseminated through school lessons, songs, and approved works of literature, history, and race' – a spirit to be revived in the 'Nazi East'.[75] In 1934, the Nazi publication *Reich Agriculture* declared that 'National Socialism starts out from the fundamental understanding that soil is not a commodity but the living space (*Lebensraum*) of the people (*Volk*).'[76] In the 'Nazi East', Hitler envisaged the creation of an agrarian 'Garden of Eden'[77] where the German colonist would live 'on handsome, spacious farms'.[78]

Hitler had been fascinated – indeed, obsessed – with the American 'frontier' since his youth, and, like many of his fellow Germans in the 1920s, he was enthralled by the United States (or, as he referred to it, 'the American Union'). His initial awareness of the American assault on 'native' indigenous populations came from his lifelong reading (and re-reading) of Karl May, the German cowboy western novelist. In short, Hitler was fascinated by what a recent historian has termed 'the North American precedent', and he was captivated by its 'Nordic' settler pioneers who drove Early American westward expansion.[79] For the future Nazi *Führer* and leader of the German government, the 'Nordics' of North America, who had ruthlessly pushed aside the 'inferior' Indian 'race' to secure new land and soil, would be the model for future German expansion. If pushing westward in North America at the expense of 'native' indigenous peoples had been necessary for the 'Nordic' Americans, Hitler reasoned, it was equally 'logical' for German settlers to acquire 'space' for themselves at the expense of indigenous Slavs and Jews in order to create their own *Lebensraum* in 'the East'. Before and during the Third Reich, the mystique of the American 'frontier' would become an addiction among many other National Socialist 'true believers'. In their view, the eastern *Lebensraum* would be to Germany what the 'frontier' was to America: the foundation of future global power.[80]

Hitler's notion of *Lebensraum* was implicitly imperialist as well as social Darwinist and racist, resting on the idea that 'superior' races had the right to conquer and subjugate 'inferior' races. Following Ratzel, Hitler saw the struggle for existence between the races as, first and foremost, a struggle for 'living space'.[81] By regarding Bolshevism as 'Jewish rule', he combined his pathological antisemitism with Germany's need for land in 'the East'.[82] As party ideologue and propagandist, Hitler offered his listeners/readers a vision of his – and ultimately Germany's – 'mission'. He did not, however, offer concrete policies. On the 'social question', Hitler offered the German people a 'national community' (*Volksgemeinschaft*) based on 'racial purity'; on the 'Jewish question', he advocated 'getting rid of the Jews' (*Entfernung der Juden*); and, on the 'land question', he sought 'living space' (*Lebensraum*) in Eastern Europe to secure Germany's future.[83] Taken collectively, these strands came together in a personalized worldview that would drive Nazi policies of expansion, conquest, and 'racial purification'. In his ideological pronouncements, Hitler blended his obsessive antisemitism (aimed at the destruction of 'Jewish bolshevism') with the concept of a war against the Soviet Union for 'living space' (needed by the 'master race' to sustain itself). His idea of *Lebensraum* (a much-radicalized version of pre-existing ideas) combined the most brutal tenets of late nineteenth-century imperialism, racism, and antisemitism into a 'new' twentieth-century imperialist ideology of 'race' and 'space'. As we shall see in subsequent chapters, Adolf Hitler's twin goals of racial purification and continental territorial expansion were interlinked and intimately related to 'war'.[84]

In securing support for his notions of 'race' and 'space', Hitler looked to other historical models and examples. In a January 1932 address to German industrialists, Hitler spoke of the political supremacy of the white race as foundational for past colonial expansion. England, he told his audience, ruled in India with the 'most brutal ruthlessness'; furthermore, it did not, he argued, acquire India in a lawful and legitimate manner and ruled there 'without regard to the natives' wishes'. In Hitler's view, 'the settlement of the North American continent was similarly a consequence not of any higher claim in a democratic or international sense, but rather of a consciousness of what is right', an idea he noted 'which had its sole roots in the conviction of the superiority and thus the right of the white race...to organize the rest of the world'.[85] To be sure, nineteenth-century colonial expansionism provided the Nazis with a number of historical models and precedents. In the end, however, the conquest and colonization of the 'American West' provided the closest model for Hitler's *Lebensraum* project in 'the East'.[86]

During 1937, there was a marked increase in the number of references to *Lebensraum* in Hitler's public speeches.[87] For example, in a

21 November 1937 public speech in Augsburg subsequently reprinted in *Völkischer Beobachter* (*Nationalist Observer*), Hitler spoke of the 'too confined *Lebensraum* of the German *Volk*'. The National Socialist government faced a new task, he announced to his audience: to procure 'this vital right of ["living space" for] the German *Volk*'. If the 'whole Party and the whole nation' would 'unite behind the leadership', he declared, 'this vital right... would one day be understood by the whole world'.[88]

Earlier, on 5 November 1937, Hitler addressed his generals in a closed session. According to notes taken by his adjutant, Colonel Friedrich Hossbach, Hitler spoke of the necessity of establishing new colonies in 'the East' to serve as the *Lebensraum* of the German people. He told his audience that he had made an 'inalterable decision' to solve the problem of 'living space' by the use of force no later than 1943–5. The 'German racial community', he asserted, had the 'right to a greater living space'. 'Solving' the 'need for space' was crucial to Germany's future, with the 'security of [Germany's] food situation' as the 'principal question'. 'The only remedy', Hitler declared, 'and one which might appear to us as visionary, lay in the acquisition of greater living space – a quest which has at all times been the origin of the formation of states and of the migration of peoples.' In Hitler's view, 'space' could 'only be sought in Europe' and not in the 'exploitation of [overseas] colonies'. 'It is not a matter of acquiring population', he noted, 'but of gaining space for agricultural use.' Hitler told his generals that he was determined to solve the 'German problem' by 'means of force' (a strategy not without its 'attendant risks'); it was 'only the question of "when" and "how" '. Similar economic issues, he noted, were driving recent Italian and Japanese expansion. 'We [are] living in an age of economic empires', he concluded, 'in which the primitive urge to colonization was again manifesting itself.'[89]

Hitler made no secret of his plans for 'solving' what he called 'the problem of our *Lebensraum*'. In his May Day speech of 1 May 1939, for instance, he told his audience that 'the foundations for the life of a people are not to be found in doctrines or theories, but in its *Lebensraum*'. 'The commandment of the hour', he declared, 'is the securing of German *Lebensraum*', for which he was arming Germany 'with all my might'.[90] Likewise, in the run-up to the attack on the Soviet Union, on 18 December 1940, Hitler addressed the annual rally of young officer cadets at the Berlin *Sportpalast*. As reported by the German News Bureau, Hitler spoke (at length) of the relationship between population and 'living space'. The need for expanding Germany's 'living space', he noted, was a function of the 'discrepancy between the *Volk's* numbers and the available *Lebensraum'*. A 'healthy people', he continued, must enlarge its *Lebensraum*. Rather than 'adjusting' the *Volk's* numbers to the 'available *Lebensraum'*, Germany would, he said, 'adjust' its 'living space' to 'accommodate the increase in the *Volk'*. Hitler called the 'adjustment' of Germany's 'living space' to its numbers 'the natural way and the one willed by Providence'. The 'Anglo-Saxon', he reminded his audience, 'is nothing other than a branch of our German *Volk'*; after all, it was a 'tiny Anglo-Saxon tribe [which] set out from Europe, conquered England, and later helped to develop the American continent'. While the 'American Union' encompassed about nine and a half million square kilometres, the German people, he complained, had less than 600,000 square kilometres of *Lebensraum*. Celebrating past conquests and hinting at more in the future, Hitler boasted that the National Socialist movement had 'brought about the creation of a new empire in Europe', and its officers and soldiers must be ready to die in 'the most decisive battle for our *Volk'*.[91]

Hitler's ideology of 'race' and 'space' was very much in tune with widely held views and aspirations in German society concerning the construction of a German empire in eastern lands, based on racial and social Darwinist principles. The idea of *Lebensraum* was the most constant ideological current in Hitler's expansionist vision; in a similar sense, the conquest of 'living space' in 'the East' was the fixed, basic tenet underpinning Hitler's foreign policy ideas. For his part, Hitler amalgamated and radicalized previously existing *Lebensraum* elements into a congruous system of thought that prescribed eastern spatial expansion as an all-embracing solution to Germany's perceived domestic and international problems. In addition, he popularized the previously marginal and somewhat vague idea of *Lebensraum* by placing it in the vanguard of the Nazi political programme.[92]

As Chancellor and *Führer* of a rearmed German nation, Hitler would act on the Pan-Germanist fantasies of his youth and on his later dreams of a German continental imperium and a German-dominated, racially purified *Lebensraum* in 'the East'. As leader of Germany's Third Reich, from 1933 to 1945, he would mobilize an entire national government – its military, diplomacy, and bureaucracy – behind the realization of his obsessive notions of 'race' and 'space', as embodied in the Nazi *Lebensraum* imperialist ideology. At its core, Nazism would become a 'doctrine of perpetual empire'.[93]

Adolf Hitler would hold on to his *Lebensraum* obsession until the very end. In a final message to his followers on 29 April 1945, in the last hours of his life and with his self-proclaimed thousand-year empire crumbling around him, he declared that 'the efforts and sacrifices of the German *Volk* in this war were so great that I cannot believe that they were in vain. It must continue to be the objective to gain space [*Lebensraum*] for the German *Volk* in the East.'[94]

Agents of empire

To realize their respective visions of empire, the Early American and Nazi-German nation-states would need to employ various 'agents of empire' to carry out specific continental imperialist policies. In both cases, individuals and institutions served this vital function. Both land-based empires clearly needed settler pioneers willing to settle and fight in the new 'living space'. But they also needed the indispensable men of action, to organize and lead military and paramilitary forces for the purposes of opposing potential and actual indigenous resistance to the taking and occupation of their lands. In many ways, Andrew Jackson and Heinrich Himmler were the prototypical 'westerner' and 'easterner', respectively, who would help provide the military and paramilitary means to enable empire-building in the 'American West' and the 'Nazi East' by opposing indigenous resistance to the taking of their lands for future settlement. The dynamics of empire-building in the Early American Republic required corresponding assaults by 'white' settler pioneers and national policymakers, while Nazi empire-building called for initial military assaults to clear the way for subsequent settlement by 'Aryan' settler pioneers.

Early America

In many ways, the history of American westward expansion is the biography of Andrew Jackson. As a young frontier lawyer seeking financial success and social advance, Jackson acquired land as rapidly as possible. Like all westerners, he caught the contagion of 'land fever', which, in turn, determined his negative attitudes towards Indians, Spanish, and English who, in the frontiersmen's view, were barriers to American western expansion. Migrating to the western frontier in search of a better life, the young Jackson became 'a fire-breathing frontiersman obsessed with the Indian presence and the need to obliterate it'.[95] Like many western frontiersmen, he demanded a substantial government contribution – but subject to his lead – in 'eliminating' the Indian presence, and he became contemptuous of Congress for, in his view, failing to help protect the settlers against Indian attacks. As a western land speculator and Congressman, Jackson was antagonistic towards both England and Spain who, he claimed, thwarted further American expansion – by encircling the new American nation on the north, south, and west – and who, again in his view, constantly encouraged Indian attacks along the young nation's frontiers.

Where other expansionists offered the transcontinental vision, Jackson provided the military means by which that vision could be converted into reality; in short, he provided the rigid determination and essential military conquests to realize America's expansionist dreams. While the Jeffersonian expansionists were men of intellect, Jackson was the crucial man of action – with an absolute will – who made their visions realizable. The politicians in Washington came to rely on Jackson, America's greatest Indian fighter, for the efficient subjugation and dispossession of the 'natives'. More than anyone else, before or after, Andrew Jackson determined the course of American expansion. He was, asserts biographer Robert Remini, the 'greatest expansionist of them all .... Without Jackson the leap across the continent was unlikely if not impossible.'[96]

In the Early American Republic, there were two chief agents of westward expansion: American policymakers who sought to gain title to a continental empire stretching from coast to coast, and pioneers who moved into 'frontier' areas to transform settlement into permanent land ownership and possession.[97] Andrew Jackson was the embodiment of both – an early settler on the frontier, an Indian fighter, a general who fought the English and the Spanish, and a president who made Indian policy. In the early days, frontier settlers (like Jackson) were visibly the vanguard of empire.

When indigenous peoples sought to resist white encroachment, military and paramilitary forces were needed to protect the settler colonists. Before, during, and after the War for Independence, Americans on the ever-advancing 'frontier' fought as Indian fighters, as members of ad hoc organizations formed for special operations and then disbanded at their conclusion. These specialized units for Indian fighting (called 'rangers') waged a series of 'Indian wars' on the 'frontier' that 'only occasionally, and usually reluctantly, saw the participation' of the British or American regular armies.[98] Another fundamental institution and agent of empire was the local, state, or territorial militias – the armed 'citizen soldiers' who provided much of the military power on the empire's frontiers from the first colonial settlements to the mid-nineteenth century. In wartime, this 'armed citizenry' was used to form volunteer companies of 'special forces' to support the regular army. All along the advancing western 'frontier', local militia units defended settler communities and engaged Native Americans in a bloody contest for the land. Owing its existence to the American frontier, the regular army also played a significant role in the westward expansion of America's 'empire of liberty'. As instruments of Congress and the president, they were, above all, agents of empire whose chief work was on the Indian frontier as an official and indispensable instrument in the enforcement of 'Indian policy'. In addition, they were also so-called 'advanced pioneers' who opened up the westward-moving 'frontier' of the new American 'empire', serving as policemen, farmers, road builders, scientists, explorers, and lumbermen.

By the early 1840s, politicians and propagandists promoting aggressive territorial expansion became the primary agents of empire, although settler pioneers continued to play a significant role in expansion. In the course of Early American expansion, frontier settler pioneers alone did not take possession of the entire North American continent, nor did policymakers in the metropole single-handedly 'acquire' it. The particular dynamics of empire-building in the Early American Republic required two complementary assaults, by national political leaders and individual settler pioneers to ultimately achieve America's continental empire.[99] Indeed, far from being the forceful and lively agent of westward expansion, the poorly armed 'frontier' settler was more often cast in the role of a client who very much depended on the effective exercise of state authority and federal government power to 'acquire' the new 'white' settler 'living space' (via war and diplomacy), to help gain secure land titles, to provide protection from Indians, and to secure slave labour for agriculture. Importantly, as a lightly populated nation seeking to build a continental empire, maximizing women's reproductive capacity was a high policy imperative, with George Washington, the 'father' of his country, urging settlers of 'the West' to fulfil, in his words, 'the first and great commandment, *Increase and Multiply*'. In the American experience, fecund women, a high birth rate, continued immigration from Europe, and a fertile continent all combined to provide the foundation for America's western continental empire.[100]

Nazi Germany

Adolf Hitler's most ardent follower was Heinrich Himmler. Himmler became active in the NSDAP from 1925 onward, held a number of different positions within the Nazi Party, and was appointed *Reichsführer-SS* in January 1929. He claimed to be one of the first to buy Hitler's book, *Mein Kampf,* and found that, in his words, 'there's an incredible amount of truth in it'.[101] Like Hitler, the fight against the Jews and the German conquest of additional 'living space' in 'the East' were two of Himmler's great lifelong causes. And, like his *Führer* (leader), Himmler dreamed of colonizing eastern lands with 'racially pure', 'Aryan' German settlers.

As a young man, Himmler was drawn to 'the East' and the 'frontier experience'. In 1919, he decided to become a *Lebensraum* pioneer (that is, a warrior-farmer who would colonize 'the East'), and he made plans to work on a farm and study agronomy. That same year, he confided to his diary that 'I will live my life in the East and fight my battles as a German far from beautiful Germany.'[102] Two years later, after hearing General Graf Rüdiger von der Goltz speak about the recent *Freikrops* (Free Corps) military campaigns in the Baltic, Himmler wrote in his diary, 'Now I know more definitely: if there is a campaign in the East again, I will go along. The East is the most important thing for us', he continued, 'we must fight and settle in the East.'[103] A qualified agriculturalist and former district leader of the *Artaman* League (a German back-to-the-land movement), Himmler saw the rural lifestyle as a means of restoring the German nation to 'health' and advocated the farmer-peasant life as a precondition for the nation's renewal and preservation. Adopting these ideas fully, he also embraced the *Lebensraum* imperialist ideology calling for seizure of land and colonial settlements in conquered eastern lands.

In Himmler's vision, 'the East' was to be 'cleared' in order to create a huge settler-colonial territory for Nazi Germany. The Nazi strategy for *Lebensraum*, to him, meant 'cleansing' the eastern lands of the indigenous populations all the way to the Ural Mountains through war, murder, enslavement, and deliberate starvation. This strategy also meant that indigenous peoples in the 'Nazi East' were to be reduced to the lowest level of culture. Himmler aimed at colonizing and taming the 'Wild East' with SS *Wehrbauern* (soldier-farmers) who would be charged with defending the Reich from the 'Asiatic hordes' – meaning Slavs and Jews. In his view, his *Wehrbauern* settlements of SS and German peasant-warriors were necessary to assure the existence of Adolf Hitler's proclaimed thousand-year Reich. Himmler's own racial, agrarian-utopian schemes were based on romantic notions of the 'frontier' inspired by the North American example.[104] For the *Reichsführer-SS* and like-minded Nazi agrarians (including Hitler), '[t]he yeoman on his own acre' is, in Himmler's own words, 'the backbone of the German people's [future] strength and character'.[105]

Hitler's *Lebensraum* imperialist ideology was implicitly based on a series of wars to win 'living space' in 'the East', requiring a large, loyal, and like-minded military force. Like the Nazis, Germany's military elite shared the geopolitical, social Darwinist view that Germany must gain eastern *Lebensraum* to make itself blockade-proof and secure its position as a world power; they viewed Slavs as 'inferior' peoples and appropriate objects of colonial exploitation and domination; they were obsessed with anti-communism; and they accepted Hitler's equation of the Bolsheviks with the Jews.[106] The most modern, innovative and efficient military machine of its time, the German armed forces (or *Wehrmacht*) was Hitler's armed instrument and the willing tool of the Nazi regime in implementing National Socialist foreign and racial policies. Even more than civilians, the *Wehrmacht*'s 'ordinary' combat soldiers were more likely to be supportive of the regime, its ideology, and its policies, including Hitler's dreams of an aggressive war of expansion and colonial 'empire' in 'the East'.[107]

In addition to the military, Hitler had other agents of empire available to him, most notably Heinrich Himmler's SS (*Schutzstaffel*). Himmler's SS embodied the mixture of racism and expansionism, captured in Hitler's twin goals of 'race and space'.[108] It was to be both a secret police and a warrior elite, an instrument for 'cleansing' the new German empire of its internal and external 'enemies', and the agency for settling conquered eastern lands with German soldier-farmers. From 1939 onwards, the SS controlled two of the most important areas of Nazi foreign and racial policy – population policy and *Lebensraum* policy, including the colonization of the conquered territories in 'the East'. Operating behind the lines of regular army troops, *Einsatzgruppen* (SS mobile killing squads) sought to maximize territorial coverage in the colonized space, often killing indigenous peoples under the guise of carrying out 'anti-partisan operations'. The *Einstazgruppen* also participated in the occupation and pacification of conquered eastern territories where they promptly assumed responsibility for the 'fundamental cleansing' (*Flurbereinigung*) of 'unwanted' indigenous populations – that is, Jews and Slavs. The military combat wing of the SS, the Waffen-SS, was also available for 'antipartisan actions' against indigenous peoples. Indeed, in the words of *SS-Gruppenführer* Otto Hoffman of the Race and Resettlement Office, 'The East belong[s] to the SS.'[109]

Similarities, differences, and links

Anchored by their visions and fantasies of 'empire' in the 'American West' and the 'Nazi East', respectively, the expansionist ideologies of Manifest Destiny and *Lebensraum* were founded on strikingly similar notions of 'space' and 'race' – embedded, in both cases, in a broader continental imperialist discourse. In both the Early American and Nazi-German contexts, continental territorial expansion was driven by these respective racial-imperialist discourses. As ideologies of colonial expansion, moreover, both discourses were predicated on the 'taking' of the indigenes' land, the founding of settler colonies, and the 'removal' of the indigenous populations from the settler 'living space'. Both the Manifest Destiny and *Lebensraum* ideologies were based on a notion of 'empire', which required extending their frontiers and national space – often by force – in an aggressive agenda of territorial expansion. Both the Early American and Nazi-German imperial projects, moreover, were 'colonizing' missions to settle 'the West' and 'the East' at the expense of the local indigenous populations. Both political elites shared the conviction that a nation needs to secure adequate 'space' in order to assure its economic and national survival. In constructing these ideologies, both American and German ideologues found a convenient rationale for limitless territorial expansion and for the brutal (even murderous) treatment of indigenous peoples. To be sure, both ideologies were examples of ideological thinking and propaganda designed to rationalize, legitimize, and justify continental expansion and conquest, and both were models of social engineering and population politics, aimed at the attainment of racial homogeneity, unlimited expansion, and continental empire. A belief in the nation's own righteousness and providential destiny was the common ideological prerequisite. Both ideologies sought to exploit the opportunities provided by territorial expansion into a contiguous landmass, and both aimed to make the most of the potentialities afforded by a dynamic territorial 'frontier'. In both cases, the political leaders whose ideas drove continental expansion relied on powerful agents and instruments of 'empire' to drive their policies, which were founded on like notions of 'space' and 'race'.

Despite these numerous similarities, however, there was also a subtle (yet crucial) difference between the two ideologies of continental imperialism, a difference which would, as we shall see, ultimately shape the course of expansion and conquest, as well as the evolution of settler colonial and 'out-group' policy in the colonized space. At the end of the day, American Manifest Destiny was primarily an ideology of 'space' (albeit with a strong racial component). Nazi-German *Lebensraum*, on the other hand, was an ideology of 'race' and 'space' – that is, of co-equal elements of 'racial purification' and territorial expansion, which intertwined to form the driving force of Nazi policy in 'the East'. Hitler's goal was to reconstruct Europe as a racial entity, with a blending of the metropole and its colonies into a racially defined empire.[110] In the Nazi *Lebensraum* project, race and empire became interlocking imperatives.

The Early American variety of continental imperialism stood at the beginning of the development of the racial-imperialist discourse. Heavily influenced by the North American precedent and model, the Nazi-German variety of continental imperialism was, I would argue, the logical culmination of the earlier Anglo-American continental imperialist ideology, with a number of prominent – as well as disturbing – points of ideological convergence.

The historical lessons and example offered by American westward expansion would not be lost on Hitler and other Nazi 'true believers'. In the Third Reich, Nazi imaginings of the new 'Aryan' paradise in 'the East' – especially those of Hitler, Himmler, and party ideologue Alfred Rosenberg – contained frequent laudatory references to the North American 'frontier', and Nazi propaganda photos and films featured ethnic German settlers driving covered wagons eastward decorated with portraits of the *Führer*.[111] Nazi songs glorified settler wagons rolling east into an eastern 'alien wilderness'. Konrad Meyer, a leading Nazi SS planner and author of the notorious General Plan East (describing Nazi intentions towards 'native' indigenous populations in the 'Wild East'), wrote that the 'America' of the Germanic peoples lies in Eastern Europe.[112] In *Der Untermensch* (*The Subhumans*), one of Himmler's SS publications, eastern *Lebensraum* was described as 'black earth that could be a paradise, a California of Europe'.[113] Echoing the advice given to young men in Early America to 'Go West, Young Man, Go West!', the headline of a wartime article in a German newspaper carried the title 'Go East, Young Man!'.[114] In their pursuit of additional 'living space' in 'the East', Nazi officials would emulate and exploit the language and practices of the American 'frontier'. In the end, Hitler, Himmler, and other like-minded Nazi leaders were 'true believers' in the mystique of the 'American frontier' and in the evocative link between the 'American West' and the 'Nazi East'. For them, it was a strong ideological obsession underpinning their racial and expansionist fantasies of large-scale eastern agrarian settlement; an obsession which, as we shall see in subsequent chapters, would exert a strong influence on planned and actualized Nazi policies and practices in the 'Wild East'.

2
Racial 'Othering': 'Manufacturing Difference'

In both Early America and Nazi Germany, each nation-state constructed a hierarchical social structure, using 'race' as the primary organizing principle for society and based on a racial worldview founded on notions of racial 'difference' and 'otherness'. In both cases, specific historical and cultural contexts nourished ideas of racial 'difference', promoted racial ideologies (linked with territorial expansion), and offered up racial worldviews supporting the alleged 'superiority' of the 'white'/'Aryan' races and their 'right' and 'duty' to subjugate 'inferior' 'natives' in the new 'living space' of the 'American West' and the 'Nazi East'. A race-centred worldview, in both cases, gained increased power and influence from specific political developments. In pre-Civil War Early America, the Jeffersonian and Jacksonian political elites (mostly politicians from the south and west who benefited from territorial expansion as well as the extension of slavery) occupied the White House and directed the course of American continental imperialism. In Germany, the Nazi ascension to power in 1933 guaranteed that a race-centred worldview (as expressed in Hitler's *Mein Kampf*) would be a driving force behind the empire-building and 'racial cleansing' at the heart of the Nazi agenda. The Early American 'western empire' and the Nazi-German 'eastern empire' involved the 'racial remaking' of 'living space', both in the metropole and in the colonial territories. Thanks to this process of racial 'othering', both 'ordinary' Americans and 'ordinary' Germans developed a deep-seated sense of belonging to a 'superior' and privileged collective, feelings that would render most of them 'indifferent' to the fate of allegedly 'inferior' peoples.

In each specific historical context, however, 'race thinking' became operationalized in different ways. In Early America, the ideology of race was compatible with the power relationships, political goals, and economic interests of the political elites.[1] Premised on the rights of property, the American Revolution – its causes, motivations, and objectives – would allow the 'white' settlers to pursue their 'happiness' by 'obtaining' Indian lands and black slaves. In the nineteenth century, the ideology of race became fully operationalized, as American continental imperialists turned to the authority of science to buttress and expand their arguments for continued territorial expansion and extension of slavery. During this century, a racial worldview became firmly entrenched, with the ascendancy of an aggressive racial Anglo-Saxonism. In Nazi Germany, two distinct campaigns served to operationalize 'race thinking' as part of efforts to mobilize popular support for Hitler's racial aims (at home and abroad). During the years 1933–9, the Nazis undertook massive public relations campaigns to popularize racial thinking and to create a race culture; playing on emotions of ethnic fear and racial pride among 'ordinary' Germans, these campaigns called for a 'Germany for the Germans' and a 'living space' cleansed of 'alien' 'others'.[2] And during the years 1939–45, Nazi propaganda campaigns effectively legitimized war and genocide to 'ordinary' Germans as necessary pre-emptive measures (of retaliation and defence) against an alleged 'threat' (posed by 'international Jewry' and the Soviet 'Judeo-Bolshevist' state) to the existence and survival of the German nation.[3]

In tune with America's expansionist consensus, a deepening process of racial 'othering' in American political and popular culture provided both a justification and an ideological rationale for past, current, and future westward territorial expansion, across lands occupied by North America's indigenous peoples. In the three centuries of colonial settlement and westward expansion, 'Indian-hating' and empire-building called for the 'elimination', one way or the other, of indigenous peoples who stood in the path of Anglo-American expansion. To be sure, American expansionist policy was firmly 'based on assumptions of racial and cultural superiority, as well as on an insatiable desire for land, expansion, and empire'. Rather than their inclusion and integration, it emphasized the exclusion of Indians from the dominant 'white' society as well as from the 'white' settler 'living space'.[4]

Thanks to the work of Nazi propagandists and racial theorists, 'the Jews' and other 'out-groups' were not understood as human beings but as – in the chilling words of Nazi ideology – 'life unworthy of life' whose 'elimination' would benefit the 'Aryan national community'. Built on what has been called an 'ethnic fundamentalism', a racial culture spread throughout the Third Reich, which endorsed Nazi racial beliefs and shaped the worldview of 'ordinary' Germans, allowing them to accept the Nazi-promised future of a Greater German Reich and Nazi empire 'cleansed' of racial and ethnic 'aliens'. With the onset of wars for *Lebensraum*, the Nazi racial culture served as a backdrop for the openly proclaimed 'race war' in 'the East' and prepared 'ordinary' Germans to tolerate – and some to participate in – racial crime.[5]

Antecedents

In both the Early American and Nazi-German cases, racial themes, concepts of 'race', and notions of racial 'otherness' had important antecedents embedded in their prehistories that formed a background for later racial categories and processes of 'manufacturing difference'. In the American case, notions of 'otherness' (not yet defined by 'race') were an important part of English colonizing efforts in North America from the very beginning of its settlement. These notions of 'otherness' would lead to the emergence of a harsh racial underpinning to life in British Colonial America, along with the creation of the 'frontier' as a racial boundary separating the 'living space' of indigenous peoples and 'white' settler colonists. In the German case, early notions of 'otherness' focused mainly on Germany's small Jewish population, with antisemitism mostly occupying the fringes of German politics and society. These notions of 'otherness' soon led to the construction of a full-blown antisemitic ideology which, while situated at the peripheries of German life, was fully capable of moving to the centre of German political culture at times of economic and political crisis.

Early America

In their colonizing efforts, English settlers would encounter 'other' peoples in Ireland, Virginia, and New England, resulting in social constructions of 'civilization' and 'savagery'. Like the Irish, the native peoples of North America were viewed as the 'other', but this 'otherness' was not yet definitely fixed by 'race'. In British North America, the social construction of race appeared within the economic context of competition for Indian lands. To be sure, to deny the humanity of the Indians, to define them in non-human terms, and to picture them as 'Godless savage beasts' made it easy for the Euro-American invaders and settler colonists to argue that these non-peoples were 'disqualified' from the right to possess land.[6] But, as historian Daniel Richter points out, clear-cut 'racial' categories of 'white' and 'red' had to be constructed, and 'whites' and 'Indians' had to '*learn* to hate each other'.[7]

Euro-American settlers in the 'New World' fashioned different codes of race relations, based on their own needs, prejudices, and attitudes concerning how people should be classified, treated, and separated. For their part, colonizing Englishmen maintained themselves as an ethnic caste, enforcing colonialism upon the subject indigenous peoples of their geographic vicinity. Along with the settler colonists, there were Africans imported as plantation slaves and indigenous peoples in their tribal communities who lived within the claimed territory of a colony. The Indians and the Africans were, as separate castes, excluded from 'civil society' and its legal structures. There was, indeed, a hard racial underside to life in British North America. Distinctions, however, were initially based on religion (not on race); the colonists were Christians, while Indians and Africans were 'heathen'. When some of those red and black 'heathens' chose to accept white Christianity, however, race (identified by skin colour) became the basis for necessary distinctions between the privileged conquerors and the so-called 'inferior' races. In the colonies Indians and Africans were seen as 'alien' 'others', suitable subjects for convenient conquest and ruthless exploitation. In British North America, then, religion and God were used as justification for both the colonization of North America and the brutally harsh treatment of the Indians.[8]

With the British defeat of France in the Seven Years' War (known as the French and Indian War in North America), there was a steadily hardening definition of racial categories. Over time, Indian lands had become a bone of contention between colonists and the ruling empire in the London metropole. Tired of costly wars to protect white settlers in the western lands, Britain's King George III specifically prohibited further white settlement west of the Appalachians in his Proclamation of 1763. As white settlements continued to expand, white racism followed the moving 'frontier' into 'Indian country'. From the time of the earliest settlements until the eve of the American Revolution, ugly patterns of racial antagonism took root between whites and Indians. Importantly, the Proclamation Line of 1763 became a racially defined 'frontier line', a racial boundary extending from Maine to Georgia and roughly following the crest line of the Appalachian Mountains. In ethnic and racial terms, the Proclamation Line of 1763 signalled the emergence of a racial frontier, which attempted to separate and delineate the 'living space' of indigenous peoples and Anglo-American settler colonists.[9]

With this dividing line between 'savage' Indians and 'civilized' whites, Indian and white worlds became increasingly defined, contested, and racial. Although concepts of 'race' remained ill-formed throughout the late eighteenth century, both 'whites' and 'Indians' on the 'frontier' increasingly viewed and defined each other in 'racial' terms. Among both colonists and Indians, there was an increasingly pervasive view that 'whites' and 'Indians' were 'different', 'incompatible', and, therefore, could never peacefully share the North American continent. After 1763, the once-shared Euro-Indian transatlantic imperial world – with its 'middle-ground', accommodationist vision of native European coexistence – would disappear, as the newly independent 'Americans' set about constructing a future in which Native American communities and peoples had no place. On the western 'frontier', 'white' Anglo-Americans envisaged a country 'cleansed' of Indians, who (as a race) were more and more (by definition) their 'enemies'. Sadly, the cultural legacy of 1763 was the increasingly powerful belief that the North American continent must become 'white' or 'Indian' (but nevermore both).[10] By the early nineteenth century, the 'middle ground' (of white/Indian accommodation and coexistence around the Great Lakes) and the 'native ground' (in the heart of the North American continent where Indians were still sovereign over land and resources, despite the arrival of white settlers) would start to give way (in the face of overwhelming numbers of white settlers) to attitudes, practices, and policies of racism, dispossession, and exclusion.[11]

Nazi Germany

In Imperial Germany (1871–1918), practising Jews numbered around 600,000, lived in an overwhelmingly Christian society, and constituted around 1 per cent of the total population. Excluded from owning land, they were also subject to informal social discrimination, which worked to deny them access to positions in such key institutions as the army, the universities, and the top ranks of the civil service. As Jews began to convert and marry into Christian society, religious prejudice was subsumed into racial prejudice, with Jews increasingly denounced as a racial (not as a religious) minority. When economic misfortune struck, moreover, Germany's motley collection of political antisemites were quick to blame 'the Jews' and to advocate their 'total exclusion' from German society. Due to the influence of antisemitic propagandists, 'the Jewish question' was placed on the political agenda, where it became a matter subject to discussion and debate. While there was a lack of overt or violent political antisemitism, many of the ideas that would become part of Nazi racial ideology were already part of the German political discourse well before the First World War.[12]

Within Germany itself, the onrush of modernization – many conservative Germans believed – threatened the country's social structures, existing hierarchies, and traditional cultural values. Viewed as the main beneficiaries of this modernization, 'the Jews' were thus blamed for all of modernity's evils. On a scale not seen elsewhere, anti-Jewish attitudes spread into the very heart of German society, due to widespread and deep anti-Jewish hostility in economic and professional associations, nationalistic political parties, and widely influential cultural groups. Moreover, an all-embracing antisemitic ideology was systematically elaborated in Wilhelmine Germany which, in later years of crisis, would encourage more extreme ideological constructs.[13]

During the First World War, racial antisemites accused 'the Jews' of not serving in the military to defend the Fatherland from its enemies. Instead, they argued, 'the Jews' used wartime conditions to exploit patriotic Germans for their own profit on the black market. Not surprisingly, these accusations led to a noticeable upsurge in antisemitic expression and attack. German failure to win a quick victory in the war was due, said antisemites, to Jewish shirking and war profiteering. Accused of dodging the draft and avoiding service on the front, 'the Jews' were seen as unpatriotic elements that stood in the way of German victory. These sentiments soon gave rise to a new wave of antisemitism which, during the post-war years, would prove more dangerous and durable than its predecessors. In the latter part of the war, German antisemitism became a national phenomenon. In the political arena, various antisemitic, racial forces united to form the German Fatherland Party (*Deutsche Vaterlandspartei*), a right-wing party that 'endorsed a boundless expansionism, an unambiguous biological racism, and an abiding hostility towards Jews'.[14]

Racial antisemitism existed mainly on the fringes of imperial society, while a populist antisemitism found a home in the populist radical-conservative parties of Wilhelmine Germany.[15] In the late nineteenth century, German antisemitism was very much one of antisemitic peripheries – that is, an antisemitism of the provinces. There was a socio-economic antisemitism among peasants and artisans who suffered from the effects of industrialization and modernization; for its part, the bourgeoisie, in German towns, often adopted antisemitism as a cultural code to preserve their social status and prestige against an alleged Jewish cultural threat. At times of economic and political crisis, however, German antisemitism quickly moved from the periphery to the centre of German politics and society.[16]

In addition to anti-Jewish feeling, other prejudices were being constructed. A new science called eugenics grew up in Europe and North America, around the notion that modern society could be 'engineered' to assure reproduction by only its supposedly healthiest elements. A radicalization of eugenic ideas took place after the First World War: in this radicalized environment, people deemed mentally or physically handicapped were called 'living burdens' and 'completely worthless creatures'. Roma were commonly referred to as the 'Gypsy plague', as if they were a kind of disease. Within twentieth-century German society, Slavic peoples – especially Poles and Russians – were considered to be backward, uneducated, unkempt, brutish, and childlike. German anti-Slavic prejudices and suspicions were only intensified by the Russian Revolution of 1917, which linked hatred of the Jews with the 'Jewish Communists' now running the Soviet Union. Yet modern antisemitism, in both its pre-Nazi and Nazi forms, had a virulence and intensity that set it apart from these other prejudices.[17]

Early prejudices

In both the Early American and Nazi-German cases, long-standing racial prejudices hardened at critical moments in their respective national histories. In the American case, the run-up to the American War of Independence from Great Britain emphasized racial themes and fuelled the colonists' racial anxieties, while the war itself displayed elements of a racial war between 'white' settler colonists and 'native' indigenous peoples. As American studies scholar Renée Bergland writes, '[T]he birth of the American nation and the death of the Native American were as closely related as light and shadow.'[18] The prediction (and hope) that all Indians everywhere in America would 'vanish' or 'disappear' became a key component of the nation-forging ideology of the new United States. In the German case, racial prejudices against Jews exploded during the First World War, and in the post-war (and short-lived) Weimar Republic (1918–33) many Germans on the radical Right called for government action against Jews and other targeted 'out-groups'. In the early Weimar period (the years 1918–23), national humiliation, defeat, revolution, and hyper-inflation led to the rise of German mass antisemitism, a widespread infiltration of antisemitic language and arguments into German political discourse, and an alliance between overt racism and respectability in German society.[19] Along with 'the Jews', Weimar conservatives also targeted some non-Jewish Germans as dangerous 'aliens'.

Early America

The American War for Independence had unleashed a new wave of anti-Indian and anti-Negro sentiment.[20] A rationale for the extermination of the Indians was, in fact, embedded in the Declaration of Independence (published 4 July 1776), America's founding document and the great charter of 'white' American liberties. Among the bill of particulars against King George III was the provocative charge that 'he has excited domestic insurrections among us, and has endeavored to bring on the inhabitants of our frontiers, the merciless Indian savages, whose known rule of warfare, is an undistinguished destruction of all ages, sexes, and conditions'.[21] Interestingly, Jefferson was repeating a charge made by Revolutionary propagandist Tom Paine in his tract *Common Sense* (published 14 February 1776 and widely circulated in the colonies) that England was a 'barbarous and hellish power, which hath stirred up the Indians and the Negroes against us'.[22] These references by Jefferson and Paine reflected the widespread belief in much of Colonial North America that the British were scheming to loose the Indians upon the frontier's back settlements and to incite the slaves in revolt, a disturbing vision, indeed, of a violent racial war to come. Ignoring settler atrocities against peaceable Native Americans, Jefferson's vicious caricature created a generic, colonist-hating Indian ready to unleash extreme violence against defenseless white women and children on the 'frontier'.[23] More and more, 'white' settlers cast the 'civilization'/'savage' dichotomy in permanent, racialized terms.

Racial themes persisted throughout the American War for Independence, with American Revolutionaries denouncing Britain's unholy alliance with the Indian 'enemy'. The conventional war fought between the American rebels and the British along the eastern seaboard was paralleled, and at times intersected, by a brutal genocidal war without mercy on the 'frontier' fringes of the 13 rebellious colonies.[24] In the Revolutionary War's aftermath, the notion of the American Revolution as a 'racial war' assumed a dominant place in the national mythology, as periods of Indian–white peace and patterns of interdependency were soon forgotten (as were those Indians who had remained neutral or fought with the 'patriots'). In the American national memory, 'the Indians' had sided with the British in an effort to prevent American independence and were, therefore, justly deserving of past, present, and future American assaults on Indian lands, communities, and cultures.[25] At the war's end, Native American communities were left facing an Indian-hating white society on the 'frontier', which was heavily armed and obsessed with the vision of 'vacant' Indian lands in 'the West'.[26]

With American independence won, Native Americans – whether they had sided with the rebels, sided with the British, or remained neutral – became increasingly identified as 'enemies' of the young republic, and Indian resistance was widely seen as a security threat to the new nation. In the Early Republic, the fiction took hold that *all* Indians had fought for the British in order to prevent American independence. This new national mythology was used, in turn, to justify dispossession, with Indian land (along with African labour) seen as a vital resource for the new nation. For the Revolutionary generation (as well as subsequent generations of Americans), Indian land became the key to national, state, and individual wealth. Meanwhile, 'white' citizens looked forward increasingly to a homeland in the 'New World' without Indians. The new American Republic, it was clear, would be a White Man's Republic, with its Jeffersonian and Jacksonian political elites committed to supplying good agricultural land to its 'white' settler farmers.[27]

The view of the American Revolution as a racial war took on a dominant place in the national mythology of the new nation. The Revolution, in cultural terms, perpetuated the early colonial image of the Indian as a 'savage'. In 1804, John Vanderlyn's famous painting, *The Death of Jane McCrea*, showed Indians assaulting a young, white female with obvious murderous intent; the painting fuelled sexual and racial anxieties among 'whites', reminding Americans that 'Indians' were (as Jefferson had told them in the Declaration of Independence) 'merciless savages' with genocidal intent against 'innocent' white settlers. Other artistic depictions of Native American people showed them slowly 'retreating westward, suffused in the heavy imagery of setting suns, as they "faded" from history'.[28] By the end of the American Revolution, the newly independent 'white' Americans had constructed an anti-Indian rhetoric (based on fear, loathing, and hatred of their 'savage neighbours') that was genuinely worth calling racist.[29]

In 1790 the US Congress, in the Naturalization Act, defined American citizenship solely on the basis of race, limiting the rights of citizenship to 'all free white persons who have or shall migrate into the United States'. The Revolutionary era, then, witnessed an emerging hierarchy of races, based on an 'inferior' status ascribed to Native Americans and African Americans. 'At the end of the eighteenth century', as historian Kathleen DuVal writes, 'most white Americans believed that all blacks were naturally and permanently inferior to all whites, and they were rapidly expanding their analysis to Indians.'[30] There was, moreover, a growing cultural construction of 'race', based on the idea of 'races' as separate and exclusive groups, on the notion of a racial determinism in explaining history and culture (and the success of the 'American experiment'), and on an Anglo-Saxon myth of innate white 'superiority'. By the end of the eighteenth century, then, Early America's racial ideology, in both political and popular culture, had achieved critical mass. Thanks to the post-Revolutionary generation, it would attain full flowering by the middle of the nineteenth century.[31]

Nazi Germany

As leader of the rising Nazi Party, Adolf Hitler was the leading advocate of racial thinking, a race-based ideology, and a racial worldview. Darwinian terminology and rhetoric permeated Hitler's writings and speeches[32], and he took the social Darwinian myth of 'superior' and 'inferior' races to a logical extreme, calling for the 'Aryan' German 'master race' to rule the world and to 'eliminate' 'inferior' races. In particular, as both a political biography and an ideological tract, *Mein Kampf* was a clear guide to his thinking on race. In the 'Conclusion' to his book, Hitler declared that Germany, if she was 'led and organized according to ... [racial] principles', would 'inevitably win her rightful position on this earth'. In this 'age of racial poisoning', he asserted, the German nation-state 'must some day become lord of the earth', if it 'dedicated itself to the care of its best racial elements'.[33]

During the post-First World War Weimar Republic (1918–1933), Hitler and other radical antisemites denounced the Jews as an 'alien' element to the German nation and as the cause for all the problems besetting Germany, including defeat in the First World War, the Bolshevik Revolution in Russia, post-war inflation, and the Great Depression. Under the Weimar system, the antisemites claimed, German politics, economics, and culture were controlled and dominated by 'the Jews'. In the eyes of many Germans, the Weimar Republic was a 'Jewish Republic', a convenient instrument for the establishment, consolidation, and exercise of Jewish power and influence over the German people. On the radical Right, Hitler was the most consistent theorist and practitioner of antisemitism. Nazi racial theory demanded, in the words of Nazi propaganda chief Josef Goebbels, 'the rigorous weeding out of all alien elements from all areas of public life' and, in particular, the 'destruction of the dung-heap of Jewish immorality and racial degeneration'.[34] The Nazis had a simple explanation for all of Germany's military, political, and economic catastrophes, captured in their slogan: 'The Jews are to blame!'. While antisemitism played a relatively minor role in Hitler's rise to power, an antisemitic discourse during the Weimar years poisoned the minds of many Germans.

Before the Nazis came to power, eugenic and related ideologies of social engineering spread through the medical, healthcare, criminological, and social policy-making professions. During the Weimar Republic, there was a decided turn towards 'biological politics' where social, cultural, and political issues were increasingly seen in racial terms and as issues of 'racial hygiene', laying the groundwork for the Third Reich's radicalized racial policies and grandiose population schemes.[35] Ideas about selective breeding and calls for 'permission for the destruction of worthless life' (the phrase is from a 1920 book written by the lawyer Karl Binding and the psychiatrist Alfred Hoche) had become widespread during Weimar, under the guise of eugenics. By the early 1930s, the eugenics that emphasized collective health gave way to a eugenics focusing on the dangers of racial and blood pollution.

In Weimar Germany, many Germans called for government action against society's 'out-groups'. Many of these 'out-groups', like 'the Jews', were blamed by conservative nationalists in the military and elsewhere, for Germany's defeat in the First World War and for the German Revolution of 1918. Roma and Sinti were subjected to police harassment and public hostility. Germans of African descent (the so-called 'Rhineland bastards', offspring of German women and black French colonial troops from Africa who had participated in the 1923 French occupation of the Rhineland) became easy targets of German racial prejudice. Jehovah's Witnesses were seen as an annoying and offensive 'cult' by mainline Christians, both Protestant and Catholic. Conservative Germans also called for government measures against homosexuals, criminals, and other so-called 'asocials', supposedly responsible for a wave of criminal activity and deviant behaviour which, in their view, characterized 'liberal' and 'permissive' Weimar society.[36] For many Germans on the Right, then, Weimar Germany was a society of 'alien' ethnic, racial, and social 'out-groups', whose very presence was intolerable to self-defined 'racially pure' Germans.

Dehumanization

In both Early America and Nazi Germany, perceptions of 'difference' and 'otherness' (within popular and political culture) further hardened into newly constructed racial ideologies, ideologies that served as convenient justifications for policies of expansion, conquest, and racial exclusion. In both cases, political leaders opportunistically used these processes of racial 'othering' to build a popular consensus for expansionist policies on the 'frontier' peripheries of 'empire' and for policies of segregation, exclusion, and elimination aimed at targeted 'out-groups'. In British North America and the Early American Republic, the concept of race became an invented rationale for the conquest of Indian lands and policies of Indian 'removal'. By classifying them as 'non-white', the successful American Revolutionaries wanted to reduce Indians and African slaves permanently to sub-human status and to deny them a place in the new nation. Nazi racial ideology and political propaganda called for the acquisition of 'living space' and for the removal and destruction of 'racially alien pests' (especially 'the Jews'), as 'life unworthy of life' representing a mortal threat to the health and existence of the German nation. As a result of an extreme process of racial 'othering' in Nazi Germany, eliminating 'inferior' peoples became, in the eyes of 'ordinary' Germans, a culture-wide sanitation project.

Early America

It took almost three centuries for Anglo-American perceptions of Native Americans to gradually evolve from assumptions of profound cultural 'difference' to a belief in their innate racial 'inferiority'.[37] In the late eighteenth century, perceptions of 'difference' first began to harden into notions of 'racial' categories. In Early America, the racialization of Indians and Africans was built on the foundational distinction between land and labour.[38] As slaves, blacks were a labour source that allowed frontier planters to realize the value of 'vacant' Indian lands by converting the 'wilderness' into 'civilization'. To assure continued economic growth, then, the newly independent republic needed both African labour and Indian lands. Conveniently, both enslaved Africans and Indians had been excluded from legal society; they were not viewed as 'people' in the new American Republic. Settler colonists were interested, moreover, in exploiting the Africans' labour and in taking the Indians' land, seeking to increase the black slave population and to 'reduce' the Indian population. Accordingly, black slaves were inoculated against smallpox and given medical treatment in case of sickness or disease; rum was rationed at holiday time and at weekends. On the other hand, epidemic disease among Native Americans went untreated, and whites often promoted alcohol with the intention of destroying life among the Indians.[39]

The emerging hierarchy of races assigned 'superior' status to whites and 'inferior' status to Indians and blacks. In the self-proclaimed 'New World', the Indians' status was that of a conquered and oppressed population possessing few attributes or racial characteristics that would allow them to become 'civilized'; as a slave population, blacks were consigned to a permanent servile status that offered no escape. Racism and notions of 'difference' in Early America defined African Americans and Native Americans as 'non-persons' within the white settlement culture. In Early America, however, race operated differently in the case of Native Americans and enslaved Africans: for blacks, race became a structure of social control; for Indians, it became a logic for 'elimination'. Dependent upon slaves as a cheap source of labour, white society did not seek to 'eliminate' blacks but aimed, instead, at their exclusion from white society. 'Eliminatory' policies (such as warfare, separation, and removal), therefore, were characteristically applied to Indians but not to blacks. Unlike the 'red' Indians, 'black' Africans were not seen as a 'dying race', a notion that became the ideological preserve of the Native Americans.[40]

The 'metaphysics of Indian-hating', as has been observed, 'reduced native people to the rest of the fauna and flora to be "rooted out"' by white settlers.[41] Indian-hating, unsurprisingly, was strongest among those who stood to most benefit from the 'obtaining' of Indian lands.[42] In the Early American Republic, 'white' Americans came increasingly to understand the Native American as an 'ignoble savage', destined to be destroyed by God, Nature, or 'Progress' to make way for 'Civilized Man'. The American settlers' strong desire for Indian lands, as well as settler 'eliminationist' tendencies, were apparent even to foreign visitors. During a visit to the southern states in 1797, Louis Philippe (future king of France) observed that '[c]ertainly no effort is made to hide plans to strip Indians of everything, and their eagerness to get on with it leads the whites often to paint the Indians in false colors'.[43] To be sure, by the mid-nineteenth century, territorial governors and local newspapers in the settler colonies of Texas, Colorado, and California openly called for the 'extermination' of 'the Indians' and for an 'exterminatory Indian war', echoing a popular sentiment among many 'white' western settlers.[44]

Within the broader political culture, certainly, views were more divided. While a few 'humanitarians' sought eventually to assimilate Indians into Anglo-American society, most settler colonists thought them 'inferior' and inassimilable. Other political theorists (notably Thomas Jefferson) offered the possibility of assimilation, as an *alternative to extermination.* Even the discourse of assimilation, however, was premised on the view that Indian ways of life were 'inferior' and that Indians were an 'inferior race' destined to 'disappear'. As such, the assimilationist discourse was 'linked to increasingly systematized theories of racial classification and hierarchy that tended to reinforce ontological thinking about race'; this discourse also 'facilitated fatalistic ideas about the inevitability of [the] Indians' disappearance'.[45] Even those nineteenth-century Americans who were somewhat favourably disposed to the Indian believed that, due to divine intervention or the laws of nature, the Indian, in the end, must 'disappear' from the American continent. White settlers, from their perspective, saw Indians at best as a nuisance and at worst as a real danger to the advance of western settlement. For their part, most intellectuals of the era were convinced of the Indian's 'racial inferiority'. As Thomas Gossett notes, in his classic study, however, differences in views were 'more apparent than real'. While the settler looked forward to – or was indifferent to – the Indians' extinction, most intellectuals were convinced that, because of their racial inferiority, the Indians must ultimately 'vanish'.[46]

Within popular culture (that is, stories, songs, paintings and engravings, domestic and commercial objects), the colonial image of native peoples was carried over into the popular culture of the new American nation. To settlers in British North America, Indians were seen either as traditional, fierce, and wild 'enemies' or as exotic, strange 'savages' and unlawful roamers of the North American continent – in either case as formidable foes who stood in the way of settler expansion. In the Early Republic, the racially constructed 'Indian' provided legitimacy for the conquest of the North American continent, for the eventual sovereignty of the United States over most of the continent, and for the 'Indian wars' of conquest and expansion. In opposition to the 'white' settlers, the image of the 'wild', 'uncivilized', and 'savage' Indian was, indeed, a vision of the 'Other'. A racial stereotype soon emerged of the Indian as captive to despair and addicted to alcohol, depravity, wildness, and violence, a stereotype that helped to perpetuate the belief that the Indian was inassimilable. Even more ominously, stories and images of Indian atrocities provided a basis and rationale for dispossession or forced removal (or worse) of Native Americans.

In Early America, as both a political theorist and a political leader, Thomas Jefferson was central to the formulation and dissemination of attitudes about race. On a personal level, Jefferson fully accepted the newly emerging ideas of Anglo-Saxon 'racial purity' and 'superiority' and found them helpful to assuage occasional doubts about slavery and the dispossession of indigenous peoples.[47] As we have instanced above, Jefferson's political rhetoric towards Native Americans during the American Revolution conjured up images of violence on the western 'frontier', images of white women and children being slaughtered, captured, and tortured by 'merciless savages'. In these images, Indians became despised objects of a powerful hate and were therefore declared ineligible for citizenship in the new American family. Jefferson's images and views often placed him on the side of Indian-hating western frontiersmen. As a political theorist, Jefferson had a geopolitical mind, driven by an exacting view of American destiny. His aim was a 'proper arrangement of the races' to be achieved by the creation of a racially homogenous, ethnic homeland of 'white' yeomen farmers: a nation (in Jefferson's words in an 1801 letter to James Monroe) 'free from blot or mixture'.[48] When it came to the Native Americans, Jefferson was a benevolent zealot who would do almost anything to ensure the survival and growth of his ethnically exclusive White Man's Republic of Anglo-Saxon yeomen. There was, however, a distinctly darker side to Jefferson's geopolitical vision. In the end, his attitudes and beliefs towards Native American peoples were premised on the 'disappearance' of a 'doomed red race', a 'red race' destined to cultural (if not physical) extinction.[49]

The Native American was commonly thought of as the 'vanishing American', a trope that became a persistent theme in Early American literature, popular culture, and political culture. As an 'inferior race', the future of the native peoples, many Americans believed, was predetermined: they would simply 'vanish' or 'disappear'. The idea of the Indian as a 'vanishing American' was a constant in Early American thinking, achieving the status of a cultural myth. This cultural myth became a convenient explanation for the 'red' man's 'inevitable fate' in what had now become a 'white' man's world. After 1814, with the end of the War of 1812 (America's Second War for Independence), the idea of the Indian as a 'vanishing' American (doomed to 'utter extinction') won wide public acceptance in popular culture, due to the collective efforts of poets, novelists, orators, and artists. This idea of the 'vanishing red race' owed much of its popularity to a simple realization among 'white' Americans that the Indians would have to disappear in order to make their lands 'available' for the 'white' settlers, making it convenient and easy to believe that God truly 'intended' the 'red' man's 'extinction'. In the end, the notion that the Native American peoples were destined to 'vanish' (leaving no trace behind) became a chillingly self-fulfilling prophecy.[50]

Nazi Germany

In the Third Reich, there was an ever-expanding aggregation of 'community aliens' – all of whom were targeted for maltreatment and violence. Indeed, according to the Nazi Party, the German Reich had many 'enemies' and targets of attack – of whom 'the Jews' were only one. In Nazi Germany, the process of racial 'othering' targeted not only Jews but also Sinti/Roma, Slavs, the physically and mentally disabled, homosexuals, and alleged 'asocials' as 'racial enemies' of the German people. In the Nazi racial view, Sinti and Roma ('Gypsies'), like 'the Jews', were 'carriers of alien blood' and, therefore, to be excluded from the 'national community'. In addition to a 'Jewish question', there was, the Nazis said, a 'Gypsy question', which needed to be resolved on a Reich-wide basis. In accordance with what the Nazis called criminal-biological/racist criteria, beggars, vagrants, and the homeless were categorized as 'disorderly wanderers' while so-called 'asocials' were accused of 'deviating' from the 'healthy instincts of the *Volk*'. The Nazis declared homosexuality to be a 'degenerate and racially destructive phenomenon' that must be 'eradicated' from German society.[51] Nazi racial prejudices and propaganda against all of the targeted 'out-groups' followed similar patterns, echoing and broadening familiar hatreds and linking them to current anxieties and concerns within broader German society.[52]

Before Nazi policy mandated physical death for the Jews, German public culture in the pre-war years made Jews suffer social death every day, through racism, discrimination, and social ostracism.[53] Most Germans, in the Nazi era, took cultural antisemitism – or a polite Judeophobia – for granted, even if they did not necessarily share the radical antisemitism of Nazi 'true believers'. In the mid-1930s, there was a dramatic increase in antisemitism in public culture, as Germans were deluged with 'proof' of the 'Jewish danger' and Jewish 'otherness' in books, documentary films, exhibits, and educational programmes. These efforts led to the construction of a so-called 'respectable racism', a deceptively mild form of racism that caused German citizens to expel Jews from the community of moral obligation and to view their Jewish neighbours and colleagues as a 'racial enemy' deserving of expulsion (or worse). As a result, a carefully invented race culture spread throughout the Third Reich, serving to prepare 'ordinary' Germans to tolerate decisive, brutal (and even criminal) measures against 'Aryan' Germany's declared 'racial enemies'.[54]

In the wider public culture, ethnic Germans – members of the supposedly 'superior' 'Aryan' race – were encouraged to reject citizens deemed 'alien' and to ally themselves only with people certified by the state as racially 'valuable'. Nazi Germany's public culture was characterized by an 'ethnic fundamentalism', based on Nazi racial beliefs and a concept of 'ethnic virtue' that promoted both 'Aryan' ethnic pride and a promised glorious future cleansed of ethnic 'aliens'. In what they called the 'battle for public opinion', the Nazis relied on precise public relations campaigns to popularize racial thinking and to imbue public culture with not only 'Aryan' racial pride but racial contempt for its targeted 'enemies'. The cumulative effect of these efforts was the creation of a public culture that effectively disabled empathy for these ethnic, racial, and social 'out-groups'. The public culture created by the Nazis was so compelling, moreover, that, even if one disagreed with one or another aspect of Nazism, it became easy to accept the notions of a racial hierarchy and hatred of racial 'out-groups', as well as the desirability of territorial conquest in 'the East' and subjugation of its 'inferior' indigenous populations.[55]

Within the Third Reich, professional elites in science, medicine, and the law were enlisted in the cause of 'manufacturing difference'. By helping to construct a fabricated hierarchy of racial types, anthropologists, for instance, helped bolster Nazi racial ideology and, ultimately, provided a theoretical foundation for euthanasia, 'racial hygiene', and the annihilation of Jews and other so-called 'impure' racial 'out-groups'. With such 'scientific' legitimation, in the Greater German Reich – as well as in the occupied territories in 'the East' – 'unwanted (*unerwünscht*) groups' would be moved, placed, positioned, or 'eliminated' to meet the needs of the Nazi racial state and to support Nazi projects of social and biological engineering.[56] 'The Jews', in particular, were seen as biological 'enemies', as a 'public health menace', and as 'racial pollutants'. The work of the professional elites in medicine[57], science, and law, led to the construction of a cultural consensus on the need to 'eliminate' Germany's supposed biological and racial 'enemies'. To win the support of the elites and the masses, racial 'othering' needed, above all, both a scientific stamp and a legalistic sanction. The German scientific community gave an academic validation to racism and identified Nazi racial enemies as 'inferior' and 'unworthy of life', as well as 'dangerous' to the 'Aryan national community'. For its part, the legal profession provided new legal theories to legitimate the Nazi regime's racial policies. In historian Omer Bartov's words: 'Thus, while the doctors sanctioned murder, the lawyers legalized crime.'[58]

Within the scientific community itself, German scientists in the fields of eugenics, racial hygiene, racial anthropology, psychiatry, human genetics, and population science all contributed to the formation of Nazi racial ideology, helping to mould and legitimate the process of racial 'othering'. Many German racial anthropologists, for instance, participated in the various aspects of Nazi and SS racial policy in the occupied eastern territories (including the 'Gypsy problem', the 'Slav problem', and the 'Jewish question'), providing support and inspiration for its murderous racial policies.[59] National Socialism conceptualized and practised racial hygiene as part and parcel of Nazi racism.[60] Within this framework, Nazi ethnic racism targeted groups considered 'inferior' on ethnic grounds, including Jews, Gypsies, and Slavs. Crucially, doctors and scientists who became Nazi converts believed – like the top Nazi leadership – that a racialized concept of 'health' justified antisemitism as well as plans for territorial expansion.[61] Quickly coming to terms with the Nazi regime, many German racial hygienists eagerly worked to validate Nazi racial theories, and some participated directly in the implementation of Nazi racial policy.[62] With the start of the wars for 'living space' in 'the East', racial hygienic supporters of *Lebensraum* initiated and endorsed population policies for replacing Poles, Slavs, and Jews with German settlers. In fact, many racial researchers aimed to be at the forefront of Nazi policy-making on 'depopulating' and 'repopulating' the 'Nazi East'.[63] The 'logic' of Nazi racial theory and racial ideology gave them, they believed, the 'right' to displace and annihilate 'inferior' races and peoples in Hitler's empire.

In the Third Reich, compulsory studies in Nazi 'racial science' were introduced into German schools. Under the Hitler regime, the schools themselves became sites for the teaching and practice of Nazi ideology and racial policy. In the classroom, German youth were taught the basic principles of Nazi racial ideology: ethnic arrogance in their Aryan 'superiority', racial contempt for Jewry and all 'lesser' races, and Germany's right to *Lebensraum*. Outside the classroom, Nazi youth organizations aimed at the total control, education, and indoctrination of the German youth. As young adults, many of these young people would carry these racial ideas and attitudes into the *Wehrmacht* or other Nazi organizations as fighters, pioneers, or colonizers in the 'Nazi East'.

For many biomedical scientists and others in the German medical profession, National Socialism was simply 'applied biology', a term used by Hitler deputy Rudolf Hess. Many in the medical profession viewed the 'Jewish question' as a 'medical problem' requiring a 'medical solution'. In 'the East' and in the Reich itself, 'unwanted' groups were portrayed as 'health hazards' to the 'Aryan' German population. Crucially, Nazi racial policies (including 'Jewish policy') were explicitly expressed in biological and medical terms and 'sold' to the German public as 'public health measures', measures aimed at 'cleansing the Fatherland' and the new eastern *Lebensraum* of supposed biological threats to the 'racial health' and 'purity' of the Greater German Reich and the Nazi empire. In the end, these ideas provided Nazi occupation forces with a convenient medical rationale for the 'concentration' and then the 'extermination' of 'the Jews'.[64] In a 1934 book honouring Eugene Fischer, director of the Kaiser Wilhelm Institute (KWI) for Anthropology, Human Heredity, and Eugenics, two German 'race scientists' made a plea for the 'application' of this 'biology', declaring that 'German science has given the politicians [in the person of German *Führer* Adolf Hitler] the necessary tools' to 'apply the knowledge of the biological foundations of nations – race, heredity, and selection'.[65] Within the Reich itself, as well as in the 'Nazi East', Hitler and the Nazi leadership would ruthlessly 'apply' this 'knowledge' to 'eliminate' 'Aryan' Germany's declared internal and external 'enemies' (especially 'the Jews').

During the so-called period of peace (that is, between the years 1933 and 1939), antisemitism was progressively diffused throughout German society. In these years, much of society had internalized the Nazi regime's antisemitism, by accepting the idea that a 'Jewish question' existed, which called for a 'solution'. While radical antisemitism probably influenced no more than a minority of Germans, enough 'ordinary' Germans did become affected by a strong Judeophobia, thus assuring the regime of a sufficiently wide consensus regarding its anti-Jewish policies. In both political and popular culture, the Nazis constructed a veritable culture of resentment against 'the Jews', a culture that resonated widely among the population generally and that turned a perception of Jewish 'otherness' into a very real sense that 'the Jews' presented a 'threat' to the very existence of the German nation. Tragically, this culture of resentment was to block even a minimum of fleeting compassion for the 'fate' of European Jewry.[66]

From the mid-1930s, then, a racist, antisemitic tone became a pivotal element of the Nazi regime's ideology and propaganda, as more anti-Jewish measures were taken by the regime. In these years, Nazi ideologues and propagandists mounted radical antisemitic propaganda campaigns, aimed at arousing the hatred of the German people against 'the Jews'. Demonizing and denouncing 'the Jews' as 'racial enemies' of the German *Volk*, these antisemitic campaigns were aimed at ethnic Germans on the homefront and in the armed forces. In this context, Nazi anti-Jewish policy could be (and actually was) presented as a set of justified protective and defensive (and even pre-emptive) measures against an alleged 'Jewish danger'. By 1939, due to these campaigns, an antisemitic consensus had become widespread in German and Austrian society, creating an indispensable reservoir of public hatred, contempt, and indifference towards 'the Jews'. By conscious design, Nazi ideologues and propagandists were engaged in the production and diffusion of a radical antisemitic discourse whose aim was to so enrage Germans against 'the Jews', that 'ordinary' Germans would support (or at least be indifferent to) measures taken (or to be taken in the future) against the fundamental 'racial enemy'.[67]

Radicalization

In both Early America and Nazi Germany, specific historical circumstances brought about an escalation and radicalization in the process of racial 'othering', as political leaders elected to pursue ever more aggressive policies of territorial expansion. A new 'racial science', in both cases, reinforced the Early American belief in white supremacy and the Nazi-German belief in Nordic or Aryan superiority. In Early America, 'race' was a social or cultural invention that had been used variously and opportunistically since the eighteenth century, mainly as a new form of social stratification and a rationalization for inequality in North America. By the 1840s, however, a categorical racism had gained respectability in the Early American Republic. In Early America, concurrently developing sciences played a key role in legitimizing race thinking, while scholarly and popular writings helped to disseminate and institutionalize a racial worldview. By the end of the 1930s, Germany had become the laboratory of a vast experiment to create a racist and antisemitic society. Crucially, it was Hitler's launching of a war for *Lebensraum* in 'the East', however, which made it possible to produce the nucleus of a genocidal community from within an apartheid German society.[68]

In both cases, this radicalization of racial 'othering' within Early American and Nazi-German popular and political cultures produced similarly strong notions of the inevitable 'disappearance' of targeted 'out-groups', thus making 'ordinary' citizens more likely to support (or at least be indifferent to) even more radical policies designed to 'hasten' the 'disappearance' of those identified as racial and ethnic 'enemies' of the nation-state. In the Early American case, an extinction discourse was to be found whenever and wherever 'white' American settler colonists 'encountered' indigenous peoples. Within this discourse, the 'demise' of the Native American populations was seen as 'inevitable' and, like the nation's own expansion, as the design of 'Providence'.[69] In the Nazi-German case, long-standing cultural prejudices and inherited feelings against Slavs and Jews, along with Nazi propaganda, helped to per-suade many to support Hitler's 'war of annihilation' in 'the East'. Thanks to the success of the process of racial 'othering', by 1940–1, Germany and German society had become a veritable reservoir for Daniel Jonah Goldhagen's 'willing executioners' of European Jewry.[70]

Early America

Within American political culture, there was a continued racialization of the notion of Indian 'savagery', due, in large measure, to the influence of Andrew Jackson and his followers. Jackson was viewed by his Early American contemporaries as a 'frontier American' and a 'child of the frontier West', and he was, in fact, the first president to achieve prominence west of the Appalachian Mountains. A brash frontiersman, unapologetic slaveholder, and fierce Indian fighter, his views on, and antagonism towards, Native Americans were representative of most, if not all, of his frontier neighbours. As a fire-breathing frontiersman, Jackson was obsessed with the Indian presence and the need to eradicate it.[71] He saw Indians as a 'disease' which, in his words, was 'constantly infesting our frontier'.[72]

The new American Republic, it was fervently believed, had a special racial destiny. A new racial ideology would be used by many of the new nation's political leaders and opinion makers to justify the permanent enslavement of blacks and the expulsion – and possible 'extermination' – of the Indians. In the 1830s, a sense of Anglo-Saxon racial destiny and of irreversible distinctions between the races was beginning to occupy the popular consciousness of 'ordinary' 'white' Americans.[73] The alleged 'superiority' of Anglo-Saxon 'racial' traits became a stimulus for American expansion and for notions that Americans, as God's 'chosen people', were destined to dominate others.[74] Indeed, by the mid-1840s, the use of the term 'Anglo-Saxon' in a racial sense became commonplace in the political discourse and political arguments of the day. Given the widely held racial and cultural prejudices against Indians, Americans on the western 'frontier' of empire did not want and would not accept the mass assimilation of Indian nations into the dominant 'white' society. Even the most acculturated Indians, the Cherokees, were an 'unwanted', 'alien' population in the 'white' settler 'living space'.

Another catalyst in the creation of a race-based Anglo-Saxon politi-cal ideology of expansion was the 'encounter' of white Americans with

Mexicans in the south-west. Like Indians, the Mexicans, according to many white Americans, were unwilling or unable to make 'proper use' of the land, and they were seen as a 'mixed, inferior race'. One of the most fervent believers in the destiny of a 'superior' Anglo-Saxon race was Sam Houston, a Jackson protégé and president of the newly independent Texas Republic. In 1844, Houston told a newspaper correspondent that the Mexicans would, like the Indian race, 'yield to the advance of the North America race'. Repeating this opinion in New York, two years later, Houston claimed that 'the Mexicans are no better than Indians, and I see no reason why we should not go in the same course now, and take their land'.[75] In the Jacksonian racial hierarchy, Mexicans became lumped together with Indians and black Africans as an 'inferior' race. In expanding their settlements westward, the supposedly 'superior' Anglo-Saxon race would 'inevitably' replace these 'inferior' races.

Within popular culture, generally, newspapers and popular books about life on the 'frontier' offered these racial views to a highly literate mass audience. In his 1832 novel, *Westward Ho!*, James Kirke Paulding, a prominent novelist and chronicler of the 'Frontier West', wrote of 'the red men' receding before the 'irresistible influence' of the 'wise white man' who 'carries with him his destiny, which is to civilize the world, and rule it afterwards'.[76] In pre-Civil War American literature, Indians became comfortable and comforting stereotypes, forming part of an Early American national ideology of expansion. As American studies scholar Louise Barnett writes, 'as noble savages, Indians could be remembered with a vague regret; as good Indians, they could helpfully initiate whites into the wilderness milieu before falling victim to their inherent inferiority; and as bad Indians, they deserved the harsh fate actively meted out to them by the conquering race'. Within a new genre of 'Indian hater fiction', she notes, an 'underlying racist climate' made Indian killing 'acceptable and even laudatory'.[77] While some writers continued the eighteenth-century image of the Indians as a 'noble savage', on a popular level this view was largely trumped by the depiction of 'the Indian' in so-called atrocity and captivity literature as an 'inferior' and expendable 'wild beast'. While the literary view of the Indian was mixed, both sides shared a commonly held assumption that the Indian was doomed to 'inevitable disappearance'.[78]

Beginning in the 1830s, pre-Darwinian American race scientists – in the emerging fields of natural history (embracing both geology and biology), economics, and anthropology – contributed to the development of a 'racial' discourse by supporting the notion of a racial hierarchy in which the 'civilized' strong exterminated or enslaved the 'savage' weak.

These new 'scientific' theories were seen to justify the enslavement of African Americans, the decimation of Native Americans, the conquest of northern Mexico, and the 'right' of Anglo-Saxons to the entire North American continent. Scientific racialist thinking provided a retroactive justification for policies and practices based on racial difference as well as a future justification for white domination and subordination of 'inferior' races and the expected 'disappearance' of non-white races.[79] The scientific attack on the Indian as 'inferior' and 'expendable' served to give authoritative backing to long-held popular beliefs, and presented the 'replacement' of an 'inferior' by a 'superior' race on the North American continent's 'living space' as fulfilment of the laws of science and nature.

During the mid-nineteenth century, the notion of 'civilization' was increasingly seen in racial terms, especially among scientific advocates of 'race'.[80] In the 1840s and 1850s, a debate about 'race' raged (inside and outside science) between the monogenists (who believed that all men are of one race and shared the same origin) and the polygenists (who believed that there are different races of men, who were separately created). A growing number of American ethnologists embraced polygenism and promoted the existence of 'race' and 'racial types', channelling ethnological research into the service of racial causes. Not surprisingly, this debate spilled over into US Indian policy – with monogenists generally supporting programmes of Indian 'civilization', education, and Christianization, with some polygenists supporting calls for Indian 'removal' (as the next logical step towards Indian 'extinction'), and with others calling for their outright 'elimination' by war or 'extermination'.[81]

In early 1854, five years before Darwin's *The Origin of the Species* appeared, Josiah C. Nott and George R. Gliddon published *Types of Mankind*, one of the first white supremacist narratives in American science. In this book, they saw racial determinism as the driving force behind human history. According to Nott and Gliddon, there were different 'races' of mankind: 'superior' types of mankind ('Caucasian races', bearers of 'civilization') and 'inferior' types of mankind (non-whites, 'savages'). Anticipating the notion of racial purity, Nott asserted in 1854 that 'it is evident...that the superior races ought to be kept free from all adulterations, otherwise the world will retrograde, instead of advancing in civilization'.[82] Embracing a belief in the innate inferiority of the Indians and of other 'non-white' races, polygenists – such as Nott and Gliddon – argued that the Indians were an 'inferior' species of man, incapable of further 'progress' or of being 'civilized'.

Racial and biological differences, they argued, were divinely ordained and immutable. Polygenist beliefs were held by many in nineteenth-century America (especially among the political elite), with even the prominent historian Francis Parkman ascribing the Indian's inevitable 'extinction' to their 'biological inferiority'. In a passage that justified the ongoing war on the racial 'frontier' and the decimation of Native Americans, Nott himself wrote that: 'looking back over the world's history, it will have been seen that human progress has arisen mainly from the *war of [the] races*. All the great impulses which have been given to it from time to time', he noted, 'have been the results of *conquests and colonizations.*'[83]

Nineteenth-century Americans were obsessed by the idea of 'race' and racial difference.[84] Anxious to justify the enslavement of blacks and the displacement (and possible extermination) of the Indians, many American politicians and writers in the popular press eagerly welcomed the scientific proof provided by the intellectual community, warmly embracing notions of racial difference and America's new racial ideology (based on a limitless expansion by a 'superior' American Anglo-Saxon race). By and large, however, it was Americans in direct contact with blacks and Indians who embraced scientific theories of black and Indian 'inferiority' and the new rationales developed by American theorists on race. In this context, these new racial ideas both reflected and influenced popular and political attitudes and opinion. By 1850, the inherent inequality of the races was accepted as a scientific 'fact' by most 'ordinary' Americans.[85]

To most Americans, 'Indians' were innately 'red', racially distinct, and 'inferior'. In the Early American Revolutionary, early national, and antebellum periods, the 'white' perception of Indian 'inferiority' was widespread (albeit not universal). By the middle of the nineteenth century, the dominant shift in Anglo-American perception had reached its logical conclusion: the racially 'inferior' Indian, most Americans had concluded, was 'resistant' to civilization, education, or missionary efforts and would never be able to be assimilated into the Anglo-American community.[86] An 1854 article in *DeBow's Review* declared that 'the doctrine of the Unity of the race, so long believed by the world is [now] ascertained to be false. We are not all descended from one pair of human beings .... The negro till the end of time will still be a negro, and the Indian still an Indian.' Another *DeBow's* essayist, in the same year, asserted that the Indian's 'race is run, and probably he has performed his earthly mission. He is gradually disappearing, to give place to a higher order of human beings.'[87]

From the 1860s onwards, the extinction discourse lent support to social Darwinism and its recent offshoot, the eugenics movement. In turn, Darwin and his followers produced new ideas that only served to strengthen the extinction discourse. According to the 'evolutionists', those races on the lower rungs of the evolutionary ladder were 'doomed' by the 'inexorable laws of nature', were 'slated for extinction', and, in fact, deserved their pending demise. With this discourse, the gulf between 'savage' and 'civilized' humans became almost unbridgeable, making the extinction of primitive races highly likely (if not inevitable). In short, the 'elimination' of 'inferior' human races had very much become a matter of 'scientific' inevitability.[88]

America's new racial ideology was increasingly useful to justify the sufferings or deaths of African Americans, Mexicans, and Native Americans, as well as assuage feelings of guilt about the mass violence that accompanied American expansion.[89] Within American political and popular culture, it should be noted, however, that a subtle (but important) distinction in 'out-group' status was also slowly emerging in this racial ideology. Comparing 'the negro' with 'the Indian', an 1854 article in *DeBow's Review* allowed that, while 'the negro' cannot 'be made civilized or made a white man', his condition 'can be ameliorated, and he can indirectly enjoy the benefits of civilization'. 'The Indian', on the other hand, like 'the savage beasts among whom he lives', was destined 'to disappear before the new tide of human life now rolling' westward across the North American continent.[90] While some eastern 'humanitarians' hoped to 'save' the Indian, in the eyes of most westerners the Indians were irredeemable peoples.

Nazi Germany

With their accession to power in January 1933, the Nazi regime undertook a programme to spread and reshape antisemitism. As a result of their efforts, many more Germans became antisemitic, and anti-Jewish prejudice became firmly entrenched in the broader German society. After 1933, anti-Jewish prejudice became a 'norm' in Germany. Under Nazi antisemitism, 'the "otherness" of the Jews was exaggerated and exalted into an essential "malignancy"'.[91] But it was during the war years (1939–45) that Hitler and leading Nazi Party propagandists and ideologists used radical antisemitic propaganda to persuade German citizens that 'the Jews' represented both a political and racial 'threat' to the German nation, an invented threat that conveniently reinforced the need to 'eliminate' European Jewry.

Within the plans for a racialized Nazi 'New Order' in Europe, the antisemitic driving force remained central, as did the notion of a 'war against the Jews'. Unlike other Nazi racial enemies, 'the Jews' were targeted for planned total physical extinction on a global scale. In Nazi eyes, 'the Jews' were *the* central enemy. Crucially, the Nazi regime's 'attitude toward the different groups, murderous though it was in every case, was', as has been suggested, 'different in the case of the Jews'.[92] In the racial fantasies of Nazi 'true believers', 'the Jews' were seen as an existential threat to the security of the 'Aryan race'. Unlike the Nazi regime's other racial enemies, 'the Jew' was a Satan, an incarnation of the Devil, which had to be destroyed root and branch – that is, every man, women, child, and infant. Up to 1941, 'the Jews' were one target among many, and, indeed, a lot of the Nazi regime's most radical measures had been taken against other targeted 'out-groups'. But with the war for *Lebensraum* in 'the East', 'the Jews' would now be positioned centre stage.

During the war years, a relentless anti-Jewish propaganda made its way into every crevice of German society; a propaganda whose slogans – mainly in the context of the racial war in 'the East' – became partially internalized among hundreds of thousands of 'ordinary' Germans.[93] There was, moreover, an enthusiastic acceptance of Nazi racial beliefs among many segments of German society. As a result of this intensive propaganda campaign, and due to the moderate antisemitism that was so common in German society, the Nazis were able, in a very short time, to advance their brand of radical antisemitism from a quasi-religious belief held by a small minority into a conviction that was accepted by ever larger numbers of 'ordinary' Germans. In a few short years, a murderous consensus developed within German society. Reaching this consensus, involved education, preparation, and propaganda based on the radicalization of pre-existing forms of prejudice against segments of the population that now became targeted for murder (partial or total). With great care, the Nazi regime organized these pre-existing elements and prejudices into a consensual racist, antisemitic ideology, based on a radical (though not necessarily murderous) antisemitism.[94]

Under the Nazis, radical antisemitism would be used to justify a policy of continent-wide mass murder. To this end, racial 'othering' became part of the definition of German collective identity in the Third Reich. Defined and shaped by Nazi propagandists and ideologists, there was, throughout the 12 years of Nazi rule, an omnipresent image of 'the Jew' as the fundamental 'racial enemy'. After 1941, 'the Jew', in both professional and popular literature, took on the position of an impending and major 'blood threat' to the 'racial health' of 'Aryan' peoples. In particular, the texts and images of Nazi wartime ideology and propaganda evidenced a radicalization of Nazi Germany's public language about the Jews, asserting that 'Jewry' was responsible for starting the Second World War and that a 'Jewish international conspiracy' was intent on destroying Germany and the German people. The National Socialist government successfully projected a genocidal policy onto 'the Jews' and 'international Jewry', arguing that *all* Jews were at war with Nazi Germany and aimed at destroying the Nazi regime and murdering the German people, thus compelling the Nazis to wage a 'war of retaliation' against European Jewry.[95]

Between 1933 and 1945, Nazi Germany sought to construct a racially organized state and society, an effort which ultimately led to the systematic and brutal persecution of the regime's alleged 'racial enemies'. The success of the Nazis' barbarous persecution of its racially determined victims was due, in large measure, to the success of its own aggressive process of racial 'othering'. As we have seen above, Nazi racial 'othering' grew out of a worldview that defined targeted 'out-groups' as 'life unworthy of life' and that targeted 'alien elements' who were deemed a 'threat' to the 'racial purity' and 'racial health' of the 'Aryan' German ethnic collectivity. Unlike its predecessors and imitators, Nazi racism had a comprehensive character. In a 1936 speech to Nazi agrarian functionaries, Darré declared to his audience that the 'axis of all National Socialist thinking [was] National Socialism's faith in blood, e.g. in race'.[96] In Hitler's Third Reich, racialism became the official doctrine and policy of the Nazi state; in Nazi Germany, to be sure, we see the creation of a functioning racial state. Far more than an indifference or apathy to the fate of the victims of Nazi persecution, there was within the broader German society a deliberate unwillingness to see or experience the very visible suffering of the racially defined 'Other'.[97]

In the Third Reich, Nazi racism also defined attitudes towards 'inferior' groups and 'sub-humans' outside of the German metropole, on the 'frontier' peripheries of 'empire'. Depictions of 'inferior' and 'hostile' Slavs – above all, Poles and Russians – had been cultivated by German intellectuals for decades, serving as justification for historic aggressive pre-Nazi designs upon 'the East'. Throughout the nineteenth century, Prussian politicians equated Slavs with Indians (or, as they called them, the 'American redskins'); a familiar stereotype of the day also distinguished between the 'manly' and 'active' Germans and the 'feminine' and 'passive' Slavs.[98] For their part, the Nazis gave these age-old stereotypes and prejudices a new racist edge. Indeed, some Nazis from the borderland regions, like *Warthegau Gauleiter* Arthur Greiser, saw the 'Slavs' as as threatening as the 'Jews'. For them, the Nazi project in 'the East' would be more than the destruction of European Jewry.[99] In a similar way to the American Indians, the Slavs were perceived as 'enemies' standing in the way of colonial expansion.

Unlike the Jews, there are few signs in Hitler's writings of his intentions towards the Slavs. While Slavic racial 'inferiority' was central to the notion of *Lebensraum*, prior to 1939 most Nazi leaders held only a vague notion of Slavic lowliness. After the launch of the war against Poland, however, these views hardened as Poles became the declared 'enemies' of the German Reich by 'blocking' the path leading to new German 'living space' in 'the East'.[100] In private, Hitler was more open about his intentions in the 'Wild East'. As he told his close associates, 'the real frontier is the one that separates the Germanic world from the Slav world. It is our duty to place [the frontier] where we want it.... It is inconceivable', he continued, 'that a higher people should painfully exist on a soil too narrow for it, whilst amorphous masses, which contribute nothing to civilization, occupy infinite tracts of a soil that is one of the richest in the world.' Under such circumstances, he concluded, it was Germany's 'right' to extend Germanic space further and further east, by a 'permanent war' in 'the East' as a 'dike against the Russian flood'.[101] In Nazi racial ideology, during the years 1939–45, Slavic peoples standing in the trajectory of Hitler's wars for *Lebensraum* – most notably, all Russians and Poles – were declared 'inferior' races and 'sub-humans' and would be the target of a brutal wartime anti-Slavic crusade.

In Nazi racial theory and discourse, 'Reich Jews' were never cast as a 'colonial other'. Within the Greater German Reich, the Nazis were fighting off a perceived Jewish penetration and domination of German life (by an already 'Westernized Jew'). On the 'frontier' colonial peripheries of 'empire', however, the Slavs and the *Ostjuden* (Eastern Jews) filled the role of the 'colonial native'. In Nazi eyes, the *Ostjuden* in the needed *Lebensraum* incorporated both the 'native other' (in the classical colonial sense) and the 'colonizing other' (of supposed German ancestral land, the greatest threat to the German settler colonizer).[102] In the 'Nazi East', both Slavs and Jews were recast as 'Indians' by their Nazi conquerors and occupiers, who frequently expressed the attitude of a settler-colonial racist. For instance, in Hitler's words, 'the East's' Slavic inhabitants were to be regarded and treated 'as American Redskins', and Hans Frank, head of the General Government of Poland, called Jews in the occupied eastern territories 'flat-footed Indians'. 'The East', the Nazis believed, was the reservoir of 'world Jewry'. Nazi theorists classified the indigenous inhabitants of 'the East' as 'Indians', as 'history-less peoples', as 'nomads' (rather than tillers of the soil), as 'savages', as 'passive' and 'child-like', and as 'cunning' and 'cruel'.[103] In their colonial fantasies, Nazi leaders would recognize Slavs and Jews as East European 'Indians', and the Nazis would fight their own 'Indian wars' in an attempt to tame the 'Wild East'. When they resisted German encroachment of their 'living space', the indigenes of the 'Nazi East', as we shall see, would be subject to similar practices of dispossession, displacement, and violence as visited on indigenous peoples in the 'American West'. In the Nazi racial world, however, 'the Jew' held a unique position: within the Reich itself, 'the Jew' was the fundamental 'enemy' of the 'Aryan national community'; in the 'Nazi East', the *Ostjuden* were seen as the carriers of the 'Judeo-Bolshevist contamination'. In either case, Nazi 'true believers' ultimately decided, 'the Jews' could not be allowed to live.

Similarities, differences, and links

Both Early America and Nazi Germany hierarchically organized a racist society. In both nation-states, the political leadership encouraged the creation of this hierarchical social structure, similarly constructed on the principles of racial 'difference' and 'otherness'. Racial 'othering', in both these contexts, became a collection of representations used to negatively define a collective aggregate as a political, economic, racial, cultural and/or security 'threat' to the nation-state. Thanks to these 'eliminationist' discourses, many 'ordinary' Americans held dehumanized beliefs about Indians ('savages'); for their part, many 'ordinary' Germans held dehumanized beliefs about Slavs ('sub-humans'), Sinti and Roma ('racial mishmash'), the disabled (lives 'unworthy of life'), and dehumanized/demonized beliefs about 'the Jews' ('racial enemy no. 1'). In both cases, science supplied guidelines, data, and arguments to justify racial thinking, providing political elites with scientific rationalizations that conveniently supported their beliefs, political goals, policies, and practices. In both cases, these processes of racial 'othering' led to a cultural and political consensus on the desirability of an America 'without Indians' and a German Reich and Nazi empire 'free' of 'racially alien', 'unwanted' peoples (especially 'the Jews'). In both societies, this process of racial 'othering' – in both political and popular culture – would render ordinary citizens passive, indifferent, or complicit in the 'fate' of the targeted 'out-groups'. Many 'willing' American and German citizens, in fact, would 'help' these 'unwanted' ethnic and social 'out-groups' 'disappear', as they 'faded from history'. In both cases, leading voices in the political culture argued that the 'alien' element (that is, 'the Indians' and 'the Jews') were supporting a genocidal policy aimed at the majority society; both political leaderships succeeded in projecting aggressive genocidal intention onto the indigenous 'Other'. In both dominant societies, the 'American West' and the 'Nazi East' operated as spatial, racial, cultural, and colonial constructs, defining the 'frontier' as 'hostile' lands inhabited by 'inferior' peoples unworthy to occupy these 'spaces'. Convinced of their own 'racial superiority', 'ordinary' Americans and 'ordinary' Germans in the new 'living space' were not to be constrained by moral or ethical norms that might guide their behaviour towards others higher in the racial hierarchy. In both contexts, 'race', race thinking, and racial 'othering' acted as necessary (but not sufficient) conditions for 'eliminationist' assaults, as part of nation-state projects of territorial conquest and racial cleansing. As we shall see below, other factors – in both contexts – would provide the triggers and catalysts for 'eliminationist' violence against indigenous 'others' in the 'American West' and the 'Nazi East'.

While race became *the* organizing principle for both Early American and Nazi-German societies, there were important differences in their conceptions of racial 'otherness', differences that would ultimately influence government policy towards the respective indigenes and targeted 'out-groups'. In Early America, 'race' was a socially accepted concept; in Nazi Germany, 'race' was proclaimed as a 'biological fact'. From the beginning of the American nation's founding, Indians were denied rights of citizenship and possibilities of assimilation. Nazi Germany, on the other hand, had to formally annul the legal protections of already assimilated Reich citizens on the basis of what the National Socialist government defined as their 'race', 'ethnicity', or 'asocial' status. In North America, race ideology suggested that human physical and cultural differences *need* not be tolerated; the extremes of Nazi race ideology, however, declared that these differences, in fact, *would* not be tolerated.[104] In Early America, indigenous peoples could be saved only by ceasing to be Indians in any discernible way, by knowingly choosing a path of non-resistance to 'white' settler colonial expansion, or by attempted assimilation into white society.[105] In the 'Nazi East', some Slavs would serve as slaves to their Nazi masters, a few deemed 'racially valuable' would be eligible for assimilation, and most would be decimated. The Jews of the Greater German Reich metropole, of the 'Nazi East', and of Nazi-controlled Europe, on the other hand, could not be saved. In Holocaust historian Raul Hilberg's memorable words, 'The missionaries of Christianity had said in effect: You have no right to live among us as Jews. The secular rulers who followed had proclaimed: You have no right to live among us. The Nazis at last decreed: You have no right to live.'[106]

Throughout the Third Reich, the National Socialist leadership would display a resolute consistency to the long-term Nazi goal of racial purification. In the end, the Nazis sought a radical reordering of the European continent along racial-biological lines. In the process, Hitler's Third Reich became the first state in human history whose dogma and practice was racism.[107] But the Nazi 'racial state', nonetheless, had important roots in the broader landscape of Western history. In terms of racial theory, Nazism joined together the two paradigmatic figures of 'otherness' in the Western world: the Jewish 'other' of the 'civilized world' and the Slavic sub-human (*Untermensch*) 'other' of the 'colonized world'.[108] In its essentials, the Nazi race ideology, as we have seen above, contained the basic ingredients of the racial worldview of the late eighteenth century. It was, in many ways, the logical outcome of the race ideology first developed by the eighteenth-century 'white' Anglo-American settler society.[109]

Part II
Settler Colonialism

Introductory note

Within an overall imperial project, 'colonialism' is a relationship of domination by which the invader rules the indigenous inhabitants of colonized 'living space', according to the wishes and dictates of national elites in the imperial metropole. In the literature, as recently noted, 'most common definitions of colonialism describe a general process in which a nation-state expands its territory as well as its social, cultural, and political structures into extant territories beyond its own national boundaries'. As a structure of domination and oppression whereby one group of people benefits from the exploitation and subjugation of another, it is 'a process in which one power exerts and maintains control over what ultimately becomes a dependent area of people'.[1]

As a variety of colonialism, 'settler colonialism' denotes a method of conquest and expansion, as well as policies and practices toward indigenous inhabitants in the new settler 'living space'. In different historical contexts, the notions of 'space' and 'race' were the two overriding preoccupations of settler colonialists everywhere.[2] Rather than imperial expansion undertaken for primarily military advantage or trade, settler colonialism involves the presence of a settler population intent on land seizure.[3] The impetus for settlement is the land and the wealth that land could bring. In settler colonialism, the metropolitan country encourages or dispatches colonists to 'settle' the territory of indigenous peoples. As such, it 'implies displacement [of those peoples] and occupation of [their] land'.[4] In a settler colonial context, there is a continuing 'land grab' of indigenous 'space'. In this context, moreover, invasion is a structure (not an event); the colonizers come to stay. In lands already occupied by indigenous people, settlement is premised on 'removal' and 'replacement' of the indigenous peoples, as well as on what Patrick Wolfe calls a 'logic of elimination' – a logic which ensures that spatial coexistence of invaders and indigenes is highly improbable. Disturbingly, it is characterized by what he terms a 'sustained institutional tendency to eliminate the indigenous population'.[5] The 'logic of elimination', then, becomes the 'essential characteristic of the settler-colonial project'.[6] Caught in the maelstrom of settler colonialism, 'native' indigenous peoples would be subjected to ethnic transformation, spatial displacement, slow death via attrition, and/or immediate death by killing.

Political scientist Daniel Jonah Goldhagen is correct when he asserts that 'eliminationist' beliefs, desires, ideologies, discourses, acts, and policies have been a 'central feature of all eras of human history and all sorts of societies'.[7] In many (but not all) cases, the result of settler-colonialist practices and policies is the dissolution (and often the destruction) of indigenous communities and societies, achieved by various modalities of violence (often working in tandem), including massacres, selective killings, forced expulsions, coerced labour, destruction of indigene villages and food supplies, disease, malnutrition, and starvation.[8] Driven by its primary logic of 'elimination', settler colonialism is, to be sure, 'prone to genocide'.[9] In this context, 'planting' settler colonies invariably means 'supplanting' the indigenous inhabitants. This process of 'supplanting', what is more, has an 'inherent genocidal imperative' – that is, a 'potential for extreme forms of genocide that [sadly] is all too often realized'.[10]

As an historical phenomenon, settler colonialism changed over time.[11] In most past conceptualizations, settler colonialism was seen by historians as a pre-twentieth century phenomenon informing colonization by western nation-states, including the English conquests of Ireland and British Colonial America, the Anglo 'settler democracies' of the United States and Australia, and European colonialism in Africa (for example, the French in Algeria and the Germans in Southwest Africa).[12] Reaching across specialization, however, two scholars of colonialism have recently argued (convincingly, in my view) of 'the continued centrality of settler projects to the histories of nations and empires in the twentieth century', including the Nazi national project in 'the East'.[13]

The next three chapters of the book provide an overview of the methods, policies, and practices of settler colonialism, as carried out by the Early American and Nazi-German nation-states in their respective 'western' and 'eastern' empires. On the North American continent, settler colonialism occurred in uneven chronological and geographical phases, in Britain's North American colonies and in post-independence America.[14] For its part, the Nazi 'eastern empire' was designed to be run according to the model of 'settler colonialism',[15] based primarily on the North American example (as understood by Hitler).

Chapter 3, 'Conquest and Expansion', recounts the acquisition of new 'living space' for the American 'western empire' and the Nazi 'eastern empire'. It sketches other colonial expansionist episodes which preceded the Early American and Nazi-German national projects of territorial expansion. It also examines the diplomatic tactics (often premised on the threatened use of force), as well as actual episodes of naked military force, used by political leaders in each nation-state to acquire additional 'living space' for their growing continental empires. And it describes the disturbingly similar ways of war used by the Early American and Nazi-German nation-states, ruthless ways of war which accepted, legitimized, and encouraged murderous attacks upon enemy non-combatants (including women and children) as well as the intentional destruction of indigene villages and agricultural resources.

Chapter 4, 'Colonization', reviews the proposed colonization plans for, and actual settlement practices in, the 'American West' and the 'Nazi East'. It sketches prior colonization efforts in the earlier histories of Early America and Nazi Germany which served as antecedents for later colonization in the 'Wild West' and the 'Wild East'. It describes colonization plans developed to settle, control, and govern the new settler 'living space' in the Early American 'West' and the Nazi-German 'East'. It also shows how America's 'western empire' and Hitler's 'eastern empire' were linked to the common notion of a 'people's empire' which would benefit, as well as provide new opportunities for, 'ordinary' Americans and 'ordinary' Germans. And it examines the actualities of 'settlement' ('unsettlement'?) in the 'American West' and the 'Nazi East'.

Chapter 5, ' "Out-Group" Policy', looks at the policies and practices political leaders adopted in dealing with ethnic and racial 'out-groups' in both metropolitan and colonized 'space'. It describes the almost constant wars of 'pacification' to 'clear' indigenes from the land in advance of, or as part of, the actual 'settlement' process in the 'American West' and the 'Nazi East'. It depicts deliberate 'eliminatory' national policies of separation and segregation to 'cleanse' metropolitan and colonized 'living space' of 'alien' and 'unwanted' ethnic and racial 'out-groups'. It also examines totalizing 'territorial solutions' to the 'out-group problem' which were actively considered (but not adopted) by Early American and Nazi-German policymakers. And, finally, it explores the 'final solutions' ultimately embraced by these policymakers in the metropole after various 'territorial solutions' were no longer feasible or viable.

3
Conquest and Expansion: 'Obtaining' New 'Living Space'

In both the Early American and Nazi-German cases, continental expansionist preoccupations were underpinned and prescribed by comparable expansionist ideologies of 'space' and 'race'. In pursuit of these expansionist ambitions, as well as motivated by similar aspirations, Early American and Nazi-German political leaders used markedly similar strategies and tactics to pursue continental expansion. Both actual expansionist trajectories were, of course, influenced by specific national developments, as well as aided or constrained by strong historical forces (both domestic and international) prevailing at the time. In both cases, however, actual policies and actions were strongly influenced and shaped by guiding ideological principles and beliefs embedded in the respective continental imperialist discourses – discourses that ultimately influenced American and German policymakers' predispositions, tendencies, options, and priorities.

Both the Early American and Nazi-German nation-states pursued aggressive policies of conquest and expansion, policies driven by racial-imperialist ideologies founded on the 'taking' of land from allegedly 'inferior' indigenous peoples to create 'living space' for their settler colonists. In both cases, prior histories of 'western' and 'eastern' expansion, respectively, provided important historical antecedents and legacies, which informed and, in the eyes of latter-day expansionists, legitimized their own expansionist visions and agendas. In addition, both Early American and Nazi-German governing elites used surprisingly similar diplomatic methods, means of military conquest, and ways of war to further their imperialist goals: diplomatic methods often premised on the threatened (or actual) use of military force and ways of war and conquest that accepted, legitimized, and encouraged extreme violence and murderous attacks upon enemy non-combatants (including women and children), as well as the destruction of indigene villages and agricultural resources.

In the Early American case, aggressive territorial expansion often involved acquiring extensive lands in a single action, as well as in much smaller increments.[1] America's expansionist presidents consistently pursued a cycle of acquisition, often threatening war but then settling by treaty and/or purchase or, in the case of Mexico, by provoking and winning a war.[2] In Early America's 'imperial surge', American political leaders, as historian Thomas Hietala notes, employed a wide range of tactics, including 'open diplomacy, intrigue by secret agents, economic leverage, intimidation, [covert military pressure], and offensive war' to achieve their expansionist goals. The expansionist policies of both Jeffersonian and Jacksonian presidents, he observes, were based on similar strategies of territorial expansion – 'subjugate the natives, acquire their land by purchase or conquest, then remove the survivors to remote and poor areas of no interest to the whites'. Rather than the visible 'hand of God' (as the Manifest Destiny ideologues asserted), policymakers, politicians, propagandists, soldiers, and settlers guided the nation's territorial expansion and growth. Far from being 'inevitable', 'destined', or 'fated', the continental expansion of the United States was the result of deliberate planning and action – that is, it was a matter of purposeful political, diplomatic, and military policy, the result of 'manifest design' (and not of 'manifest destiny'). Earlier scholarly notions about the assumed benevolence and innocence – as well as the supposedly accidental nature – of American expansionism, as Hietala rightly argues, tend to minimize or ignore much of the historical evidence.[3]

It is no longer accurate to say that American expansion was not imperialistic. Racism, aggression, war, and conquest were all essential factors in American westward continental expansion. As recent scholarship convincingly demonstrates, it was the result of deliberate actions by political, diplomatic, and military leaders – that is, a matter of purposeful policy and endeavour. Conscious policy and deliberate actions – not 'fate' or 'destiny' – were its actual driving forces. Far from being benign expansionism, Early American western expansionism was a violent, imperialistic process by which lands were wrested from the indigenous peoples. Both purposeful federal policy and ruthless political and military power were necessary prerequisites to the conquest of the entire North American continent.[4]

In the Nazi-German case, the conquest of *Lebensraum* was the core of Hitler's policies of conquest and expansion at all times.[5] Nazi expansionist aims and policies were not a series of limited diplomatic and/or military actions to revise the territorial provisions of the Treaty of

Versailles but, instead, were aggressive territorial expansions (predicated on a series of wars) to secure sufficient 'living space' for the German people in 'the East'. *Contra* the revisionists, Hitler desired *Lebensraum*, not border revision. As noted above (Chapter 1), the German *Führer* was a self-described '*Raumpolitiker*' (space politician) whose goal was to seize vast areas for German settler colonies, and he had only disdain for the so-called '*Grenzpolitiker*' (border politicians) whose aim was merely to undo the territorial arrangements of the Treaty of Versailles and the post-First World War political settlement. Hitler could (and did), in fact, pursue both revisionist and expansionist sets of foreign policy objectives simultaneously, disguising his ultimate objectives from other major European powers. In light of more recent scholarship, it is becoming increasingly difficult to distinguish between a revisionist and expansionist phase of Nazi foreign policy. Instead, we can discern 'a phase of concealed preparations for aggression until 1937, a period of open and violent expansion from 1938, the unleashing of war in 1939, and the plans for a step-by-step creation of a "Greater German Reich" by way of military and terroristic violence as well as economic exploitation and financial integration'.[6]

Hitler's expansionist policies were characterized by tactical adroitness, the gambler's bluff, the bold leap, elements of surprise, the bold coup, intimidation, and the *fait accompli*, as well military force (both threatened and actual). Perpetual, limitless expansion was the very essence of Nazism. Both Hitler's 'intentions' (as expressed in his ideological views) and 'structural' factors (that is, conditions and forces inside and outside Germany) shaped the implementation of the *Führer*'s intentions to acquire 'living space' in 'the East'.[7] While Hitler was opportunistic in terms of short-term political and diplomatic moves, most of his actions in the run-up to the Second World War were based on long-held policy goals derived from Nazi continental imperialist ideology, as expressed in his writings and speeches.[8] In the Nazi-German context, 'ideology' largely functioned as general ideas driving Nazi expansionism (rather than a stage-by-stage blueprint for action).[9] While there were varying centres of influence in Nazi foreign policy (as well as differing views as to aims, methods, and timing), Adolf Hitler's continental imperialist ideology and intentions were, in the end, the crucial and determinant elements.

Antecedents

In both the Early American and Nazi-German cases, recent historical examples of 'western' and 'eastern' trajectories of conquest and expansion provided important precedents, models, and justifications for future continental expansion in the 'American West' and the 'Nazi East', respectively. Both prehistories, in fact, were replete with numerous historical examples of colonial conquest and expansion predicated on the 'taking' of indigenous lands, the 'planting' of settler colonies by the invaders, the 'supplanting' of the indigenes, and the use of 'the sword' against any indigenous inhabitants (both combatants and non-combatants) standing in the way of, or openly resisting, the expansionist projects.

In the American case, the conquest and colonization of Ireland became a model that English metropolitan sponsors and investors consciously sought to employ in their North American settlements and colonization projects.[10] Indeed, a number of veterans of the Irish campaign were prominent among those who set out to 'conquer' North America. Military adventurers in the 'New World' brought the brutal tactics of the 'Irish wars' to the early 'Indian wars' on the Anglo-American 'frontier'.[11] Following from the Irish experience, early English maritime expansion was part of a broader transatlantic and imperial background, as England and its imperial rivals – the Netherlands, France, and Spain – all looked to 'plant' settler colonies in the 'New World' of the Americas. In the Nazi-German case, thirteenth-century and early twentieth-century antecedents offered the Nazis their main historical examples and justifications for a new German 'drive to the East'. German invaders of 'the East' during the First World War, as well as the post-war German Baltic *Freikorps* fighters, saw themselves as resurrected thirteenth-century Teutonic Knights, the crusading military order who conquered territory in the eastern Baltic lands during the Middle Ages. In their propaganda and ideology, the Nazis – particularly those top leaders who had fought in the war and/or the *Freikorps* – declared that they would follow the path of the Teutonic Knights as they sought new 'living space' for the German people in 'the East'.

Early America

Beginning in the sixteenth century, English imperialists began to advance on their country's 'borders', 'peripheries', 'marchlands', and 'frontiers'. England's first imperial adventures took place in the British Isles, with 'border adjustments' and 'conquests' seen as essential to the nation's security and economic well-being. In the late sixteenth and early seventeenth centuries, an expanding Tudor state looked to 'incorporate' the Scottish borderlands, the Welsh marches, and the western island of Ireland into its growing imperial dominion. In the 'frontier' zones of Scotland, Wales, and Ireland, English and indigenous cultures stood opposed, with the English committed to 'obtaining' 'native' lands and imposing their ways of life on the indigenes (whatever the cost in 'native' lives). In these contexts, wars of conquest became a constant requirement for English expansion, settlement, and subsequent colonization.

The goal of English imperialism in Ireland was to bring the island under English control and make it 'British'. The conquest and colonization of Ireland was based on an agreed plan of action, a plan centred on: military conquest, local control by demobilized English soldiers, 'removal' of indigenous Irish populations from 'forfeited' lands, and large-scale colonization by dispatch of British settler colonists.[12] The Irish generally were held to be 'savages', 'aliens', 'enemies' of England, and 'weeds' to be eliminated.[13] In the English metropolitan view, the 'wild Irish' were 'unsettled' semi-nomads who did not properly cultivate their land, giving 'superior' English settler farmers the 'right' to take it. The English colonial project in Ireland required the displacement of 'native' indigenous populations, a policy that led to widespread resistance by Irish 'rebels' and 'extirpative war' by the English. In this context, English tactics against the 'savages' included a scorched earth policy aimed at the destruction of 'native' crops and houses, as well as genocidal massacres targeting men, women, children, the sick, and the disabled.[14]

The Elizabethan conquest of Ireland was simultaneous with, and ran parallel to, the English colonization of North America. In the eyes of Sir John Davies, the English attorney general for Ireland, the Ulster plantation was but 'the most inland part of Virginia'.[15] Ireland and America, to be sure, shared a common ideology of English colonization.[16] On the 'frontier', the English conceptions of 'the Irish' and 'the Indians' were, in fact, quite similar. In the English view, 'Indian' and 'Irish' indigenous populations were 'idle', 'lazy', 'dirty', and 'uncivilized', 'barbarians' who did not make proper use of the land; in English eyes, both 'the Irish' and 'the Indians' were 'heathens' and 'savages', 'wasteful' and, therefore, undeserving of their lands. In both contexts, the English used notions of 'native' 'inferiority' to justify conquest and dispossession of 'native' lands, as well as to establish pretexts for 'extirpation' of 'native' combatants and non-combatants. These notions of 'native' inferiority, in their view, absolved them of any need to use normal ethical restraints in dealing with 'the natives'.[17] Any 'natives' who resisted English settlement and colonization, moreover, would be put to the sword, combatants and non-combatants alike (regardless of sex or age).

While metropolitans, in both contexts, claimed to want to 'civilize' the 'natives', the settler colonists increasingly saw 'the Irish' and 'the Indians' as incapable of being 'civilized'.

During the first century of English settlement in North American, roughly the period 1585–1685, English settler colonists competed with American Indians in the Chesapeake Bay region and in New England for control of land and resources on the first Anglo-American 'frontier'. Metropolitan Englishmen (in both Britain and the colonies) looked to spread English Christianity and English 'civility' among the 'New World's' 'native' inhabitants (a vision that required peaceful relations with the Indians and avoidance of costly 'Indian wars'). At the same time, the metropolitan English sought to defend their colonial possessions from other European 'enemies' and to establish English dominion in North America by building strategic alliances and establishing intricate trade networks with the indigenes. Locked in competition with 'natives' for control of Indian ancestral lands, English settler colonists on the 'frontiers' of the Anglo-American empire, however, viewed the Indians as irredeemable 'savages' and often looked to 'eliminate' (and sometimes kill) the very same Indians the metropolitans were hoping to 'convert' and 'civilize'. For their part, most Indians had little interest in adopting English values, religion, and ways of life and openly resisted (violently, at times) the English settler conquest of their lands.[18] In Early Virginia and Early New England – the first successful English North American settlements – conquest and expansion meant the subjugation and dispossession of 'the natives' by force, their segregation and removal from 'white' settlement zones, brutal attacks on warrior combatants and non-combatants (regardless of sex or age), and slavery for the Indian survivors.

The Anglo-French contest for North American dominion focused on Indian homelands between the Appalachian Mountains and the Mississippi River. This contest culminated in the French and Indian War (1756–63), a conflict that became a global war – known to the Europeans as the Seven Years' War – fought on four continents and three oceans, which resulted in the defeat of France and her Spanish ally. In February 1763, the Treaty of Paris extended Britain's North American possessions from the Atlantic (in the east) to the Mississippi (in the west) and from Hudson Bay (in the north) to the Gulf of Mexico (in the south). Parties to the war but not the peace, the Indians were stunned when they received news that their French allies (most – but not all – Indian tribes had sided with the French) had handed over their homelands to the British, without so much as consulting them. With the French and their

Indian allies defeated, Anglo-American settler colonists looked to 'settle' on the newly acquired 'western' lands, serving to intensify the competition between Anglo-American settlers and Indian peoples for Indian homelands.[19] Tired of costly colonial wars, King George III issued a Royal Proclamation in October 1763, aimed at restricting and regulating further settler expansion onto Indian lands (a move that angered George Washington and other fellow Virginian speculators in western lands) and at creating a so-called 'reserve' for eastern Indians beyond the Appalachian Mountains. Viewed by the Anglo-American colonists as a British attempt to prohibit 'white' settlement 'west' of the Appalachians, the Proclamation became a major cause of the American War for Independence from British rule (1775–83), as the Anglo-Americans looked to build their new nation and 'western empire' on lands 'obtained' from Indians. In an atmosphere of escalating racial hatred between white settlers and Indians, the earlier 'middle grounds' on the edges of the Anglo-American 'frontier' – based on relative peace, coexistence, trade, and mutual dependence – were fast disappearing.[20]

Everywhere in British North America, conquest and expansion left a legacy of Indian subjugation, dispossession, 'elimination', enslavement, and the indiscriminate killing of non-combatants (regardless of sex or age). A defining feature of the first Anglo-American 'frontier', the clash of 'metropolitan' and 'frontier' interests would also be evident in subsequent American 'frontiers' in 'the West'.[21] Like the early Anglo-American metropolitans, the post-Revolution metropolitans (leaders such as George Washington, Henry Knox, and Thomas Jefferson) hoped for an 'orderly' and 'peaceful' 'settlement' of their new 'western empire' and looked to a 'civilizing' and 'Christianizing' of the American Indians by offering benevolent metropolitan plans of acculturation. In post-independence America, however, settlers on the 'frontier' cared little about bringing 'civilization' and 'Christianity' to the 'natives'; they wanted immediate 'settlement' and 'obtaining' of Indian lands, even if that meant fighting the occasional 'Indian war' when 'the natives' resisted the taking of their homelands. Constant settler pressure on Indian lands only led to mounting Indian resistance to white conquest, a dynamic featuring mutual and reciprocal genocidal violence against both Indian and settler combatant and non-combatant populations. Fatefully, the early Anglo-American settler colonists of coastal North America bequeathed to post-independence Americans over a century's experience in waging 'extirpative war' against Native Americans, a 'way of war' that would shape the 'Indian wars' of the late eighteenth and nineteenth centuries.[22]

Nazi Germany

In Germany, the idea of territorial expansion was focused eastward, on lands adjacent to the German nation-state – especially in Poland and the Baltic States – in what was viewed historically as Germany's 'frontier' territories. The new German imperialist *Lebensraum* ideology, in its numerous manifestations, 'signified a return to the pristine, lost past of the Teutonic Order and Frederick the Great, and heralded a[n eastern] paradise to be regained'.[23] For many Germans, the turn to 'the East' was a 'return', a chance to complete the plan started by their thirteenth-century ancestors when crusading Teutonic Knights had conquered and Germanized 'the East' by 'the sword'. The example of the Teutonic Knights and their Baltic crusade would provide a powerful historic precedent for twentieth-century Germans committed to continuing what they saw as the inevitable and timeless German 'drive to the East' (*Drang nach Osten*) and expansion onto Slavic lands.

When war broke out in Europe, in August 1914, a debate between *Weltpolitiker* and *Lebensraum* imperialists quickly ensued over the question of German war aims in the First World War. The so-called 'September Programme' of German Chancellor Theobald von Bethmann-Hollweg was centred on the *Weltpolitik* economic imperialist notion of a central European economic union (popularly called *Mitteleuropa*) and extensive acquisitions in Central Africa (popularly called *Mittelafrika*). On the imperialist right, Heinrich Class, leader of the Pan-German League, drew up his own memorandum on German war aims, advocating a *Lebensraum*-oriented policy based on extensive additions to German territory on the European continent (especially in 'the East') and the massive settlement of German peasant farmers (mostly war veterans and urban workers) on large areas of agricultural land to be annexed primarily in Eastern Europe. Class also insisted on the 'clearing' of 'native' populations from German-annexed lands in the Baltic and Poland, with Slavs sent to a Polish state under German control and with Jews sent to a specially designated Jewish state carved out of Russia or part of the Ottoman Turkish empire. The *Lebensraum* annexationist war-aims position ultimately triumphed in July 1917, when Bethmann resigned and the political vacuum was filled by the Army High Command under General Paul von Hindenburg and General Erich Ludendorff.[24]

While the war on the Western front was effectively stalemated, unexpected military victories on the Eastern front brought large areas of the Russian empire (in what would become the post-war Baltic States and Poland) under German military control, fuelling German imperialist visions of vast territorial gains in 'the East'. The German eastern victory against the Russian Army in 1914 was named the Battle of Tannenberg, redeeming, in the eyes of many German expansionists, the 1410 defeat of the Order of the Teutonic Knights by a combined Lithuanian and Polish force. With assistance from the German supreme command, Bolshevik leader Vladimir Lenin returned to Russia and seized power on 7 November 1917, promising to immediately remove Russia from the war. The Treaty of Brest-Litovsk, signed on 3 March 1918, brought one-fourth of the territory of the Russian empire under German domination and control (an area even larger than that which the Nazis would later conquer during the Second World War). In the occupied territories, beyond Germany's eastern borders, the army established a German military state called '*Ober Ost*' (after the title of the supreme commander in the east, *Oberbefehlshaber Ost*). Reflecting his *Lebensraum* propensities, Ludendorff envisaged the occupied eastern territories as German colonial land, and plans for settlement were begun. In the fall of 1918, however, these plans were cut short by an Allied victory on the Western front.

While the collapse of the German Army on the Western front brought military defeat and an end to the war, dreams of German expansion in 'the East' continued into the post-war period. In Germany, the newly created Weimar Republican government was forced to use former soldiers and students too young to have fought in the war as paramilitary fighters (right-wing German freebooters and military adventurers known as the *Freikorps*) against a perceived internal and external Communist threat. Count Rüdiger von der Goltz, supreme commander of all the *Freikorps* in the Baltic, saw the *Baltikum* (that is, German lands along the Baltic Sea) as the place where Germany could continue her self-described 'Eastern politics', securing land in 'the East' for German expansion and settlement. According to von der Goltz, Germany – defeated in 'the West' but victorious in 'the East' – required 'German settlers to cultivate [the border provinces'] fertile soil'[25], and he promised his recruits eastern lands in return for their service fighting 'Bolshevists' in 'the East'. Intoxicated with 'the East', the Baltic *Freikorps*, as one of its members later recalled, saw themselves as resurrected Teutonic Knights, as a 'new race of military farmerhood, a battle-ready chain of colonizers, which believed that it had a Teutonic Knight mission to fulfill'. To another *Freikorps* fighter, their Baltic adventure was a 'small-scale war of Indian-style wildness, accompanied by a Wild West romanticism'.[26] While the Baltic adventure ended in defeat, frustration, and bitter disillusionment, many *Freikorps* members remained committed to a 'military politics' that acted to the detriment of the Weimar Republic and to the benefit of Hitler and the Nazis.[27] Drawn by a Nazi programme promising (among other things) expansion and war in 'the East', former *Freikorps* fighters formed a small but important part of Hitler's initial support.[28]

With the Nazi assumption of power in January 1933, the historical examples of the Teutonic Knights, the First World War's Eastern front, the *Ober Ost* military state, and the *Freikorps* Baltic adventure would come together, as Hitler's National Socialists made the *Lebensraum* racial-imperialist ideology the focal point of their foreign policy aims. In 'the East', the Nazis would re-enact the First World War with a new ending – a Nazi-German empire to last a 'thousand years'. Under National Socialism, Hitler wrote in *Mein Kampf*, his new Reich would 'march on the road of the Knights of the Teutonic Order of yore' to obtain new 'living space' in 'the East' for the German people.[29] In 1921, as instanced above, after hearing a talk by General von der Goltz, leader of the *Freikorps* Baltic adventure, the young Heinrich Himmler became obsessed with a future in the 'German East' to regain lost German lands. Numerous *Freikorps* fighters rose to prominent positions in the Nazi regime, and the post-war *Freikorps* were hailed by Nazi historians and leaders as 'the first soldiers of the Third Reich'.[30] Hitler's second war for 'living space', the assault on the Soviet Union – launched on 22 June 1941 – was named Operation Barbarossa after a crusading twelfth-century German emperor. In Nazi Germany, the Teutonic Knights became the model for Himmler's SS, and, in their propaganda, the Nazis portrayed the Teutonic Knights' crusade as the forerunner of Hitler's wars for 'living space' in 'the East'. Citing historical precedent, the Nazis saw themselves as *re*conquering land that the German Teutonic Knights had won and settled many centuries before; they were merely 'taking back' land that had once been 'German' and, in Hitler's spatial fantasy, making this land 'German again'.[31]

Diplomacy

Both Early American and Nazi-German political leaders used diplomatic tactics (backed by a strong readiness to go to war) to drive so-called 'border adjustments' and to acquire 'living space' for their growing land-based continental empires. In both cases, diplomatic moves aimed at 'border adjustments' and a reordering of political boundaries, so as to create springboards for further expansion. In both cases, political leaders threatened military action, and both nation-states carried out intimidating military actions and manoeuvres in their border areas. Leaders in both Early America and Nazi Germany were quite willing to use internal subversion to prepare the way for conquest and expansion. Political leaders, in both cases, were able to exploit weaknesses in their great power opponents, who were unwilling to risk – or go to – war in order to stop continental expansion by Early America or Nazi Germany.

In the American Republic, both political leaders and propagandists openly proclaimed their true expansionist objectives, seeking to create a national consensus in favour of western continental expansion. Early American presidents, as well as expansionists in Congress, ran on political platforms favouring the acquisition of lands inhabited by indigenous peoples and claimed by European colonial powers (who would have to be 'persuaded' to give way to American territorial expansion). In Nazi Germany, Hitler used subterfuge and deceit to disguise his purposes, but he revealed his true intentions in secret directives and conversations with subordinates. On a public level, however, the Nazis took steps to cover up their true intentions. The German press were told that Hitler's *Mein Kampf* was merely 'an historical source', and they were instructed not to cite those sections pertaining to foreign policy. For their part, German diplomats reassured their foreign counterparts that a reading of *Mein Kampf* would only lead to erroneous conclusions about Nazi foreign policy, a policy whose publicly declared goals were 'peace', 'reconciliation', 'equal status' for Germany, and the 'restoration of German honour'.[32]

Early America

Louisiana purchase

Prompted by perceived fears that European powers sought to limit further American westward expansion, President Thomas Jefferson, in 1803, sought to purchase New Orleans (in the Louisiana territory) and the province of West Florida from France. America's political leaders were united in the desire to 'acquire' New Orleans and secure navigation rights to the Mississippi. While the Federalists favoured 'immediate conquest', Jefferson (a Republican) 'preferred an assertive diplomatic campaign to buy the city, using threats, bullying, and explanations of cold realities, mixed with occasional pleas, to close the deal'.[33] In Congress, both Federalist and Republican senators proposed 'war plans' calling for the raising of as many as 80,000 state militia.[34]

The president was determined to have New Orleans, by whatever means necessary. At the same time he sent negotiators to Paris to discuss purchasing New Orleans, Jefferson also sent regular army troops to the border of the Louisiana territory, in case it became necessary to use military force to accomplish his goals. Understanding the cold realities of their position, the French surprised the American negotiators by agreeing to sell them *all* of the Louisiana territory (not just New Orleans) at a price of about four cents per acre. Jefferson took a great gamble by convincing Napoleon that the United States was prepared to go to war, should the French try to retain possession of New Orleans. What has been called the 'largest real estate deal in history'[35] was, in fact, built on the threat of war. With the 'purchase', the United States eliminated the French and the Spanish as colonial powers in the lower Mississippi and secured American hegemony in eastern North America, setting the stage for further continental expansion.[36] And, as we shall see below, it was the lands provided by Jefferson's Louisiana Purchase that ultimately – and conveniently for the 'white' settler state – made an official federal policy of Indian 'removal' feasible.[37]

Florida

The eastern boundary of the Louisiana Purchase (bordering the Spanish-controlled Floridas) was left deliberately ambiguous. Claimed by Spain but dominated by British agents and merchants, the Floridas were the remaining south-eastern centre of resistance to American expansion. President Jefferson was intent on 'acquiring' Florida by making a claim that it was included in the Louisiana Purchase and then threatening to seize it; he let it be known to the Spanish that he would forego the use of military force if Spain would agree to sell the territory, and Spain agreed to negotiations. Tired of waiting for the government, so-called 'filibustering' expeditions of private citizens invaded Florida, without the explicit authority or approval of the federal government.

While negotiations with the Spanish continued, Andrew Jackson, commander of the southern US Army, under orders from President James Monroe to 'protect' American interests, invaded the Spanish provinces of East and West Florida in March 1818, supposedly in pursuit of 'hostile' Indians and runaway black slaves (who, it was alleged, might inspire a slave revolt in the United States). Characterized by supporters as a 'defensive invasion' of Florida (but, in reality a war of conquest in present-day Alabama and Florida), Jackson's campaign won de facto American military control of the region.[38] Denying that the United States had been the aggressor in Florida, Secretary of State John Quincy Adams claimed that the United States had been the victim of a conspiracy of Spaniards, Britons, and Indians, forcing the United States to attack 'mingled hordes of lawless Indians and negroes' who had 'visited ... renewed outrages' and 'savage war' on peace-loving American settlers.[39] While almost derailing negotiations, Jackson's invasion ultimately served to demonstrate to Spain that the American Republic could 'seize' Florida if it wished. Deserted by the British (who protested weakly against Jackson's invasion of Florida but who were unwilling to risk another war with the Americans) and with Jackson occupying East Florida, Spain finally capitulated to the Americans. In the Adams–Onís Treaty of February 1819 (also called the Transcontinental Treaty) Spain formally agreed to 'sell' the region to the United States, ceding all Spanish south-eastern lands east of the Mississippi River to the Americans.

Oregon

Under the Convention of 1818, the British and Americans agreed certain 'border adjustments' to the US–Canadian border and, at the same time, declared the Oregon territory of the Pacific Northwest to be 'free and open' to both British and American 'settlement'. Suffering from what was called 'Oregon fever', thousands of American settler colonists flocked to 'the Oregon country' on the continent's West Coast, in order to 'acquire' beautiful, high-quality farmland. As more Americans settled in Oregon, the British and the region's Indian inhabitants looked to block further American expansion. While the British looked for an 'equitable division' of Oregon country – which, by prior agreement, was jointly occupied by both British and Americans – American expansionists called for 'all of Oregon', viewing the possession of Oregon as a 'providential right'. Claiming that 'our title to the country of the Oregon is clear and unquestionable',[40] President James K. Polk moved to confront the British, confident that they would not risk war over the distant territory.

While publicly supporting demands for 'all of Oregon', Polk privately kept open the possibility of compromise, while keeping his eye firmly on further expansion in Texas and California. Fearful of perceived British designs in the Pacific Northwest, he directed Secretary of State James Buchanan to negotiate a treaty with the British minister to the United States, hoping to avoid war. Facing the increasing likelihood of a war with Mexico over Texas and California (and not wanting to have to fight both the British and the Mexicans simultaneously), Polk held out an olive branch to the British, offering to agree to a boundary at the 49th parallel (rather than holding out for 'all' of the Oregon country).[41] The Oregon Treaty (1846) established the 49th parallel as the US–Canadian border, running from the Continental Divide to the Pacific Ocean; more importantly, it cleared the way for war with Mexico.

Texas

In the case of Texas and Oregon, expansionists used the phrases 'reoc-cupation' and 'reannexation', implying that these areas had always been part of America's 'providential' domain.[42] As in Oregon, land-hungry settlers were attracted to Texas by cheap and fertile agricultural lands. Encouraged by the Mexican government – who wanted more 'white' settlement in their northern provinces as a 'buffer' against fur-ther US expansionism – emigrants from the United States streamed in, establishing a large colony of Anglo-Americans in the northern Mexican province. In 1836, with unofficial encouragement from the US gov-ernment, American settler colonists launched a revolt against Mexican rule, declaring their 'independence'. In a clear violation of American neutrality laws, men, money, and supplies for the Anglo-Texan rebels poured across the Louisiana border into Texas in support of the set-tler colonists in the new 'Lone Star Republic'. In a brief war, American settler colonists defeated Mexican government forces in their own 'war of independence', a revolt welcomed by the president and most of the American government.

But it did not take long before the white settlers in the self-declared Republic of Texas began to push for annexation by their 'sister American republic' to the north. For their part, in the early 1840s, American expansionists in Washington cited new 'dangers from abroad' to kick-start the Texas annexation debate. When rumours of a 'Mexican plot' to invade Texas proved false, expansionists cited British commercial ties with the Lone Star Republic and British abolitionist interest in end-ing slavery in Texas as evidence that Britain would seek to bring the independent republic into its sphere of influence, effectively block-ing American expansion to the south-west.[43] While most Democrats (mainly in the south and west) supported annexation, most of their Whig opponents opposed it, fearing the creation of another 'slave' state.[44] For the moment, Texas remained outside the American Union, and the 'Texas question' quietly simmered, awaiting a solution accept-able to both the Texas settler colonists and their political allies in Washington.[45]

Nazi Germany

Austria

Determined to annex Austria (the land of Hitler's birth) by one means or another, the Nazis aimed at complete Austrian 'union' with Germany, the incorporation of Austria, and the creation of a 'Greater Germany'

(*Grossdeutschland*). The German government was more than willing to use pressure from inside Austria to assist the process, and the Nazis launched a massive pro-Nazi and pro-annexation propaganda campaign in Austria. Following an abortive putsch attempt by Austrian Nazis, Hitler turned to a policy of watchful waiting, as well as making efforts to remove Italian objections to a German–Austrian union. When Mussolini dropped his objections, Hitler began bullying the Austrian government and threatened to invade the country if his demands were not met. Clothing German moves in a mantle of legality, Hitler claimed that German assistance was necessary for the restoration of 'law and order' in Austria. As German troops moved across the Austrian border unopposed, the era of Nazi territorial expansion began.

The annexation (*Anschluss*) of Austria by Germany was a watershed for the Third Reich and for Hitler. For Nazi Germany, it was a triumph of enormous political and psychological significance: a country created by the Versailles peace settlement disappeared, but the land taken had not been former German land 'lost' by the Treaty of Versailles, and the threatened use of force had sufficed.[46] It was also a defining moment in the history of the Third Reich: after the *Anschluss*, Hitler believed that he could take on the world – and win. The *Anschluss* proved that he could do anything he wanted, that his instincts were right, that the Western democracies were powerless, and that (however they might protest) they would not intervene to block his plans. It served to make Hitler impatient for more and set the roller-coaster of continental expansion moving.[47] And finally, it drove Hitler's popularity in Germany to new heights, and it bolstered his self-confidence – reinforcing his belief that he had been chosen by 'Providence' to 'save' the Fatherland.[48]

Sudetenland

After the *Anschluss*, Hitler's attention quickly shifted to Czechoslovakia. Ethnic Germans in Czechoslovakia were referred to as Sudeten Germans and constituted a German-speaking minority who began to look to Hitler's Third Reich to protect their security and welfare. In their propaganda campaign claiming Czech mistreatment of ethnic Germans, the Nazis would both exploit and invent alleged injustices done to the Sudeten Germans. From Hitler's perspective, he could conveniently use the Sudeten Germans as a pretext for the destruction of Czechoslovakia (his ultimate goal), with its arms industry, skilled labour, and plentiful raw materials. For now the Sudeten Germans would form a cover for any German attack, an attack that could be made to appear as a 'defensive measure' to 'protect' the Sudeten Germans.[49]

To the world, Hitler portrayed his desire to incorporate the German-speaking areas of Czechoslovakia into the Greater German Reich as a justifiable and reasonable 'border adjustment' in line with American President Woodrow Wilson's post-war doctrine of national self-determination (one of Wilson's so-called 'Fourteen Points'). In seeking the Sudetenland, Hitler displayed his willingness to gamble for high stakes, to take 'go for broke' risks, and to even risk war, in order to accomplish his expansionist objectives. In this case, a more cautious approach advocated by Nazi leader Hermann Göring led to a diplomatic settlement. While the Munich Agreement of September 1938 detached the Sudetenland from the rest of the Czech state, it thwarted Hitler's primary intention of taking Czechoslovakia by force and temporarily interrupted his drive for the total destruction of the Czech state. But the Munich accord left the Czech state friendless and, with its border fortifications lost, virtually defenceless as well. After the Munich Agreement, Hitler's drive to war was unabated. The next time, he told himself, he would get his war and would not succumb to last-minute diplomatic manoeuvres.[50] Indeed, the Munich Agreement would only cause Hitler to speed up the pace of German expansion.

Czechoslovakia

After Munich, Hitler promised that the Sudetenland had been his 'last territorial demand'. Yet the day after the Munich Agreement was signed, Hitler privately revealed his intention to annex the remaining Czech territory at the first opportunity. Within weeks after the Munich settlement, Hitler moved to liquidate the Czech state. Denied the opportunity to 'obtain' the Sudetenland by force, Hitler's aim was a limited war with the Czechs. In the case of the rump Czech state, the Slovaks would play the role that the Sudeten Germans had played earlier – that is, an 'aggrieved minority' who needed Germany's help and protection.[51] While the Czech government was willing to become a German satellite, Hitler was intent on smashing the remnants of the Czech state in a two-stage plan to 'acquire' the whole of Czechoslovakia and then to use it as a platform for further eastern expansion.[52]

Hitler's plan to smash Czechoslovakia (a hated Slav state allied with the Bolshevik arch-enemy) by military action marked a shift in course. It made clear that Nazi Germany was no longer embarking on a 'readjustment' of what the Germans (and many Europeans) saw as the unfair and punitive territorial provisions of the Treaty of Versailles of 1919 (ending the First World War).[53] With the Czech crisis, Hitler demonstrated that he was prepared to go beyond the revisionism and national integration, instanced by the incorporation of the Sudetenland into the

German Reich, to the military destruction of the Czech state itself. The conquest of the Czech rump finally destroyed the fiction that Hitler's policies were aimed at uniting German-speaking peoples into a single state.[54] In Hitler's mind, destruction of the Czech state (giving Germany full control of Bohemia and Moravia and effective control of the Slovak satellite) was a subsidiary, short-term goal on the road to his larger aim of the conquest of vast 'Aryan' German 'living space' in 'the East'.[55]

Memel

Memel, a seaport on the Baltic with a largely German population, had been taken from Germany by the Treaty of Versailles and given to Lithuania. Employing his usual bullying tactics, Hitler threatened the Lithuanian foreign minister with military force if his demands for the immediate return of Memel were not met. The Lithuanians were quickly 'pressured' into yielding and agreeing to the Nazi takeover of Memelland, Hitler's last annexation without bloodshed.

Military conquest

In addition to diplomatic moves, both Early America and Nazi Germany used naked force and brutal military conquest to gain 'living space' for their settler colonists. In the American case, far from being exceptions to America's past (as most Americans and some historians like to think), imperialism, empire, war, and conquest were central to Early American expansionism. Victory against Britain in the War of Independence opened up lands 'west' of the Appalachians to 'settlement'. Often ignored or minimized in the traditional narrative of American history, the War of 1812, the Mexican War, and the three dozen or more 'Indian wars' were all imperial wars that expanded the geographical domain of the new American Republic. As 'wars for empire', they were, in fact, wars to extend American power and to conquer vast territories for the young nation.[56] As well as a contest of cultures and two distinct ways of life, what historian Colin Calloway has called the Indian–settler 'War for America' was primarily a struggle for land and resources.[57] In the German case, to be sure, war had been objective of the Nazi leadership from the moment they came to power in 1933.[58] In defiance of the Treaty of Versailles, Hitler rearmed Germany and then, in early 1936, sent German troops to remilitarize the Rhineland (an area in the western part of Germany that had been established as a demilitarized zone by the Treaty). Between 1937 and 1939, Hitler began preparing for a series of wars, wars whose purpose was to 'acquire' agricultural lands in 'the East' for settlement by German settler colonists. These years would see a radicalization of Nazi foreign policy in accordance with Hitler's foreign policy views outlined in *Mein Kampf*: Germany's need for 'living space', he declared, could only be solved by 'the sword' (that is, by the use of outright military force). The attack on Poland, in September 1939, was thus conceived as a necessary first step in 'acquiring' *Lebensraum* farther 'east' (not as a desire for a general European war).

Early America

The revolutionary era

In the Royal Proclamation of 1763, as noted above, the British promised to keep white settlers from encroaching on Indian lands beyond the Appalachian Mountains, alienating both gentry land speculators and Indian-hating backwoodsmen in the American colonies. British attempts to regulate its colonial subjects – whether Indians or colonists – only produced resistance among both groups, igniting 'wars of independence' in both 'Indian country' and in Britain's American colonies.[59] Frustrated by Britain's refusal to open the western lands to white settlement and colonization, many American colonists joined the War for Independence from Great Britain to defend (among other things) their right to expansion, settlement, and colonization 'west' of the Appalachians.

In simplest terms, the War for American Independence (1775–83) substituted an aggressive American empire (the new 'United States') for the defeated British colonial empire.[60] Like so many previous wars on the North American continent, it was also (primarily?) a war about Indian land. The end of the war opened the way for a renewed invasion of Indian lands by American settler colonists; meanwhile, a great smallpox epidemic killed Native American peoples by the thousands in the 'West', clearing the region for American occupation and settlement. The Treaty of Paris (ending the war) not only recognized the independence of the 13 Anglo-American colonies but also granted America a western boundary along the eastern bank of the Mississippi River, creating a vast western imperial domain for the new American empire and immediately doubling the size of the original 13 colonies. After 'independence' itself, the fertile American midcontinent, from the Appalachians to the Mississippi, was the 'greatest prize of the Revolution'.[61]

In the aftermath of the American Revolution, the former colonial subjects became colonizers themselves in their own 'western empire'. Despite frequent clashes, as well as recurrent differences of opinion, the Early American political elite and 'ordinary' Americans ultimately became allies in the national project of conquest and expansion.[62] The 'winning of the West', both groups realized, would require the participation of the state. Western settlers looked to the state to secure 'the West' by subjugating the Indians and removing them from 'white' settlement areas. Unlike their former British colonial masters, the new, more powerful American state, the new 'American Leviathan', would always put the settlers' interests first and would prove quite willing to kill Indians to retain 'the West'.[63]

War of 1812

In the years following the War for Independence, the British had not only harassed American ships on the high seas, but had aided and abetted Indian resistance to the continued westward expansion of the American Republic. While these traditional maritime freedom-of-the-seas issues were important, recent scholarship has rightly stressed the desire of settlers in the Old Northwest (embracing modern-day Ohio, Indiana, Illinois, Michigan, and Wisconsin) to stop the British from continuing to support Indian resistance to white settler expansion, as well as the desire of settler colonists in the Old Southwest (embracing modern-day Alabama and Mississippi) to expand into Florida and the Gulf Coast regions still held by Spain.[64] Pressured by militant western House members, the United States declared war against Britain in June 1812, including the conquest of Canada and Florida in its war aims.

Manifest Destiny began (we now know) west of the Appalachians in the War of 1812 – not west of the Mississippi in the 1840s. The War of 1812 effectively ended a long series of border wars for control of the vast western territory between the Appalachians and the Mississippi, from the Great Lakes to the Gulf of Mexico. 'In many ways', as historian Mark Joy notes, 'the fighting in the War of 1812 in the western parts of the United States was basically a continuation of the Indian wars that had been going on there since American independence.'[65] In retrospect, the War of 1812 – known at the time as the 'Second American War for Independence' – was a war of conquest by which the Early American Republic secured control of the eastern half of the North American continent and effectively destroyed the resistance of the American Indians east of the Mississippi River.[66] It helped cement 'the West' (as then defined) to the young American nation.[67]

Mexican–American war

Rather than speaking of the conquest of Texas (like Andrew Jackson protégé Sam Houston), many American expansionists, like Jackson himself, spoke of 'adjusting the border' between the United States and Mexico. Many militant expansionists, again like Jackson, believed that borders were best defended 'in the territory of the enemy'.[68] While diplomatic recognition was extended to the newly declared Texas Republic, anti-slavery forces in Congress – many of whom also opposed any further territorial expansion – refused to countenance formal annexation, forcing those favouring annexation and an expansion of slavery to look for another solution. In 1844 James K. Polk, a committed expansionist and champion of Andrew Jackson's political agenda, was elected president. Like Jefferson and Jackson, Polk claimed that Texas had been part of the original Louisiana Purchase and advocated 'reannexation' of the region. He also wanted to 'acquire' the California coast and deny its spectacular harbours and ports to the British.

The compromise settlement with Britain on Oregon conveniently freed Polk's hand to aggressively pursue American expansion in the south-western and western lands now owned by Mexico (following its recently won independence from Spanish control). At a 30 May 1845 White House meeting (as he recorded in his diary), Polk declared to his cabinet 'my purpose to acquire for the United States California, New Mexico, and perhaps some others of the Northern Provinces of Mexico' by 'military possession'.[69] In the United States, expansionist voices called for the conquest of 'all Mexico', envisioning a vast American settler colony to the south. Ignoring Mexican warnings that the annexation of Texas would be equivalent to a declaration of war, the US Congress voted to annex the independent Republic of Texas.

In May 1846, seeking a justification for going to war, President Polk used a border incident (in disputed territory) between American and Mexican forces to declare that 'American blood has been shed on American soil' and to persuade Congress to formally declare war on Mexico.[70] In his 'war message' to Congress and the public, Polk charged that 'Mexico has invaded our territory',[71] clearly casting the war as a defensive rather than offensive measure. In reality, however, Polk deliberately provoked a war and then lied, in order to blame Mexico for starting the conflict.[72] Despite Polk's claims and pretensions, the Mexican War was not a defensive struggle but a war of conquest.[73] Ostensibly begun as a limited war for limited objectives, it soon became a far-reaching war of conquest, with principal theatres of operation in northern Mexico, New Mexico, and California.

Weakened and exhausted by its own 'Indian wars' in its northern provinces, Mexico was no match for the US Army. Backing Polk, American expansionists pointed to Mexico's inability to 'control' the

Indians as justifications for their own actions in Texas, as well as in the whole of the Mexican north. The Anglo-American invaders actually posed as 'liberators' to Mexican inhabitants of the north, offering them 'protection' from future Indian raids. As in prior conquests, Americans invoked their self-proclaimed God-given 'natural right' to seize territory which, like Texas and the Mexican north, they declared, was 'empty' and 'not properly cultivated'. Mexico had, the expansionists argued, surrendered its moral claims to these lands by failing in its own attempts to settle and develop its northern territories.[74]

The Mexican War of 1846–8 was a pivotal event in Early American westward expansion and, as many expansionists at the time believed, an expression of America's racial (as well as continental) destiny.[75] Under the terms of the Treaty of Guadalupe Hidalgo (1848), Mexico ceded roughly a million square miles of its territory to the United States – an area larger than the Louisiana Purchase – and confirmed the annexation of Texas. The United States paid Mexico $15 million and acquired half of Mexico (including the present-day states of Arizona, California, Colorado, Nevada, New Mexico, and Utah); it also gained recognition of the Rio Grande River as the border between Texas and Mexico. In 1853, additional territory was purchased from Mexico by James Gadsden (a railroad executive hoping to use the newly acquired territory as part of a transcontinental railroad). The so-called Gadsden Purchase formally ended the continental expansion of the United States.

Indian wars

In the first 100 years of its existence, the newly independent United States waged three dozen or more 'Indian wars' by which settler colonists of the Early American Republic 'appropriated' lands that native peoples had called home for a thousand generations. In the settler colonial context, these 'Indian wars' were about who should own and occupy the land. Throughout the period of Early American conquest and expansion, Indian homelands became imperial borderlands, as the new nation began to build and expand its own empire (based on the concept of 'liberty' for 'white' settler colonists and the 'acquisition' of Indian lands). Often with troops at their backs, American negotiators demanded Indian lands 'by right of conquest', and when the Indians resisted white settler intrusions, they were subjected to what the Americans termed 'just and lawful wars'.[76] Rather than individual wars or distinct incidents, the 'Indian wars', spanning almost a century, were part of a single overarching campaign to establish American dominion over the entire North American continent.[77]

Nazi Germany

War in 'the East'

On 23 May 1928, as a political outsider, Adolf Hitler announced his intention 'to lead our people into bloody action, not just for an adjustment of boundaries, but to save it into the most distant future by securing so much land and ground that the future receives back many times the blood shed'.[78] On the evening of 3 February 1933, within days of his appointment as German chancellor, Hitler suggested to army leaders that he preferred to use his newly acquired political power and his planned build-up of German armed forces for 'the conquest of new living space in the East and its ruthless Germanization'.[79] Even during the so-called 'peace years', Hitler remained totally committed to launching a war of conquest and expansion in 'the East' at the first opportunity. Hitler sought war in 'the East' to acquire *Lebensraum* at Poland's and Russia's expense. War for territorial gain was, to be sure, intrinsic to the notion of *Lebensraum*.[80] During the war, in a speech to his army commanders, Hitler described the war in 'the East' as a 'fight for *Lebensraum*. Without this *Lebensraum*', he declared, 'the German Reich and the German nation cannot endure.... For in the end man lives from the earth and the earth is the prize Providence gives to those people who fight for it.'[81]

The Nazi vision of protracted war aimed at military conquest extending across the entire European continent. On 5 November 1937, Hitler presented his programme for war to the supreme military commanders and foreign minister – a programme founded on his broad ideological vision. While not a war plan, it was, nonetheless, a clear statement of Hitler's intention to launch a European war inspired by racial ideology. 'The aim of German policy', Hitler declared, was 'the safeguarding and maintenance of the racial group (*Volksmasse*) and its propagation.' It was, in his view, a problem of 'space'. Therefore, 'Germany's future', he asserted, was 'wholly conditional upon the solving of the need for space.'[82] In a speech on 10 February 1939, Hitler told his army commanders that 'I have taken it upon myself to solve the German question, i.e. to solve the German problem of space.' Convinced that 'this question must be settled one way or the other', he told his audience that 'I thereby would never shrink from the most extreme measures.' 'The next great war', he boldly announced, would be a 'pure war of ideology' (*Weltanschauungskrieg*), that is consciously a 'war of peoples and races' (*Volks- und Rassenkrieg*).[83] Hitler's wars for *Lebensraum* in 'the East' were very much a product of his plans and intentions[84] and were inextricably entangled with Nazi racial goals.[85] Genocidal in their implications, Nazi military and imperial conquests in the years 1939–42 were premised on the relocation, deportation, and murder of millions of civilian non-combatants in the new eastern *Lebensraum*.

Poland

Hitler's first territorial demands in 'the East' were the return of lands 'lost' to Poland after the First World War. In the Nazi view, Poland was the racially backward, bastard child of the post-war peace settlement and an important source of 'living space' for Germany's settler colonists. In the case of Poland, Hitler vowed, there would be no diplomatic settlement, no new Munich; he would not be cheated once again of the war he had always intended. Having been deprived of war in 1938, he was all the more determined to have it in 1939.[86]

In the early stages, there was no plan for invasion and conquest, with even Hitler more interested in a negotiated settlement that would bring Poland into the German orbit, that would allow for the return of Danzig to the Reich, and that would permit road and railway access through the Polish corridor (land that Germany was forced to cede to Poland after Versailles and that gave Poles access to the sea but detached East Prussia from rest of the Reich). Hitler expected the Poles to yield after the usual bullying, with Poland becoming a German satellite and then an ally against the Soviet Union. Unlike the Sudeten crisis, some generals favoured military measures and an aggressive war against Poland. When Poland refused to make any concessions – backed by assurances from England and France – Hitler's approach to Poland changed markedly. On 23 May 1939, Hitler told his generals that the coming war against Poland was not about Danzig or access.[87] 'For us', he declared, 'it is a matter of the expansion of living space in the East and the securing of our food supply.'[88]

In a real sense, Poland was a dress rehearsal for the final drive for *Lebensraum*, a dress rehearsal for the war of conquest, plunder, subjugation, and mass violence in the Soviet Union. On the eve of the invasion of Poland, claiming 'frightful persecution' of ethnic Germans in the 'ancient German lands' given Poland by the Treaty of Versailles, one German general exhorted his troops to take back 'this living space of the German people for the honour and existence of the [German] fatherland'.[89] Identifying with Nazi ideological goals, one *Wehrmacht* soldier wrote home from Poland, saying that German troops 'carry the borders of German *Lebensraum* even farther to the East with every step they take'.[90]

Russia

As early as December 1922, Hitler called for the 'destruction of Russia' in order to 'give Germany sufficient land for German settlers'.[91] Hitler's racially based need for *Lebensraum* became the impetus for the decision to attack the Soviet Union in 1941 (Operation Barbarossa), fed by Hitler's desire to radicalize the war. A war of conquest, enslavement, and annihilation, the Russian campaign aimed at the conquest of *Lebensraum* and colonies for the Third Reich, liquidation of 'Jewish-Bolshevik' elites and 'the Jews', slaughter and enslavement of the Slavic masses, and the creation of a vast colonial empire in Eastern Europe providing security and food for the Greater German Reich. The acquisition of 'living space' in Eastern Europe at the expense of the Soviet Union was to be achieved 'by the sword', as Hitler had repeatedly reminded his readers and audiences since the late 1920s.

The fate of Russia was determined, in the minds of Hitler and the Nazi elites, by the ideological and economic imperatives of Nazi imperialism. In Nazi eyes, Russia was the cradle of Germany's ancient racial enemies (the Slavs) and now new racial and political enemies (the 'Jewish Bolsheviks'). Facing a numerically superior enemy, the war in the Soviet Union would, of necessity, be a war of annihilation against the Reich's political and racial enemies. Germany aimed not only to defeat armed enemies on the field of combat but also to conquer, subjugate, and exploit the indigenous peoples (that is, Slavs and Jews). Barbarossa envisioned the physical destruction of Soviet state, the deliberate starvation of tens of millions of Slavs, enslavement of the surviving remnant, extermination of the Jews, and a struggle to the death between two opposing world views: National Socialism and 'Jewish-Bolshevism'. Accordingly, German troops and security forces would be given free rein to 'defend themselves ruthlessly against every threat by the hostile civilian population'.[92] Violent acts against civilian populations, it was mutually understood, would go unpunished. Soviet political commissars (the proclaimed principal carriers of the alleged 'Bolshevik infection') and all 'perpetrators of resistance' (both real and imagined) would be 'finished off with weapons immediately as a matter of principle'[93] and, it should be noted, without regard for international law.

In Poland, between 1939 and mid-1941, the Nazis fought a war that they limited territorially and that its propagandists described as a defensive, preventive war. The attack on the Soviet Union (June 1941), however, signalled a growing radicalization of Nazi foreign and racial policy. From now on, foreign and racial policy would be pursued in strict accordance with the demands of the Nazi *Weltanschauung* (worldview). A war instigated and relentlessly pursued by Hitler, it was, above all, a war for racially reconstituted 'living space' for Germans in 'the East'. For the Nazis, the Soviet Union was the 'Wild East', a savage region ripe for conquest and expansion, its 'sub-human' indigenous inhabitants destined for extermination or helotry. For Nazi expansionists, Russia promised land and resources on a far greater scale than Poland had provided; it would also provide a far greater scale of mass death as well. Indeed, violence towards the civilian populations in the Soviet Union would be far more systematic and wholesale than in Poland.[94] In a pre-invasion directive to his troops, General Erich Hoepner called the war against the Soviets a war for 'the existence of the German nation', a battle of 'the Germanic against the Slavic peoples' to defend 'European culture' and repel 'Jewish-Bolshevism', and a battle in which German troops must possess 'an iron will to exterminate the enemy mercilessly and totally'.[95] With the invasion of the Soviet Union, the centre of Hitler's continental empire moved farther and farther eastward.

Way of war

Historians of both America and Germany discern an unambiguous continuity in the nature of military campaigns and operational warfare over different historical eras in the respective national histories. In the colonial, Revolutionary, and early national periods, American war-making on the 'frontier' was waged against indigenous 'enemy' non-combatant populations and their agricultural resources, as well as against armed combatants. Significantly for this investigation, successive generations of Anglo-American settler colonists, both soldiers and civilians, made the killing of Indian men, women, and children an important part of a shared American identity.[96] In the 'Wild East', the German National Socialists and their military forces waged a self-described 'war of annihilation', fought against civilian populations – and not just against enemy armies and their war-making capability. On the Eastern front, entire peoples were to be disposed of during or after the phase of military conquest. Waging war against civilian populations was part of a German historical tendency (a tendency not uniquely 'German', it should be noted), one that had been given a twentieth-century update by the *Wehrmacht*, and ultimately perfected by Nazi ideological warfare.[97]

Early America

The American War for Independence from Great Britain was not limited to the military confrontation between patriot armies and the British and their hired forces. Indeed, a series of small but brutal wars between frontiersmen and Indians ran concurrently with the War of

Independence in the trans-Appalachian West and along the New York 'frontier'. These 'Indian wars' on the southern, western, and New York 'frontiers' focused on destroying Indian fields, food supplies, and civilian populations and were characterized by horrific violence.[98] During the American War for Independence, American patriot military leaders embraced a philosophy of 'total war'. This embrace of 'total war' by American patriots was not new, having been used by early settler colonists, as noted above, in their attacks on Indian villages in areas coveted by white settlers in the 'New World'. Unlike the colonial precedents, however, the intent of the American patriots was not to punish the Indians or force them to sue for peace but, rather, to drive them off lands coveted by white settlers. The 'way of war' practised by American patriots against Native Americans who had taken up the hatchet as British allies, was the modern equivalent of murderous ethnic cleansing, built around an ideology of political and ethnic solidarity among 'white' settler colonists on the 'frontier'.[99]

In their inexorable march across the North American continent, Anglo-American military, paramilitary, and settler colonist militia formations embraced warfare shaped by extreme violence and focused on conquest of Indian lands. On the frontier of empire, warfare against the indigenous 'Other' was characterized by face-to-face shootings, random atrocities, and 'reprisal' killings. The 'first American way of war', as historian John Grenier convincingly demonstrates, 'accepted, legitimized, and encouraged attacks upon non-combatants [as well as] the destruction of villages, and agricultural resources', in 'shockingly violent campaigns to achieve [Early American] goals of conquest'. When the US Army proved unable or unwilling to drive Indians from western lands, he notes, white settler colonists frequently 'took matters into their own hands', unleashing 'spasm[s] of extreme violence' against indigenous 'native' peoples, including 'enemy' non-combatants (irrespective of sex or age).[100]

In the mid-nineteenth century, the Mexican–American War involved US military campaigns against Mexican armed forces and the civilian population, using methods similar to America's 'first way of war' in the brutal campaigns against Native Americans. Behind the battle against regular Mexican Army forces, a hidden dirty war was waged against Mexican civilians in the countryside. Although formal military resistance by the Mexican Army and government collapsed within a year of the commencement of hostilities, fighting continued against Mexican civilians. US state-sponsored murder, moreover, was committed against Mexican civilian populations by American forces, with many instances of unprovoked racial and sexual depredations upon the Mexican people.

In particular, the Texas Ranger companies were notorious for establishing a reign of terror in the Mexican countryside. Any military resistance to American occupation by Mexican civilians or guerrillas brought swift reprisal attacks in which wholesale massacres were carried out to avenge the death of even one murdered ranger. The nature of warfare and occupation in Mexico was often characterized by a racist brutality, involving the looting of the Mexican countryside by American regular army and volunteer militia soldiers and the commission of racial and sexual atrocities against Mexican civilians by the occupation forces.[101]

Throughout the nineteenth century, waging war against Indian non-combatants on the 'frontier' continued to define American war-making, with the US taking war straight to the 'enemy's' civilian populations in the brutal military conquest of the trans-Mississippi west.[102] Anglo-American military leaders quickly discovered that destruction of supplies and infrastructure was as effective in conquering the Indian 'enemy' as defeating his troops in battle. Throughout the so-called 'Indian wars', the US Army found small mobile special operations units more successful against Indian warriors than pitched battles against large formations. Having to transport their own supplies, as well as protect their women and children, Indian warriors were susceptible to 'economic warfare'. For its part, the US Army used 'economic warfare' aimed at destroying the Indians' ability to wage war, including destruction of Indian crops and stored supplies, as well as mounted attacks against Indian villages and Indian encampments.[103]

In the 'American West', regular military forces and settler paramilitary forces adopted a strategy of murdering chiefs, burning villages and crops, and killing non-combatants. As practised against indigenous peoples who stood in the path of Anglo-American expansion, the Early American 'way of war', then – in the colonial, Revolutionary, and early national periods – condoned the use of extreme violence against 'enemy' non-combatants, including women, children, and the elderly. It also entailed destroying 'enemy' villages, fields and crops, as well as intimidating and/or killing 'enemy' non-combatant populations. In short, America's 'first way of war' was the primary engine of Early American conquest and expansion in the settler–state drive to gain dominion over the entire North American continent.[104]

Nazi Germany

The Nazi-German war in 'the East' was, above all, a racial war, prosecuted by the Nazis with the utmost ruthlessness and brutality. As a political movement and ideology, German National Socialism was inseparable from war and violence. In the Nazi worldview, war and racial struggle were the same. Racial war lay at the core of Nazism; it was also the essence of the Nazi setter-colonial project.[105] For Nazi leaders, the war of annihilation in 'the East' was a struggle of ideologies, a battle 'to the death' against the 'Jewish-Bolshevist enemy'.

The Nazis were prepared to wage war against any groups who, in their view, stood in the way of their often-stated goals of a racially pure Germany and the colonization of the 'Nazi East' with racially superior 'Aryan' settler colonists. In 'the East', the Nazis waged ideological war, aimed at removing entire peoples and cultures from the designated German 'living space' and redrawing the racial map of the European continent. Far from being the product of defeat or desperation, waging war against civilians was part of the German strategy from the beginning in Poland, throughout the years of victory, and, indeed, to the bitter end.[106] While less systematic than the destruction of Jews, outrages against non-Jewish civilians rivalled the Nazi Judeocide in the degree of death and suffering they produced.[107] While some historians (such as Andreas Hillgruber) see the genocide of the Jews as a 'separate theatre of war', others (such as Omer Bartov and Christopher Browning) more rightly note a symbiotic relationship between the Nazi Judeocide and the war in 'the East'.[108]

Hearkening back to Frederick the Great's 'harrowing of Saxony' in the Thirty Years' War, the Germans prosecuted the war in 'the East' with a high degree of ruthlessness towards the civilian population, as well as towards enemy armed forces. In the 'Wild East', terrorizing the civilian population wherever possible was a vital tool in the *Wehrmacht's* arsenal. In prosecuting the war in 'the East', the Nazis aimed not at mere military victory but at the destruction of indigenous peoples and their way of life. Unleashed by Hitler, with the willing complicity of higher military echelons, the war in 'the East' was a ruthless, ideologically charged war: a destructive war aimed at entire civilian populations and seeking the total annihilation of some and the decimation or enslavement of others. It was, moreover, a multifaceted war: a war of annihilation against certain enemy populations (political leaders and POWs); a war of extermination against the Jews (all of whom were marked for death); a war of enslavement against Slavic peoples (mostly Poles and Russians); and a ruthless war of subjugation and occupation against indigenous peoples who survived the initial onslaught.[109] Bolstered by a strong sense of superiority, as well as the imagined bestiality and inhumanity of the racial and ideological 'enemy', the German Army, special mobile killing units, and security forces committed acts of extreme violence against civilian populations frequently and on a massive scale. Unarmed men, women, and children were shot and killed at murder sites on the outskirts of a village or town, many civilians were executed as 'partisans', and many others were left to die of starvation. In short, the German way of war in 'the East' was marked by systematic murder.

From the start, the war launched against Poland was a war of racial conquest, subjugation, and extermination. But Poland was, as noted above, merely a dress rehearsal for the attack on the Soviet Union. Before the campaign against the Soviet Union began, the *Wehrmacht* High Command annulled any possibility of international law protection for the civilian populations in any occupied territory; in effect, they declared war against the civilian population. Under certain conditions, civilians who exercised (or were suspected of exercising) armed resistance were to be dealt with as soldier combatants; these so-called 'irregulars' could be shot 'in battle' or 'while escaping'. Unarmed civilians, if suspected, counted as 'irregulars', as suspected perpetrators of resistance subject to 'collective reprisal measures'. The Nazi war in the 'Wild East' also countenanced (and often implemented automatically) the shooting of hostages and the burning of entire villages.[110] The *Wehrmacht* leadership, in an order dated 23 July 1941, called upon German troops in Russia to 'spread the kind of terror which is the only suitable means of suppressing any inclination towards resistance in the population'.[111] Throughout the Russian campaign, the German Army increasingly institutionalized the ruthless treatment of civilians in the occupied territories.[112] In Nazi eyes, 'the Jews' were seen as supporters of the partisan movement: that is, every Jew was (by definition of the occupation forces) a partisan or a supporter of the partisans, subject to immediate execution. To the very end, the Nazis were committed to effecting a racist 'war of annihilation' in 'the East', a campaign of extraordinary devastation and brutality.

Similarities, differences, and links

Both Early American and Nazi-German territorial expansion were intended and planned projects of settler colonialism: that is, their respective drives for conquest and expansion similarly aimed at placing indigenous lands and resources at the disposal of their settler colonists (regardless of the consequences for indigenous life and culture). In both cases, policies of territorial expansion and conquest were preparatory steps for American and German population expansion. The aim of Early

American and Nazi-German colonizers, in fact, was to remove and/or decimate (not assimilate) the allegedly 'inferior' indigenous populations in the areas to be colonized, in order to seize land and resources for their settler colonists. In both cases, successful expansion and military conquest only added more indigenous peoples to the colonial empire, requiring, as we shall see below, further 'measures' to preserve the 'racial purity' of the new 'living space'. In both cases, the respective trajectories of conquest and expansion displayed disquieting parallels, as similar projects of settler colonialism. The dynamic of both Early American and Nazi-German expansionism meant that there was no fixed 'frontier' but rather a political border to be continually expanded outward; in both cases, then, the process of territorial expansion was intended as a continuous process. With other powers reluctant to take firm action against American and German expansion, both nation-states accomplished a great deal of expansion via annexation, without resorting to military conflict or without immediate bloodshed (although the threat of force was frequently used). In both cases, treaties were at most temporary instruments that could, and would, be quickly broken when they had lost their usefulness in the struggle for 'living space' or when they no longer met the requirements of 'space' policy. Outside the national borders, 'Americans' in Oregon, Texas, and California and 'Germans' in Austria and Czechoslovakia were used as a pretext for aggression, in order to protect alleged 'rights of self-determination'. Where necessary, incidents were encouraged or staged by Early American and Nazi-German political leaders in order to provide a pretext for war. Drawing no distinction between soldiers and civilians, both the Early American and the Nazi-German 'ways of war' backed aggressive expansionist policies of territorial aggrandizement and racial purity, as both nation-states became engaged in brutal enterprises of settler colonization and subjugation of indigenous peoples. In both cases, prior histories of conquest and expansion in 'the West' and 'the East', respectively, legitimized brutal military conquest and extreme violence against combatant and non-combatant populations, as justifiable methods of 'obtaining' indigenous lands and resources.

Differences between the actuality of conquest, expansion, and settlement in these two cases mainly involved timing and sequence. In the American case, crucially, disease acted as an invisible army, decimating Native American communities and often allowing settler colonists to swarm over Indian lands in advance of formal expansion and/or actual military conquest. In the German case, by contrast, military conquest for *Lebensraum* preceded actual settlement, due to the very large numbers of indigenous peoples in the desired 'living space' who had to be 'pacified' before actual 'settlement' could begin.

Despite these differences, the Early American and Nazi-German cases of settler colonialism shared markedly similar trajectories, policies, and practices. Moreover, the legacies of the Early American settler project (as perceived by Hitler and Himmler, especially) served as an example and model for the planned Nazi-German settler project in 'the East', with numerous Nazi policies in the eastern *Lebensraum* versions (albeit more radical and extreme) of those practised in the 'American West'. For some expansionists in pre-Nazi Germany, the analogue of the German 'East' and the American 'West' was used as an argument for overturning the Treaty of Versailles and for establishing German influence in 'the East'. The Nazis, as usual, thought in more radical terms. Casting the indigenous inhabitants of the 'Nazi East' – Slavs and Jews – as 'Indians', many Nazi leaders were fascinated by the opportunities in the 'Wild East' and by the idea of 'heroic settlers' on the 'frontier'. The mystique of the 'Wild East' was for some an irrelevance, for others a useful fiction, and for others a legitimizing ideology with definite propaganda potential.[113] For Hitler and other 'true believers', however, it was a true driving force of belief and action. German military conquest and expansion in 'the East' would proceed, in Hitler's words, 'as in the conquest of America'. In August 1942, Hitler equated the struggle with partisans in 'the East' with 'the Indian wars in North America'; three weeks later, he returned to this theme, calling the partisan struggle in 'the East' a 'real Indian war'.[114] These links, to be sure, can work both ways. As historian Michael Geyer rightly suggests, the Nazi way of war in 'the East' is beyond the American imagination. However, it is not, he sadly notes, beyond the collective ethnic memory of quite a significant group of North Americans – the indigenous Native American peoples – who stood directly in the path of Anglo-American expansion.[115]

4
Colonization: 'Peopling' the Empire

Early American plans for a 'western empire' and Nazi plans for an 'eastern empire' were both predicated on 'peopling' the empire with settler colonists and 'removing' indigenous peoples who stood in the way of their national expansionist projects. In both cases, legacies of prior settlement episodes provided useful legacies and convenient justifications for future 'settlement' schemes. In the 'American West' and the 'Nazi East', political leaders envisaged a 'people's empire' that would benefit 'ordinary' citizens – as well as, of course, the political elites – which, in turn, would provide economic security for the nation-state. In both cases, the settlers' 'pursuit of happiness' was to be achieved at the expense of 'inferior' peoples who would be required to 'disappear' from the new settler 'living space'. Political leaders, in both Early America and Nazi Germany, developed colonization plans that outlined general settlement goals in 'the West' and 'the East'. And, finally, both nation-states shared a similar settlement model, based on settler self-interest in striving for prosperity and material security for themselves and their children.

In the Early American case, the expectation of land in 'the West' proved more powerful than military might in 'settling' western lands.[1] As early as 1837, eastern newspaper editor and spokesman for the western movement Horace Greeley advised, 'Go West, young man, go forth into the Country.'[2] Many an American settler would head 'west' with Greeley's words 'go West, young man' ringing in their ears. By the 1830s, however, there were two completing and conflicting agrarian visions: one of an American society composed of 'white' yeomen farmers, and the other of a plantation slave system as practised in the older slave states of the Atlantic seaboard. The Northern victory over the South in the American Civil War would transport the Jeffersonian ideal of the idealized western yeoman and the vision of a western utopia of 'white' yeomen farmers into the trans-Mississippi 'west' and all the way to the Pacific Ocean.[3]

In the Nazi-German case, military might and force were a necessary condition for 'settlement' given the vast numbers of 'natives' in the 'Nazi East'. In Hitler's view, 'our Colonizing penetration must be constantly progressive, until it reaches the stage where our own colonists far outnumber the local inhabitants'. The German colonist, in his mind, was 'the soldier-peasant'; after 12 years of military service, the professional soldier would be provided a 'completely equipped farm' in 'the East', with his own 'patch of ground'. In a conversation with dinner guests, on 12 May 1942, Hitler declared that his long-term policy aim was to eventually have 'a hundred million Germans settled in [our Eastern] territories'. In a decade, his hope was that '20 million Germans' would have settled in eastern territories either already annexed to the Reich or occupied by German troops.[4] Under Hitler's National Socialists, the 'opening up of space in the East' for German settlers would take colonization and 'settlement' to new extremes in a radical new kind of colonial empire.

Antecedents

The histories of Early America and Nazi Germany both contained a 'prehistory' of actualized and/or intended settler colonization and 'settlement' episodes in colonized 'living space'. In British Colonial North America, the first settler-colonial projects were targeted for Atlantic coastal areas: coastal regions neglected by the French and Spanish in their own colonization efforts. Pre-Nazi-German colonial projects, both on the African continent and in Central and Eastern Europe, were predicated on agricultural settlement and the founding of settler colonies, as well as on the vision of the 'soldier-farmer'. In both cases, these 'prehistories' left important legacies and histories to be exploited by later advocates of national projects of territorial expansion and settler colonization in the 'American West' and the 'Nazi East', respectively.

Early America

During the mid-sixteenth century, English imperialists were preoccupied with the conquest and colonization of Ireland. Many potential investors and settler colonists, in fact, viewed colonizing the nearby island as more desirable than colonizing North America.[5] From the

1580s to the 1640s, British investors from England and Scotland established numerous settler colonies in Ulster and Munster, attracting more than 100,000 immigrants who proved unwilling to move to the distant North American settlements. Irish 'native' resistance and rebellion was finally broken by Oliver Cromwell and his New Model Army, who defeated the 'natives', confiscated millions of acres of their lands, and expelled, deported, or enslaved the tens of thousands of survivors. Emboldened by the success of colonization efforts in Ireland, English imperialists looked to extend their colonial ambitions across the Atlantic to the North America continent.[6] The colonial 'plantations' of Ireland served as the model for very similar 'plantations' in England's original settlements in North America. In the thrall of Ireland's example, the English rejected strategies of accommodation and adopted aggressive attitudes and actions as part of a colonization model aimed at 'planting' settler colonies on indigene lands 'cleared' of the 'native' inhabitants.[7]

The Spanish, British, and French empires in North America were all empires of conquest, based on largely on territorial expansion through subjugation of the 'natives'. But unlike its imperial competitors in North America, an insatiable settler-colonist hunger for land became the defining feature of English colonization. Given this insatiable 'land hunger', the 'settlement' and colonization of British North America depended upon subjugating and dispossessing the American Indians. With regard to the 'natives', the Spanish aimed to make them a pliant labour force, the French sought to incorporate them as trading partners, and the English sought to exclude them from their North America colonies.[8] Unlike its French counterpart, the English North American empire was built largely in opposition to – rather than in co-operation with – native peoples, as the English settlers shunned cultural engagement in favour of separation. As long as Spain, Britain, and France competed for dominance in North America, Indians were needed as trading partners and allies in 'imperial wars', fostering attitudes of mutual dependency between 'white' settler colonists and the 'natives'. Over time, British North America became the 'most populous, prosperous, and powerful colonial presence on the continent', eventually overpowering its competitors.[9]

During the seventeenth century, English settler colonists secured a foothold on the Atlantic coast. Initially, colonial promoters looked to a region they called 'Virginia' (so-called because they believed their queen, Elizabeth I, to be a virgin) and a region to the north they named 'New England'. English settler colonists in Virginia and New England viewed Indian land use as 'unproductive' and, therefore, felt free to confiscate 'native' lands. At the same time, colonist notions of Indians' 'savagery' justified, in their view, brutal wars of expiation and land dispossession. In Virginia and New England, Indians who resisted 'settlement' and colonization of their lands would be treated, as in Ireland, like 'wild' and dangerous 'beasts'. The success of the Virginia and New England settlements soon provided a base for further expansion and settler colonization. A new colony, called Maryland (after the queen of English monarch Charles I), was founded at the northern head of Chesapeake Bay. In the mid-seventeenth century, the English 'settled' and colonized the so-called 'middle colonies', lying between Chesapeake Bay and New England (comprising present-day Pennsylvania, New Jersey, and New York). In New England, settler colonists from Massachusetts Bay founded adjoining colonies in Connecticut and Rhode Island. South of Virginia, West Indian planters, under the sponsorship of English aristocrats, founded a new colony called Carolina to honour King Charles II (a colony that included present-day North and South Carolina and Georgia). By the end of the seventeenth century, 'white' settler colonists had conquered, stolen, or bought Indian tribal coastal lands and had built densely populated settlements from Massachusetts to the Carolinas.

With a large and growing colonial population on the Atlantic seaboard, English settler colonists would soon break thorough the Appalachian Mountains into 'Indian country'. English metropolitans in London and in the colonies eagerly promoted colonization of the western borderlands, in order to establish a 'buffer zone' – running from Nova Scotia to the Carolinas – to protect English settlements from the French, from the Spanish, and from Indians living west of the Appalachians.[10] During the eighteenth century, colonists began to 'settle' the vast backcountry that stretched from northern New England to Georgia, building farming settlements in the foothills and across the Appalachian Mountains. In the eyes of the English settler colonists, the original royal and colonial charters gave them rights not only to lands on the Atlantic coast but also to almost limitless 'western' territory. Soon the attraction of cheap 'frontier' land further 'west', coupled with growing land scarcity and high land prices near the Atlantic coast, attracted some colonists to 'settle' the western borderlands.

But dreams of 'frontier settlement' were dealt a severe blow when the British, in the Royal Proclamation of 1763, declared that no settlement should occur west of the Appalachians and then, in the Quebec Act of 1774, placed the limits of Canada's southern boundary at the Ohio River. Prominent and influential western land speculators in trans-Appalachia and the Ohio country (including George Washington and Benjamin Franklin), as well as 'ordinary' Anglo-Americans anxious for western lands, were greatly angered by these British actions, actions that bolstered the arguments of those favouring 'independence' from the mother country. During the War for Independence itself, brutal warfare in 'the West' temporarily ended 'frontier' migration and 'depopulated' the western-most Anglo-America settlements, driving settlers eastward. After the war, however, settler colonization of the western 'frontiers' and western 'farm making' resumed and intensified.[11]

British North America and the experience of its settler colonists left powerful legacies for the new 'United States' – legacies that would empower its nineteenth-century conquest and colonization of the entire North American continent. By the time of the American War for Independence, Anglo-American settler colonists, both native-born farmers and European immigrants alike, came to believe that the ownership of Indian lands was their birthright.[12] Like their colonial counterparts, post-independence 'Americans' denied that Indians had any 'right' to the soil. In times of war, moreover, Anglo-American settler colonists tended to attack all Indians, both 'hostile' and 'friendly'. In the end, the former British 'colonists' and their descendants would become the American 'colonizers' of the indigenes who stood in the path of their 'western empire'.[13] Following the example of their ancestors, children, grandchildren, and later descendants of the original settler colonists, as well as hordes of landless immigrants and their descendants, would move 'west' to 'obtain' 'frontier' lands newly wrested from the American Indians.

Nazi Germany

Following the 1772 partition of Poland between Russia, Austria, and Prussia, Frederick II ('the Great'), King of Prussia (1740–86) sought to 'plant' colonists on reclaimed land in what was called 'the East', specifically on the marshlands of the north German plain – lands that had once been conquered and settled by the Teutonic Knights.[14] Under his auspices, recruitment stations advertised Prussia as a 'promise land' for hardworking immigrants. As part of what has been called *Peuplierungspolitik* (population policy), peasant settlers and craftsman were solicited from Germany, as well as from German-speaking Europe. Frederick's agents recruited German farmers with the promise of free land, and Frederick himself looked to replace Polish nobles with Prussian ones. He also sought to gradually 'get rid' of all the Poles, and aimed to expel the 25,000 Jews living in West Prussia at the time.[15] During the course of his reign, some 300,000 emigrants 'settled' on new lands 'won' for Prussia, establishing 1,200 new villages and rural settlements. These colonists were one of Frederick's driving passions: he followed their journeys with intense personal interest, and he visited his new eastern colonies often. As the man who had transformed Prussia into a major European power and had colonized 'the East', Frederick the Great, not surprisingly, was one of Adolf Hitler's heroes, and the *Führer's* study had a picture of Frederick on the wall.

Modern Germans first put the idea of *Lebensraum* into practice during Wilhelmine-era conquest and colonization in Africa. In the fantasies of German colonial enthusiasts, colonization by 'white' German settlers would lead to a 'New Germany in Africa'. Both German Southwest Africa (GSWA; present-day Namibia) and German East Africa (GEA; present-day Tanzania) were settler colonies, areas designated for extensive future settlement by late nineteenth-century Germans.[16] In both GSWA and GEA, lands seized from the local indigenous populations would be given to German settlers and colonial land companies, while the indigenes would be confined to restricted reservations and kept alive as labourers for the colonial economy. Both settler colonies were predicated on a 'white' settler community dominating an African helot class. Indigene fear of settler intentions and colonizer fear of indigenous uprisings, however, led to the outbreak of colonial wars in both GSWA and GEA in the early twentieth century – genocidal wars that led to mass death among indigenous populations due to outright killing, starvation, and disease. In both wars, settler campaigns against the 'natives' also featured the burning of villages and destruction of food supplies. In these conflicts, some 60,000 Herero and 10,000 Nama in GSWA and up to 250,000 Africans in GEA lost their lives. In many ways, the Nazi blueprint for 'the East' broadly replicated the earlier colonization of Africa: 'planting' settler colonies, 'supplanting' the indigenes, destroying those who resisted German settlement, and enslaving the survivors.[17]

During the First World War, German planners in Berlin, in 1915, called for Germany to assume, under the cover of 'the present war', a 'colonization mission in the East' that would involve a 'resettlement of large masses of people',[18] as part of a wartime scheme to push the German–Slav racial 'frontier' further eastwards and 'settle' German farmers on Polish land. While actual settlement would have to wait until after the war, plans for settlement were begun during it. These settlement plans called for the depopulation of indigenous ethnic populations, permanent possession of their lands by new German settlers, and exploitation of these territories as German colonial land. In 'the East', settler colonists would be soldiers turned into farmers, on the model of the medieval *Wehrbauern* – that is, 'fighting farmers', taking, holding, and cultivating the land with 'sword and plow'. The new colonial land, in General Erich Ludendorff's vision, offered ground for 'large-scale German settlement activity', new 'food supply possibilities', and new manpower sources for 'Germany's military and economic security'.[19] Baltic barons of German ancestry in the region agreed to cede a third of their collective lands for German settlement. German military defeat on the Western front, however, ended the First World War, as well as Ludendorff's proposed settler-colonial project. The *Ober Ost* vision of eastern colonization, however, was later revived, harnessed, built upon, exploited, and radicalized by Hitler and the Nazis, who made the acquisition of new 'living space' in 'the East' an integral part of their ideology and foreign policy aims in the 1920s and 1930s.[20]

Following the end of the First World War, some German soldiers, as well as men too young to have fought in the war, were recruited into so-called *Freikorps* (Free Corps), volunteer paramilitary units – each owing allegiance only to its commander – used by the post-war German government to fight Communists within Germany, as well as 'Bolshevists' in the Baltic lands of 'the East'. Elaborate recruitment campaigns in the Reich carried advertisements promising volunteers a 'wonderful settlement opportunity' to 'own [your] own estate in the beautiful Baltic', as well as 'excellent colonization opportunities'.[21] While some went to the Baltic to 'fight Bolshevism', others like the Rossbach *Freikorps*, according to their leader's biographer, 'fought for nothing else than for German land, for German conquest and for German colonization on the Baltic sea'.[22] Older so-called 'homesteader-volunteers' went to the Baltic to fulfil lifelong dreams of owning their own land. Baltic *Freikorps* Commander von der Goltz established *The Drum*, a soldier's newspaper, to discuss colonization opportunities in 'the East'. For their part, the local German landholders in the Baltic offered *Freikorps* fighters lectures and courses on agriculture. According to its participants, the Baltic fighting was a stereotypical colonial war, which some compared to an 'Indian war', while others insisted it 'was much more comparable to an expedition in the interior of Africa'.[23] Nonetheless, the colonial war in the Baltic was a 'pivotal experience for many freebooters who went on to join the Nazis'.[24]

In the 1930s, the Nazis would use and exploit these actual and intended episodes of past German colonization, as examples and justifications for their proposed 'drive to the East'. The Nazi revolution, said

Hitler and Nazi propagandists, meant the restoration of German greatness in the tradition of Frederick the Great. During the Nazi era, books and films glorified prior conquest and colonization in German Africa.[25] Nazi propaganda also recalled *Ober Ost*'s wartime rule in 'the East' and its intended colonization efforts, identifying the then-attempted 'German ordering of the East-space' as the 'German task' of the future for an 'Aryan' 'race united in National Socialism'.[26] In many respects, Nazi intentions in 'the East' also mirrored the earlier Baltic *Freikorps* aims of conquest, expansion, settlement, and colonization, a fact that motivated many former *Freikorps* fighters to join the Nazi movement. In the eyes of Hitler, Himmler, and other 'true believers', the Nazis would make good on the failure of wartime and immediate post-war eastern plans with their own terrible new plan for 'the East'.

A people's empire

Over the centuries, the main purpose of European imperialism was to provide wealth to the 'mother country'. In Early America and Nazi Germany, however, many of the benefits of the respective 'western' and 'eastern' empires were designed to accrue to 'ordinary' Americans and 'ordinary' Germans whose 'settlement' would, in turn, provide economic and national security for the nation-state. In both cases, there were immediate economic gains for 'ordinary' people from nation-state policies of territorial expansion, dispossession, racial war, and extreme political violence. To this extent, both the Early American 'western empire' and Hitler's 'Nazi empire' were linked to the promised notion of a 'people's empire' – that is, to policies of territorial expansion and subjugation of 'inferior' peoples that would benefit, as well as provide new opportunities for, 'ordinary' Americans and 'ordinary' Germans. Given these 'benefits' and 'opportunities', it would be much easier for 'ordinary' American and 'ordinary' German citizens – both in the metropole and on the 'frontier' edges of 'empire' – to ignore, turn away from, be indifferent to, or participate in the extreme violence being visited on the 'natives' in the new settler 'living space'.

Early America

In Early America, empire-building involved the occupation and 'settlement' of the American continental landmass. Early on in the new nation, politicians, land speculators, and 'grass-roots' settlers set their gaze westward, to ancestral lands occupied by Native Americans. On the 'frontier' peripheries of America's 'western empire', the prospect of owning land and thus securing a measure of economic security attracted both native-born and foreign-born migrants to 'the West'.[27] Initially, small groups of 'pioneers' – encouraged by politicians, promoters, and propagandists – moved westward to lands outside the nation's political boundaries, motivated by self-interest and hopes of a better livelihood. Faced with 'hostile' Indians resisting their invasion, these settler colonists quickly sought the protection of the US government and, ultimately, annexation of their former settler colonies and territories by the United States.

As we have seen (Chapter 1), Jefferson's vision for the new American republic was one of 'extensive empire', an 'empire of liberty' built by his beloved 'white' yeomen farmers, the 'chosen people of God'.[28] Rather than a country of wealthy landlords and poor tenants (like Europe), the United States would be a nation of small freeholders eager to own their own land, a nation of small commercial farmers.[29] The Jeffersonian vision was of a nation of independent, self-subsisting small farmers whose own prosperity would feed the new nation's progress, growth, and national destiny. Writing in 1786, Jefferson's vision was that the Atlantic settlements would serve as the 'original nest' from which the entire North American continent would be 'peopled'. Whenever a certain population density is obtained (that is, ten persons to the square mile), Americans, he observed, 'become uneasy, as too much compressed, and go off in great numbers to search for vacant country'. Within 40 years, he estimated, the territory east of the Mississippi would be 'settled' and occupied by his yeomen farmers. Eventually, settler colonists would 'settle' beyond the Mississippi and, ultimately, spread into South America as well.[30] Andrew Jackson built on Jefferson's vision and created his own vision of a populist, nationalist empire benefiting 'ordinary', 'white' settlers.[31] Viewing himself as champion of the common man, Andrew Jackson 'believed that the federal government's first obligation was to expand opportunities for "white" Americans to improve their situation in life, most especially through owning and developing land'.[32]

Promotional tracts, like that written by schoolmaster John Filson in 1784, spoke of 'the West' as a new 'land of promise, flowing with milk and honey' where 'you shall eat bread without scarceness and not lack anything', inspiring thousands of native-born settler colonists to head 'west' over the Appalachians. In a later book, early pioneer Daniel Boone was celebrated by Filson as a 'pathfinder', as 'an instrument ordained to settle the [western] wilderness', and as an example to future 'settlers'.[33]

European immigrants to Britain's North American colonies came hoping to glean opportunities on American 'frontiers' that they thought would be greater than those in Europe itself. In a best-selling book, *Letters From an American Farmer* (1782), J. Hector St. John de Crevecoeur, a French immigrant writing in the guise of a simple American farmer of the 1770s, declared that the new American nation would find its destiny and immigrants would find 'happiness' in 'the West'. Abundant American lands, Crevecoeur wrote, had 'enticed so many Europeans who have never been able to say that such a portion of land was theirs' to 'cross the Atlantic to realize that happiness'. After building his first farm, the small and middling farmer, he noted, 'determined to improve his fortunes by removing ['west'] and sought to buy as much land as will afford substantial farms to everyone of his children'.[34]

In letters, speeches, and pamphlets, potential western settler colonists heard stories of unlimited opportunities in 'the West'. Land speculators advertised their western landholdings with handbills, pamphlets, and newspaper stories. In addition, mass-circulation newspapers and magazines advertised western lands available for 'settlement', and travelling exhibitions at state and country fairs, as well as specially hired travelling agents, spread the word about the land and opportunities available in 'the West'. A report by John Charles Fremont, the 'Great Pathfinder', promoting western expansion and 'empire' became a national bestseller. Letters from those in 'the West' were passed from hand to hand within families, and western family members or neighbours promoted 'the West' on visits 'back East'. Early in the nineteenth century, travel accounts and guidebooks were available to prospective emigrants to 'the West'. In the last half of the nineteenth century, railroads, states and territories actively promoted western migration. State and territorial agencies hired representatives who distributed pamphlets, trumpeting the abundance of 'cheap' farm lands; some sent emissaries abroad to recruit settler colonists. Railroads also enthusiastically promoted 'settlement' along their western routes, luring prospective 'settlers' with pictures of bountiful fields, prosperous farmers, and easy rewards.[35]

Embedded in the American Declaration of Independence was a Jeffersonian promise that the new 'Americans' would be 'free' to 'pursue' their own 'happiness'. Believers in the Jeffersonian promise, many 'ordinary' Americans looked to move 'west', 'acquire' fertile and cheap land, and achieve personal betterment. For most colonists, individual decisions to 'go west' were personal ones, largely contingent on circumstances.[36] Some, like the Mormons, sought a religious utopia and economic security. Others believed themselves to be agents of 'imperial republicanism', apostles of republican institutions in the Jeffersonian tradition. For most 'westering' Americans, however, land was the attraction: the vision of a lush farm and a prosperous family. Hoping for 'success' and 'happiness' in 'the West', western 'settlers' also desired to improve themselves materially and spiritually. In the simplest terms, common folks craved a patch of land. Most 'ordinary' Americans saw 'the West' as a 'land of opportunity' where the promise of free, inexpensive, or more fertile land offered hopes of material gain and 'doing better'. For 'ordinary' American 'settlers', 'the West' was a world of great economic possibilities. In the 'American West' lay cheap land and precious metals (such as gold and silver). In 'the West', settlers would better their economic possibilities and improve their lives. Although pursuing their own individual 'manifest destinies', 'westering' Americans were also fulfilling Jefferson's vision of an agrarian 'western empire' 'peopled' by his 'white' yeomen farmers.

Unlike Europe, Jefferson told French philosopher Jean Baptiste Say, America has an 'immense extent of uncultivated and fertile lands', which 'enables everyone who will labor, to marry young, and to raise a family of any size'.[37] In the nineteenth century, a familiar pattern developed, which would do much to assure the populating of the 'people's empire' in 'the West'. 'Ordinary' Americans married early and had large families. Soon the oldest children also married and had their own children, and the new families headed off to 'settle' their own lands and live as independent landowners in 'the West'. In turn, their children repeated the process, leaving for a still farther 'west'. By the end of the nineteenth century, British Foreign Secretary Viscount Castlereagh's prediction that the Americans would win new lands in 'your bedchambers', rather than on battlefields, had largely come true. Driven by a high fertility rate, as well as sizeable European immigration, the US non-Indian population had grown from about 250,000 in 1700, to over 4 million in 1790, and to some 63 million in 1890, a population explosion unprecedented in human history.[38]

Nazi Germany

The Nazi *Lebensraum* project promised future prosperity and material well-being for the 'Aryan' Germans. Under National Socialism, 'ordinary' Germans were promised equality within the national racial community, a community to be 'cleansed' of its 'alien' and 'inferior' elements in both the metropolitan and colonized space. The Nazi goal of levelling out class differences found its clearest expression in Nazi settlement plans in 'the East' – plans designed to provide 'ordinary' Germans with more and better opportunities for self-advancement. The Nazi project in 'the East' aspired to create new opportunities of upward mobility for 'ordinary' Germans. Nazi ideology promised that 'the East' would be conquered for the benefit of 'ordinary' Germans, not for the benefit of landed Prussian Junkers or rich industrialists.[39] Nazi plans for eastern empire offered to satisfy the material interests of millions of 'ordinary' Germans, by offering desirable lands for settlement, cheaper food, new opportunities, and cheap labour. In return, millions of 'ordinary' Germans 'served their Nazi leaders with all their strength' and supported the Nazi national project in 'the East'.[40] The expulsion of Poles and Jews meant farms, houses, and businesses for the newly arrived German settlers. In the 'Nazi East', in fact, the dispossession of 'inferior' peoples had 'the euphoria of a [western] gold rush'.[41]

Crafted largely by Hitler and Himmler, the Nazi vision of a 'new East' was based on a German peasant culture, on 'resettlement' of ethnic Germans to conquered territories, and on the displacement of 'alien' Slavs and Jews. Hitler believed that rural settlement could solve the problem of urban unemployment, an idea that gained momentum during the Depression of the early 1930s. Himmler's vision was based on a system of *Wehrbauern* and SS settlements in eastern Poland and in western Russia, military strong points in the midst of 'alien' and 'unwanted' peoples. Hitler and Himmler aimed to attract precisely those types of people who, in an earlier period of Germany history, migrated to the 'American West' in search of freedom, opportunity, and land. On the surface, Nazi dreams of small yeomen farmers in 'the East' were at odds with the interests of the Junkers, aristocratic large landowners with estates near Germany's 'frontier' borderlands. However, such conflicts did not really bother radical Nazi 'true believers'. Hitler looked to the 'younger generation' for the 'repopulation of our Eastern territories'. Accordingly, said the *Führer*, 'We must imbue them with a feeling of pride in being invited to go to a country where we expect them to build up something truly magnificent.' By emigrating in this fashion, he argued, 'they will find opportunities for promotion infinitely more rapid than those of their less enterprising comrades who remain quietly at home, content to follow the beaten track'.[42]

Hitler told his close associates that, under the Nazi 'New Order', Europe, rather than America, would be the new 'country of boundless possibilities'.[43] Among many in the Nazi Party, in the SS, and in the planning organizations, there was already a strong *Ostrausch* (or 'intoxication of the east').[44] Hitler realized that 'ordinary' Germans would have to

'acquire' this *Ostrausch*. Accordingly, he suggested tourist trips be organized for Reich Germans to visit the Crimea and the Caucasus, in order
for them, in his words, to 'acquire the feeling for the great, open spaces'
of the 'Nazi East'.[45] Under the sponsorship of Strength Through Joy, the
giant Nazi leisure and tourism agency, Nazi tourists acquired a taste of
the prosperous future promised by the regime once *Lebensraum* in 'the
East' had been acquired and secured.[46]

Nazi propaganda depicted 'the East' as an exciting land of opportunity for German settler colonists. The 'freedom and opportunities' of
'the East' were promoted in schoolbooks, popular histories, and Nazi
party propaganda. The 'pioneer' spirit of the 'wide open spaces' of the
'German East' was also celebrated in fictional 'settler novels' of the
1930s.[47] Magazine articles were used to popularize the resettlement programme in the Reich metropole, and, in late 1940, the regime even
introduced tax breaks in order to attract Reich Germans to 'settle' in
'the East'.[48] Nazi propagandists proclaimed that 'our destiny calls us to
make the land in the East bloom for us as it did for our forefathers'.[49]
German recruiting agents and propaganda articles painted a rosy picture
of peasant life in the 'Nazi East', of uninhabited farmhouses awaiting
the 'resettlers'. For their part, Nazi organizations promoted 'the East' as
a land of opportunity where its activists could advance their careers and
make long-term homes. A tourism advertisement for East Prussia used a
Teutonic Knight as a marketing tool to entice tourists to visit 'the East',
and recruitment adverts for 'settlement advisers' proclaimed 'The East
needs You!'.[50]

While Himmler wanted to hold eastern lands 'in trust' for war veterans, Göring publicly decreed that all Polish farms in Nazi-occupied
territory were subject to confiscation. The Nazis hoped that so-called
'land hunters' from the Reich would be attracted by a sense of self-
interest and by the prospects of participating in an old-fashioned 'land
grab' on a massive scale.[51] In the 'Germanized' eastern territories, 'settlers' attracted to 'the East' by party propaganda expected to receive
the keys to a Polish farm or to a Jewish apartment. Nazi activists and
organizations began recruiting women and students as settlement advisers, teachers, and nurses to help make the 'Nazi East' into a 'German
homeland', by performing education and welfare tasks aimed at fostering community-building among ethnic German settlers. A sense of
patriotic duty and ideological commitment to support the 'German
mission' to colonize 'the East' drove many genuine volunteers; others less ideologically inclined were induced to join by organizational
or peer pressures.[52] For many party functionaries especially, the 'Nazi

East' became a 'frontier' of unlimited possibilities, promising a level of prosperity few could have imagined possible.[53]

The Nazi vision of settler colonies in 'the East' appealed to many 'ordinary' Germans, including soldiers fighting in the eastern campaign. Many soldiers, in fact, 'welcomed the Nazi colonial project, envisioning settlements of armed German farmers, who would exploit the labor of Slavic helots' and 'imagin[ing] themselves as the landowner-settlers of the future'.[54] Writing to his mother from a military hospital at the end of 1943, the young Heinrich Böll (future German writer and Nobel Prize winner) opined that, while he longed for the German homeland, he often thought about the 'possibility of a colonial existence here in the East after a victorious war'.[55] At the beginning of the 1940s, many Germans dreamed of a 'country estate in the East' and of a future life as 'militia farmers' in what was popularly called (at the time) 'the black-earth country'.[56] By 1942, soldiers' wives could dream of spacious farms and estates in 'the East', while children of German settlers were staging imaginary cowboy-and-Indian gunfights in the eastern *Lebensraum*.[57] Within the Reich itself, children played a board game in which armed farmers competed for the fertile 'black earth' of Ukraine.[58] Meanwhile, two German authors of children's books mulled over a primer 'for beginning readers' that would 'acquaint small children with the ideas behind the settlement plan and transfer the cowboys-and-Indians romanticism [of the "American West"] to eastern Europe'.[59]

A primary goal of Hitler's *Lebensraumpolitik* was to increase the 'Aryan' population by 'obtaining' land for German settlers and providing sufficient food for Germany's growing population. 'The highest aim of [a National Socialist] foreign policy', Hitler announced in *Mein Kampf*, will be *'to bring the soil into harmony with the population'*.[60] He clearly recognized the link between the conquest of 'living space' and the ability and willingness of Germans to reproduce, to 'multiply' enough to populate the new *Lebensraum*. By gaining the 'inexhaustibly fertile soil' in 'the East', Hitler told his closest advisers, the Nazis would help 'create conditions for our people that favour its [the people's] multiplication'. In Hitler's view, population expansion was both necessary and beneficial. 'The essential thing for the future', he declared, 'is to have lots of children.' Hitler thought that increasing the birth rate in Germany – and thereby gaining more future soldiers – was crucial to achieving his foreign policy goals. German war losses, moreover, would be 'paid for several times over by our colonization in the East. The population of German blood', he claimed, 'will multiply itself richly.'[61] Not only would increasing the birth rate improve the biological quality of the

Volk, he believed, it would also allow Germany to expand eastward at the expense of 'inferior' indigenous peoples.[62]

Colonization plans

Both Early America and Nazi Germany developed plans to control and govern the new 'living space' they planned to conquer in the American 'West' and the Nazi-German 'East'. In the American case, these plans for colonizing what used to be called 'Indian Country' were put forth by two of the nation's 'Founding Fathers' – George Washington and Thomas Jefferson – and called for the administration of much of the 'American West' as a colony of the United States. In the German case, much more detailed plans were developed by Nazi bureaucrats, based on the vast numbers of indigenous peoples who would have to be 'cleared' from the settlement areas. In Early America, colonization involved vast but thinly populated regions called 'territories', which, after being sufficiently populated by white settlers, would eventually become 'states' of the new Union. In Nazi Germany, colonization involved vast but highly populated regions, which were to be administered as either 'incorporated' or 'unincorporated' territories.

Both Early American and Nazi-German colonization plans were viewed as long-term projects of settler colonialism that required the 'depopulation' of the indigenous inhabitants. In the American case, the settlement of the trans-Appalachian and trans-Mississippi 'wests' was a repeating cycle of frontier migration, Indian warfare, Indian 'removal', and farm making. As long as lands could be 'obtained' from the Indians, it was a process that could (and would) be repeated continuously for more than a century.[63] While influenced by prior instances of frontier or colonial settlement, the Nazi experiment in colonization was, at once, radical and modern.[64] This new German 'living space' was to be populated, in the decades after the war, by ethnic Germans living abroad and repatriated to the Reich and by settlers from the Greater German Reich itself. Looking forward to a 'mass migration' of settler colonists, the Nazis intended to colonize the conquered territories in 'the East' and make these areas thriving Germanic provinces.

Early America

In his 1893 famous lecture on the 'frontier thesis' of American history, American historian Frederick Jackson Turner used the phrase 'the colonization of the Great West' to describe the Early American process of conquest, expansion, and 'settlement'.[65] The 'colonization' of the 'American West' was a state-sponsored process of 'white' settler expansion and Indian dispossession that operated on several levels: on the one hand, it was a migration of thousands of 'ordinary' people (who migrated 'west' for their own reasons); on the other hand, it was an intentional and planned process, which required the participation and active promotion of the national government. In short, after the American Revolution, the former 'colonial subjects' became 'colonizers' themselves, as 'ordinary' Americans and policymakers became allies in a deliberate process of conquest and settler colonization.[66]

Even before the War for Independence was won, the Americans began planning for the future settlement of 'the West'. Early in 1783, before the formal end of the war, General George Washington described his own 'plan of colonization' for the lands between the Appalachians and the Mississippi. In his plan, Washington proposed to use 'disbanded Officers and Soldiers of the [Continental] Army' – 'a brave, a hardy and respectable Race of People' – as 'our advanced Post', to 'connect our Government with the frontiers' and to 'extend our Settlements progressively'. These men 'would be always ready and willing (in case of hostility) to combat the [Indian] savages and check their incursions'. These 'advanced Posts' would, he continued, 'give security to the frontiers, the very name of it would *awe* the Indians, and more than probably prevent the murder of many innocent families'.[67] In this vision, the coveted western lands – denied to the rebellious colonists by the French and then the British – would finally belong to the new American nation who would use violence (as required) to take and keep them. But the post-independence 'settlement' of the Old Northwest was not, as Washington had hoped, a 'peaceful' settlement of 'unclaimed' and 'vacant' land but rather a costly and prolonged five-year war of conquest.[68]

At the end of the Revolution, Thomas Jefferson outlined his own vision for westward expansion and colonization, in his 'Plan of Government for the Western Territory', which called for the formation of 16 new states in the trans-Appalachian 'west'. His plan for the new western territories – in his envisaged 'empire for liberty' – called for settler colonization on both sides of the Mississippi River. 'When we shall be full on this [eastern] side', he wrote, 'we may lay off a range of states on the Western bank... and so, range after ranger, advancing compactly as we multiply.'[69] Jefferson's views influenced subsequent colonization plans, outlined in the so-called Northwest Ordinances, which detailed how the Old Northwest would be organized for territorial government and eventual statehood. According to the plan, Indian lands in 'the West' were to be formed in the image of the original 13 colonies, excepting that the new western colonies of the United States were to be called 'territories'. As it grew, the new and rapidly expanding American empire would be colonized and administered under the provisions of these Northwest Ordinances.

The final Northwest Ordinance of 1787 stipulated that, after passing through 'territorial status' with their own territorial governments and reaching a population of 60,000 inhabitants, the regions would become 'states' of the American union.[70] These new states were, the ordinances said, to be equal in all respects to the original 13 states, with equal citizenship rights for ('white') citizens and with no class of colonial dependents (since the Indians, it was assumed, would simply 'vanish').[71] The ordinances, as two recent scholars have noted, provided a 'robust institutional framework for the American colonization' of Indian lands north and west of the Ohio River and established 'an empire capable of indefinite expansion'.[72] On paper, at least, the Northwest Ordinance of 1787 promised that Indian lands and property 'shall never be taken from them without their consent' and that the Indians 'shall never be invaded or disturbed, *unless in just and lawful wars* authorized by Congress'.[73] Unfortunately for American Indians, such authorization would not prove difficult to obtain.[74]

For Jefferson, the settlement process seemed quite simple. As he wrote in an 18 February 1803 letter to a friend, 'While [the Indians] are learning to do better on less land, our increasing numbers will be calling for more land, and thus a coincidence of interests will be produced between those who have lands to spare, and want other necessaries, and those who have necessaries to spare, and want lands.'[75] Settler–state notions of the Indians' willingness to give up long-inhabited ancestral lands proved false, in many cases, leading to wars of resistance to 'white' settlement and to settler–state policies of ethnic cleansing. Rather than a seemingly benign process of territorial expansion based on 'voluntary' Indian 'land sales' (as often portrayed in the 'master narrative' of American history), American 'settlement' was predicated on the active and intended dispossession, subjugation, and control of Indian peoples who were treated as 'colonial subjects' without citizenship rights or legal status.[76]

In the Early America settler-colonial model, treaties would be 'negotiated' with the Indians to retroactively validate the 'taking' of Indian lands by white settler incursions or by 'just and lawful wars'. In Colonial America and Early America, they served, as one scholar has recently noted, as a 'legal procedure to acquire lands and remove Indians, both backed by [military] force'.[77] In pre-independence British North

America, however, the Anglo-Indian treaty system of the early 1760s was largely based on accommodation, mutual compromise, and coexistence. Post-independence, however, it became very much a colonial treaty system which, between 1796 and 1871, served to secure the domination of the Indians by the American 'white' settler–state, by transferring land from Indian ownership to ownership by the United States. In the hands of the new American government, this new treaty system functioned for the new United States as a 'license for empire'.[78] For the white settlers, as well as for the federal government, these treaties gave an aura of legality to the forced dispossession of Native Americans and their 'removal' further 'west' onto reservations. For their part, American treaty negotiators, as a recent scholar notes, 'operated from the premise that the question was not whether the Indians would be removed [from their lands] but how and when they would be [re]moved and confined to their own reserves'.[79] In the nineteenth century, the status of the Indian tribes evolved from independent 'nations' capable of making treaties to powerless colonial subjects.[80]

While sharing similar aims, the nation's governing elites and its settler colonists engaged in differing discourses. Government officials usually masked their desires and actions in rhetoric; frontier people spoke plainly about their 'land hunger' and took a harder stance against the Indians. The people on the frontier, after all, were, 'engaged in the dirty work of empire on behalf of those who stayed behind'.[81] While settler colonists on the frontier and high government officials in Early America were certainly of one mind on their desire for expansion, conquest, and settlement of fertile Indian lands, they often differed on means. The nation's 'Founding Fathers', for the most part, envisaged settler colonization of 'the West' as a 'gradual' and largely 'peaceful' process. While some early political leaders advocated for eventual Indian inclusion into the American Republic – based on notions of a 'civilization' policy – white settlers and their political supporters in 'the East' had very different ideas. In 'the West', white settlers 'rejected *any* notion of land sharing, labeled *all* Indians as "savages", and defined *all* Indians as "the enemy" '.[82] Rather than the hoped-for 'gradual' settlement founded on 'peaceful' change (or, at least, on some idea of coexistence), the reality quickly became explosive, chaotic, and rapid settlement, resulting in almost constant Indian–settler violence. Cultural contacts and negotiation, as historian Douglas Hurt rightly concludes, gave way to 'territorial conquest achieved by violence that escalated to total war before the nineteenth century ended'. As a result, the American 'frontier' was no longer an inclusive, intercultural borderland but an area of conquest, subjugation, and exclusion. On the edges of American empire, the intercultural borderland of the 'middle ground' ceased to exist.[83]

Nazi Germany

As Adolf Hitler said, and 'blood and soil' Nazi ideologues like SS leader Heinrich Himmler and agricultural minister Richard Walther Darré often repeated, 'the Third Reich will either be a realm of farmers (*ein Bauernreich*) or it will perish'.[84] Although both shared an essentially agrarian-based ideology, Darré and Himmler, two of the Nazis' foremost 'Easterners', had very different visions of Nazi expansion and colonization in 'the East'.

Dreaming of a Jeffersonian Republic of small farmers, and inviting explicit comparison with American colonization of 'the West', Darré's vision was deeply Jeffersonian in tone, stressing the ideal of a self-sufficient, racially homogeneous yeoman peasantry. Darré did not support the invasion of Russia. Opposing what he called 'foreign adventurism', he favoured, instead, a limited war in 'the East' focused on the acquisition of the Baltic lands. Darré would confine 'settlement projects', he said, to German territory, as well as the settlement of German farmers in East Prussia and the Baltic. In his view, 'the East' was to become a substitute for Germany's 'lost colonies' after the First World War. He strongly opposed Himmler's *Wehrbauern* concept, which the SS leader based on the notion of an armed frontier peasantry living in fortified model villages of some 30 families each, governed by two or three SS men. According to Darré, 'settlement questions' were to be considered solely on the basis of 'agrarian realities', rather than 'matters of inspiration or romance'. For his part, Himmler declared Darré 'too theoretical'.[85] While Darré looked to settlement taking place within an enlarged German border, Himmler looked to armed conquest, SS-dominated expansion, and an SS-ruled empire in Poland and Russia. Like his *Führer*, Himmler was an imperialist with strong racial overtones, dreaming of a pan-European Greater Germanic empire organized on strict Nazi racial principles.[86]

Rather than follow Darré's plan for more limited colonization and 'settlement', Hitler, on 7 October 1939, appointed Himmler to the additional position of Reich commissar for the strengthening of germandom, granting the SS and its Race and Settlement Office a leading role in the deportation and 'resettlement' schemes for conquered Polish territory. With Himmler's appointment, Darré became increasingly more marginalized; viewed as a 'pessimist' by Himmler, he was finally sidelined from any position of influence.[87] Himmler's successful fight to gain control of Nazi-German 'resettlement' policy ultimately meant that his much more radical and brutal view of 'colonization' would be carried out in the 'Nazi East'.

In the late nineteenth and early twentieth century, much European overseas colonization was predicated on the notion of a 'civilizing' mission to bring 'order', 'cleanliness', and 'culture' to the 'dirty' and 'ignorant' 'native' populations of Africa and Asia. Rather than a 'civilizing' mission, however, the Nazi-German 'mission' in Eastern Europe would be a radical 'colonizing' one, where, Hitler said, 'land' – but not 'peoples' – would be 'Germanized'. In the 'Nazi East', 'spaces' would be taken by military force, and 'unwanted', 'alien', and 'inferior' 'races' (that is, Jews, Gypsies, and Slavs) would be 'cleared' and 'eliminated' – via deportation and murder – to make way for 'superior', 'Aryan' German settlers.[88] *SS-Oberführer* Konrad Meyer, Himmler's planning chief, summarized the totalizing and radical nature of the Nazi 'colonizing' mission in 'the East': 'It is not enough', he declared, 'to settle our race in those areas and eliminate people of an alien race. Rather, these spaces have to take on a character that corresponds to the nature of our being.'[89]

Nazi colonization plans were built on a decidedly settler-colonial model. Hitler defined the task in 'the East' as 'Germaniz[ing] this [space] by the emigration of Germans, and to look upon the natives as Redskins'. He defined his long-term policy aim as 'having eventually a hundred million Germans settled in these territories.... In ten years' time', he continued, 'we must be in a position to announce that twenty million Germans have been settled in the [eastern] territories already incorporated in the Reich and in those [areas] which our troops are at present occupying.'[90] Nazi deputy leader Hermann Göring proclaimed that 'the newly occupied eastern regions will be exploited economically from colonial points of view and with colonial methods'.[91] In 'the East' itself, *Gauleiter* (regional party leader) Arthur Greiser of *Warthegau* enthusiastically asserted that, 'in ten years' time, there will be no patch of land which will not be German; every homestead will belong to German colonists'.[92] According to fellow *Gauleiter* Hans Frank, the territory of the *Generalgouvernement* would also be 'totally Germanized'. It would become, Frank announced, the site of 'great settlements' and 'major military centres'. 'Unwanted ethnic aliens', he stressed, would be 'transported to the east'; 'immigrant Reich and ethnic Germans' would 'put down roots' while 'ethnically alien elements' (that is, Poles and Jews) would be 'squeezed out'.[93]

In his views on the indigenous populations of 'the East', Hitler expressed the typical attitudes of a settler-colonial racist. 'Anyone who talks about cherishing the local inhabitant and civilizing him', he declared, 'goes straight off to a concentration camp.'[94] 'Compulsory vaccination will be confined to Germans alone', Hitler told close associates, 'and the doctors in the German colonies will be there solely for the purpose of looking after the German colonists'; health services, it was clear, would not be available to 'the subject races'.[95] 'We must take all necessary measures to ensure that the non-German population does not increase at an excessive rate', he said, including the 'use of contraceptives and denial of health services and inoculations or other preventative measures'. It would be the task of local Nazi officials to persuade 'the natives' that vaccinations are 'really most dangerous'.[96]

As the most literal advocate of Hitler's racial, population, and settlement policies in 'the East', as well as the Nazi leader most responsible for the attainment of Nazi eastern racial and territorial goals, Himmler spoke of a 'settlement ground in the East which gives [Germany] enough air and space to live', describing 'the East' as a 'plantation of pure Germanic blood, the melting pot of all German and Germanic tribes'.[97] 'After the war', Himmler told SS colleagues in October 1943, 'we'll be ready to proceed with the great work of the future...we will colonize' the eastern *Lebensraum*. He called on the SS, 'together with the farmers', to 'colonize the East, in bold strokes, without inhibition, not inquiring about traditional methods, with revolutionary drive and impetus'.[98] Himmler's colonization and 'settlement' vision was even more expansive than his *Führer's*. In 1942, he told SS and police leaders in the Ukraine that 'this German East as far as the Urals has to be the nursery of German blood so that in 400 to 500 years there will live 500 to 600 million Germans and Germanic people instead of 120 million'.[99] Nazi settlement plans for 'the East' were succinctly captured in Himmler's own slogan, 'Today colony, tomorrow settlement area, the day after tomorrow part of the Reich!'[100]

The Nazi agenda for further 'Germanization' of 'the East' was outlined in various wartime drafts of what was called the *Generalplan Ost* (the General Plan East, or GPO),[101] produced by Himmler's Reich Security Main Office. In the GPO, Nazi planners put forth far-reaching proposals for what they called the 'opening-up of the East', built around planned colonization by German settler colonists, the expulsion of 'alien' ethnic groups (that is, Slavs and Jews), and the 'Germanization' of some 'selected' portions of the 'primitive' indigenous populations. In the initial draft of the GPO, Konrad Meyer wrote that 'the Reich now views as its most noble task the building up of these [conquered eastern] areas in the shortest possible time into full-fledged *Reich Gaus*. For this purpose the first precondition is *rural colonization* and the creation of a healthy peasantry.'[102] The GPO, an SS design for a 'blood and soil' utopia in 'the East', was a ruthless vision of a radicalized twentieth-century settler colonialism.[103] In addition, as historian Elizabeth Harvey correctly points out, the GPO linked, both ideologically and practically, the Nazi drive to 'Germanize' Eastern Europe with the Nazi goal to destroy the Jews. The murder of the Jews, in turn, provided an important precedent for the eventual displacement and destruction of other 'unwanted', 'native' populations.[104] While the GPO was a long-term 'settlement' plan for the 'Nazi East', Himmler began to implement its first stages during the war. In Himmler's hands, the GPO was a 'grand design for exterminatory colonization'.[105]

Settlement

In both the 'American West' and the 'Nazi East', situational factors influenced the outcome of the settlement and colonization of the new 'living space'. In the Early American case, the pace and extent of actualized 'settlement' exceeded even the most optimistic expectations of the nation's 'Founding Fathers'. In Early America, 'settlement was the key to America's conquest of the [North American] continent'.[106] The process of turning western Indian lands into Early America's agrarian empire was, moreover, a continuous process of occupation and settlement. Land-hungry settler colonists accomplished the 'settlement' of the nation's coast-to-coast continental empire in less than a century – a pace that would have astounded even Jefferson. In the Nazi-German case, there was a wide 'gap' between Nazi 'settlement' plans and actualized accomplishments. In the 'Nazi East', the realities 'on the ground' proved very different to Hitler's and Himmler's eastern settlement fantasies. In the end, grandiose Nazi projects for German 'Aryan' settlements in 'the East' collapsed in the wake of Germany's defeat at the hands of the Red Army on the Eastern front. Plagued by Nazi jurisdictional rivalries and ideological disagreements, Nazi-German colonization and 'settlement' of 'the East' was a goal that would be only partially attained.

Early America

In the nation's first 100 years, American 'settlement' was 'occupation' of Indian lands, the dispossession of the indigenous inhabitants, and their displacement further 'west'. As noted earlier (Chapter 3), Early America acquired legal sovereignty to western lands by diplomacy/purchase, annexation, or outright war. They had the 'right' and 'duty' to take the land, they believed, because they would make it more productive than 'inferior' Indian American peoples had done. America's success in 'settling' 'the West' rested largely on four situational factors that combined to assure the success of the national expansionist project: (1) Indian 'removal' from metropolitan and colonized 'living space'; (2) benevolent federal land laws; (3) high 'frontier' birth rates and immigration rates; and (4) a self-serving expansionist ideology, fortified by racist assumptions of Anglo-Saxon 'superiority'.[107]

The history of Early American 'frontier' settlement involved 'settling' the nation's successive 'wests', a process which in less than a century extended the nation's national boundaries from coast to coast. In the American imagination, 'the West' was settled by independent and self-reliant 'pioneers' and 'settlers'. The actuality of American settlement, however, reveals the significant role of the federal government in the 'peopling' of the nation's western 'empire'.[108] For the most part, 'white' native-born Americans dominated western migration, but foreign-born immigrants – mostly northern Europeans and Canadians – formed a large but important minority of western settler colonists. In the nineteenth century, 'colony' was a term used by contemporaries to describe both highly organized settlement ventures as well as clustered family settlements. Colonizing families included members of a family line, often in conjunction with a larger group of relatives or kin. Formal colonization schemes, then, were a feature of virtually every newly developing western region throughout the century, whether organized by land or transportation companies, by religious groups, by voluntary organizations, or by a group of colonizing families.[109]

Settlement patterns in the 'American West' followed what, over the next century, would become a familiar and similar pattern of: 'settler' incursions, Indian resistance, military 'pacification' to 'protect' the 'settlers', an 'Indian war' resulting in Indian land cessions to the 'whites', a 'treaty' conveying land title to the United States, subsequent Indian 'removal' further 'west', and a flood of 'white' 'settlement' to the new national 'living space'. Taken together, this repeating pattern of acquisition, dispossession, 'settlement' and displacement, in the new nation's successive 'wests', was a 'continental imperialism' that allowed the United States to complete its coast-to-coast expansion, from the Atlantic seaboard all the way to the Pacific, in an astoundingly short seven decades. In the new nation's successive 'wests', then, the overall pattern was the same: 'white' settler incursions would spawn Indian resistance; the US military would be dispatched to protect the settlers; eventually, the Indians would fall back, sign a treaty 'ceding' their lands to the federal government, and be 'removed' further 'west'.[110] The 'acquired' lands would officially become a US territory, ready for the mass migration of settler colonists. In the 'American West', 'settlement' assumed the metaphor of a constant migratory stream of native-born and foreign-born settler colonists flooding 'the West'.[111]

In the early eighteenth century, Britain's North American colonies were expanding rapidly. Between 1700 and 1750, the number of settler colonists – clustered in settlements dispersed along the Atlantic coast – grew from 250,000 to more than 1.3 million. Over time, these isolated coastal settlements became connected colonies. As the amount of land available for purchase or inheritance diminished, the prospect of greater opportunities beckoned on the 'frontiers', causing many small and middling farmers to head 'west', seeking cheap land and better prospects. Besides a high birth rate among native-born Americans, large numbers of immigrant German and Scots–Irish settlers moved to the western fringes of English 'settlement', pushing into the 'backcountry'. The combination of growing land shortages and high land prices near the coastal settlements, coupled with an abundance of cheap land on the 'frontier', led to increased 'settler' migration 'west'. In the vast backcountry stretching from Maine to Georgia, squatters trespassed on Indian lands, cleared the lands, and began to farm, 'squatting' on lands for which they had no title and creating settler communities strong enough to withstand Indian warfare and to attract more settlers.[112] In the sparsely colonized 'borderlands' between the coastal settlements and the Appalachians, 'frontier' land seemed free for the taking.

At the end of the War for Independence, fewer than 25,000 'settlers', or about 1 per cent of the total US population, lived in Indian lands between the Appalachian Mountains' western slope and the banks of the Mississippi – an area that was an Indian 'homeland' for between 200,000 and 250,000 Native Americans. Fully 70 per cent of the new nation's land area created by the Treaty of Paris (1783) formally ending the War for Independence was 'west' of the Proclamation Line of 1763 in what was called the trans-Appalachian 'west'.[113] During and after the war, 'white' 'settlers' surged into the 'settlement area'. At the end of the American War for Independence, native-born farmers and European immigrants caught the 'fever' for American 'frontier' land and rushed to these north-eastern and western frontiers to 'obtain' Indian lands. After vicious Indian–settler warfare, a settler 'land grab' was followed by 'acquisition' by land developers, states, and the federal government. Land-poor or landless families dreamed of making farms on fertile Indian lands they believed were 'empty'. As historian Allan Kulikoff writes, 'as long as unimproved land could be stolen from the Indians, the cycle of land development and land scarcity in older areas, Indian removal from their farms and hunting grounds, migration to new frontiers, pioneer squatting, followed by purchase and development of land, could be repeated endlessly'.[114] In the space of two or three decades, 'white' settlers greatly outnumbered Indians. In the eighteenth century, white 'settlement' became a repeated cycle of Indian warfare, Indian 'removal', 'frontier' migration, and farm making. This 'western empire' of 'white' yeomen farmers continued this same cycle for another century in the 'American West', making the young American Republic into a 'farmers' nation'.[115]

In the lands 'west' of the Mississippi River, the so-called trans-Mississippi 'west', rapid settlement was driven by what Congressman Andrew Kennedy of Indiana called in 1846 'the American multiplication table'. 'Go to the West and see a young man with his mate of eighteen, and [after] a lapse of thirty years, visit him again, and instead of two, you will find twenty-two', he asserted.[116] American settlement 'west' of the Mississippi drew native-born and foreign-born immigrants. Western 'settlers' in the American trans-Mississippi 'west' included pioneer farmers, cattle and sheep herders, and gold-seekers. In the post-Civil War period, eastern journalist Horace Greeley and other western promoters advised 'young men' to 'go west' in search of opportunity. *Contra* the national mythology, the federal government led pioneers westward, guiding and moulding their settlement.[117] After 1863, land was 'free' under the terms of the Homestead Act, which granted 160 acres of land to citizens and non-citizens alike who agreed to reside on and improve the land for a period of five years. On the eve of the American Civil War, in 1860, nearly 1.4 million Americans lived west of the Mississippi, as compared to about 360,000 Indians. By the end of the nineteenth century, though, some 8.5 million 'Americans' lived in the 'Far West', while the Indian population had been 'reduced' to less than 250,000.[118]

Actualized 'settlement' in 'the West' constituted of nothing short of a 'white' American demographic onslaught, as 'white' Americans quickly outnumbered the 'natives'. Indian 'removal' had 'cleansed' much of the metropolitan and colonized 'space', leaving many states 'Indian-free'. According to the Office of Indian Affairs, in 1855, some 315,000 Indians lived within the nation's borders (which now stretched from coast to coast); of this total, however, only 8,500 lived east of the Mississippi

River. In addition, benevolent federal land laws had made 'cheap' lands available to 'westering' Americans, allowing for an efficient distribution of the public domain and greatly facilitating the national expansionist project. Between 1790 and 1890, high birth and immigration rates caused a nearly 16-fold increase in the non-Indian population, from 4 million to 63 million. And the self-serving expansionist ideology of 'Manifest Destiny', in the eyes of 'white' Americans, provided an ideological justification for the occupation, dispossession, and 'settlement' of non-white lands in 'the West'.

Nazi Germany

'If Russia goes under in this war', Hitler predicted, '[the Nazi "New Order" in Europe] will stretch eastwards to the limits of German colonization.'[119] While they fought over nuance, tactics, and jurisdiction, the multiple German agencies with a stake in 'the East' shared the policy goal that the 'Nazi East' would provide the Greater German Reich with food, land for settlement, resources, and forced labour.[120] In the 'Nazi East', Hitler favoured the 'creation of purely and exclusively German settlements'.[121] Claiming to take back lands that once had been 'German', the Nazis called their settler colonists 'resettlers' (*'Umsiedler'*). Hitler and Himmler hoped that many ethnic Germans (*Volksdeutsche*), as well as citizens of the Greater German Reich (*reichsdeutsch*), would answer 'the call to the East'. The Eastern European colonial territories were viewed by radical Nazis as an 'organic' expression of Germany's 'racial core' (not as distant possessions). In 'the East', the Nazi empire was to be erected around the Jewish Pale of Settlement, an area which, not coincidently, as we shall see in later chapters, became 'the core of [Nazi] genocide and its main object'.[122]

In the 'Nazi East', the SS was to be the motor and driving force of 'Germanization' and 'settlement' of 'the East'. Accordingly, a newly created Reich Commissariat for the Strengthening of Germandom (RKFDV) was placed under Himmler's control, and the SS was given primary responsibility for the colonization and settlement of the 'Nazi East'. In his *Führer* decree of 7 October 1939, Hitler assigned three primary tasks to Himmler as 'settlement commissioner' and head of the RKFDV: (1) to 'repatriate' Germans 'resident abroad' deemed 'suitable' for 'permanent return to the Reich'; (2) to 'eliminate' the 'harmful influence' of 'alien' populations who constitute a 'danger to the Reich and to the German national community'; and (3) to form 'new German settlements by the transfer of population and, in particular, by settling persons of German race or nationality returning from abroad'.[123] Given this sweeping brief, Himmler's RKFDV would be the bearers of the 'German mission' in 'the East'. In his new capacity, Himmler's racial and spatial fantasies would run wild.[124]

In the 'Nazi East', Hitler and Himmler looked to 'Germanize' (*'Eindeutschen'*) the newly acquired 'living space' through a massive programme of 'native' expulsions and 'resettlement' by repatriated and local ethnic Germans and Reich Germans. Nazi colonization and 'settlement' plans called for the 'removal' of much of Eastern Europe's non-German populations in order to free up lands for Himmler's yeomen farmers. All ethnic Germans were subject to a 'screening and processing procedure' in their place of origin, on arrival in the Reich, or at 'reception camps' in the eastern territories, in order to determine who was 'suitable' for eastern settlement. It was the job of Nazi 'screeners' to match 'right' settler with 'right' opportunity at the 'right' time and to make sure that settlers were early contributors to the war effort as well as to the 'Germanness' of the region.[125] In the 'Nazi East', the settlement process involved screening and separating – on the basis of 'blood' and 'racial quality' – the population into 'Germans' and 'aliens', the displacement of non-Germans, the appropriation of non-German lands and property for the benefit of those German 'resettlers' who met Nazi racial criteria, and the deportation of Poles and Jews further 'east'. Those refused permission to 'settle' in 'the East' due to lack of racial and/or political fitness were sent to the *Altreich* as labourers. Those deemed 'settlement material' were sent to resettlement camps to await the confiscation of indigenous land and resources for their use. In Polish towns, 're-settlement specialists' requisitioned Polish and Jewish homes and businesses for the new settlers; in the countryside, they confiscated Polish farms for the Nazi-German settler colonists.

In Hitler's view, the 'immense spaces' of the 'Nazi East' encompassed a vast 'Russian desert' waiting to be populated by German settler colonists. The Nazis envisaged a number of different sources of so-called 'settlement material' (*'Siedlungsmaterial'*). In their visions and plans, the 'Nazi East' was to be 'settled' by a combination of Reich Germans, 'Nordic' peoples from northern Europe, and local *Volksdeutsche* (ethnic Germans living beyond Germany's pre-1938 borders). Ethnic Germans brought 'home to the Reich' were to be a major source of settlers for newly 'acquired' lands in western Poland. Germans living beyond the Reich's borders would no longer serve, in Hitler's words, as a 'cultural fertilizer' for foreign states; instead, this 'valuable German blood' would be returned 'in order to strengthen the Reich'.[126] Hitler also looked to attract other 'Nordic' peoples – Norwegians, Swedes, Danes, and Dutch – to Nazi Germany's eastern territories as settler colonists. The 'two or three million men' needed to colonize 'the East', Hitler declared, would come 'from Germany, Scandinavia, the Western countries and America'. In German-occupied territory, he indicated, 'natives' would be 'screened' and 'the Jews' driven out.[127] In a larger sense, Hitler wanted to redirect European emigration from America to the 'Nazi East'; 'Aryan' Germans, Hitler declared, would not be allowed to emigrate to America. Himmler, too, hoped to 'recall' Germans whose ancestors had emigrated to North and South America.

In the aftermath of the military victory over Poland, former Polish territory won by the Nazi-Germans – up to the agreed border with the Soviet Union – was divided into two areas: the incorporated territories, and the non-incorporated territories. According to a decree by Hitler, large areas of western Poland were formally incorporated and annexed into the Greater German Reich. These so-called 'incorporated territories' included two new provinces (*Reichsgau*) formed and annexed to Germany: West Prussia (later called the *Reichsgau Danzig-Westpreussen*) and Posen (later called the *Reichsgau Wartheland*, or *Warthegau*). Within the incorporated territories, the Nazis pursued a radical programme of 'Germanization', a programme that met with some (albeit small) measure of success. That part of German-occupied Poland not annexed to Germany was given the name General Government (*Generalgouvernement*). Originally viewed as a reservoir for Reich labour and a 'dumping ground' for 'unwanted' populations of Poles and Jews evicted from the annexed territories, the General Government also emerged as an area for German settlement as German armies and the Reich's borders drove further 'eastward'.

Radical Nazi 'true believers', however, would never be satisfied with limited territorial gains in areas contiguous to Germany. Their colonial ambitions compelled them to seek additional settlement territory in Russia, drawn by past dreams of the *Baltikum* and the Ukraine as German 'colonial territories'. Both Hitler and Himmler were consumed with the idea of turning European Russia into a German colonial settlement area.[128] With the onset of the war for *Lebensraum* in Russia, SS planners, drawing deeply 'from a geographical imagination that was stimulated for decades by visions of the American frontier',[129] drew up schemes for new German 'colonies' in the Baltic provinces, in the Ukraine, and in the Crimea.

For Nazi 'true believers', Russia was 'the promise land'. In the Occupied Eastern Territories 'acquired' subsequent to the June 1941 attack

on the Soviet Union, four new settler colonies were envisaged by radical Nazis. In the newly conquered areas, the Nazis created two new
provinces: the Reich Commissariat Ostland and the Reich Commissariat
Ukraine. The Reich Commissariat Ostland was comprised of the three
Baltic states of Estonia, Latvia, and Lithuania and the northern parts of
Belarus. The Reich Commissariat Ukraine was projected to be Germany's
largest settler colony, incorporating Ukraine, parts of eastern Poland,
and southern Belarus. Hitler's plans for the Crimea envisaged the region,
in his words, to be 'cleared of all foreign elements and colonized by
Germans'.[130] Two additional provinces – one for the Caucasus and one
for the region around Moscow – were planned, but these provinces were
never established, due to insufficient German military control in these
areas.

In the 'Nazi East', the settlement process proved to be painfully slow
and the results meagre. Changing wartime security and economic needs
foiled many colonization and 'settlement' plans. According to RKFVD
statistics, almost 500,000 ethnic Germans had been repatriated to the
Old Reich or to the newly incorporated eastern territories by December 1940. Subsequent to the attack on the Soviet Union, an additional
300,000 ethnic Germans were added to the pool of potential settler
colonists, bringing the total to some 800,000. Of these, 408,000 were
successfully 're-settled' in the newly annexed eastern territories during
the war, while another 74,000 were 'settled' in the *Altreich*. The remaining 316,000 were awaiting 'settlement' or had been judged not suitable
'settler material'.[131] For the most part, radical National Socialist fantasies
of 'eastern settlement' remained largely unfulfilled.

Nazi colonization efforts in 'the East' were disrupted by mounting partisan warfare in the new 'living space', including increased
partisan attacks on German settlers. Nazi settlement plans, in fact,
often had to be repeatedly changed or divided into short and long-
term plans.[132] German fortunes of war cut off the GPO's 'settlement'
and 'depopulation' schemes in embryo. After the German defeat at
Stalingrad, Hitler put settlement planning 'on hold', and many of
Himmler's settlement schemes were put 'on ice'. By the end of 1942,
Nazi 're-settlement' schemes in western Poland had come to a halt.
In the Ukraine, ethnic German settlers were driven out by Ukrainian
militias and partisans. By mid-1944, as the Red Army continued its
advances on the Eastern front, German settler colonies were abandoned
from the Baltic to the Crimea. While frustrated in his 'settlement' efforts,
Himmler would achieve much more success as respects 'the Jews', as we
shall see in subsequent chapters. To be sure, 'the Jews' and the 'final

solution of the Jewish question' now became his top priority. Crucially, conquest and colonization in 'the East' (with its spatial logic of 'removal' and deportation) would provide both the opportunity and the context for 'ridding' German 'living space' of the 'Jewish enemy'.[133]

Similarities, differences, and links

In both Early America and Nazi Germany, prior colonization and settlement efforts, both actualized and intended, provided historical legacies that informed and drove the respective national expansionist projects in the 'American West' and the 'Nazi East'. In both cases, dreams of a 'new life' in the 'American West' and the 'Nazi East' were motivated by settler self-interest in striving for prosperity and material security for themselves and their children. Ultimately, plans for the colonization of the 'American West' and the 'Nazi East' were based on the collective aggregate of the individual settler 'manifest destinies'. Top political leaders, in both cases, promoted visions of a 'people's empire' offering 'boundless opportunities' and promised economic benefits to 'ordinary' American and 'ordinary' German settlers. Thus, many 'ordinary' citizens, in both cases, became 'invested' in their respective national projects of territorial expansion and settler colonization – projects which, as we shall see in subsequent chapters, unleashed violent 'eliminatory' campaigns against the 'natives' in the 'American West' and in the 'Nazi East'. Given the potential and actual economic gains, it was easy, therefore, for 'ordinary' citizens of Early America and Nazi Germany to become complicit in government-sponsored projects of conquest, dispossession, and settlement. Indeed, both groups of 'settlers' would profit from their eager participation in the 'elimination' of 'useless inferiors' in the 'American West' and the 'Nazi East', respectively.

While Early American and Nazi-German settlement visions shared very similar goals and objectives, the outcome was quite different. While both Early American and Nazi-German political leaderships crafted visions and plans to guide the colonization of their respective 'western' and 'eastern' empires, situational factors, in both cases, determined the very different outcomes. In the 'American West', these situational factors worked to assure the success of American colonization plans. In the 'Nazi East', on the other hand, the on-the-ground realities worked against Nazi 'settlement' schemes. Efforts at German colonization were hindered by wartime exigencies, resource limitations, few eligible and willing ethnic Germans, and political opposition from within Alfred Rosenberg's Ministry for the Occupied Eastern Territories. As historian

Donald Bloxham rightly notes, however, 'the most important limit put on German colonial plans was that the [Nazi] empire was constructed at war'.[134] Unlike its Early American counterpart, Nazi-German settler colonialism, in the end, would prove 'a goal more anticipated than achieved'.[135] There would be no history of 'The Winning of the East', nor any movie of 'How the East Was Won'.[136]

While the actualities of settlement in the 'Nazi East' fell well short of Nazi fantasies of future settlement, Hitler's and Himmler's partially realized visions for the 'Nazi East', and their future intentions as revealed in SS colonization plans, confirm the fundamentally settler-colonial nature of the Nazi project in their eastern empire – a project modelled firmly on the USA settlement model. Fifty years ago, two early historians of the 'Nazi East' hinted at its essentially colonial nature. While seeing Nazi practice in 'the East' as 'unabashed colonialism', Alexander Dallin, however, believed that Hitler's 'favourite analogy' was the German East and British India, with Russia as 'Germany's India'.[137] The 'Nazi East', according to Robert Koehl, was a 'cross between the American Wild West and British India'.[138] Nonetheless, much recent historiography, in a view which I share, sees the USA settlement model as primary and determinant, in both theory and practice, for Hitler and Himmler and other like-minded Nazis. In private conversations, for instance, Hitler's utterances about America and 'the West' are 'even more common than analogies with British India when [he] talks about eastern Europe'.[139] As the world's leading example of modern colonial settlement, the United States of America clearly provided the settlement model and foremost historical example for Hitler and Himmler in the 'Nazi East'.[140] As understood by the *Führer* and his most devoted follower, successful settler colonization in 'the East' would give Germany a continental land empire 'fit to rival the United States, another hardy frontier state based upon exterminatory colonialism and slave labor'.[141]

Illustration 1 Covered wagons headed 'west'. A 'wagon train' of American 'settlers' heads 'west' across the northern plains to seek their individual 'manifest destinies' in America's 'western empire'.
Source: Nebraska State Historical Society, photograph # RG1764-3.

Illustration 2 Covered wagons headed 'east'. A covered 'waggon convoy' of German 'settlers' stops to rest before resuming their journey to a new life in the Nazi 'eastern empire'.
Source: Ullstein Bild/The Image Works, Inc.

Illustration 3   Pioneers in the 'American West'. A family of 'homesteaders' on the northern plains pose for a photo in front of their new home (called a 'sod house') in Custer County, Nebraska.

Source: Nebraska State Historical Society, photograph # RG2608-1784.

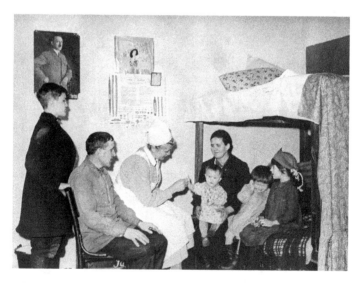

Illustration 4   Pioneers in the 'Nazi East'. In the *Reichsgau Wartheland* (areas of western Poland annexed by Nazi Germany), a 'settler' family is visited by a nurse from the National Socialist Volunteers (NSV).

Source: *Sueddeutsche Zeitung* Photo/The Image Works, Inc.

Illustration 5 Forced 'removal' in the 'American West'. US Army troops oversee a group of Navajo Indians who have been forcibly 'removed' from their homes and 'force-marched' to a military reservation at Fort Sumner, New Mexico.
Source: US National Archives, photograph # 111-SC-87964.

Illustration 6 Forced 'removal' in the 'Nazi East'. German police and SS personnel oversee the forced 'removal' and forced 'resettlement' of Poles from their homes in Sol, Katowice, Poland, to an internment camp.
Source: USHMM, photograph # 81234, courtesy of Instytut Pamięci Narodowej.

Illustration 7 Attrition in the 'American West'. Indians line up to receive their often inadequate food rations on 'ration day' at the Pine Ridge Agency Reservation in South Dakota.
Source: Nebraska State Historical Society, photograph # RG2845-8-12.

Illustration 8 Attrition in the 'Nazi East'. Jews in the Lodz Ghetto (Poland) wait outside Kitchen #452 to receive their meagre food rations.
Source: USHMM, photograph # 24895, courtesy of Jehuda Widawski.

Illustration 9   Mass shooting in the 'American West'. Sioux Indian civilians shot by the US Army Seventh Cavalry during the 1890 Wounded Knee massacre in South Dakota are buried in a mass grave.
Source: Nebraska State Historical Society, photograph # RG2845-13-12.

Illustration 10   Mass shooting in the 'Nazi East'. Men from an unidentified unit of an *Einsatzgruppen* mobile killing squad execute a group of Soviet civilians kneeling by the side of a mass grave.
Source: USHMM, photograph # 89063, courtesy of National Archives and Records Administration, College Park.

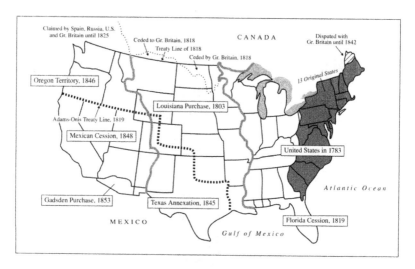

Map 1 Conquest and expansion in the 'American West'. This map shows America's 'successive wests' across the new nation's expanding continental empire.

Source: William Earl Weeks, *Building the Continental Empire: American Expansion from the Revolution to the Civil War* (Chicago, IL: Ivan R. Dee, 1996), p. 51.

Map 2 Conquest and expansion in the 'Nazi East'. This map shows Hitler's *Lebensraum* empire in 'the East' at its zenith (that is, at the end of 1941).

Source: David Blackbourn, *The Conquest of Nature: Water, Landscape, and the Making of Modern Germany* (New York: W. W. Norton, 2006), p. 276.

5
'Out-Group' Policy: 'Eliminating' the 'Natives'

In both the Early American and Nazi-German cases, settler-colonial projects were premised on 'obtaining' needed 'living space' by taking the indigenes' land and on the 'elimination' of the indigenous owners of that territory. In both cases, moreover, continuing wars of racial-imperialist conquest served only to enlarge the size and scale of the 'out-group question', by increasing the number of 'Indians', 'Slavs', and 'Jews' under colonial control. Underpinned by similar ideologies of continental imperialism, the long-term goal that all 'Indians', all 'Slavs', and all 'Jews' would 'disappear' – either immediately or eventually – from the metropole and from the new settler 'living space' was widely accepted by the expansionist political elites; therefore, it remained only for policymakers to decide the timing, policies, and methods for accomplishing their 'disappearance'. While both nation-states sought to 'eliminate' the indigenous populations, 'elimination' was not – in either case – necessarily premised on any particular method or strategy. In both contexts, policymakers and planners always considered a wide range of 'eliminationist' strategies for 'solving' their 'out-group problem'. Both Early American and Nazi-German political elites favoured 'totalizing solutions' for 'solving' the 'Indian question', the 'Slav question', and the 'Jewish question'. In both cases, as we shall see, Early American and Nazi-German policymakers would use strikingly similar policies and practices for dealing with 'alien' peoples in the metropole and with 'unwanted' peoples on the 'frontiers' of empire.

In the Early American case, as the numbers of white settlers – as well as their political power – grew, they continually pressured Congress and the federal government to 'remove' the 'natives' further 'west', freeing more land for white settlement.[1] The fundamental nature of Early American settler colonialism was the 'depopulation' of Indian lands for settlement, which involved 'clearing' the 'former inhabitants' and 'replacing' them with 'white' settler colonists in a continuous process of dispossession. The only questions, as historian Reginald Horsman has suggested, were 'how, when, and under what terms actual Indian dispossession would be arranged'.[2] The US government, as an editor of the *Army and Navy Journal* observed, when facing the Indians has one hand holding 'the rifle' and the other holding the 'peace pipe', and we 'blaze away with both instruments at the same time'. While many in the East favoured the 'peace pipe', settler colonists in 'the West' overwhelmingly preferred 'the rifle'.[3] Thus, while policymakers in Washington developed paternalistic policies that relegated the Indians to the status of colonial subjects, settlers on the 'frontier' treated them as 'enemies' to be 'eliminated'. Often the western states and territories took matters into their own hands, forcing the federal government to react to locally initiated directives.[4]

In the Nazi-German case, Hitler's vision of 'space' and 'race' was a colonial one – imperialistic and exclusionary, with strong genocidal tendencies.[5] In 'the East', Nazi 'out-group' policy called for 'Germanization' of locals found to be 'racially suitable', for colonization by ethnic German settler colonists, and for the 'resettlement' of all 'racially unwanted elements'. In the Nazi view, this was a process that might take decades. Under the cover of war, however, the Nazis would further the long-term colonization goal by killing or deporting the 'natives'. Nazi 'out-group' policy was closely linked to the acquisition of 'living space' and to its colonization. In late December 1941, for instance, the training journal of the Order Police told its readers that the 'gigantic spaces of the east' would not only be the site of German 'colonization' but would also serve to 'facilitate the definitive solution of the Jewish problem in the near future'.[6] At the metropolitan centre, Nazi elites and policy planners formulated ambitious 'resettlement' schemes, which required the 'removal' of 'the East's' indigenous inhabitants from the newly conquered *Lebensraum*, while in the 'Wild East' itself, Nazi administrators were left to deal with the on-the-ground realities as well as the inconsistencies of Nazi racial and settlement policy.[7]

'Pacification'

In both Early America and Nazi Germany, settler-colonial expansionist projects meant that indigenous populations would have to be 'cleared' from the land in advance of, or as part of, the actual 'settlement' process. As a result, wars of 'pacification' against the indigenes were a constant requirement of 'out-group' policy in both the 'American West' and the 'Nazi East'. Armed resistance to the invaders often led to mass shootings of indigenous populations, as well as to the destruction of their villages and crops. Wars of 'pacification' against indigenous peoples typically made no distinctions between armed enemy soldiers and unarmed civilian populations. On the 'frontier', 'pacification' involved physical violence, intimidation, and destruction of indigenes' property and agricultural resources. In both cases, these wars of 'pacification' frequently involved organized killing actions directed at largely unarmed, civilian non-combatant populations. Early American and Nazi-German strategies of 'total war' subjected non-combatants – women, children, infants, and old people – to death or cruel suffering. In both cases, 'pacification' of the indigenes was part of long-term plans for 'resettlement' and the 'shifting' of ethnic populations. In Early America, the 'Indian wars' were a series of more than three dozen wars to 'pacify' the new 'living space' and clear the way for the onslaught of more 'white' settler colonists, while the Nazis used 'pacification' to 'reduce' 'native' numbers and 'cleanse' settlement areas in advance of actual colonization by ethnic German settlers. While occupational terror in the 'American West' and the 'Nazi East' sought to 'discourage' indigenous peoples to take up arms to defend their homelands, it had (unsurprisingly), in both cases, the opposite effect.

Early America

Devastating wars against the North American continent's indigenous populations in America's successive 'wests' – known in the master American historical narrative as the 'Indian wars' – were a constant feature of the first 100 years of the nation's national history. During the 'Indian wars' of the late eighteenth and nineteenth centuries, 'pacifying' the 'frontier' involved 'extirpative war' (the term used at the time) aimed at driving the Indians from their lands. While most American leaders hoped for an 'orderly and peaceful' advance of the 'frontier' boundary, they nonetheless proved willing to use military force (as required) to 'pacify' the 'American West'. As conditions on the frontier 'got out of hand', the US government used both militia and standing army troops as a striking force to 'overawe' (a word also much used at the time) and 'pacify' the Indians.[8] As noted earlier (Chapter 3), the 'first [American] way of war' against Indian non-combatants (that is, destroying 'enemy' villages and fields and killing and terrorizing non-combatant populations) was a defining feature of American conquest and 'pacification' of 'the West' – from the first 'Indian war' in Virginia (1609) to the last military engagement between Indians and whites at Wounded Knee (1890).[9]

A carry-over from the colonial period, extirpative war-making accompanied settler-colonial expansion into 'Indian country' and was characterized by the killing of 'enemy' non-combatants (including women and children) and destruction of Indian villages, homes and agricultural resources (fields, crops, and food supplies). In addition, specialized units for Indian fighting, called 'rangers', were specifically created to 'pacify' the hinterlands of the American 'frontier' and pave the way for further expansion and settlement by settler colonists. As instanced above, extirpative wars against indigenous peoples on the American 'frontier' paralleled – and ran concurrent with – the American War of Independence (1775–83). In the words of one scholar, 'murder gradually became the dominant American Indian policy' in the 'American West', both during and after the American Revolution.[10] During the Federalist era of the 1790s, the US Army fought wars of 'pacification' in the Upper Ohio Valley and on the Tennessee and western Georgia 'frontiers'. When they failed in efforts to 'secure' the 'frontier', backcountry settlers took matters into their own hands, focusing on destroying Indian villages and food supplies. Again, in the 1810s (overlapping the War of 1812), American settler colonists – frustrated by the US Army's inability or unwillingness to 'solve' the 'Indian question' – unleashed a spasm of extreme violence to complete the subjugation of the Indians in the trans-Appalachian West, laying these lands open to further American 'settlement'. During the Second Seminole War (1836–7), an early version of 'search and destroy' missions (similar to the Vietnam War in the 1960s) was carried out by US forces, during which Seminole villages and crops were put to the torch. And during the American Civil War (1861–5), when federal troops were needed to fight Southern rebels, state and territorial militias continued the 'pacification' campaigns against Indians in 'the West'.[11]

American–Indian conflict in the years 1783–1890 contains many examples of 'total war' – that is, waging war on entire 'enemy' populations, including unarmed civilians (regardless of sex or age). It was US Army Generals William Tecumseh Sherman and Phil Sheridan, however, who ultimately sanctified it as deliberate policy in the decades following the American Civil War. Both generals believed in waging 'total war' against the entire Indian population, in a strategy reminiscent of a similar one that they had used against the South in the last years of the American Civil War (1864–5). The Sherman–Sheridan concept of 'total war' was based on the strategy of severely undermining the Indians' collective will to resist, by killing the 'enemy' and by destroying their food, clothing, shelter, and horses. The centrepiece of the strategy was surprise attacks on Indian villages, which meant, in most cases, the killing of unarmed women and children in addition to armed warriors. The aim of these attacks was to force the survivors to surrender, scatter, or retreat to a reservation, under the impact of military attack, climatic extremes, and/or psychological stress.[12]

Following the close of the Mexican War (1848), 'Indian wars' were fought to support the official Indian policy of 'concentration', a policy that sought to 'clear' Indians from their 'unceded' lands and concentrate them on 'reservations'. Virtually every major 'Indian war' in the post-Civil War era was fought to force Indian communities on to the newly created reservations or to make them return to reservations from which they had recently fled.[13] During these years, the main role of the regular army was enforcing the reservation system by forcing the West's entire indigenous population on to the reservations and keeping them there. Nonetheless, Indian resistance to the reservation policy led to all-out war in many regions of 'the West'. From the Indian perspective, the 'Indian wars' of 1846–90 were a conscious rejection of the reservation system and a desperate, last attempt to maintain their traditional ways of life on small parcels of often barren land, which were unwanted – for the moment – by the 'white' settler colonists.

Nazi Germany

For Hitler and other Nazi expansionists, Poland (a 'bastard child' of the post-First World War peace settlement) and the Soviet Union (the cradle of Germany's Slavic and 'Judeo-Bolshevik' 'enemies') were to become the key sources of additional 'living space' for 'Aryan' Germans. Although there were obvious differences in scale and targeting, the SS policy of using mass murder to 'pacify' conquered territory was applied in a relatively similar fashion in both Poland and the Soviet Union, leading to the selective murder of indigenous Poles, Russians, and Jews.[14] In this context, so-called SS mobile killing squads (the *Einsatzgruppen*) were focused on behind-the-lines 'pacification' and on other so-called 'special tasks' (which often involved mass killings); supplementing these SS mobile killing squads, German police battalions and auxiliary police units from the local populations would form the core killing squads on the Eastern front. In the 'Nazi East', the 'pacification' of the indigenes served as a legitimization for mass murder, characterized by a massive push for physical 'elimination'. In particular, anti-Jewish measures were presented as 'cleansing actions', part of a wider Nazi policy of 'pacifying' German-occupied territory in the 'Wild East'.[15] To Heinrich Himmler, the chief executor of Hitler's spatial and racial policies in the eastern *Lebensraum*, the 'pacification' of 'the natives' and the 'elimination' of 'the Jews' were merely preconditions to the principal task of settling and Germanizing the 'Nazi East'.[16]

On 16 July 1941, in a meeting with *Reichsleiter* (National Leader) Alfred Rosenberg, Reich Minister Hans Lammers, Field Marshal Wilhelm Keitel, and Reich Marshal Hermann Göring, Hitler outlined his plans for 'the East'. At this meeting, the *Führer* declared his intention to occupy, dominate, and exploit conquered Russian lands but cautioned that this intention must be concealed from the world. In 'pacifying' the new *Lebensraum*, he ordered, Nazi occupation forces were to 'take all necessary measures – shooting, resettling, etc.'; the Nazis would use the Russian order for partisan warfare, moreover, as a justification to 'eradicate anyone who opposes us'. 'The East' would have to be 'pacified as quickly as possible', Hitler asserted, and 'the best solution was to shoot anybody who looked sideways'. Portions of the Crimea, Galicia, the Volga colony, and the Baltic territories, he further declared, would be 'Germanized' and annexed to the Greater German Reich, a process that would require 'extermination measures' (such as mass shootings and executions), as well as 'resettlement' of the indigenes. The ultimate Nazi goal, Hitler announced, was to 'create a Garden of Eden in the newly-occupied eastern territories' for the benefit of ethnic German settler colonists.[17]

The Nazis were careful to hide their true intentions in the 'Wild East' from the German public and the world. In a directive issued by Josef Goebbels, the propaganda minister, he specifically instructed *Reichsleiters*, *Gauleiters*, and *Gau* propaganda leaders to 'hide' Nazi plans for 'the East' from the German people and other European nations, calling observations 'to the effect that Germany will establish colonies in the East and follow a colonial policy in which the land and its inhabitants will be regarded as an object of exploitation' 'completely inappropriate'. Fearful that it might 'strengthen the will to resist of the eastern peoples and the Soviet troops and aid Soviet propaganda', there was, 'above all' to 'be no discussion about the deportation of the long-established inhabitants'. Nothing was to be said or written, he warned, which might support Soviet claims that 'Germany was placing the nations of the East on the same level as Negroes'.[18]

The earliest victim of Nazi-German military attack, Poland, suffered the longest period of German occupation. It was the site of most of the Holocaust, and it was the country that suffered the highest percentage of human loss during the Second World War. During the brutal five-year occupation, Nazi 'pacification' and 'resettlement' policies in Poland led to the murder of millions of Polish Christians and the near-total extermination of Polish Jewry, as part of the Nazi intention to 'erase' the Polish state, nation, and culture from the face of the earth. In Poland, the Nazis looked to use terror, mass killings, and confiscation of Jewish property to force Jews out of German-occupied territory, as part of its broader effort to 'cleanse' the new 'Nazi East' of indigenous peoples deemed racially, ethnically, and culturally 'inferior'. They adopted a policy of terror (*Schrecklichkeit*) against civilians at all levels of Polish society, unleashing a murderous wave of violence against Poland's population (both Jewish and non-Jewish). As part of this 'pacification', Polish elites and those segments of Polish society deemed capable of challenging German rule (political leaders, educators, nobility, priests, and intellectuals) were to be immediately exterminated. In many ways, Poland served as a kind of dress rehearsal for Operation Barbarossa (the attack on Russia of 22 June 1941). Seen in this light, the Polish 'pacification' campaign was a significant first step in the ongoing escalation of Nazi 'out-group' policies, which ultimately resulted in mass genocide and the *Vernichtungskrieg* (or War of Annihilation) against 'Jewish Bolshevists' in the Soviet Union.[19]

Following the attack on the Soviet Union, 'pacification' through terror became part of wider Nazi occupation policy in the 'Wild East'. The self-declared Nazi War of Annihilation was a war with no distinction between combatants and non-combatants – truly a 'total war'.[20] On 2 July 1941, Himmler told his SS and police officers that their immediate goal was the political pacification of the newly conquered *Lebensraum*, using terror as their principal weapon to 'crush every will to resist among the [native] population'. According to Himmler, 'All persons suspected of supporting partisans are to be shot; women and children are to be deported; livestock and food are to be confiscated and secured. The villages are to be burned to the ground', he said, casually adding that 'the eastern territories are to be freed of Jews'.[21] At any sign of even the slightest resistance from the occupied population, *Wehrmacht* and SS troops would carry out collective reprisals against civilian populations. A ruthless 'pacification' policy of terror, subjugation, and exploitation led to mass requisitioning of livestock, the razing of villages, and mass killing in large-scale mobile operations. At first, the Nazis faced no outright resistance or partisan threat to speak of in the 'Wild East'. Over time, however, Nazi 'pacification' and occupation policies engendered bitter popular resistance, and anti-partisan warfare in the German-occupied Soviet Union became part of the 'pacification' of Nazi *Lebensraum*.[22]

Following a more radicalized version of the earlier Polish model, 'pacification' campaigns in the Soviet Union remained the primary focus of Nazi 'out-group' policy. Under this policy, the 'Jewish-Bolshevik' elites were to be 'liquidated' immediately, Soviet Jews (at first only men) were to be 'liquidated' by police and security units, and the Soviet masses were to be enslaved or slaughtered. Nazi conquest would lead to 'obtaining' *Lebensraum* and to the establishment of settlement colonies, and the occupied areas would serve as a springboard for further eastward expansion. Importantly, in order to ensure army co-operation, Jewish actions were always made to appear part of the 'pacification' and anti-partisan campaign. In 'the East', Nazi policies of 'pacification' would lead to the deaths of millions of civilians (Jewish and non-Jewish), partisan fighters, and Red Army prisoners of war (POWs) due to outright murder, starvation, disease, or exposure to the elements.

Separation and segregation

In both Early America and Nazi Germany, selected 'out-groups' were purposely separated from the dominant society by deliberate national policies formulated and carried out by the government. For those 'out-groups' residing in the metropole (that is, acculturated so-called 'civilized' Indians such as the Cherokees living in Georgia and assimilated Jews living in the Greater German Reich) 'out-group' policy was centred on 'de-assimilation', a process that denied them, or stripped them of, citizenship rights and ultimately mandated their 'removal' outside the 'white'/'Aryan' 'living space'. Throughout the first century of the American nation's existence, the 'Indian question' was, in simplest terms, what to do with the Indians who stood in the way of westward settler expansion.[23] While advocates for both 'assimilation' and 'separation' of Indians were present within the political leadership, those favouring 'separation' became dominant in the early years of the American Republic. In Nazi Germany, anti-Jewish segregation policies began to be implemented upon the National Socialist assumption of power in 1933. Until the war, the Nazi frame of reference in respect to the 'Jewish question' was the Greater German Reich (which included Jews in Germany, Austria, the Sudetenland, and the Protectorate of

Bohemia and Moravia), as the Nazis sought a 'solution' that would ensure the Reich was 'free of Jews' (*judenfrei*). In both societies, the 'out-groups' became socially and legally separated from the dominant society. While Early American separation was always linked with western expansion, Nazi racial 'cleansing' would begin in the Reich itself prior to the campaign for 'living space' in 'the East'.

Early America

Under the new constitution, American Indian policy in 'the West' – described as 'foreign' relations with Native American tribes – became the domain of the federal government, under the authority of the executive branch (specifically, the president and his secretary of war). President George Washington and Secretary of War Henry Knox advocated the Federalist Party policy of 'civilizing' the Indians and of 'orderly' white settlement of Indian lands in 'the West' – a policy that Thomas Jefferson (a member of the Democrat Republican Party) observed when he became president. Sharing the Enlightenment beliefs of Washington and Knox, Jefferson believed that Indians could be 'civilized' and, as individuals, might enter 'white' society, and he supported the 'civilization' policy – encouraging Indians to become peaceful farmers, to abandon their cultures and adopt American ways of thinking, and to 'willingly' sell their lands to white settlers.[24]

But Jefferson's policy of 'civilization' and 'assimilation' applied only to so-called 'friendly' tribes willing to 'cede' their lands to the white settler colonists. Indian refusal to 'cede' lands to the settler colonists drove Jefferson to contemplate harsher measures; recalcitrant Indians would, in his words, 'be exterminated, or driven beyond the Mississippi'. 'They will kill some of us', Jefferson noted in a letter to a friend, but 'we shall destroy all of them'.[25] In reality, Jefferson's Indian policy was a plan for 'obtaining' Indian lands for continuous westward expansion and white settlement. For his part, Jefferson strongly favoured the 'separation or elimination, of disparate ethnic groups – Indians and blacks – who refused to disappear through civilization and assimilation, or were, in his view, incapable of participating as citizens of the republic'.[26] In effect, Early American Indian policymakers gave Indian peoples two choices: resist American expansion and risk extermination, or assimilate into the white culture. Either way, the Indians would 'vanish' from the 'American West', and their traditional ways of life would 'disappear'. Furthermore, regardless of their final 'choice', ethnically distinct Native American communities would eventually be 'cleansed' and 'erased' from the North American continent. In the end, the supposed 'choice' offered Native Americans was really no choice at all.

The new US government was totally committed to allowing (as well as encouraging and promoting) settler-colonial expansion 'west' from the Atlantic coast. Short of both money and military force and plagued by moments of conscience, the new nation's leaders – men like Washington, Jefferson, and Knox – were sensitive to moral considerations and to possible internal and external criticism; the outright extermination of the Indians, they feared, would tarnish the 'honour' of the new nation. As a result, they sought to cloak conquest and expansion in a fog of Enlightenment assimilationist rhetoric about bringing 'civilization' to the 'savages'. The Indians, they concluded, would be encouraged to give up not only their lands but also their ways of life – ways of life that 'white' Americans viewed as both 'different' and 'wrong', or as 'wrong' because they were 'different'.

These early policymakers, in many ways, practised a form of 'conquest by kindness'. In the shaping of government Indian policy, they eagerly embraced what one scholar has called 'expansion with a good conscience'.[27] The white settler colonists in 'the West' and their representatives in Washington, however, did not share these 'good intentions' and were not the least bit concerned about acting with a 'good conscience'. While policymakers looked to formulate an Indian policy that would allow for 'orderly and peaceful' western expansion and that would also reflect favourably on the proclaimed egalitarian ideals of the new American Republic, white settler colonists openly advocated the 'extermination' or 'removal' of the indigenous peoples. Early American Indian policy foundered thanks to the compulsive land hunger of the white settler colonists, as well as Indian unwillingness to give up their lands and their ways of life (coupled with their willingness to take up arms to defend their homelands). Given these obstacles, the Early American policy of peaceful westward expansion and Indian assimilation failed, as did the federal government's attempt to control expansion and make it an orderly process.

The inherent contradiction of US Indian policy was most clearly exposed in the case of the Cherokee Indians living in the state of Georgia. Widely understood to be the most acculturated and 'civilized' Indians, the Cherokees built farms, homes, churches, and schools, and their large landowners (who had adopted white farming methods) used white indentured labour or black African slaves on their plantations. Despite their adoption of the 'civilization' policy, the Cherokees were seen by Georgians and their political allies in Washington as 'savages' and as 'enemies' of American 'progress' and white expansion. A special police force, the Georgia Guard, soon became a central element in a state-sponsored programme of harassment and intimidation of Cherokees living within Georgia's borders, as the state's 'white' citizens resorted to outright theft of Cherokee property and land.[28] When the Cherokees refused to 'cede' more lands to the whites, the federal government acted to force their 'removal'. The 'removal' of the Cherokees from their lands was a breach of faith, as well as a breach of Jefferson's promises to the 'friendly' Indians, a betrayal of proven friends, and a violation of stated federal policy (that is, Jefferson's 'civilization' policy), and federal officials knew it at the time.[29] For the Cherokees and other so-called 'civilized' tribes, acculturation was no barrier to dispossession and displacement.

Ultimately, the central contradiction in US Indian policy (between 'freeing' land for 'white' settlement and preparing Indians for eventual assimilation) was never resolved. When forced to choose between these contradictory goals, the federal government always sided with its 'white' settler colonists (*without exception*), opting for forced Indian land 'cessions' and Indian 'removal'.[30] At the end of the day, policymakers conveniently decided that it was not possible (or desirable) for white settler colonists and Indians to coexist on the vast lands east of the Mississippi. In their search for a 'solution' to the 'Indian question', they looked to a new policy of Indian 'removal' – a programme of voluntary and forced emigration of Indian tribes from the territory of the United States (whose western boundary was then the Mississippi River). 'Removal' was a policy with a new goal: the permanent separation of Indians and white settler colonists by drawing a definite boundary line between them and offering to 'protect' Indians against white settler encroachment – a promise that proved impossible to fulfil due to the white settler colonists' insatiable appetite for more land. On a more practical level, 'removal' allowed policymakers to avoid the rhetoric of assimilation as well as avoid officially endorsing a declared policy of extermination.[31] In the final analysis, it was, and always would be, a policy of permanent separation (true to its original intention).

Nazi Germany

Upon assuming power in 1933, the Nazi regime began the implementation of a systematic policy of segregation and persecution against its Jewish citizens. Anti-Jewish decrees and legislation issued between

1933 and 1935 aimed at excluding 'the Jews' from the 'Aryan' 'national community' and at putting an end to allegedly 'inordinate' Jewish influence in German life. In these years, the Nazis aimed at the growing persecution of German Jews, at a permanent framework of discrimination, at the segregation of 'Jews' and 'Aryans' within German society, and at making Jewish life in Germany painful and, ultimately, both untenable and unsustainable.[32] Discriminatory measures against the Jews were enacted in many areas of social and professional life – measures that sought to deprive them of their civil rights and to bring about their 'social death' within German society. For the Nazis, these measures were seen as mere first steps in what would be a growing radicalization of anti-Jewish policy, as well as a programme of ever-escalating Jewish persecution.

The Nuremberg Laws (15 September 1935) segregated 'the Jews' according to 'racial' criteria and placed the German Jewish community under 'alien status' within the borders of the Greater German Reich. Representing a major step in the separation policy, these laws aimed at the legal enshrinement of political and social inequality between 'Jews' and 'Aryans' and looked to reverse Jewish achievements in the post-Emancipation era. Crucially, the Nuremberg Laws introduced an official distinction of status between 'Germans' and 'Jews', similar to the colonial distinction between 'citizens' of the metropole and 'subjects' of the colonized lands and space.[33] In Hitler's words, the Nuremberg Laws were a 'legislative solution' to the 'Jewish question', aimed at a further segregation of 'the Jews' and at a formal annulment of their citizenship rights. On a broader basis, the Nuremberg Laws codified the racial 'otherness' of the Jews, Sinti, Romas, and other mixed-raced Germans, denying full citizenship rights to Nazi-designated 'persons of alien blood'.[34]

In the wake of the Nuremberg Laws, Hitler still saw the limitation of 'Jewish influence', the separation of 'the Jews' from the 'Aryan' 'national community', and 'more vigorous emigration' as the goals of Nazi anti-Jewish policy. In 1936, Nazi anti-Jewish policy entered a new phase, focused on three major initiatives: accelerated 'Aryanization' (that is, expropriation of Jewish property and businesses), increased efforts to compel Jewish emigration, and a propaganda campaign aimed at winning popular recognition of the imminent 'Jewish threat'. The *Reichskristallnacht* pogrom (9–10 November 1938) was a massive, Nazi-coordinated physical assault on Germany's Jews: a terrifying, nationwide outburst of violence and destruction aimed at 'encouraging' Jews to leave Germany and providing justification for their

final, total expropriation and complete segregation. In the wake of
Reichskristallnacht, the National Socialist regime introduced further anti-
Jewish measures to promote the total expropriation and plundering of
Jewish property and to deny 'the Jews' even the most basic forms of
subsistence. Making Jewish life in the Reich untenable was part of a
wider strategy to advance and accelerate voluntary Jewish emigration.
Privately, however, some Nazi leaders began to talk of forced emigration, using more violent official pressure and, in Himmler's words,
'unparalleled ruthlessness'.[35] In a 6 December 1938 speech to party leaders, Deputy Führer Hermann Göring – citing Hitler's expressed orders –
declared that we must 'rid ourselves of the Jews as quickly and effectively
as possible, to force emigration with the utmost vigour and to remove
all possible obstacles to emigration'.[36]

In the 1930s, Nazi 'out-group' policy used two different but complementary methods to achieve the complete exclusion of racially
dangerous groups from the Volksgemeinschaft (the 'Aryan' 'national community'): segregation and expulsion on the one hand, sterilization on
the other. In this context, segregation and expulsion were used primarily against Jews, Gypsies, and homosexuals, while sterilization was used
against the physically and mentally handicapped and against those who
were considered to be 'racially contaminated' individuals. In the years
1933–9, then, Nazi anti-Jewish policy was a chronology of persecution,
segregation, emigration, and expulsion: a combination of humiliation
and violence (both actual and threatened).[37] On the eve of the first war
for Lebensraum in 'the East' (September 1939), the overall declared goal
of Nazi anti-Jewish policy was to hasten the Jews' departure from the
Reich through voluntary or (if necessary) forced emigration. 'Solving the
Jewish question' in the German Reich (at this time) meant their forced
emigration from Reich 'living space'. During these years, then, Nazi
Jewish policy (Judenpolitik) was, for the most part, conducted according
to the 'spatial' logic of 'removal'.[38]

At first glance, Nazi persecution of Reich Jews seems to have little
connection with the plans or practices of settler colonialism in the 'Nazi
East'. Subject to local variations, nonetheless, the same Nazi measures
of segregation, expropriation, and exclusion that applied to targeted
'out-groups' in the German Reich were extended into the territories
in 'the East' occupied by Nazi Germany, its allies, and satellites – policies that would eventually impact the Jews more than any other ethnic,
racial, or social 'out-group'. At home, in the Reich metropole itself, the
domestic component of the Nazi imperial project focused on the 'elimination', marginalization, or destruction of targeted political and racial

'enemies' (the foremost 'enemy' being 'the Jews'). The 'cleansing' of the Reich metropole of these 'aliens' and 'undesirables', moreover, was intrinsically linked to the wars for *Lebensraum* as necessary measures and preconditions, to unify and purify the German *Volk* in advance of the war for empire in 'the East'.[39]

In Nazi parlance, 'after the war' and 'the East' operated as complimentary notions of time and place for the realization of Nazi racial and settlement fantasies,[40] fantasies that conjoined the 'solution' of the 'Jewish' and 'Slav' 'questions' in the context of ethnic German settler colonies and 'Germanization' in 'the East'. Recognizing this intimate connection, on 3 September 1941, Rolf-Heinz Höppner, head of the Central Resettlement Office in Posen, wrote a memo to Adolf Eichmann, an SS expert on Jewish emigration, in which he announced that the '[post-war] large-scale deportation of populations groups' would include 'undesirable' groups from the Greater German Reich and 'the final solution of the Jewish question', as well as 'racially non-Germanizable members' of the indigenous peoples 'within the German settlement sphere'.[41] Seen in this light, the 'Jewish' and 'Slav' questions were both subsets of a broader and more general Nazi population policy (or *Volkstumspolitik*).

In the former Polish areas incorporated into the Reich, there was to be a ruthless segregation of 'German' from 'alien' blood, the settlement of ethnic Germans, and the 'removal' of Jews and Slavs to a 'dumping ground' in the Polish territories not annexed to Germany (the so-called Government General) – a reservation where they would be allowed to exist only as long as the Reich needed their labour. In the Russian territories conquered by Germany, non-Germans were to be segregated from the Germanic population in order to prevent the 'Aryan' Germans from being 'contaminated' by 'alien' and 'inferior' blood. While Jews and Gypsies were to be 'removed' completely, those Slavs not deemed suitable for 'Germanization' were to be 'retained' temporarily as slave labour and, when no longer needed, were to be subject to 'removal' and 'elimination' – eventually meeting the same fate as Jews and Gypsies.

The premeditated goal of radical Nazis – the radical 'removal' of the Jews from the Greater German Reich and their physical annihilation – could not have been carried out on German soil or during peacetime, given Hitler's real concern about not alienating German public opinion. Ultimately, the 'Nazi East' would provide the opportunity, location, and 'methods' for radically 'solving' the Reich's 'Jewish question', out of sight of the German public in the Reich metropole.

'Territorial solutions'

Both Early American and Nazi-German national policymakers attempted 'territorial solutions' to their 'out-group problem', based on remarkably similar notions of 'removal' and 'concentration'. Characterized as an alternative to 'disappearance', Indian 'removal' made it clear that there was no longer room for a common world that included independent Indians living with whites – any common world of Indians and whites could not and would not be allowed to continue. The later reservation system of 'concentration' was an improvisation and evolved on an ad hoc basis as a way to halt conflicts between Indians and whites, to enforce continued separation of the races, and to open up Indian lands for further settlement.[42] In Early America, forced 'removal' of Indians from white lands and their 'concentration' on 'reservations' sparked renewed indigene resistance and triggered continuous 'Indian wars' in 'the West'. In the Nazi-German case, the so-called 'territorial solution to the Jewish question' focused on various deportation schemes: to a 'Jewish reservation' in Lublin (Poland), to the French island of Madagascar (off the east coast of Africa), or to inhospitable regions of the conquered Soviet Union. In 'selling' these schemes to 'the Jews', Adolf Eichmann, Heydrich's deputy, purposefully and skilfully traded on Zionist rhetoric of 'territorial solutions', the idea of 'returning to the land', and the formation of self-governing 'colonies'.[43] The later policy of 'concentrating' Jews in ghettos was always viewed by policymakers – at both the centre and the periphery – as a holding action, pending a more definitive and lasting 'solution' to the 'Jewish question'. In the settler-colonial context, policies of 'removal' and 'concentration' of indigenous populations operated, to borrow a phrase, as 'spatial stop-gaps'.[44] In both Early America and Nazi Germany, then, policies of 'removal' and 'concentration' were mainly viewed as 'temporary solutions' or 'holding actions' on the road to some (as yet undetermined) 'final solution' to the 'out-group problem'.

Early America

In their search for a 'territorial solution' to the 'Indian question', American policymakers looked to 'remove' indigenous peoples from white areas of settlement to lands further 'west' of the settlement zones. In the words of the leading scholar of American Indian policy, 'removal was the policy adopted to solve the problem of *alien groups*'.[45] As a practical matter, 'removal' involved inducing the Native Americans to 'exchange' their lands for territory in 'the West', leaving the vacated areas 'clear' for immediate white settlement.[46] In the first phase of settlement, white settlers in the trans-Appalachian territories and states wanted Indians 'removed' west of the Mississippi River, while, in the second phase, white settlers in the trans-Mississippi states and territories wanted Indians 'removed' beyond their borders. Federal officials acquiesced to their requests *every time*.[47] Indeed, at the end of the nineteenth century, *The New York Times* would rightly conclude that 'the history of the Indians in this country is a wearisome repetition of removals of tribes from point to point, each remove taking them further toward the [western] sunset'.[48]

In 1787, Secretary of War Henry Knox reported to Congress that 'the deep rooted prejudices, and malignity of heart and conduct, reciprocally entertained and practised on all occasions by the Whites and Savages will ever prevent their being good neighbours'. As a result, he noted, 'either one or the other party must *remove* to a greater distance, or Government must keep them both in awe by a strong hand, and compel them to be moderate and just'.[49] After completion of the Louisiana Purchase (1803), President Jefferson began to contemplate the 'removal' of the Indians, expelling them from the trans-Appalachian West, as an alternative to 'civilizing' them. In his view, 'removal' was the 'solution' of choice for, and fate of, Indian tribes who refused to participate in the 'civilization' programme or who chose to wage war against the United States; he also considered 'removal' as an answer to recurring bloodshed and violence on the 'frontier'. As articulated in 1803, Jefferson proposed to 'remove' the Indians from the eastern to the western side of the Mississippi River to lands not (yet) inhabited by whites. Under his proposal, this territory would be designated 'Indian country' and would be separated from white America by a 'Permanent Indian Frontier'. Jefferson, however, did not act upon his ideas.

As a formal policy, Indian 'removal' would only be implemented during the administrations of Presidents Andrew Jackson and Martin Van Buren. While not a new idea, Andrew Jackson's aggressive removal policy of the 1830s was, in fact, the culmination of an idea that had been steadily gaining popularity among policymakers for more than three decades. 'By persuasion and force', Jackson pointed out, the Indians in the East had become extinct or reduced to remnants; for their own survival and preservation, he proposed, surviving Indians east of the Mississippi should be made to 'retire' (voluntarily) west of the river, beyond the reach of the whites.[50] In the past, some Native American communities voluntarily chose to emigrate west of the Mississippi, independent of any official removal policy. While Jackson himself hoped that emigration would be 'voluntary', realists understood that force would be inevitable. Disappointed with the pace of 'voluntary' removal, the first priority of newly elected President Andrew Jackson was crafting a comprehensive removal plan. As finally implemented, forced 'removal' was carried out against the southern Indian nations and Indians north of the Ohio River, all of whom were 'removed' to the 'Indian country' west of the Mississippi River. For those Indians who had embraced white notions of 'civilization', the reality of 'removal' was an especially bitter pill to swallow. As Secretary of War James Barbour forthrightly wrote in 1826, '[The Indians] see our professions are insincere...that our promises have been broken; that the happiness of the Indian is a cheap sacrifice to the acquisition of new lands.'[51] Like a giant bulldozer, the process of Indian 'removal' pushed eastern native peoples west of the Mississippi.

As an official policy, Indian 'removal' was cut short by new forces of expansionism in the 1840s and 1850s and, ultimately, by the American Civil War. Despite enormous efforts, it had not proved possible to 'solve' the 'Indian question' by the convenient, time-honoured scheme of repeated Indian 'removal'. At the time, some correctly saw its future outcome. As *North American Review* editor Jared Sparks realized, the '[removal] project only defers the fate of the Indians. In half a century their condition beyond the Mississippi will be just what it now is on this side. Their extinction', Sparks concluded, 'is inevitable.'[52] In a broader context, as historian James H. Merrell provocatively argues, the early national period (the first half of the nineteenth century) can be read as 'the Age of Removal', as the poor were placed in workhouses, the mentally ill in 'insane asylums', and the criminals in penitentiaries. Among the governing elite, Jefferson and others contemplated 'Negro removal' to Africa, the West Indies, or across the Mississippi River. In this context, as Merrell suggests, 'Indian removal' – rather than an aberrant episode – was part of a 'larger culture of removal in American life', with Native Americans 'removed' to an 'Indian asylum' in 'the West'.[53]

When continued westward expansion made Indian 'removal' unfeasible, policymakers looked to other 'territorial solutions'. Initially, the idea of a permanent 'Indian country' focused on lands west of the Missouri River, where each Indian nation would have its own clearly bounded territory. It envisaged the creation of a permanent and specific boundary line (like the British Proclamation Line of 1763) separating the white and Indian worlds – a barrier that Indians at the time referred to as the 'strong fence'. The idea of a permanent 'Indian country' was short-lived, falling victim to further American expansionism and to the white settler colonists' unappeasable appetite for Indian ancestral lands. In the wake of constant white encroachment on Indian lands, another 'territorial solution' introduced the idea of northern and southern 'Indian colonies' in the West, divided from each other by an American corridor, which would allow settler colonists passage on their way to Oregon and California. Indeed, some officials and humanitarian reformers went so far as to propose an 'Indian state' in 'the West' that might eventually become part of the United States. But, as in the past, all such suggestions and recommendations eventually came to nothing. In reality, rather than an act of benevolence, the attempt to create a congressionally designated refuge for 'displaced' Indians was, instead, little more than an illusory stop-gap that only lasted until the needs of Early American western expansion outweighed the need to 'solve' the 'Indian problem'.[54]

By the end of the 1840s, it was clear to many policymakers that neither the systematic removals of the 1830s nor the 'barrier philosophy' of an 'Indian country' would, in the end, provide a workable, 'permanent solution' to the 'Indian question'. As in previous expansionist phases, the final expansionist push of the 1840s brought the US government face to face with more and more Indians, leading to the end of the 'removal' policy and the beginning of the 'reservation system'. In 1848, Polk's Indian commissioner, William Medill, offered a scheme for 'Indian colonies' in which to 'concentrate' the Indians; an idea that evolved into the 'reservation' policy – the foundation stone of later federal Indian policy. In his Annual Report (1850), the Indian commissioner advised Congress that, with respect to the 'wilder tribes', it is 'indispensably necessary that they be placed in positions where they can be *controlled*, and finally *compelled* by stern necessity to resort to agricultural labor *or starve*'.[55] Finally, in 1851, Secretary of the Interior Alexander Stuart declared that 'the policy of removal, except under peculiar circumstances, must necessarily be abandoned. The only alternatives left', he concluded, 'are to civilize or exterminate them. We must adopt one or the other.'[56] Rather than a large, separate 'Indian country', there would be a series of small 'Indian countries' (called 'reservations') scattered across 'the West', continuing – albeit in a modified form – the old policy of Indian segregation.

The new approach of 'concentration' and 'segregation' on 'reservations' called for the 'reserving' of small parcels of land for Indian habitation. The reservation policy was viewed as a means to further 'segregate' and 'concentrate' Indians on federal reservations, freeing the 'ceded' lands for white settlement and exploitation. In the words of the commissioner of Indian affairs (1856), it provided the means by which to 'colonize' the Indians.[57] Hoping to avoid the expense of 'Indian wars', the reservation policy mandated compulsory 'relocation' of western tribes to federal land reserves, where permanent residency under strict government control would be obligatory. As a practical matter, it would further reduce Indian lands as well as facilitate white expansion and settlement. Moreover, if any Indians resisted this policy, the US government was fully prepared to use the army to enforce the 'concentration' policy. Arguing that it was cheaper to feed the Indians than to fight them, the federal government was willing to provide rations to 'reservation Indians', but the rations provided were often insufficient and/or poor in quality. In the quarter century after the Civil War, starvation and near-starvation conditions were present on most of the 60-odd Indian reservations.[58] Rather than nurseries for 'civilization', government-managed reservations effectively became poverty-stricken 'concentration' sites for dispossessed and displaced Native Americans. In the end, the US governing elites were content to 'relocate' the Indians to the most undesirable lands and leave them there to rot and slowly die out. As early as 1853, one Indian agent, Thomas Fitzpatrick, had branded the federal reservation system as 'the legalized murder of a whole nation...expensive, vicious, inhumane'.[59] That same year Fitzpatrick accurately predicted that the Indian reservations would become 'hospital wards' of cholera, smallpox, and other diseases.[60]

Intended as 'factories of cultural transformation',[61] the reservations, instead, became sites of abject hunger, rampant disease, and humiliating subjugation. Packaged by the political leadership as an 'alternative to extinction', the federal reservation policy in the case of the majority of Indian tribes came too late, since the destruction of many Native American communities was already far advanced and many resisting Indians had already been overwhelmed or crushed by military force. The results of the reservation policy were mixed. As a 'civilization' programme for surviving Indians, it was consistently 'too little and too late' and usually failed to provide the rations, farm equipment, and education promised in the treaties.[62] It was extremely successful, however, in further reducing the Indian's land base, allowing (in the words of one Indian commissioner) 'superior' whites to 'obtain' 'so large [a] proportion of our territory' from its 'savage' and 'barbaric' 'aboriginal inhabitants and made the happy abode of an enlightened and Christian people'.[63]

Nazi Germany

While the Nazis' successful military campaign against Poland freed-up more 'living space' for German settlement, it created complications for Nazi anti-Jewish policy. In a memo sent to the German Foreign Office on 15 August 1940, the Reich Security Main Office (RSHA) concluded: 'Now that the masses in the East have to be included in the total, any prospect of settling the Jewish problem by emigration has become impossible.'[64] If the 'Jewish problem' could no longer be solved by emigration, then 'a territorial final solution' (*'eine territoriale Endlösung'*), in SS leader Reinhard Heydrich's words, had now become advisable.[65] According to Heydrich's boss, *Reichsführer-SS* Heinrich Himmler, moreover, outright extermination was not a realistic policy option, since physical extermination was, in his view, a 'Bolshevik method' and would, therefore, be 'un-German'.[66]

In the wake of the Nazi military victory on 21 September 1939, Hitler approved the 'expulsion' of all Poles, Jews, and Gypsies from the Polish *Lebensraum* and the 'settlement' of these areas with ethnic German settler colonists. Most Poles were to be 'removed' eastward and their leadership elites were to be executed, with only 'racially suitable' Poles eligible for 're-Germanization'. As part of this plan, 'the Jew' was to be 'removed' to the Lublin region (between the Bug and Vistula rivers and close to the German–Soviet border agreed by Hitler and Stalin in the Molotov–Ribbentrop Pact of August 1939), to what the Nazis called a *Judenreservat* (Jewish reservation). In a speech on 15 January 1939, Nazi Party ideologue Alfred Rosenberg called on 'friends of the Jews' (most notably in the Western democracies) to support the idea of a 'Jewish reservation' as a 'territorial solution' to the 'Jewish question'.[67] In this fluid environment, Heydrich himself floated the idea of establishing a 'Jewish reservation' in the area around Lublin, as a site for the 'relocation' of some 300,000 Jews from Germany and Austria. As envisaged by Heydrich, it was not to be a Jewish state or even an autonomous region but rather a 'concentration' of 'unwanted' Jewish populations under SS supervision. Despite the initial enthusiasm, Nazi schemes for a 'Jewish reservation' in eastern Poland ultimately collapsed, due to organizational difficulties, as well as opposition from local Nazi occupation authorities in Cracow. (In the annexed Polish territories, it should be noted, officials also briefly experimented with Polish 'reservations' but soon gave up on the idea when many Poles fled the 'reservations' due to poor living conditions.[68])

On the 'periphery', local occupation authorities in Poland had, from the outset, viewed the 'concentration' and ghettoization of Eastern

European Jews as a 'transitional measure' and instead favoured a pro-gramme of mass resettlement as the ultimate 'solution' to the 'Jewish problem'. At the 'centre', policymakers in Berlin looked for another 'ter-ritorial solution' and quickly devised the so-called Madagascar project (*Madagaskar-Projekt*) in the summer of 1940. The conquest of France (May 1940) had given fresh impetus to the old antisemite idea of 'removing' the Jewish population to Madagascar and establishing a Jewish colony there. In the words of one Nazi relocation official, the project aimed at the establishment of 'a Jewish homeland under German sovereignty', with the Jews living under German police supervision.[69] The original idea, as conceived by the German Foreign Office, was for the 'removal' of the Jewish population of Western Europe to Madagascar. The RSHA version, however, expanded the plan to include the Jews of Nazi-controlled Eastern Europe as well, and it proposed a Jewish colony to be run, not surprisingly, as an SS police state.[70] Under SS aus-pices, the *Madagaskar-Projekt* envisaged the 'removal' to the island of the some 4 million European Jews then under Nazi control; including another million Jews from Palestine and another 1.5 million from other parts of the world (excluding the Soviet Union and the United States of America), the island of Madagascar, under the Nazi plan, would even-tually become a 'homeland' for a total of 6.5 million Jews. Heydrich justified the *Madagaskar-Projekt* as a viable means to 'eliminate' the Jews. Echoing his boss, Himmler, he noted that 'biological extermination ... is undignified for the German people as a civilized nation. Thus ... we will ... transport the Jews along with their belongings to Madagascar or elsewhere.'[71]

Under the slogan 'all Jews out of Europe',[72] Madagascar was a plan for a comprehensive 'removal' and deportation of all European Jews, marking a watershed in Nazi thinking. Even though the military sit-uation soon made the Madagascar project impracticable, it was clear to many policymakers that the Jews would be 'disappearing' from the European continent. Although this idea eventually died, due to mili-tary circumstances, the so-called *Madagaskar-Projekt* had, nonetheless, been taken seriously, and discussed at the highest levels, by the Nazi leadership.[73] While it was not a comprehensive plan to murder Jews, it was, nonetheless, genocidal in its implications (that is, the Jews in the 'super-ghetto' of Madagascar were expected to die of starvation and dis-ease), and it was an important psychological step on the road to the Nazi 'Final Solution'.[74]

With Madagascar no longer a viable option, Nazi leaders contin-ued the search for a totalizing 'territorial solution'. At the 'centre',

Russia was now seen as an alternative 'reservation' site for 'unwanted' Jewish populations, once the German armies were victorious in 'the East'. In the run-up to the invasion of the Soviet Union (June 1941), Nazi planners were told to formulate plans for the expulsion of Jews into 'a territory yet to be determined' – code language for conquered Soviet territory.[75] In a speech on 28 March 1941, Alfred Rosenberg alluded to the deportation of Jews 'under police surveillance' to a territory that 'could not be mentioned for the time being' (given the secrecy surrounding the upcoming invasion).[76] The war against the Soviet Union, Nazi leaders hoped, would open up the possibility of making other regions available for a 'territorial final solution', offering vast spaces in which to 'dump' 'unwanted' Jewish populations. As the latest 'territorial solution' of the 'Jewish problem', an SS plan called for a 'final evacuation of the Jews' and foresaw the mass deportation of 'approximately 5.8 million Jews' to an inhospitable area of Russia.[77] In a memorandum of 26 March 1941, Heydrich formally proposed that 'the Jews' be deported into conquered areas of Russia. But the plan for deportation to the empty spaces of Siberia soon evaporated, as the German invasion, so optimistically launched that June, faltered in late autumn 1941.

The Third Reich's declining military fortunes, as the tide began to turn in 'the East', ultimately frustrated Nazi hopes for a 'territorial solution' to the 'Jewish question'. But as historians Götz Aly and Suzanne Heim have suggested, these projects had given a 'massive boost to the continuing marginalization of the Jewish population', their very failure (as well as the deteriorating military situation on the Eastern front) making the need for new 'solutions' appear all the more urgent to Nazi leaders both in the 'centre' and at the 'periphery'.[78] In their unrelenting drive to 'solve' the 'Jewish problem' and to 'cleanse' German 'living space' of targeted 'enemies' of the German *Volk*, Nazi planners and policymakers would continue to search for new, innovative, and even more radical 'solutions'.

'Final solutions'

In practice, as surveyed above, both Early American Indian policy and Nazi-German Jewish policy evolved through a series of hoped-for 'final solutions' to the 'out-group question', featuring 'eliminatory' policies and practices aiming at the 'separation', 'removal', and 'concentration' of the indigenes. With the closure of the US frontier (in the 1880s) and the Soviet victory in the 'Nazi East' (1944/1945), there was no 'space' left for the 'removal' option; in these circumstances, mass killings or assimilation became the only eliminatory options available to policymakers in Early America and Nazi Germany.[79] In the Early American case, policymakers turned to assimilation. With the demise of the 'frontier', US Indian policy turned from 'eliminating' Indian tribes to 'killing' the individual 'Indian' identity. Driven by a comforting vision of an 'Americanized' Indian, humanitarian reformers in the late nineteenth century looked to 'civilize' and 'Americanize' the surviving Native Americans – in much the same way as the white European immigrant. While some in the East looked to 'protect' and 'civilize' the Indians, most in 'the West' still looked to further accelerate Indian land loss and 'obtain' *all* Indian ancestral lands, using threatened and actual extermination against any Indians who opposed the 'taking' of remaining Indian lands. In the Nazi-German case, 'the Jew' was widely proclaimed by Nazi ideology to be inassimilable: mass killing, in the end, was the only remaining option. While Nazi genocide and mass murder began at the 'periphery', policymakers and planners at the 'centre' in Berlin were beginning to visualize 'the East' as a site for finally 'solving' the 'Jewish question'. As respects the indigenous inhabitants of 'the East', the 'civilizing mission' was never an option for the German *Führer*: anyone 'who talks about cherishing the local inhabitant and civilizing him', Hitler told his party elite, 'goes straight off to a concentration camp!'.[80] Despite their obvious differences, these two 'final solutions' were both very consistent with the model of settler colonialism and its 'logic of elimination' of 'alien' and 'unwanted' peoples.[81]

Early America

In the 'American West', an outright war of extermination against indigenous peoples had always been a policy option for achieving a 'final solution' to the 'Indian question'. While President George Washington and Secretary of War Henry Knox hoped for 'orderly and peaceful' settlement, they recognized military force as an essential ingredient of US Indian policy, but had specifically rejected a war of extermination as too costly in terms of men and money. On the 'frontier West', however, the press, as well as numerous public officials, openly called for the 'extermination' of the remaining Indians. In the East, though, national policymakers agreed, in 1867, that the American people 'will not for a moment tolerate the idea of extermination'. Calls for outright extermination of the 'natives' from western settler colonists and military commanders on the 'frontier' were ultimately rejected by US government officials responsible for 'Indian affairs'.[82]

While officially rejecting the idea of an annihilationist assault, 'war' nonetheless became a preferred instrument of US Indian policy. In the view of one Indian commissioner, the use of military force was 'discipline' (not 'war'). Rejecting the idea of a 'general Indian war', he nevertheless insisted that the 'aborigines' of the North American continent 'must yield [to white settlement] or perish'. If they oppose the 'progress of civilization', he insisted, 'they must be relentlessly crushed.'[83] Humanitarians and reformers – so-called 'friends of the Indian' – also did not shy away from the use of coercion and force, in certain instances. When a new round of 'Indian wars' broke out on the plains, in the summer of 1868, they took a strong stand against 'hostile Indians', recommending the use of 'military force' against 'all such Indians as may refuse to go' on to the government-run reservations.[84] While forced displacement and 'removal' became the nineteenth century's 'preferred catchall solution' to the 'Indian problem', exterminatory violence was, in practice, an 'alternate, final solution' for 'hostile natives' who resisted 'concentration' on 'reservations'.[85]

US Indian policy after the Civil War was to save the 'remnant' of the Indian tribes – that is, those who had survived the prior 'Indian wars' as well as earlier attempted 'solutions' to the 'Indian problem'. As the failure of the reservation system became widely recognized at the centre, many policymakers began to think that the answer to the 'Indian problem' lay in assimilation – not segregation. In the early years after the American Civil War, the US government would be influenced by the ideas of assimilation and acculturation and by a policy of 'civilization' advocated by Indian reformers in the East. Despite these 'good intentions', white indifference was, in some ways, the Indians' worst enemy. As the Indian Peace Commission, a group of unpaid philanthropists, lamented, '[n]obody pays any attention to Indian matters...when the progress of settlement reaches the Indian's home, the only question considered', they noted, 'is, "how best to get his lands"...when [the Indian's lands] are obtained the Indian is lost sight of.' For their part, white settlers 'have grown rich in the occupation of former [Indian] lands', they pointed out, lands 'too often taken by force or procured in fraud'.[86]

An 1875 *New York Times* editorial summarized the 'two methods of dealing with the Indians': (1) a 'manifest-destiny' policy, which recognizes no future for 'the Indian' but 'extermination' as 'the destiny of an inferior people'; and (2) a policy of 'humanity', which sees 'the Indian' as a human being and cedes to him 'a portion of the territory once occupied wholly by him'. The *Times* went on to castigate 'our Government' for 'generally treating [the Indian] as an encumbrance to be got rid of'.[87] In the end, the *Times* recognized that there was a great deal of public apathy, boredom, and indifference to 'the Indian problem' and that the prevailing public opinion – particularly in 'the West' – was mostly at variance with the newspaper's own more humanitarian views.[88]

The government's official goal of assimilation required a state-directed policy of cultural genocide, with a stated aim of 'killing the Indian but saving the man' by making Native Americans into 'white' Christian farmers. The assimilation project also involved sending Indian children to boarding schools to destroy their Indian identity,[89] and prohibiting traditional Indian religious and cultural practices among the tribes. From a political standpoint, assimilation sought to 'detribalize' the Indians; there was no thought given to racial assimilation, since Indians would continue to live separately from 'whites'. As in the Jeffersonian era, moreover, the 'civilization policy' would be underpinned by the threat and actual use of force. President Grant's 'peace policy' (1870), for example, was a two-edged sword: any Indians 'disposed to peace' would not be dealt with by force of arms, but 'those who do not accept this policy', Grant promised, would find the US government 'ready for a sharp and severe war policy'.[90] Should the Indians refuse to 'cede' their lands, oppose American expansion, or decline to embrace 'civilization', even assimilationists agreed that the federal government should call out 'mounted troops for the purpose of conquering the desired peace'.[91] Paradoxically, violence was an intrinsic part of Grant's 'peace policy'. America's remaining Indians would be subjected to, in General Sherman's words, 'a double process of peace *within* their reservations and war *without*'.[92]

The leading scholar of US–Indian relations, Francis Paul Prucha, sees 1880 as a crucial divide in US Indian policy, marking the end of an era of diplomatic dealings and almost non-stop 'military encounters' in one or more regions of the 'American West' and the beginning of a movement aimed at the 'ultimate acculturation and assimilation of individual Indians into white society'.[93] Secretary of Interior Henry M. Teller noted in 1884 that 'the time has passed when large and valuable tracts of land fit for agriculture can be held by Indians either for hunting or grazing to the exclusion of actual settlers'.[94] As applied to the land itself, assimilation took the form of the General Allotment Act (or Dawes Act) of 1887, which envisioned dividing up reservation lands into private plots: parcels of land 'owned' by individuals or families. Any 'surplus' land would, of course, be 'given' to the white settler colonists. As implemented in the 'American West', the Dawes Act did not promote (or result in) the civilization or assimilation of the surviving Native American communities; in fact, it only served to swiftly move Indian land into white hands, reducing the lands still held by Indians to fragmented, unproductive parcels, which prevented 'the Indian' from becoming a self-sufficient farmer.[95] In practice, neither the federal government nor the settlers ever let the Indians alone: the settlers were constantly pressuring Indians to 'sell' their allotments, while the federal government continued purchasing allotted lands from Indians for 'resale' to white settlers. Ultimately, settler colonists and land speculators, not the Indians, were the 'winners' of the allotment policy. By the 1880s, America's indigenous peoples retained virtually no land in the entire North American continent that was not part of a 'reservation'.[96]

While 'assimilation' was the oft-stated purpose of US Indian policy, it repeatedly functioned in the Early American settler-colonial context as a convenient rationale for the taking of Indian lands, for the 'elimination' of the natives, and for a policy to 'kill the Indian' ways of life – and sometimes Indians, regardless of sex or age – in the name of a national homogeneity.[97] Indeed, assimilation, as Patrick Wolfe rightly asserts, involves a Faustian bargain: in exchange for a 'place' in 'civilization', the indigene gives up his soul. It is, in reality, a kind of death.[98]

Nazi Germany

After the September 1939 attack on Poland, there was a noticeable and rapid escalation in Nazi anti-Jewish policy from the immediate pre-war policy of forced emigration towards a 'final solution', an escalation that finally called for the murder of every Jew within the German grasp – men, women, children, infants, and the elderly. At the time of the June 1941 attack on the Soviet Union, forced resettlement was still the 'solution' to the 'Jewish question' envisaged by the Nazi leadership. The decision to invade Russia ended the era of expulsion and led to the beginning of the era of mass murder. German anti-Jewish measures in the occupied Soviet Union followed the Polish model of dispossession, exclusion, and separation. From the beginning of Operation Barbarossa, however, these policies were directly linked with acts of mass murder. A policy of selective mass murder at the onset, this would soon be transformed into a more comprehensive policy aimed at the wholesale destruction of Jewish life in the occupied parts of the Soviet Union.[99]

In Nazi-occupied Western Europe (France, Belgium, the Netherlands, Italy, Denmark and Norway), the Nazi goal, following the outbreak of war in the West in April 1940, had been to encourage or force Jews to emigrate to Palestine or beyond the borders of Germany's frontiers, leaving their property behind. Nazi policy towards the roughly half a million West European Jews was always subsidiary to their policy towards the *Ostjuden* (Eastern Jews), and was determined, above all, by strategic, rather than ideological, concerns. Until the Wannsee Conference, in January 1942, the Nazi top leadership 'had [eastern] Jews on their minds'.[100] After vacillating over the fate of the Reich Jews, Hitler ordered their 'removal' from Germany, Austria, and the Protectorate in mid-September 1941 to ghettos in Poland, White Russia, and the Baltic. Hitler's order to 'remove' the Jews from the Reich, however, specifically prohibited their murder. A month later, emigration was forbidden for West European Jews, and they began to be interned in holding camps – awaiting deportation 'east' to an, as yet, undetermined location and fate.

After being 'removed' to ghettos in 'the East', indigenous *Ostjuden* were to be killed in mass shootings to 'make room' for the Reich Jews. In the 'Nazi East', mass murder by shooting was fast becoming a 'standard procedure of occupation policy'.[101] Within the SS leadership, the mass shootings in Russia were increasingly seen as a viable alternative or adjunct to the new 'removal' scheme. The mobile killing squads of the *Einsatzgruppen* and the police battalions unleashed an onslaught against Soviet Jewry using shooting and firing-squad methods, beginning with Jewish men. Then, in August 1941, an increased targeting of Jewish women and children began, signalling a transition from selective to total mass murder of Soviet Jewry. As the mass executions continued, however, 'problems' developed with the killing of Soviet Jewry by traditional colonial methods of shootings and mass reprisals: first, it required considerable manpower; second, the killing of women and children imposed 'undue' psychological burdens on the killers; and, finally, the process was too public – as word of the killings reached the Reich metropole itself via letters, postcards, pictures, and soldiers on leave.[102] In response to these various 'problems', Nazi planners and innovators began to conceptualize a potential solution: the extermination camp (*Vernichtungslager*) – that is, stationary gas chambers to be located in 'the East' in which to carry out the 'total eradication' of European Jewry.

At a moment still debated by historians (September–October 1941 at the earliest or January–May 1942 at the latest), Hitler, Himmler, and Heydrich decided that the local massacres and regional genocides should be combined and enlarged into a European-wide extermination programme. At the Wannsee Conference of 20 January 1942, according to Eichmann's minutes, Heydrich outlined the prior history of the Nazi struggle against 'the Jews'. Nazi *Judenpolitik*, Heydrich said, had initially focused on their 'exclusion' from the 'individual spheres of German life' and from the 'living space of the German people'. The regime's goal, he reminded his audience, had been to 'purge' 'the Jews' from 'Germany's living space' in a 'legal fashion', by voluntary or forced emigration. But now, Heydrich noted, 'the East' provided fresh 'opportunities' to 'solve' the 'Jewish question'. As a result, the 'evacuation of Jews to the East', he asserted, had now emerged as the proposed 'final solution of the European Jewish question'. Henceforth, Heydrich announced, local genocides would be coordinated under SS auspices – as he carefully and repeatedly emphasized – into a pan-European extermination project.[103]

From the end of 1941, specially designed extermination centres were built on Polish soil in the 'Nazi East'. Starting in the summer of 1942, brutal 'ghetto clearances' deported victims to these killing factories. Almost 1 million Jews were shot in wild shooting sprees during these 'clearances'; in addition, tens of thousands of Jews who had fled from ghettos were shot after being captured.[104] Millions of European Jews would spend months (or sometimes years) in ghettos in 'the East' or in transit camps or assembly areas in Western Europe, before being transported to the extermination centres for 'processing'. In the extermination centres themselves, full-scale, 'industrialized' mass extermination began with the gassing of Jewish men, women, children, and infants – the corpses buried in mass graves, cremated in ovens, or burned in the open. In the end, the Nazi 'final solution' became an organized continent-wide murder campaign, meaning death by extermination in eastern 'killing factories' for entire Jewish communities in Nazi-occupied Europe.

In retrospect, the Nazi campaign against Slavs and Jews was the defining feature of Nazi empire-building in the 'Wild East'.[105] In the settler-colonial context, Nazi wars for *Lebensraum* in 'the East' effectively became a general war against Slavs and Jews. For instance, in the Ukraine – the largest Nazi settler colony – Himmler told his SS and police officers to 'clean the territory...for the future settlement of Germans', calling for the immediate destruction of all Jewish communities and for the Slavic population to be brought to a 'minimum'.[106] As a leading scholar of Hitler's empire rightly concludes, we can no longer 'maintain that there was any significant distinction after 1941 between how the SS and the *Wehrmacht* treated Jews and Slavs in the occupation'.[107]

The actual fate of 'the Jews', however, would be markedly different from the Russian 'Redskins'.[108] Although we can point to numerous similarities in Nazi plans for and actions against Jews and Slavs, there was and remained one crucial difference: as a matter of Nazi racial ideology, the Jews (unlike some of the Slavs) could never be saved, converted, or assimilated.[109] In the case of the Slavs, given the requirements of the German economy, mass murder was not an explicit Nazi goal but rather a implicit means to implement their continental racial-imperialist goals in 'the East'. In the case of European Jewry, racial-ideological motivations were primary and drove policies aimed at the Jews' immediate death.[110] Nazi policies towards the Slavs involved constant improvisation and were balanced by considerations of both opportunity and ideology. As the logical culmination of the National Socialist ideological predisposition, the Nazi 'final solution' to the 'Jewish question' was total and uncompromising in nature, and dominated by ideological considerations.[111] Slavic groups in 'the East' (that is, Poles, Russians, White Russians, and Ukrainians) were seen as a potential source of labour (a 'leaderless work force' in Himmler's words) to be denationalized and brutally treated, with the certain expectation (and hope) that they would ultimately 'fade away' during the next generations. But there was no policy of intended, complete eradication of the Slavs. Unlike the Poles, the Russians, and the Ukrainians, the Jews were not subject to 'general selection' for the purposes of determining their individual 'racial worth'. Depending on their 'racial quality', Slavs faced deportation 'further east', exploitation as slave labour, or extermination. The separation of Jews into those 'fit' and those 'unfit' for labour only determined, as historian Götz Aly notes, the order in which they were to die.[112]

Unlike its policies towards other 'out-groups', the Nazi extermination of the Jews was, at the same time, systematic (that is, centrally organized) and urgent (that is, it had to be completed before the end of the war).[113] Isabel Heinemann is right when she writes, 'The fundamental difference between Nazi racial policies against Jews on the one hand and Slavs on the other consisted in the degree of totality that was applied in theory as well as in implementation.'[114] The Jews were the main victim group of the Nazi occupation and the only one immediately targeted for instant and complete extermination. In the end, the Nazi genocide of the Jews contained both a 'spatial' goal ('removal' of the Jews from the German 'living space') as well as an 'existential' goal (the intended physical destruction of every Jewish man, woman, and child within the Nazi grasp).[115]

In the 'Wild East', Nazi policy had shifted from 'exterminatory colonialism' to 'extermination as such'. At the same time, Hitler's dream of eastern colonization and Himmler's notion of 'racial shifting' had been transformed into a programme of Jewish extermination. Following the lead of the *Führer*, Nazi propaganda had recast the war as a war against 'the Jews' (rather than a war against Slavic 'sub-humans' and 'Jewish Bolshevists').[116] Wide-ranging discussions among Nazi leaders on the intended 'reduction' of the Slavic population (by 'tens of millions') continued well into 1944. After 1941, however, there were few discussions on the 'final solution of the Jewish question'.[117] After all, no discussion was necessary: the fate of European Jewry had already been decided – they were to be murdered *without exception*.

Similarities, differences, and links

Both Early American and Nazi-German societies accepted the idea that there was an 'Indian question', a 'Slav question', and a 'Jewish question', which all called for 'solutions' in order to assure the continued expansion and racial purity of the nation-state. 'Pacification' campaigns and wars against whole civilian populations (including women and children) were common practices in both the 'American West' and the 'Nazi East'. For the most part, in both Early America and Nazi Germany, 'out-group' policy involved the exclusion of the indigenous 'Other' and their forced expulsion from the metropole and its newly acquired 'living-space'; in both cases, the nation-state undertook policies of deliberate ethnic cleansing – which the Early Americans called 'removal' and which the Nazi-Germans called 'resettlement'. In both cases, alternatives to outright extermination – that is, policies of separation, removal, and concentration – were not only considered but adopted (in full or in part). Furthermore, continental-imperialist expansion and military conquest rapidly increased the new 'living space' in both the 'American West' and the 'Nazi East', adding growing numbers of indigenous peoples to the 'Indian problem', the 'Slav problem', and the 'Jewish problem'. As a result, current 'solutions' to these growing 'problems' often fell short or no longer proved feasible, driving the search for new kinds of 'totalizing solutions'.

In the Early American case, US Indian policy was often torn by differences between policymakers and public opinion in the East (which generally favoured 'peaceful' solutions) and settler colonists in 'the West' and their political supporters (who almost always preferred 'military' solutions), with the US government often unable to decide which approach to choose or, frequently, pursuing both approaches at the same time. In Early America, while the nation-state (in the form of the federal government) officially sponsored assimilation of the 'friendly' Indian and 'elimination' of the 'hostile' Indian, the settler colonists advocated extermination of *all* Indians, and thus US Indian policy reflected elements of both approaches. In Early America, there was some open questioning of Indian policy in the metropole on religious and humanitarian grounds. In the Nazi-German case, by contrast, an 'eliminationist' 'out-group' policy, as embodied in Nazi racial ideology, became the official dogma and policy of the state. Accordingly, Nazi-German policymakers faced no moral dilemmas. In the conquered territories of 'the East', Nazi planners envisaged only death – either immediate or eventual – for the 'native' indigenous populations. Unlike its Early American counterpart, the Nazi-German settler-colonial project, as we shall see, was capable of limitless and constant mass political violence against unarmed civilian populations.

As instanced earlier (Chapter 1), on the evening of 17 October 1941, Hitler privately remarked that indigenous peoples in the Soviet Union should be treated like the 'Red Indians' in the 'American West'. In 'the East', Nazi plans called for brutal methods of occupation and rule, similar to those imposed on conquered indigenous peoples by Euro-American imperialists in the vast colonial spaces of the nineteenth century. In particular, Nazi-German 'removal' and 'resettlement' plans for *Ostjuden* (Eastern Jews) and indigenous Slavs – especially the anticipated placing of Jews on 'reservations' and the use of non-colonized 'space' as a 'dumping ground' for 'unwanted', 'alien' populations of Slavs and Jews – follow the Early American tradition of demographic re-engineering and ethnic cleansing, although on a much larger scale. Upon closer examination, Nazi 'out-group' policies and practices appear as radicalized, more extreme versions of those found in Early America. Indeed, the 'North American precedent', in the eyes of Nazi 'true believers' – like Hitler and Himmler – may well have served to legitimize Nazi policies and practices in 'the East'. Until the opening of the extermination centres and the beginning of 'industrialized killing' (late 1941/early 1942), Nazi-German 'out-group' policies and practices were very much a calculated adaptation – albeit a radical and more extreme adaptation – of the Early American settler-colonial model.

Part III
Frontier Genocide

Introductory note

Central to the existence of empires, the 'frontier' constitutes a site of imperial politics at the edge of empire, a site crucial to both national security and national prestige. An important spatial feature of territorial empire, it also serves as a springboard for future expansion and/or a defensive barrier for consolidating the expansion previously obtained.[1] In the era of the modern nation-state, the 'frontier' can function as a marker of national identity, as an instrument of state policy, as an 'imagined community' (part of a nation's political beliefs and myths), or as a term of discourse (whose meanings can change over time). In some historical contexts, it functions as an emotional and psychological divide, as well as a political-geographical line.[2] Under settler colonialism, the 'frontier' was no longer an intercultural zone of contact but was, instead, perceived as new 'living space' into which settlers could continually migrate without regard to indigenous ways of life or to indigenous lives. The coming of 'frontiers', to be sure, brings a terrific 'unsettling' to indigenous peoples, along with a reordering of power, lands, and resources.[3]

In a world historical context, the 'frontiers' of empire often erupt in violence, warfare, and bloodshed, as the 'frontier' becomes the site of widespread and brutal killing, uprooting, and destruction.[4] In the academic literature on 'violence', scholars have traditionally defined and characterized 'violence' as the use of force with an intention to inflict bodily harm, with an emphasis on inter-state war and war-making (against both combatants and non-combatants). In more recent studies, however, scholars have broadened the concept of 'violence' from physical harm and killing to other forms of violence used by the modern nation-state in both metropolitan and colonized 'living space' (including coercion, a more 'measured' use of force, and various forms of social control).[5]

As comparative historian Charles S. Maier notes, empire's ambitions, its territorial agenda, and its problematic frontiers 'create an intimate and recurring bond with the recourse to force' and extreme political violence. As a result, these imperial projects, he observes, 'claim their toll of those who resist and often those who are merely in the way'. For the most part, empire's zones of violence, he claims, almost always lie outside the metropole itself – beyond the 'frontiers', in the colonial periphery. For those in the metropole, then, the violence and bloodshed were far away and often not visible. Thus, it was, he says, both 'easy and necessary to look away from violence erupting at the periphery'. In modern times, he concludes, empires 'depend upon distance' and upon 'rendering violence remote'.[6]

In many settler-colonial contexts, genocide is closely linked to the processes of imperialism and colonialism.[7] In the broader scope of human history, I would not necessarily argue for (or subscribe to) an overdetermined link between settler colonialism and genocide. I do, however, share Patrick Wolfe's reasoned view that, for 'alien' and 'unwanted' indigenous populations, 'settler colonialism is inherently eliminatory but not invariably genocidal'. To be sure, there can be genocide in the absence of settler colonialism, as Wolfe notes; indeed, many other genocidal episodes are not (or do not seem) assignable to settler colonialism. Likewise, genocidal outcomes are not inevitable in settler-colonial projects. That being said, in a number of different historical settings, as Wolfe concludes, settler colonialism and genocide have converged, and settler colonialism has manifested as genocide.[8] In the settler-colonial context, especially, genocide is a process, rather than an event or a single decision.[9]

'War' and 'genocide' have been called the 'Siamese twins of history'. Most scholars of mass political violence, furthermore, recognize intimate connections between the two phenomena.[10] In the contemporary world, 'war' and 'genocide' are the two most prevalent forms of organized killing in modern society. As such, they are closely related, with numerous links and connections between the two modes of action.[11] In addition, genocide is a major tendency of modern war. Given the 'general hybridity' of war and genocide, 'genocidal war', as historical sociologist Martin Shaw suggests, is 'probably *the* most common form of genocide and *a* very common form of war'.[12] Many genocide scholars position 'war' as genocide's greatest single enabling factor.

Crucially, in many instances, 'war' provides a convenient 'smokescreen' for 'genocide' – that is, 'war' becomes the perpetrator's excuse and rationale for 'eliminationist' and 'exterminationist' assaults against targeted civilian non-combatant populations.[13] 'Wartime', as genocide scholar Robert Melson notes, often 'provides some of the conditions facilitating the formulation and implementation of the decision to commit genocide.'[14] Indeed, most 'genocide' occurs in contexts of more general 'war'.[15]

'War' and 'genocide' are both forms of armed conflict. In his original conception of 'genocide', the Polish jurist and historian of mass violence Raphael Lemkin (who coined the term in 1943) rightly argued that 'genocide' not only most often occurs within the background of 'war', but is, in fact, a form of warfare. The main distinction between the phenomena, in his view, 'lay in *who* the war was being waged against'.[16] The key difference between them, then, lies in the nature of the 'enemy': In 'war', the 'enemy' is another state or armed force; in 'genocide', however, the 'enemy' is a group of civilian non-combatants or targeted 'out-groups' ear-marked for 'reduction', 'elimination', or 'annihilation'. As historical sociologist Martin Shaw suggests, these 'out-groups' are often defined as 'enemies' in the fundamentally military sense of the word, justifying the use of extreme physical violence against largely unarmed civilian populations. Even in peacetime, he rightly observes, 'genocide' is a form of 'war' against targeted 'out-groups'.[17]

The final part of the book looks at how 'continental imperialism' and 'settler colonialism' manifested as 'genocide' in the 'American West' and the 'Nazi East'. In both cases, 'war' provided both the cover and the pretext for 'genocidal' assaults against allegedly 'inferior' and 'unwanted' 'out-groups'. Social actors, in both cases, used the term 'remove' to describe the radical removal of 'unwanted', 'alien' peoples from metropolitan and colonized 'living space', and they used the terms 'extirpation' and 'extermination' to describe the destruction of indigenous peoples who stood in the way of the settler state 'obtaining' new *Lebensraum*.

Chapter 6, 'War and Genocide', describes how 'settler colonialism' and 'genocide' converged within the specific historical contexts of Early America and Nazi Germany, as a distinct form of 'war' against civilians aimed at the intentional social destruction of targeted 'out-groups' by means of killing, violence, and coercion. It examines the similar dynamics driving genocidal violence in the 'American West' and the 'Nazi East'. It surveys the wide range of similar genocidal measures used by both nation-states to 'remove' 'alien' 'others' from the metropole and to 'control' and 'reduce' indigenous populations in the newly colonized 'living space'. It also considers deliberate acts of systematic, exterminatory violence carried out – by both state and non-state actors – against non-combatant indigenous populations on the 'frontiers' of 'the West' and 'the East'. And, finally, it explores the intentions, legitimations, and outcomes of genocidal violence in the 'Wild West' and the 'Wild East'.

6
War and Genocide: 'Cleansing' the *Lebensraum*

The question of 'genocide' in US history is quite naturally a threatening and disturbing one for contemporary Americans, one that calls into question the very nature and consequences of the Early American national project in 'the West'. Recognition of such a 'genocide', moreover, would severely discredit our national belief in America's 'exceptionalist' past. Among historians of Early America and the American 'West', the dispossession and destruction of Native American communities is far from a consensually accepted case of 'genocide', with the vast majority of scholars objecting, sometimes heatedly, to the use of the 'g' word and others seeing it as a case of 'ethnic cleansing' – a step below genocide, as they see it, in the hierarchy of extreme political violence.[1] Outside of a few historians of the American West and some specialists in Native American history, there has been, until very recently, an almost universal reluctance on the part of mainstream American historians to consider 'genocide' in the case of the Indian Americans.[2] Within the disciplines of genocide studies and ethnic studies, however, the notion of genocide against Native Americans, in both the colonial and early national periods, is slowly gaining wider acceptance.[3]

Among both specialists of Nazi Germany and genocide scholars, the Holocaust – the Nazi destruction of European Jewry – is almost universally accepted as a case of 'genocide'. There is widespread disagreement, however, as to what 'caused' the 'genocide', as well as general disagreement as to its nature and its victims. While many early scholars of the Holocaust saw it as the culmination of Nazi racial ideology and Hitler's long-held, declared intention to 'eliminate' 'the Jews', other scholars see it as the result of an essentially unplanned process of 'cumulative radicalization' of Nazi anti-Jewish policy.[4] Within the literature, Nazi genocide is most often cited as a case of ultra-modern 'twentieth-century

179

genocide'[5] without any (or only passing) reference to its colonial context
and content. In the scholarly literature, as well as in popular perception,
the 'colonial genocide' of Slavs and Jews in the 'Nazi East' has been
overshadowed, or even disallowed, by the equating of the Holocaust to
industrial mass murder in the extermination centres. While millions of
non-Jewish – mostly Slavic – civilians also died, they are often seen as
Nazism's 'other victims' – not, or only rarely, as victims of 'genocide' or
'holocaust'.

Using the corrective lenses of continental imperialism, settler
colonialism, and frontier genocide, we can begin to discern the true
nature of the extreme political violence in the 'American West' and the
'Nazi East', as well as its remarkably common and consistent causes.
In both cases, 'genocide' (that is, the mass killing of civilians) was
a by-product of their respective national projects of territorial expansion, racial cleansing, and settler colonization. In the American 'Wild
West' and the Nazi-German 'Wild East', 'genocide' featured both 'eliminationist' and 'exterminationist' assaults against 'alien' 'out-groups'
and 'unwanted' 'native' populations; assaults that encompassed a wide
range of destructive modalities – marked by killing, violence, or coercion. In both cases, 'eliminationist' assaults aimed at the intentional
destruction of Native American, Slavic, and Jewish communities in both
metropolitan and colonized 'living space' – communities whose systematic destruction became a distinctive goal of policymakers. In both
cases, 'genocide' occurred in a war context – as largely unarmed civilians became the subject of armed violence only applied, in most
other contexts, to armed enemies. The restrictions of 'civilized society' did not exist in the 'American West' or the 'Nazi East'; in these
'spaces', the colonial invaders were able to transgress civilizational limits. In the 'American West' and the 'Nazi East', settler-colonial wars
for 'living space' featured 'genocidal war' in which openly genocidal
'exterminationist' campaigns against civilians – civilians defined as
'enemies' in a military sense – became intertwined with more conventional warfare. In both cases, then, these wars for *Lebensraum* had an
inbuilt genocidal component, making warfare against non-combatant
indigenous populations an inherent part of military campaigns.

Despite obvious differences in time and space, 'continental imperialism' and 'settler colonialism' spawned 'frontier genocide' in the
'American West' and the 'Nazi East'. In both cases, imperialism,
colonialism, and genocide converged; however, they converged in different ways – within their specific historical contexts. In the Early
American case, genocide was part of a sustained and purposeful

campaign of aggressive continental expansion carried out by the US government and its settler colonists over the first 100 years of the nation's
existence, and it was present from the very beginning of the Anglo-
American settler-colonial project. In the Nazi-German case, the Nazis
had targeted the Reich Jews for 'removal' from the Greater German
Reich. The genocide of Reich Jews deported to 'the East', most scholars
now agree, was the outcome of an unplanned 'cumulative radicalization' of Nazi anti-Jewish policy – after other 'eliminatory' strategies
proved ineffective or no longer feasible due to the Third Reich's changing and declining military fortunes on the Eastern front. The Nazi
genocide of Slavs and *Ostjuden* (Eastern Jews) in the occupied eastern
territories was part of an aggressive programme of continental expansion and planned colonization carried out by Hitler's National Socialist
government to 'obtain' new 'living space' for agricultural settlement.
Without the wars for *Lebensraum*, driven by Hitler's and Himmler's
fantasies of German settler colonization in 'the East', there would
have been no genocide of Reich Jews, *Ostjuden*, Western Jews, or
Slavs.

In both the Early American and Nazi-German cases, a similar
genocidal dynamic, as we shall see, drove its sponsors, organizers, and
perpetrators to sanction or commit genocidal violence against indigenous peoples. Despite a similar dynamic, however, 'genocide' took
different forms in the 'American West' and the 'Nazi East'. In the Early
American case, 'genocidal explosions' took the form of sporadic 'waves
of genocide' and 'genocidal moments' in 'the West' over the first 100
years of American history. In the German case, they took the form of a
daily 'genocidal orgy' of violence in the 'Nazi East' between 1939 and
1945, an intense genocide, which featured not only traditional colonial
modalities of extreme political violence but, after 1941, unprecedented
'factory line/industrial killing' in specially built extermination centres
in the conquered eastern territories.

Genocidal dynamic

In order for genocide to occur, we need what anthropologist Alexander
Laban Hinton calls 'genocidal priming' – that is, 'a set of processes
that establish the preconditions for genocide to take place within a
given socio-political context'.[6] In both Early America and Nazi Germany,
political elite preoccupations and obsessions with territorial expansion,
racial or ethnic prejudice, settler colonization, and agrarian idealism –
as expressed in a similar continental-imperialist ideological discourse –

provided the 'enabling conditions' and 'lethal ideological ammunition'[7] for settler-colonial policies and practices that manifested into 'genocide' in the 'American West' and the 'Nazi East'. In both cases, 'genocide' directly resulted from a declared settler–state policy of expansion, conquest, and colonization of the new 'living space'. In both cases, wars for 'living space' in the 'American West' and the 'Nazi East' served as the trigger for genocidal violence against indigenous civilian non-combatant populations. In the Early American case, 'genocide' was a central and defining part of the sustained, long-term process of American western expansion and colonization. In the Nazi-German case, the 'colonial-style genocide' of Slavs and Jews in 'the East' became an 'industrial genocide', which aimed at the murder of every Jewish man, woman, and child in the Nazi empire. In the 'American West' and the 'Nazi East', 'living space' for 'ordinary' Americans and for 'ordinary' Germans became 'dying space' for Native Americans and for European Slavs and Jews.

Early America

Enabling conditions

As we have seen earlier (Chapter 1), the Early American continental-imperialist ideological discourse was based on political elite preoccupations with territorial expansion, racial and ethnic prejudice, settler colonization, and agrarian idealism. These fixations were ultimately reflected in both formal government policy and in on-the-ground events in the 'American West', forming the core of settler-colonial policies, practices, and activities, which resulted in a massive loss of life for Indian non-combatants – including women, children, infants, and the elderly. Indeed, genocidal tendencies were inherent to the process of settler colonialism as practised by the United States and its citizens on the 'frontier' peripheries of 'empire' in the 'American West'.[8] In the settler-colonial context, moreover, political elite obsessions provided the necessary 'enabling conditions' for government and/or settler policies, practices, and activities that were either genocidal in their intent ('genocidal warfare' and 'genocidal massacres') or in their outcome ('removal' and 'concentration'), for tens of thousands of Native Americans. Taken together, these preoccupations reinforced genocidal thinking and action in the 'American West', as the newly independent nation spread across the entire North American continent in a brutal campaign of conquest and dispossession of Indian lands and resources.

Causality

In Early America, genocide resulted from an intended state policy and settler practices of expansion, conquest, and violent colonization of Indian lands in 'the West'. As Henry Knox, Washington's secretary of war, wrote to the new president, in 1794, the new nation's 'modes of population have been even more destructive to the Indian natives' than the conduct of the Spanish conquerors of Mexico and Peru, as evidenced by the 'utter extirpation of nearly all of the Indians in the most populous parts of the Union'.[9] In the 'American West', bands of settlers or local militias carried out genocidal massacres of Indian men, women, and children on the 'frontier', in retaliation for Indian raids or often in pre-emptive strikes. Lacking the ability and/or the will to 'control' the behaviour of white settlers on the 'frontier', government officials, by their silence and/or inaction, condoned the genocide of Native Americans. Army units and territorial militias carried out government-sponsored genocidal wars of conquest and 'pacification' in 'the West', in order to 'secure' new 'living space' for continued 'white' settlement. Both these forms of warfare exhibited deliberate genocidal intent to annihilate Indian combatant and non-combatant populations (regardless of sex and age).

Trigger/immediate catalyst

In the Early American case, genocide was contingent on conflict.[10] As we have seen (Chapter 3), insatiable settler hunger for Indian lands led to what historian Colin Calloway has called the 'war for America' and the 'war against Indian America'. Beginning in the early seventeenth century and lasting until the end of the nineteenth century, this war was driven by relentless settler 'acquisition' of Indian 'space' and, after the War of Independence, by deliberate US government policies of conquest, expansion, and colonization becoming deeply embedded in America's nation-building and empire-building processes. American westward expansion and settlement led to a constant state of warfare with, and genocidal violence against, Native American communities, who refused to accept white domination over their lands, their lives, and their destinies. The so-called 'Indian wars' were, in reality, wars for Indian lands and served as the trigger and immediate catalyst for genocidal violence against Native American communities and non-combatants. While US Indian policy was based on the 'removal' and 'deportation' of the Indian survivors further 'west', the federal government, for the first 100 years of the nation's existence, countenanced genocide as a legitimate strategy of warfare against Native Americans who defended their way of life and who resisted the 'acquisition' of their ancestral homelands.

Nature of genocide

The genocide of the North American Indians was a sustained, long-term, and intended process of group destruction involving epidemic disease (including alcoholism), genocidal warfare and acts of genocide, voluntary and forced removal/relocation, and destruction of Indian food sources and Indian ways of life. Together, these factors interacted with one another, causing a massive and sustained 'depopulation' and demographic collapse of North American Indian populations over a span of more than 300 years: a 'depopulation' that was the direct result and consequence of more than three centuries of Euro-American settler colonization and seizure and occupation of Indian lands.[11] In the Early American case, 'genocide' was a continuum of settler-colonial policies, practices, and activities, which stretched from the time of the original English settlements in the colonies through the first 100 years of the American Republic.[12] With varying levels of intensity, genocidal violence took place over a century of American continental expansion, when state and/or non-state actors considered it necessary to 'help' the Indians 'disappear' from the white settler 'living space'. In the early American case, genocide also resulted from actions allegedly taken in the 'best interests' of the Indians – such as their forced 'removal' from the white settler 'living space' and their 'concentration' on 'reservations'.

The past and ongoing destruction of Native American communities was clearly evident to American policymakers at the time. In its 26 January 1867 report on the 'Conditions of the Indian Tribes', a joint special committee of Congress openly discussed the reasons behind the 'rapidly decreasing numbers' of American Indians, citing disease, intemperance, war, and the 'steady and resistless emigration of white men into the territories of the west'. In what they called the 'irrepressible conflict between a superior [white] and an inferior [Indian] race', the committee went on to admit that whites were responsible for a 'large majority' of the 'Indian wars': 'exterminating wars', in the committee's words, which 'frequently' resulted in the 'indiscriminate slaughter of men, women and children' (in addition to the warriors). The committee also squarely placed the blame for this destruction on non-Indian 'lawless white men' along what it called 'the frontier... boundary line between savage and civilized life'.[13] While the US political elites were well aware that slow death by attrition and immediate death by killing were lethal by-products of American colonial conquest, settlement, and rule in 'the West', they proved unable and/or unwilling to take any action that would subordinate settler interests to the well-being of Native Americans and halt the 'depopulation' of American Indian communities.

Nazi Germany

Enabling conditions

As we have seen (Chapter 1), key Nazi decision-makers – particularly German *Führer* Adolf Hitler and SS chief Heinrich Himmler – were committed to a policy of 'space' and 'race', based on political elite obsessions with continental territorial expansionism, racial and ethnic struggle, settler colonization, and agrarian idealism. Under the Nazi slogan *Blut und Boden* (Blood and Soil), these 'interlocking ideological levers'[14] provided the driving force behind Nazi-German genocidal policies – policies designed to 'cleanse' the metropolitan and colonized 'living space' of racial and ethnic 'enemies'. The primary logic underlying the Nazi continental-imperialist ideological discourse was one of 'eliminating' Jews and other 'racial enemies' from the metropolitan space and 'eliminating' 'unwanted' indigenous populations from newly acquired German settler 'living space' in the 'Nazi East'. Driven by the logic of 'elimination', the Nazi leadership proved more than willing to 'resettle' racial and ethnic 'out-groups', send them to 'reservations', deport them from the 'Aryan' 'living space', or 'annihilate' them (if necessary, feasible, or desirable). As in Early America, political elite obsessions provided the enabling conditions for policies and practices that were genocidal in their intent and outcome (genocidal warfare, 'ghettoization', and 'resettlement') for millions of Jews and Slavs. The most extreme product of four centuries of European imperialism, the vision of a continent-wide Nazi empire – organized along racial lines – was directly 'linked to the destruction of indigenous, Slavic peoples whose survivors would be reduced to undifferentiated workers and slaves, and to the demolition of Jewish communities whose inhabitants would be shunted into faraway reservations or killed'.[15]

Causality

Within the Greater German Reich, war did away with the need for taking into account international opinion, allowing Nazi leaders to proceed with more radical measures against Jews, 'Gypsies', and the disabled.

In the 'Nazi East', as in the 'American West', genocide against non-combatant 'native', 'enemy' populations was the consequence of a deliberate and intended state-directed policy of expansion, conquest, and planned agricultural settlement. As genocide scholar Jürgen Zimmerer has rightly asserted, the Nazi wars for *Lebensraum* against Poland and the Soviet Union were part of the 'largest colonial war of conquest in history'.[16] Nazi settlement policy dictated the 'elimination' of 'native' populations from the new 'Aryan' *Lebensraum* – a policy that, as its planners emphasized, required wholesale ethnic cleansing and mass murder. Rather than a separate project, 'solving' the 'Jewish question' was part and parcel of a wider and broader process of Nazi racial empire-building in 'the East', but it soon gained an autonomy and priority all its own.[17] Driven by Nazi racial-imperialism and settler-colonial fantasies, the genocides of Jewish and Slavic civilian non-combatant populations would not have been thinkable (or possible) without Hitler's overriding obsession with 'acquiring' *Lebensraum* in 'the East' for German settlement and his strong desire for war.

Trigger/immediate catalyst

Given the state of public opinion at home and abroad prior to the onset of the war, it is highly doubtful that the Nazis could have pursued their radical plans for the 'elimination' of the Reich Jews on German soil or in peacetime. In the Nazi-German case, genocide of Europe's Jews was contingent on war. Should war or external conflict occur, Hitler publicly prophesied 'the destruction of the Jewish race in Europe', and Göring warned of a 'big settling of accounts with the Jews'.[18] War offered the Nazis a 'unique opportunity', in the words of a Heydrich confidant, to 'take relatively rigorous action without regard to world opinion' (or German public opinion, for that matter). As Goebbels wrote in his diary (entry 27 March 1942), the war provided a 'number of options that would not be open to us in time of peace. We must take advantage of these options.'[19]

In October 1939, Hitler signed an order authorizing the so-called 'euthanasia' programme, a programme to murder physically and mentally disabled Germans – an order that Hitler had conveniently back-dated to 1 September 1939, the day of the invasion of Poland. According to the Reich physicians' leader, Dr. Gerhard Wagner, Hitler waited until the outbreak of war to 'solve' Germany's 'euthanasia problem', because 'such a problem could be more easily solved in war-time'.[20] In the case of Reich Jews, the wars for 'living space' in Poland and Russia also triggered a 'policy radicalization', as Nazi *Judenpolitik* moved, over the next three years, from 'forced emigration' to 'resettlement' to 'annihilation'. Without wartime conditions, it is extremely doubtful that German cit-izens would have been willing to visit (or accept) widespread physical violence and mass murder against their assimilated, middle-class Jewish neighbours in the Greater German Reich. Quite simply, without the wars for *Lebensraum* in 'the East', the events we have come to know as the Holocaust would not, in all likelihood, have occurred.[21]

Nature of genocide

Broadly viewed, Nazi racial-imperialism envisaged 'dual genocide': a genocidal 'total war' to liberate Germany – and, indeed, Western civi-lization – from the Jewish arch-enemy, and a genocidal 'colonial war' to 'acquire' Lebensraum from the 'inferior' Slavs.[22] But it was only with the Nazi wars for *Lebensraum* in 'the East' that murderous, genocidal policies became thinkable and actionable, under the cover of the Nazi-declared 'war of annihilation'. In the Nazi case, genocide in the 'Wild East' was a 'colonial genocide' committed by an invading European power (Nazi Germany) against indigenous Slavic and Jewish peoples. In the eastern *Lebensraum*, the limits placed on Nazi violence in the Reich were soon discarded or ignored in a torrent of civilian killing featuring mass execu-tions by small groups of killers. In the 'Nazi East', 'genocide' manifested as colonial-style genocidal massacres involving the face-to-face shoot-ing of entire Jewish communities and the selective shooting of Polish elites, Soviet Communist leaders, Slavic non-combatants, Gypsies, and the disabled. It also included 'slow death' from starvation, malnutri-tion, and disease in the ghettos and concentration camps of 'the East'. During the war, the multiple Nazi genocidal campaigns against var-ious targeted 'alien' 'out-groups' and 'unwanted' 'native' populations were carried out simultaneously and reinforced each other in a series of actualized and planned 'serial genocides'.[23] With the decision to mur-der *all* European Jews in killing centres in 'the East', the Nazi 'colonial genocide' became an 'industrial genocide' (a form of genocide without precedent in history).

On a geographical basis there were 'three clusters of [Nazi] genocidal projects': those implemented within the Reich metropole itself, those implemented within the eastern German *Lebensraum*, and those imple-mented within the German sphere of power in western and southern Europe.[24] Within these clusters, the persecution and murder of 'the Jews' was but one (albeit central) aspect of general Nazi population policy in Hitler's continental empire, as well as of the broader *rassen-politik* (race politics) of the Reich metropole. In the eastern *Lebensraum*, as historian Martyn Housden explains correctly, 'There was not just genocide of the Jews, but of Slavic peoples as well.' As it played out, genocide, not holocaust, was to be the fate of Slavic peoples. But while the Jews were 'first in line', the East's Slavic peoples were surely to follow in their wake, had Nazi Germany won the war in 'the East'.[25] In the Nazi-German case, both Jews and Slavs were victims of colonial genocide, but only Jews were victims of industrial genocide.

Modalities of genocidal violence

Outright killing was just one of a complex of strategies visited on indigenous peoples. In the settler-colonial context, settler states and settler colonists used a wide range of genocidal measures to 'control' and 'reduce' indigenous populations, including genocidal warfare; genocidal massacres; biological warfare; introduction and spreading of disease; slavery and forced labour; mass population removals; deliberate starvation, malnutrition, and famine; and forced assimilation (including residential schools).[26] In both the 'American West' and the 'Nazi East', many of these various modalities of genocidal violence, acting in concert, helped to 'clear' the indigenous populations from the newly acquired 'living space' to make way for settler colonization. In both cases, moreover, these modalities of violence became official state policy in an intended process of social destruction aimed at 'enemy' civilian populations – with the deliberate purpose of destroying their political, economic, and cultural power by means of killing, violence, and coercion. In the end, Early American and Nazi-German modalities of violence – embedded in settler-colonial policies and practices – caused the collective mass death of indigenous populations, irrespective of which modality of genocidal violence caused their individual deaths.

Early America

Outright killing

In the 'American West', outright killing took the forms of frontier massacres and reprisal killings during the 'ethnic cleansing' of the newly acquired white settler 'living space'. It also involved the deliberate and calculated destruction of villages and food supplies, as part of strategies of 'total war' against Indian combatant and non-combatant populations. Organized modes of killing in the 'American West' also included the state-sponsored scalp hunting of Indian men, women, and children over 10 years of age (children under 10 were to be captured as slaves).[27] In Early America, indiscriminate organized killing was designed as a deliberate strategy to terrorize Native American communities and to coerce Indian leaders to accept dispossession of Indian lands and resources. In both the Colonial and Early American periods, organized groups of men attacked Indian villages with the declared purpose of killing non-combatants (regardless of age and sex) and destroying the agricultural resources available to any survivors. Driven by land hunger, racial hatred, or both, murderous settler colonists drove Indians from their lands in a process of subjugation and dispossession that was genocidal.[28] Carried out (on occasion) by regular army troops or (more frequently) by citizen settler militias or by specialized ranger units for Indian fighting, organized, outright killing of Indian non-combatants on the western 'frontier' of the American continental empire – in brutal campaigns mounted with and without the support of the state[29] – continued to define American war-making throughout the nineteenth century.

Depopulation/repopulation

In an 1813 letter to Prussian scientist Alexander von Humboldt, Jefferson argued that Indian atrocities against American settlers 'will oblige us now to pursue them to extermination, or drive them to new seats beyond our reach'.[30] Rather than general extermination, however, American policymakers opted for 'removal' – what we today would describe as 'ethnic cleansing'. In the 'American West', the US government carried out deliberate policies to 'depopulate' Native Americans from the newly acquired 'living space', in order to make room for 'repopulation' by relentless streams of white settlers. The focus of Early American population policy in the 'American West' was on what contemporaries termed 'Indian removal', both voluntary and forced. 'Removal' did not encompass a single deportation but, instead, took place over many years in a process of forced migration. During Indian 'removal', native people died during forced marches at the hands of guards or simply from the conditions of the marches. As two scholars of American Indian history have recently pointed out, Indian 'removal', moreover, was not a uniquely Cherokee experience; dozens of eastern Indian tribes – with the Cherokees accounting for about 10 per cent – were forced to surrender their traditional homelands and 'relocate' west of the Mississippi River. Forced 'removal' had, in fact, long been an important aspect of American Indian policy in a process that spanned decades. By the end of the 1800s, more than 60

Indian tribes (from the East, Midwest, and South) had been forcibly 'removed' west of the Mississippi (mostly to what is now Oklahoma).[31] Even as the eastern Indians 'relocated' west of the Mississippi, they were relentlessly pursued by land-hungry white settlers seeking more Indian lands.

Attrition

In Early America, the policy of 'concentrating' Indian survivors of genocidal war and forced 'removal' on 'reservations' was an unplanned policy of attrition and slow death, aimed at breaking the Indian will to resist continued settler expansion and to further the dispossession of Native Americans. On these barren reservations, Indians were subject to repeated cycles of mass epidemics and starvation. Early in the nineteenth century, isolated attempts were made to vaccinate certain tribes against smallpox, but these early efforts failed, due mostly to lack of interest on the part of US officials. Vaccination had some effects in reducing mortality during the late 1800s and was used to induce Indians to stay on the reservations.[32] While 'treaties' often promised that Indians would be provided with the minimum necessities of life, Indian tribes frequently did not receive what was promised, and became unable to feed their populations. Wretched living conditions on these reservations meant only 'slow death' for Native Americans. As instanced above, in the Annual Report of the commissioner of Indian affairs, in 1853, US Indian Agent Thomas Fitzpatrick described the reservation system as 'the legalized murder of a whole nation'.[33] Almost 40 years later, *The New York Times* would accuse the US government of 'starv[ing] those whom we pretend to feed'.[34]

Between 1870 and 1883, commercial hunters, aided at times by soldiers, slaughtered millions of American bison (commonly known as the American buffalo) in an extermination effort, supported by the federal government, to force the starving Plains Indians to submit to the reservation system. Aided by drought, blizzards, and other environmental factors, the hunters brought the Indians' primary resource – a source of food, clothing, and shelter – to the point of destruction and near-extinction. Like the bison, the Plains Indian was brought to the point of near extinction. White settlers took the droughts, blizzards, and grass fires of the 1870s and 1880s that aided the bisons' demise, as evidence of the 'providential extinction of the herds'; just as their 'superior' domestic livestock were 'destined' to replace the 'inferior' bison, the 'superior' 'white' settlers were 'destined' to replace the 'inferior' Indians. As one of the buffalo hunters expressed it, 'kill every buffalo you can ... [for] every buffalo dead is an Indian gone'. In the end, this strategy spared the army from having to fight the large-scale 'exterminationist' 'Indian war' that many had predicted (and some had wanted).[35]

Forced assimilation

By the end of the nineteenth century, with the Indian will to resist largely exhausted, the US government shifted from organized killing, depopulation, and attrition to assimilation of the remnant of surviving Indians. In the aftermath of the 'Plains wars', and the quashing of Indian armed resistance to the reservation system, the federal government proposed 'Americanization' as a 'final solution' to the 'Indian question'. As part of the assimilationist agenda, the federal government and various church denominations established residential boarding schools to wean Indian children from their native way of life, to strip them of their cultural identities, and to indoctrinate them into the 'American way'. As stated by its creator, Army Captain Richard Henry Pratt, it was designed and intended to be an 'education for extinction'[36] with a declared objective to 'kill the Indian, save the man'.[37] For over four decades, beginning in 1880, Indian children (as young as 4 years of age) were taken from their homes and families (often by force) and were transported to boarding schools, confined there, and held as 'captives' for a decade or more. At these 'schools', Indian children were subjected to malnutrition, overcrowding, forced labour, deficient medical care, overwork, corporal punishment, outright torture, physical violence, and sexual abuse. Some did not survive the experience. No longer needing to use genocidal warfare and outright violence, 'whites' used forced assimilation as a weapon in a new (but no less violent) form of warfare against Indian America.[38]

Disguised as a 'humanitarian' alternative, forced assimilation ultimately sought the continued social destruction of Native American communities and traditional Indian ways of life. In the end, the Early American settler state and its more 'progressive' citizens had concluded that the only way to 'save' the Indian was to 'destroy' him. In the latter part of the nineteenth century, the policy of 'Americanization' was a coercive policy of forced assimilation, a policy resting on the destruction of traditional Indian ways of life as well as the native peoples' 'Indianness'. However well-intentioned the 'whites' *may* have been, these policies meant cultural death for all Indians, and physical death for some.

Nazi Germany

Outright killing

Outright killing in the 'Nazi East' also took on several forms, many of which were very similar to the 'frontier violence' of the 'American West'. In the 'Wild East', there was 'exterminatory war' involving frontier massacres, mass shootings, and reprisal killings as part of the 'ethnic cleansing' of the new 'Aryan' *Lebensraum*; there was also deliberate and calculated destruction of indigenous villages and food supplies as part of strategies of 'total war' against both combatant and non-combatant 'native' populations. *SS Einsatzgruppen* task forces, regular *Wehrmacht* troops – under specific instructions from their officers – and local auxiliary police carried out so-called *Säuberungsaktionen* (cleansing actions) to 'clean' areas 'contaminated with partisans' and to render areas *judenrein* (clean of Jews).[39] In Poland, organized killing actions initially focused on the Polish elite – nobility, priests, and intellectuals – but also included Polish civilians who defended their villages and towns against the German invaders and who were suspected of anti-German activity; in the Soviet Union, organized killing actions targeted Jews, the Communist political elite, 'partisans' (soon to mean any 'Jew'), and any unarmed 'hostile civilians'. In the 'Nazi East', 'elite' SS task forces, police battalions, and 'ordinary' German *Wehrmacht* soldiers were daily killers of unarmed men, women, and children. 'Concentrated' in hundreds of small rural ghettos, most Jews were murdered in or near their *shtetls* or small towns.

In the 'Wild East', a series of orders and directives authorized the killing of largely unarmed civilian populations. The commander of the 4th Panzer Group, General Hoepner, told his unit, on 2 May 1941, that future warfare in the USSR was 'an essential stage in the existential battle of the German people' against the Slavs and Jewish Bolshevists and 'must be conducted with unheard of harshness'.[40] In the Barbarossa Decree of 13 May 1941, on the eve of the invasion of the Soviet Union, German troops were told that they '[were permitted] to defend themselves ruthlessly against every threat by the hostile civilian population'.[41] That same order instructed German forces that acts by 'hostile civilians' were to be dealt with 'on the spot with the most extreme measures, including annihilation of the attacker'; troops were also authorized to carry out 'collective reprisal measures' against civilian populations.[42] In a directive issued by the High Command of the 6th Army, on 10 July 1941, troops were ordered that 'civilians who are hostile in posture or action ... are to be executed as irregulars', as part of its declaration of war against the Russian civilian population.[43] A further decree issued by Hitler through the Armed Forces High Command, on 16 December 1942, ordered 'the most brutal means... against women and children also' and specifically forbade punishment of German troops for any excesses against 'native' non-combatant populations.[44] As a result of these (and other similar) orders, approximately 2 million Jewish civilians and more than 5 million non-Jewish civilians were murdered in the 'Wild East' between 1941 and 1944,[45] using the methods of 'colonial genocide'.

Depopulation/repopulation

In the Nazi-German case, settler–state plans for spatial expansion and racial purification envisaged aggressive policies of 'depopulation' and 'repopulation' of the newly acquired 'living space' for 'Aryan' settlement. As outlined in the GPO, the Nazi long-term vision for 'the East' was a radical and massive depopulation and repopulation scheme, which required the 'depopulation' and expulsion of tens of millions of Slavs (who would be forced into desolate areas, allowed to die of disease and starvation, or turned into slaves for the Nazi empire) and millions of Jews (who were to 'disappear altogether'), to make 'space' for 'repopulation' by ethnic German settlers.[46] Nazi notions of 'depopulation' were reflected in the so-called Hunger Plan (*Hungerpolitik*), a policy mandating the deliberate starvation of millions of Slavs in 'the East', in order to feed German soldiers as well as citizens of the Greater German Reich and German-occupied Western Europe. The various SS-created Jewish expulsion schemes were also genocidal in their implications, as was recognized at the time. Commenting on one of Adolf Eichmann's schemes, *The Times* of London noted on 24 October 1939 that 'to thrust 3 million Jews, relatively few of whom are agriculturalists, into the Lublin region and to force them to settle there would doom them to famine. That, perhaps, is the intention.'[47] Indeed, had a German military victory in 'the East' allowed any of these various Nazi depopulation schemes to be fully carried out, they most certainly would have been genocidal operations.[48]

Attrition

In the 'Wild East', the Nazis carried out an ambitious 'concentration' plan aimed at 'clearing' Jews from German-speaking areas, 'removing' them from the countryside, and 'concentrating' them in urban ghettos. In the ghettos, the Nazis intentionally sought to create inhuman conditions, where a combination of massive overcrowding, deliberate starvation, and outbreaks of typhus and cholera would drastically reduce

Jewish numbers through 'natural wastage'.[49] In the Nazi-German case, 'concentration' of Jews and 'Gypsies' was regarded as a 'temporary measure' in preparation for their ultimate mass migration and 'resettlement' further 'east'.[50] When the Nazis finally abandoned the notion of a 'territorial solution' to the 'Jewish question', the ghettos were emptied, and the inhabitants put on deportation trains to killing centres, sent to slave labour projects, or transported to concentration camps. Ultimately, the Jews of Poland (and Europe) were marked for murder, for had they remained in the ghettos of Eastern Europe they would surely have succumbed to the lethal conditions. The eastern ghettos were, in fact, 'slow extermination centers'.[51] For the Nazi leaders, in the end, 'slow' was not fast enough. Anxious to 'solve' the 'Jewish question' during the war, and with their military fortunes continuing to decline, they would soon opt for immediate and systematic mass murder.

Forced assimilation

In the 'Nazi East', German occupation policy was simply expressed as 'either we win the good blood that we can use and fit in with us or . . . we exterminate this blood'.[52] Rooted in Nazi racial ideology, Nazi occupation policy in 'the East' called for the forced removal to the Reich of non-German children deemed by the Nazis to be 'racially valuable' and able to provide the German people with a continuous source of 'desirable blood' to compensate for the enormous German losses of war. These children were 'racially selected' and were forcibly taken into German custody against their will. In practice, as administered by the SS, this programme amounted to 'child stealing' (*Kinderraub*) by the SS and the forced 'Germanization' (*Zwangsgermanisierung*) of thousands of Slavic children who were kidnapped from their homes, 'removed' from their families, transported to Germany, and then 'adopted' by German foster parents in the Reich.[53] Deemed 'Germanizable' children, Himmler and his minions sought out and laid claim to the indigenous Slavic 'children of good blood'; racially poor children (*schlechtrassig*) were left behind to meet 'their fate' with the older 'sub-human' people of 'the East'.

Genocidal acts

In both cases, prior colonial experience passed on a lethal legacy of 'exterminationist' violence and so-called 'extirpative war' to the Early American and the Nazi-German settler states, based on a similar colonial heritage of territorial expansion, settler colonization, and genocidal warfare. In the 'American West' and the 'Nazi East', both state and non-state actors perpetrated deliberate acts of systematic, 'exterminationist' violence against individual 'natives', as well as collective groups of indigenous peoples, on the 'frontier' peripheries of their respective western and eastern empires. For the most part, these genocidal acts took the form, in both cases, of mobile killing operations – whereby small groups or units carried out deliberate outright killing of indigenous civilian non-combatants and destruction of their villages and food supplies, as part of warfare against indigene warriors or partisans who resisted settler–state campaigns of conquest and colonization.

Early America

Colonial antecedents

Genocidal warfare against non-combatant Indian populations was part of a deadly legacy of settler-colonial policies and practices handed down to post-independence Early American settlers from their predecessors in pre-independence British Colonial America. In Colonial North America, as British 'settlement' and 'occupation' of the eastern seaboard expanded, genocide against Indian non-combatant populations sporadically erupted. During the three Anglo-Powhatan Wars in early seventeenth-century Virginia, settlers responded to Indian attacks with a policy of 'extermination' that included genocidal massacres – as well as the destruction of Powhatan towns, villages, and crops – driving the Powhatan tribes to extinction by 1685. Further north, in New England, English policy also used genocidal warfare to subdue and dispossess local Indian populations.[54] The Pequot War (1636–7), in particular, created a precedent for later genocidal wars against Native American communities.[55] In Colonial North America, (intentionally introduced?) disease[56] – acting as an invisible army – and genocidal warfare worked, in tandem, to 'reduce' Native American populations and to facilitate white 'settlement' on Indian lands. Indians were intentionally driven from their lands or reduced to quasi-slavery in a 'frontier' settlement process that was essentially genocidal.[57] Policies and practices of genocidal warfare in British Colonial America were transmitted directly to Early America settlers who emulated and practised these 'first ways of war' during the founding and expansion of the early American Republic.[58]

Mobile killing operations

In the history of Early America, there were three separate and distinct 'frontier zones', which followed the course of American western conquest and expansion: (1) the western borderlands of the original Atlantic seaboard 13 colonies (running from the western edges of the original coastal settlements to the eastern slope of the Appalachian Mountains); (2) the trans-Appalachian West (running from the western slope of the Appalachians to the eastern shore of the Mississippi River); and (3) the trans-Mississippi West (running from the Mississippi's western shore to the Pacific coastline). Over a century of relentless western expansion, Americans selectively (but widely) used genocidal warfare against Indian civilian populations within these 'frontier' zones – warfare that frequently involved acts of 'exterminationist' violence against Native Americans (regardless of sex or age) as part of conventional warfare against Indian warriors.

In the Early American case, 'ranging' by mobile killing units became a means to 'secure' the 'frontier' zones of empire, resulting in a 'large-scale privatization of war within American frontier communities'.[59] In the 'American West', horse-mounted frontier rangers helped subjugate Indian resistance to white settlement by fighting warriors on the battlefield and by withering, brutal attacks on Indian non-combatants and agricultural resources. During the more than three dozen 'Indian wars' between 1775 and 1890, regular army troops, volunteer militias, and rangers struck directly at the Indian enemy's greatest points of vulnerability: their villages, their fields, and their non-combatants – that is, women, children, infants, and elderly.[60] Both regular and irregulars units, in historian Al Cave's words, 'struck by stealth deep in enemy territory, taking few prisoners and inflicting maximum pain', often deliberately murdering neutral or 'friendly' allied Indians as well as 'hostiles'. In a uniquely American 'innovation', the use of 'scalp bounties' became an indiscriminate killing process that deliberately targeted Indian non-combatants (including women, children, and infants), as well as warriors.[61] In the Early American 'West', extreme violence and American nationhood, as well as American continental empire-building, progressed hand in hand.[62]

Revolutionary war

During the American War for Independence (1775–83), a brutal 'frontier war' between white Anglo-American settlers and Indians (allied with the British) erupted on the southern, western, and New York 'frontiers' of the rebellious colonies. Obscured within the Revolutionary War's broader history, this frontier war was at once genocidal and decisive for the Revolutionary War's course and outcome, as well as for the American nation's subsequent history. It was a 'racial war without mercy' along the colonies' western 'frontier': a war that paralleled and, at times, intersected the largely conventional war between American and British troops along the eastern seaboard. In these 'frontier' campaigns and battles, most Indian victims were non-combatants – that is, women, old men, and children – who were not spared by the 'white' settler colonists.[63] In a sentiment widely shared in 'the West', 'frontier' general George Rogers Clark – whose brother William, along with Meriwether Lewis, would later lead the famous Jefferson-sponsored 'western' expedition – declared that he 'would never spare a[n] [Indian] man, women, or child ... on whom he could lay his hands'.[64]

On General George Washington's orders, Continental Army and militia units attacked Indian towns and villages along the New York, Pennsylvania, and Ohio 'frontiers', with the goal of destroying 'native' food sources, livestock, homes, fields, and orchards.[65] In the Revolutionary era, these so-called 'burnt earth' tactics (sometimes called 'feedfight') aimed at the intentional destruction of the Indian subsistence economy and the deliberate production of mass starvation,[66] leaving the Indian survivors without shelter or food. Typical of these 'frontier' military operations was the Sullivan–Clinton Campaign of 1779. General Washington, in his orders to Sullivan, ordered the 'total destruction and devastation of [Indian] settlements'.[67] Accordingly, a combined force of 4,500 Continental regulars, rangers, and scalp hunters attacked the Seneca Indians (allied with the British); American forces burned hundreds of houses and destroyed thousands of acres of crops. As one Onondaga chief noted, the Americans had burned his town and 'put to death all the Women & Children, excepting some of the Young Women whom they carried away for the use of their Soldiers & were afterwards put to death in a more shameful manner'.[68] In the eyes of the Patriot leaders and white settlers on the 'frontier', these killings were justified as reciprocal killings for Indian genocidal massacres by Loyalist rangers and Indians against Patriot settlements on the 'frontier'. In the aftermath of the vicious border warfare, *all* Indians, whether 'hostile' or 'friendly', became, in American eyes, 'merciless savages' whose bloodletting against 'frontier' whites justified subsequent assaults on Indian lands and cultures.[69]

Trans-Appalachian West

During their final 'conquest' of the trans-Appalachian West, newly independent white American settler colonists (now 'freed' from British imperial restraint, such as it was) continued genocidal warfare and mobile killing operations against Indian tribes in the 'frontier' zone between

the Appalachian Mountains and the Mississippi River – genocidal campaigns aimed at driving the Indians from lands on the western side of
the Appalachian range. In the 1790s, during the 'Indian wars' of the
Federal period, regular army forces and rangers launched direct attacks
on Indian agricultural resources and non-combatant populations on the
'frontiers' of Tennessee, western Georgia, and the Upper Ohio Valley.[70]
Again, in the 1810s, during 'Indian wars' in the Old Northwest (present-
day Indiana and Illinois) and the Old Southwest (present-day Alabama
and Mississippi), settlers took up arms against combatants and non-
combatants to quash Indian resistance to white settlement and compel
them to accept American conquest. Andrew Jackson's war against hostile Creeks (in present-day Alabama and Mississippi) regularly attacked
undefended Indian villages occupied only by women, children, and old
men (while the warriors were in the field). During these campaigns, soldiers killed indiscriminately, regardless of age and sex.[71] A member of
a rangers' militia described the last fighting in Alabama on 25 March
1837 as an 'indiscriminate slaughter of women and children, old men
and warriors', resulting in the death of about 150 Indians. No Indian
warriors, he noted, were made prisoner, and the 'few' Indian women
and children who survived 'were made slave by their captors'.[72]

Trans-Mississippi West

In the trans-Mississippi West, deliberate acts of genocidal 'exterminationist' violence were carried out by a combination of regular US Army
troops, local militias, and volunteers over a period of half a century,
from 1840 to 1890. In Texas, the government pursued a deliberate
strategy and policy of ethnic cleansing to 'clear' Texas of indigenous
Indian and Hispanic populations. Rangers attacked Indian villages filled
with women and children and killed indiscriminately, exterminating
entire villages.[73] After the discovery of gold in 1848, settlers and miners
flooded California – which officially became a state in 1850. In short
order, both government officials and local newspapers began calling
for a 'war of extermination' against local Indian tribes. Over the next
decade, the state of California openly pursued a policy of enslaving
Indian children and exterminating their parents, in a series of mass
killings conducted by US regular forces, as well as local militias and
volunteers.[74] Genocidal massacres also took place on the Great Plains
west of the Mississippi, with Sand Creek (1864) and Wounded Knee
(1890) the most commented on at the time and the most frequently
mentioned in today's scholarly and popular literature. On the Great

Plains, US forces 'frequently employed the genocidal massacre as a war tactic, against unarmed non-combatants, women and children'.[75]

Newspapers in both 'the West' and 'the East' regularly reported acts of 'exterminationist' violence to their readers. On 18 June 1860, the *San Francisco Bulletin* reported that, in Humboldt County, California, a group of 50–60 white men had recently attacked the Digger tribes ('known as friendly Indians') at night ('when the [Indian] men were known to be absent'). The 'white' attackers fell on '[Indian] women and children, and deliberately slaughtered them, one and all', in a series of simultaneous attacks on several villages. 'Fire-arms were scarcely used', the *Bulletin* noted, 'the work being done with hatchets'. It was 'estimated that 240 were slaughtered in a single night'. The paper also reported a 'theatre of atrocities nearly parallel' in Mendocino, where 'regularly organized bodies of armed men attacked the settlements of friendly Indians... and murdered them in like manner, except that fire-arms were used and not hatchets'. In this case, as well, Indian men, women, and children were 'massacred'.[76] On 23 June 1867, a *New York Times* editorial observed that settlers in a small town in Colorado Territory had recently subscribed $5,000 to a fund 'for the purpose of *buying Indian scalps* (with $25 each to be paid for scalps *with the ears on*)' and that the market for Indian scalps 'is not affected by age or sex'. In addition, the *Times* reported, volunteers had recently been equipped (to act under General Sherman) in an organized 'hunt for red-skins'. While condemning the 'frontier settlers', the *Times* reserved its harshest criticism for the federal 'Government, which has for years sanctioned such treatment of the Indians'.[77] While often criticizing federal Indian policymakers, the *Times* recognized that the treatment of Native Americans in the 'American West' (featuring the intentional destruction of Indian villages, as well as the purposeful slaughter of non-combatant Indian men, women, and children) only paralleled patterns that began in the 'American East' a century earlier.[78]

Nazi Germany

Colonial antecedents

In the late nineteenth century, as noted earlier (Chapter 4), German South West Africa was imagined as a settler colony for increasing numbers of 'white' German settlers. After 20 years of German colonial rule (which began in 1884), a war erupted in South West Africa (1904–8) between 'white' German settlers and Herero and Nama indigenous peoples – a war in which non-combatants (that is, women and children) were seen as legitimate targets. Understood by the German commander on the ground as a 'race war', what had started as a limited war ultimately became a war of 'annihilation' and 'genocide'. During the war in South West Africa, indigenous men, women, and children were shot, thousands died of thirst after being driven into the desert, and hundreds died of deliberate neglect in the 'concentration camps' (as they were called at the time).[79] In a 1906 book on the ongoing war in South West Africa, *Schutztruppe* Captain Maximilian Bayer claimed that 'only the strong have a right to continue to exist' and that 'the weak and purposeless will perish in favour of the strong... like, for example, the end of the Indian Americans because they were without purpose in the continued development of the world'.[80] Likewise, the Herero and Nama of German South West Africa were, in this view, 'without purpose' and would 'perish'.

While most historians would agree that the German colonial war against the Herero and Nama constituted 'genocide', a controversy has broken out over the question of whether or not there are any similarities or continuities between the genocide in South West Africa and later Nazi genocidal policies.[81] In retrospect, as recent scholarship convincingly demonstrates, the German experience in South West Africa was a crucial precursor to Third Reich imperialism, Nazi colonialism, and Nazi genocide,[82] as well as an important link between colonialism and the later Nazi policy of extermination in 'the East'.[83] Crucially, notions of *Lebensraum*, genocidal rhetoric, 'annihilation war', and the use of 'concentration camps' were transmitted across time and adopted by the Nazis in the twentieth century.[84]

Mobile killing operations

The mass shootings of civilians, by mobile killing units, was used to 'secure' conquered territories in the eastern *Lebensraum* and was applied in a relatively similar fashion in Poland and the USSR.[85] In the 'Wild East', the leaders of the SS and the *Wehrmacht* had a variety of instruments of genocide available for 'special tasks' against the civilian population, including SS *Einsatzgruppen*, special police battalions, brigades of *Waffen-SS*, regular *Wehrmacht* units, and *Wehrmacht* Military Police and Special Field Police.[86] In the 'Nazi East', mobile killing operations were the primary responsibility of the *Einsatzgruppen* – special SS task forces comprising between 600 and 1,000 men each, operating behind the German lines and specifically targeting non-combatants.[87] By definition and scope, the goals of the mobile killing units were limited, their principal tasks being to 'clean' the occupied rear (behind the

advancing German army) and to terrorize the local indigenous populations into acquiescence to German rule. Under the pretext of alleged
killings of ethnic Germans in the new 'living space', they had a licence
to kill anyone suspected of sabotage or anti-German activity. By grossly
exaggerating or simply fabricating incidents of sporadic violence against
ethnic Germans on the 'frontier', these special task forces often found
eager 'helpers' among the German ethnic settlers (*Volksdeutsche*).[88]

In Poland, the *Einsatzgruppen* were responsible for securing areas
behind the advancing German army, as well as for the 'liquidation'
of the Polish political leadership, intelligentsia, clergy, and nobility.
This 'orgy of atrocities' against the indigenous Polish leadership classes
and against Polish Jews, amounted to an all-out 'ethnic cleansing' programme and foreshadowed the full-scale genocide yet to come. Overall,
the *SS Einsatzgruppen* operations in Poland established a platform for
the killing of civilians on a much larger scale, to commence with the
planned June 1941 attack on the Soviet Union.[89]

Einsatzgruppen targets in the Soviet Union included Jews, Gypsies, the
disabled, and Soviet officials (including Communist Party or state functionaries and activists). Initially, they targeted mainly adult male Jews.
Starting in August 1941 (based on verbal instructions from Himmler to
'widen' the slaughter), women and children (seen as possible 'avengers'
of the future) were generally included in the massacres. In the Soviet
Union, the *Einsatzgruppen* conducted two gigantic sweeps in a wide campaign of extermination: the first sweep was conducted – mainly by the
Einsatzgruppen – during June–December 1941, and the second sweep
began in the autumn of 1941 and continued throughout most of 1942 –
with more participation by army personnel and police battalions of
the German Order Police, augmented by local militia auxiliaries.[90] During the Barbarossa Campaign, *Wehrmacht* commanders told their troops
that 'the Jews' were the 'spiritual leaders and carriers of Bolshevism and
the Communist idea' and were to be 'exterminated'.[91] These mobile
killing operations were justified as necessary measures in the 'partisan
struggle' and, later on, as revenge for Allied bombings of German cities.
Like the industrial factory-style gassings in Poland (after 1941), colonial-
style mass shootings in the 'Nazi East' were a form of systematic mass
murder. As historian Wendy Lower convincingly argues, the legacy of
the Nazi racial-imperial project is Babi Yar (colonial-style mass shootings) as much as Auschwitz (modern industrial killings).[92] Up until 1942,
Nazi violence and killing in 'the East' 'used nothing more modern than
a rifle'.[93] In the towns and villages of the 'Nazi East', it was, indeed, a
'Holocaust by bullets'.[94]

Industrial killing

Between September 1939 and December 1941, Nazi genocidal measures in the 'Wild East' had reflected and mirrored Early American nineteenth-century settler-colonial practices – that is, face-to-face shootings, forced relocations, and destruction of villages and food resources (causing death due to disease, starvation, malnutrition, and exposure). Out of concern about the physical and psychological impact on the perpetrators of the mass shootings, the Nazi leadership looked to discover a more efficient (and less stressful) method of mass murder, as well as a way to streamline the killing operations. Utilization of killing centres with 'industrial' methods soon emerged as their method of choice. Located in the 'frontier' lands of western Poland, the killing centres marked the transformation of mass murder into a dehumanized, bureaucratic, industrial process. Beginning in 1942, the Nazi genocide in 'the East' became a full-scale 'total genocide', aiming at 'industrial genocide' of Jews in extermination factories. Contrary to popular – and some scholarly – conception, nonetheless, Nazi extermination centres complemented, rather than replaced, the mass shootings – an intimate 'colonial method' that continued until the war's end.[95] The 'conveyor belt' industrial killing of Jews marked a sharp break with the settler-colonial practices of the nineteenth century that had, up until then, shaped Nazi policies and practices against indigenous populations in 'the East'. In the history of world genocide, the Nazi killing centres were, indeed, as Holocaust historian Raul Hilberg concluded, 'unprecedented': an assembly-line process with 'no prototype, no administrative ancestor'.[96]

In letters from the Eastern front and during visits home, German soldiers spoke frankly about the mass shootings of largely unarmed Jewish and Slavic civilians in 'the East'. Knowledge about the gassings in the death camps, however, was much more imprecise or the object of vague rumour – suggesting that the Nazis wanted to keep the systematic murder of the Jews from the German people. In the Nazi metropole, 'ordinary' Germans were allowed to 'imagine' Babi Yar, but they were not allowed to 'imagine' Auschwitz.[97]

Schema of genocide

Both the Early American and Nazi-German settler-colonial projects were similar national projects of intended empire-building, motivated by the identical, perceived settler–state need for more 'living space' for agricultural settlement. In the Early American case, the vision of a continental *Lebensraum* provided the motive for American political leaders to tolerate genocide, by effectively giving settlers, militias, and regular army troops in 'the West' carte blanche to wage war against 'hostile' Native American non-combatant populations (as they deemed necessary). In the Nazi-German case, the requirements of Nazi racial-ideological warfare provided the motive for Nazi leaders to order genocidal onslaughts against Jews and Slavs in 'the East'. In both cases, 'ordinary Americans' and 'ordinary Germans' acted in a dual capacity as agents of empire and (when needed) instruments of extreme political violence and genocide, and, in both cases, they were assisted by 'native' operatives recruited from local subject populations. In the 'American West' and the 'Nazi East', genocide and other forms of extreme violence against largely unarmed civilian populations were justified as necessary measures of self-defence or pre-emption. In the Early American 'war for America' and the Nazi-German 'wars for *Lebensraum*', genocidal violence against indigenous civilian non-combatant populations was seen as a legitimate form of warfare; in both settler-colonial contexts, genocide on the 'frontiers' of empire became, in the eyes of the settler state and its agents, an ordinary sequence of attack and retaliation in war. In the broader view, genocide was justified, in both cases, as an essential pre-emptive measure to prevent genocide against the settler state and/or its agents on the ground.

Early America

Intent and motive

From a political and economic standpoint, the objective of US Indian policy was to 'clear' Indians from lands coveted by white settler farmers. From a military standpoint, the policy goal was to reduce Indian resistance to white settler encroachment, so that Native Americans no longer presented a viable military threat to American western expansion and settlement. In pursuing these multiple objectives, the US government did not mandate or order genocide; it did, however, sanction it, allow it, tolerate it, or practise it – sometimes when other tactics failed – as part of an intentional and ruthless policy of conquest, dispossession, and expansion in the 'American West'. In Early America, the US government also carried out an intended policy of ethnic cleansing to 'remove' Native Americans from settler lands; a policy that was genocidal in both its implications and consequences for American Indians. As one scholar recently noted, government officials effectively granted American settlers, militias, and regular army troops 'a license to commit murder on an ethnic basis' against Indians.[98] Motivated by greed and a hatred of Indians, many white settlers openly and eagerly carried out genocidal 'exterminationist' assaults against Native Americans in their lust for Indian lands and natural resources. In the Early American context, genocide – whether or not intended or desired by policymakers – resulted from sustained and purposeful actions undertaken by the US government and/or its agents – actions aimed at the social destruction and dispossession of Native American communities through a variety of 'eliminatory' strategies, including mass killing, forced 'relocation', and 'concentration'. Packaged as benevolent programmes of Indian uplift, policies such as 'removal' and 'concentration' were not murderous in intent; nonetheless, they resulted in the deaths of thousands of Indians from exposure, fatigue, starvation, and disease.

Genocidal agency

In the 'American West', both state and non-state actors practised sporadic genocide (when it suited their purposes) as part of a continuing government strategy to 'secure' the new 'living space', to destroy Native American communities, and to 'enforce' US Indian policy. Acting in a dual capacity as agents of empire and instruments of occasional extreme political violence, 'ordinary Americans' on the frontier – including territorial governors, militias, army regulars, reservation agents, settlers, and local vigilantes – became direct genocidal agents, both collectively and individually, as part of actions and policies aimed at 'clearing' Native Americans from the white settler 'living space'. Often settlers took matters 'into their own hands', when – in their view – the US government and its armed forces did not act thoroughly or ruthlessly enough against the 'native savages'. Throughout the conquest and expansion of the young nation's growing 'living space', regular army troops – often supported by 'volunteers' and specially recruited 'native' operatives – carried out genocidal warfare against 'enemy' Indian non-combatants as part of a dual 'War for America' and 'War Against Indian America'. A 'friendly fraternal feeling and a certain professional pride', said *The New York Times*, led army officers 'to uphold and approve' the 'massacre' of Indians, without regard to age or sex.[99] *Contra* the dominant historical narrative, the US 'state' was not merely an onlooker at, or entirely absent from, the slaughter of Native Americans. It was often an active – if sometimes reluctant – sponsor, organizer, and/or participant.

Legitimation

For both policymakers in the metropole, as well as for settlers on the 'frontier' peripheries of the American empire, genocidal violence against Native American communities and non-combatants was seen as a legitimate form of warfare against an 'enemy' who threatened the lives of white settler colonists, as reciprocal violence and reprisals for Indian resistance to white settlement, and as a required response to Indian 'frontier atrocities'. Writing to General William Sherman, General Philip Sheridan rationalized that 'if a[n] [Indian] village is attacked and women and children killed, the responsibility is not with the soldiers but with the [Indian] people whose crime necessitated the attack'.[100] For their part, white settlers in the 'American West' legitimized genocide and 'extermination', in their minds, as justified and legitimate policies of self-defence against Indian killers of white women and children. As historian Jacob P. Dunn told his readers in 1886, the killing of Indian women and children was justified by 'vengeance' and by the need to 'dampen' the enthusiasm of Indian warriors to attack white settlements and to resist American western expansion.[101] Begun by the early seventeenth-century Puritans, the 'nits make lice' rationale for killing Indian children was an Indian-war standard throughout the eighteenth and nineteenth centuries.[102] Policies with genocidal implications – such as forced 'removal' and 'concentration' – were always presented by policymakers as a basis for Indian 'survival' and as acceptable alternatives to a 'war of extermination' against Native Americans. Even among those who advocated 'peaceful' solutions to the 'Indian question', policies of 'removal' and forced assimilation were justified as 'humanitarian' alternatives to 'outright extermination' of 'the natives'. When eastern 'humanitarians' criticized acts of 'exterminationist' violence in 'the West', they were reminded that westerners were merely following historical precedent. In a 5 July 1867 letter to *The New York Times*, Mr O. J. Hollister, a resident of Colorado visiting New York City, reminded readers that the original settlers of the eastern states set 'the example' and that the current western idea of ' "extermination" originated in "the East"; a view with which the *Times'* editorial writer concurred. 'Our forefathers', noted the writer, 'did many things which will forever be a reproach to their memories.'[103]

Statistics of death

By the end of the nineteenth century, the number of Native Americans in the 'American West' (by the best estimates) had been drastically reduced, from an estimated 600,000 in 1800 to about 250,000 in 1900. Their radical numerical decline was brought about by disease (including alcoholism); periodic genocidal warfare; intentional 'depopulation events' (that is, 'removal' and 'relocation'); and intended destruction of Indian villages, food supplies, and ways of life (resulting in death by malnutrition, exposure, and starvation). These four 'general causes' closely 'interacted with one another', as anthropologist Russell Thornton notes in his demographic history of American Indians.[104] By the US government's own admission, in the 1894 Census, an estimated 53,500 Indians – men, women, and children – were killed during more than three dozen 'Indian wars' in the period 1775–1890, based on the number of bodies found by whites (adjusted by an additional 50 per cent, since, as the Bureau noted, Indians often carried away and secreted the bodies of their dead).[105] We will, of course, never know the exact numbers; nor will we ever know how many Indian deaths are attributable to each of the individual modalities of extreme political violence. What we do know is that the estimated 350,000 'reduction' in the American Indian population during the first 100 years of the nation's existence was due to the effects of genocidal Early American settler-colonial policies and practices – policies and practices that aimed at the deliberate destruction of Native American communities and ways of life in the 'white' settler 'living space' of the 'American West' – at whatever the cost in Indian lives or cruel suffering.

Nazi Germany

Intent and motive

The original Nazi intention was to 'remove' the Jews from the Greater German Reich by 'voluntary' emigration or 'forced' expulsion. With the policy of conquest and expansion in the 'Wild East' – and control of over vast numbers of more Jews – however, 'removal' and 'expulsion' became impossible without genocide, whether by slave labour, malnutrition, disease, shooting, or gassing.[106] Hitler's ideological mission to 'obtain' *Lebensraum* in 'the East' and to create a racially pure Nazi continental empire 'cleansed' of 'alien' racial 'enemies' and 'unwanted' 'native' populations, provided both the driving force and motive behind the Nazi genocidal onslaught against Jews and Slavs in the 'Wild East'. Crucially, in Hitler's mind, the desire for German 'living space' became linked to the crusade against Jews and Slavic *Untermenschen* ('sub-humans') in 'the East'. Fuelled by anti-Jewish and anti-Slavic prejudice (radicalized by the Nazis), racial-ideological warfare – embedded in the wars for *Lebensraum* in 'the East' – provided the context and motive for killing Jews and Slavs.[107] To be sure, the wars for *Lebensraum* in 'the East' had to use historian Ian Kershaw's phrases, an 'inbuilt genocidal component', making genocide an 'intrinsic part' of the German military campaign in the 'Nazi East'.[108] Central to the acquisition and settlement of the new *Lebensraum* was the need to 'clear' 'unwanted' *Ostjuden* and Slavic indigenous populations from intended settler lands – a policy that was genocidal in both its implications and consequences for the 'natives'. Under conditions of 'total war', Nazi plans for 'Germanic settlement' and 'ethnic cleansing' – even if they only met with limited success – had murderous consequences for Jewish and non-Jewish civilian populations in the occupied eastern territories.

Genocidal agency

In the Nazi-German case, genocide was organized by the higher echelons of the Nazi leadership. These organizers of genocide were what Michael Mann calls 'real Nazis' – that is, ideological and violent careerists who were radical Nazis strongly committed to Hitler's expansionist goals and to National Socialist racial ideology. Among the perpetrators of Nazi genocide, 'real Nazis' formed a nucleus of hard-core perpetrators, reinforced by a shared ideology, which eagerly carried out Nazi genocidal policy in 'the East'. Many of these 'real Nazis', Mann notes, were disproportionately drawn from German territories lost after the First World War or from the eastern border provinces of Germany itself. Genocide on the scale of the Nazi genocide, however, required more manpower – an 'army of perpetrators'.[109] In the Nazi-German case, 'ordinary Germans' from all levels of German society became agents of genocide. Schooled in Nazi racial ideology, 'ordinary Germans' in the *Wehrmacht* and in the Order Police security battalions, embroiled in a savage war in the 'Wild East', often became casual perpetrators of genocide in the killing fields and killing sites of the 'Nazi East', driven by both hierarchical and peer pressures of conformity and discipline, dislike of Slavs and Jews, and a sense of comradeship that made them eager to 'retaliate' against 'enemy' non-combatant civilian populations.[110] Ethnic German settlers in 'the East' formed paramilitary units (known as *Selbstschutz*) and worked closely with the SS. And finally, some Slavs collaborated with the Nazi invaders, joining in attacks on their Jewish neighbours or joining local police and auxiliaries to 'help' the Nazis murder Jews.

Legitimation

German leader Adolf Hitler saw 'war' as providing the perfect cover and legitimation for accomplishing long-standing ideological aims.[111] During the Second World War, the Nazis portrayed the 'total war' in 'the East' as a struggle for national survival, which legitimized brutal 'methods' of warfare against Slavic racial and ideological 'enemies' and against 'the Jews' (the perceived fundamental 'enemy' and the true protagonist in the war). In the case of the Reich Jews, Nazi radical antisemitism justified and legitimized the leap from persecution to genocide, while in the case of the Slavs and the *Ostjuden*, the requirements of 'living space' for German settlement in 'the East' justified genocide against these 'inferior', 'unwanted', 'native' populations.[112]

As news of the mass shootings in the 'Nazi East' filtered back to the Reich, Goebbels' propaganda underlings presented the killings as legitimate retaliation for the alleged massacres of ethnic Germans by Slavs and Jewish Bolshevists and against 'the Jews' who had convinced the Allies to carry out the 'terror bombing' of German cities. Indeed, after 1939, according to the Nazi-constructed narrative, a murderous, international Jewish conspiracy – united to execute a war of extermination against the German *Volk* – required the 'extermination' and 'annihilation' (*Ausrottung* and *Vernichtung*) of the 'Jewish race' in Europe. Had Hitler not acted pre-emptively, the argument went, the Bolsheviks and Jews would most certainly have massacred German civilians.[113] To support this notion, Goebbels and his propaganda minions described the invasion of Russia as Hitler's legitimate action to pre-empt an imminent Soviet attack on German 'living space'.[114] In his Posen speech to an SS group leader meeting, on 4 October 1943, Himmler asserted that the Nazis had acted with a moral right and duty to the German people 'to destroy this [Jewish] people which wanted to destroy us'.[115] In the 'Wild East', the killing of non-combatant men, women, children, and the elderly was also justified to *Wehrmacht* troops as a legitimate act of self-defence.[116] During visits to 'the East', Himmler told SS leaders that Jewish men, women, and children were to be shot and that young children, if left alive, 'could later take revenge'.[117] In the eyes of the Nazi leadership and those many 'ordinary' Germans seduced by Nazi propaganda, the Nazi genocide of Jews and Slavs was an act of fully justified retaliation as well as a policy of justified self-defence.

Statistics of death

Nazi genocide in 'the East', it is estimated, took the lives of between 5 and 6 million Jews and at least 8 million Slavic non-combatants.

During the Nazi Holocaust, over 3 million Jewish victims (about 60 per cent of the total) are thought to have died in unprecedented 'industrial killings' at the extermination centres in Poland. Colonial practices of death and destruction caused the death of the other 40 per cent: about 1.5 million were shot to death in open-air shootings during mobile killing operations in the 'Wild East'; more than 900,000 died in eastern ghettos or in concentration, transit, and labour camps; and additional tens of thousands died during deportation or on death marches in the war's final days.[118] In Poland, some 3 million non-Jewish Poles and 3 million Polish Jews were victims of Nazi warfare and genocide; in the Soviet Union, thousands of commissars, at least 2 million Jews, and more than 5 million non-Jewish Slavic civilians were murdered between 1941 and 1944,[119] using essentially 'frontier' modalities of violence. As two leading Holocaust scholars recently argued, given enough time, '[the Nazis and their collaborators] would have subjected the Slav peoples to the machinery of death we call the Holocaust'.[120]

Similarities, differences, and links

In both Early America and Nazi Germany, 'genocide' occurred[121] when political leaders, perceiving the integrity and success of their respective national projects of continental expansion and settler colonization to be threatened, sought to remedy the situation by the systematic, *en masse* 'elimination' of 'out-groups' and 'native' populations from metropolitan and colonial 'living space'. In both cases, the Early American and the Nazi-German respective political leaderships sought to 'eliminate' their 'alien' 'out-groups' and 'unwanted' populations until they were no longer perceived to be a threat (in the case of Native Americans and Eastern European Slavs) or *in toto* (in the case of European Jewry).

Colonial antecedents, in both cases, provided a lethal legacy of genocidal violence to the Early American and Nazi-German settler states, whose own genocidal acts featured mobile killing operations whereby small groups or units carried out deliberate killing of indigenous civilian non-combatants and destruction of their villages and food supplies. In both the 'American West' and the 'Nazi East', genocide became intrinsically linked to the 'acquisition' of new 'living space' for agricultural settlement. In both cases, a comparable genocidal dynamic shared strikingly similar preconditions (political elite obsessions with territorial expansion, racial and ethnic prejudice, settler colonization, and agrarian idealism), causalities (settler-colonial policies and practices aimed at the 'elimination' of indigenes from the settler 'living space'), and triggers or immediate catalysts (settler-colonial wars for *Lebensraum* in the 'American West' and the 'Nazi East'). Both cases, moreover, featured similar colonial modalities of violence (including organized killing, a declared policy of 'depopulation' of the indigenes and 'repopulation' by settler colonists, 'slow death' by attrition, and forced assimilation of 'selected' indigene children by 'Americanization' or 'Germanization'). In both cases, genocide reflected common schema of motive (an identical perceived settler–state need for more 'living space' for agricultural settlement), intent (the intention to 'eliminate' the indigenes from the settler *Lebensraum*), genocidal agency ('ordinary Americans' and 'ordinary Germans' acting in a dual capacity of agents of empire and instruments of extreme political violence), and legitimation (justification of extreme political violence against largely unarmed civilian indigene populations as necessary measures of self-defence or pre-emption in the wars for settler 'living space'). In the 'American West' and the 'Nazi East', both state and non-state actors carried out exterminationist assaults, in the form of mobile killing operations, against the indigenous inhabitants of the newly acquired settler *Lebensraum*. And, in both cases, 'concentration' centres – whether called 'reservations' or 'ghettos' – facilitated the 'removal' of 'inferior', 'unwanted' populations away from the 'living space' of the 'superior', dominant societies (to await 'their fate').

Yet despite these many similarities, there were also important differences between the two settler-colonial genocides: differences mainly of scale, intensity, and duration. In Early America, genocidal violence 'reduced' the number of Native Americans from about 600,000 in 1800 to about 250,000 in 1900. The Nazi genocidal onslaught in 'the East' between 1939 and 1945 took the lives of between 5 and 6 million Jews and at least 8 million Slavic civilian non-combatants; had the Nazis won the war against the Soviet Union, the toll of civilian casualties would undoubtedly have been even higher. On the whole, the level and intensity of violence was much greater in the 'Nazi East' than in the 'American West'. While Early American 'genocide' featured small-scale massacres of non-combatants, Nazi-German 'genocide' featured large-scale, intensely murderous campaigns against civilian populations. In addition, Early American extreme political violence against Native Americans was sporadic; by contrast, SS, police, and *Wehrmacht* units in 'the East' practised genocide on a daily basis (with daily body counts often in the thousands). In Early America, the state and its citizen settlers carried out a sustained campaign of extreme political violence against Native Americans for almost a century. The Nazi genocide in 'the

East', however, lasted only six years (ending with Germany's military defeat in 1945). Unlike the American settler-colonial genocide, the Nazi colonial genocide became an industrial genocide, a form of genocide unprecedented in history (before or since).

Nonetheless, these differences of scale, intensity, and duration were, I would argue, more a function of the historical contingencies of each case, rather than differences of sponsor, organizer, or perpetrator intent. Prior to American independence, disease, sporadic genocidal warfare, and 'slow death' by attrition in the three centuries of European expansion throughout North America had 'reduced' the Native American population from an estimated 5 million to around 600,000.[122] Even without this demographic collapse, there is no reason to believe – based on the historical record or on the trajectory and demographics of American 'settlement' – that the Early American settler state and its white citizens would have hesitated to take whatever steps were necessary to ensure the success of their nation-state and its empire-building project.[123] Likewise, in the 'Nazi East', historical contingency acted to end the Nazi genocidal onslaughts, with the defeat of Nazi Germany in the Second World War. Had Nazi Germany defeated Russia in 'the East', however, it is highly likely that genocide against indigenous populations would have continued for decades, as a victorious Nazi Germany would have carried out its plans for 'cleansing' the *Lebensraum* of 'unwanted' indigenous populations, for subsequent settlement by 'Aryan' Germans.[124]

In the topography of 'frontier genocide', the 'American West' and the 'Nazi East' shared similar mental pictures among both perpetrators and victims. For radical Nazis committed to Hitler's dual goal of 'space' and 'race', for instance, Nazi imaginings of 'reservations' as a 'solution' to the 'Jewish question' echoed similar spatial strategies on Indian 'reservations' in the nineteenth-century 'American West'. And, after the war, one of the few Jewish survivors of the Treblinka extermination centre recalled the town itself as being similar to a 'frontier' settlement in the American 'Wild West'.[125]

Conclusion

There was nothing inevitable about the actual outcomes of the Early American and Nazi-German respective national projects in 'the West' and 'the East'. As we have seen, alternative courses of action (understood at the time as realistic) did exist in both cases – alternative courses that might well have led to different outcomes in the 'American West' and the 'Nazi East'. Plausible counterfactuals exist in both cases.[1] Both historical experiences, in fact, lend themselves to plausible (and thought-provoking) counterfactual glimpses.

In the Early American case, we may ask: What if disease had not decimated many Native American communities in advance of white 'settlement'? What if American political leaders had sincerely embraced a generalized 'territorial solution'? Or what if they had ordered a general 'exterminatory war'? Without the pre-1783 demographic collapse of Indian communities, largely from disease and warfare, it is possible that the 'middle ground' of Indian–white accommodation and coexistence – based on Indians outnumbering whites – could have continued west of the Appalachians, perhaps rendering future white 'settlement' more gradual and more peaceful (as envisaged by the 'Founding Fathers'). In the first decades of the nineteenth century, had ideas for a western 'Indian territory' been implemented *and enforced* by the US government, it is possible that an 'Indian country' could have blocked, or at least slowed, the white flood of 'settlement' into the trans-Missouri West, allowing an indisputable safe haven for Indian residence on historic Indian lands. Had American political leaders ordered a general exterminatory war, as many 'westerners' wanted, the reality of the 'American West' may have approximated Hitler's vision of 'shooting down' the 'Redskins' (without the need for 'reservations').

In the Nazi-German case, we may ask: What if Darré, rather than Himmler, had been appointed 'settlement commissar'? What if the Nazis had won a quick military victory in 'the East' (as Hitler expected)? Or what if the Germans had treated 'the natives' not as 'Redskins', as Hitler insisted, but as 'allies' in the 'liberation' of these lands from the Soviet tyranny, as Rosenberg's notion of *Helfer statt Heloten* (Helpers instead of Helots) suggested? Darré's appointment as 'settlement commissar' may have resulted in a more limited and gradual (and perhaps less violent) form of eastern 'settlement', had he been able to convince Hitler of the wisdom of this approach. Had Russia been defeated as quickly as Hitler hoped, it is quite possible, as has been suggested, that the 'instant killing' of Jews via gassing might not have occurred and that 'slow death' via attrition – as part of a more generalized 'territorial solution' – might have been the agreed 'final solution' for Europe's Jews.[2] In the event, the destruction of European Jewry would have been one part of a successfully implemented General Plan East, which would have subjected tens of millions of Slavs to the full wrath and force of the machinery of destruction we call the Holocaust.[3] Given the dislike of many Slav nationalists for Stalin's Bolshevism, it is likely that many would have joined Rosenberg's proposed anti-Communist alliance, as independent, non-Bolshevik states under German control; with Germany leading this anti-Communist coalition, the prospects of defeating Stalin and the Red Army militarily – or, at least, of achieving a stalemate on the Eastern front – would likely have been much greater.

By the juxtaposition of these two historical experiences – and by viewing them through the corrective lenses of imperialism, colonialism, and genocide – we have uncovered disquieting underlying patterns of empirical similarity between the 'American West' and the 'Nazi East'. Both the Early American and Nazi-German respective projects in 'the West' and 'the East' were national projects: that is, they were led by the nation-state, they were widely supported by the nation's elites (as well as by many 'ordinary' citizens), and they commanded substantial national resources. Both the Early American and Nazi-German expansionist projects were intended and planned projects of settler colonialism. In both cases, these projects featured a 'land grab' of indigenous 'space', they required 'occupation' of indigene lands and 'displacement' of indigenous peoples, they reflected a sustained institutional tendency to 'eliminate' the 'natives', and they contained an inherent genocidal imperative (sadly realized in both cases). In their common patterns, logics, and pathologies, these two cases are prime examples of settler colonialism (fully realized in the

Early American case and fully intended – but only partially realized – in the Nazi-German case), driven by political elite obsessions with territorial expansion, racial cleansing, national security, and agricultural settlement.

In the end, I am not arguing that the Early American and Nazi-German national projects were the same. I am, however, arguing that they can (and should) be read and understood as remarkably similar national projects of 'space' and 'race', with genocidal consequences for allegedly 'inferior' peoples in metropolitan and colonized 'living space' – projects whose distinct (but linked) histories bear an unsettling and disturbing resemblance to each other. They are, to be sure, part of an historical continuum of violent national projects of territorial expansion, racial subjugation, and settler colonization that have been very much a prominent feature of the rise and history of the modern West.

Based on the evidence presented in this investigation, we can conclude that, on balance, the similarities – in both theory and practice – between these two national projects of 'space' and 'race' far outweigh the differences and that, in many ways, the similarities are far more significant than the differences. Nonetheless, there are also, as we have seen, important differences between the two historical experiences, and I want to make clear where the similarities end, as well as offer reasons for these differences.

First and foremost, the final outcomes of the Early American and Nazi-German national projects were quite different. In Early America, 'eliminationist' politics (that is, 'removing' the Indians from 'white' 'living space') never fully evolved into 'exterminationist' politics (that is, a general 'exterminatory campaign' against the American Indians); in Nazi Germany, on the other hand, 'eliminationist' politics (that is, 'removing' allegedly 'inferior' *Others* from 'Aryan' 'living space') evolved into 'exterminationist' politics (that is, into an actual general exterminatory campaign against Jews, Gypsies, and the disabled, and a planned general exterminatory campaign against Slavs). In addition, the scale and intensity of Nazi violence in 'the East' was much more widespread, relentless, and extreme than in the 'American West'. The gassing of European Jews represented a radical – and modern – departure from prior colonial experience; it was a Nazi innovation that gave them the ability to carry out massive 'instant killing' of 'alien' and 'unwanted' *Others*.

Dissimilarities in both ideological intention and structural circumstances account for the main differences between these two national projects.

In terms of ideological intention, the Early American national project in 'the West' was predominantly a 'spatial' project (albeit with a strong racial component); the Nazi-German national project in 'the East', by contrast, was based – in theory and in practice – on co-equal components of 'space' and 'race'. While Manifest Destiny, as an ideology, was based on earlier settler notions of America's providential right to continental expansion, Hitler's ideology of 'race' and 'space' was a much-radicalized version of pre-existing (largely nineteenth-century) ideas. While the Slavs, the Gypsies, the disabled, and others were 'dehumanized' 'out-groups', many of whom were destined to 'disappear' from metropolitan and colonized 'living space', the Jews were a 'demonized' 'out-group' selected by the Nazis to be totally destroyed root and branch – that is, every Jewish man, woman, and child in German-controlled 'living space'. While American policymakers could envision ethnic domination as a policy goal in 'the West' (with destruction for any indigenes who resisted), the top Nazi leadership insisted on wide-ranging planned and actualized policies of ethnic destruction in 'the East'.

In terms of structural circumstances, differences in the size of the respective 'native' populations greatly influenced the ultimate outcome of these two national projects. In the Early American case, disease acted as an 'invisible army', decimating indigenous populations in advance of the flood of white 'settlement'; the fact that the 'American West' was thinly populated greatly facilitated the 'settlement' process, allowing 'settlers' to quickly outnumber the 'natives'. After brutal military campaigns, Indian survivors were 'removed' 'west' to create 'space' for the 'settlers'. In the Nazi-German case, a heavily populated 'Nazi East' meant that large-scale deportation and 'evacuation' of the indigenes was an unavoidable prerequisite to 'settlement'; a measure difficult to undertake during wartime due to competing interests and objectives within the various Nazi agencies who claimed responsibility for the 'German East'. This much more numerous indigenous population would have rendered the Nazi-German 'settlement' task considerably more difficult than its American predecessor, even if Germany had defeated the Red Army in 'the East'. Driven by Nazi *Lebensraum* fantasies and colonial ambitions, Hitler and Himmler were blind to the very different realities that they faced on the ground in 'the East', in relation to the on-the-ground realities Early Americans faced in 'the West'.

In the end, Adolf Hitler – as documented in his writings, public speeches, and private conversations – clearly saw America's westward expansion, as well as US Indian policy, as a prototype for Nazi notions and practices of *Lebensraum* and Nazi racial policies in 'the East'. To be sure, the USA settlement model – based, as Hitler understood it, on exterminatory violence against the 'Red Indians' – was primary and determinant for Hitler and Himmler, the two key decision-makers in Nazi foreign and racial policy. In the 'Nazi East', genocidal patterns, logics, and pathologies (derived from the USA settlement model) became 'operational' and were carried to their 'logical' (albeit much more radical) extremes, according to Hitler's and Himmler's spatial and racial fantasies. Born into a world of European empire and obsessed with the 'North American precedent', Nazi leaders – especially Hitler and Himmler – could (and did) think that they were merely applying nineteenth-century Euro-American 'colonial methods' to the European continent and fighting their own 'Indian wars' in the 'Wild East'. At the end of the day, the overwhelming success of the American expansionist project invited repetition in a Nazi-German project which, in their fantasies, would one day dwarf its American predecessor.

Using the new 'optics' of transnational colonialism and genocide studies, we can plainly discern the broader implications of this study for the national histories of the 'American West' and the 'Nazi East', as well as for the events that we have come to call 'the Holocaust'.

In the Early American case, the new 'optics' allows us to see that the Early American project in 'the West' is a central part of – rather than an exception to – the histories of imperialism, colonialism, and genocide. To be sure, the 'American West' was an integral part of the high point of global Western imperialism in the nineteenth and early twentieth centuries.[4] Like other settler-colonial projects, American westward continental expansion was very much an imperialist enterprise, intent on empire-building and 'eliminating' 'inferior' Native American populations from the metropole and from newly colonized settler 'living space' in 'the West'. American imperialists, arguing for further 'westward' expansion on 'island colonies', looked to the American Indian example. In 1899, for instance, American historian Albert Bushnell Hart asserted that America had many 'colonies' already in its Indian reservations, that its Indian wars had been 'colonial' wars against 'native' insurrections, that the United States of America had been a 'great colonial power' for over a century, and that the recent Spanish–American war annexations (Guam, Puerto Rico, and the Philippines) were but 'the enlargement of a policy long pursued' against the American Indians.[5] With these understandings, and within the comparative explanatory and interpretive framework offered by this study, we can begin to integrate the history of the 'American West' into the discipline of comparative genocide studies.[6]

In the Nazi-German case, the new 'optics' allows us to understand that, far from being an inexplicable anomaly, Nazi genocidal violence in 'the East' and many of the events we have come to call 'the Holocaust' were a radicalized blend of several forms of mass political violence whose patterns, logics, and pathologies can be located in the Early American settler-colonial project, an historical episode that served as the primary model for Adolf Hitler's notions and practices of *Lebensraumpolitik* ('politics of living space') as well as for Nazi racial policies in the 'Wild East'. It also helps us recognize the fundamentally colonial origins, content, and context of Nazi genocidal violence. Within metropolitan 'living space', the persecution of 'the Jews' and others deemed 'inferior' was the internal application of an essentially imperial logic: the binary worldview of allegedly 'superior' and 'inferior' people, of 'citizens' and 'subjects'.[7] Nazi conquest and colonization in 'the East' provided both an opportunity and a context for 'ridding' the Greater German Reich of its Jews.[8] Within the newly colonized and occupied eastern *Lebensraum*, Nazi 'eliminationist' politics became 'exterminationist' politics for Slavs, Jews, and Gypsies (killings of the disabled began within the Reich's borders during the wartime euthanasia campaign). It is no coincidence that almost all of the outright killing of non-combatants committed by the Nazis took place outside the Reich's pre-1939 borders, under the cover of, and directly resulting from, Hitler's wars for *Lebensraum*.

Rather than an event unique in the history of the world, the Holocaust is part of a continuum in modern history. While acknowledging the singular aspects of the Nazi Judeocide (that is, its intended totality and its later 'modern' methods of mass extermination by gassing), we can also recognize that Nazi *Judenpolitik* was but one part (to be sure, an increasingly central part) of Hitler's and Himmler's larger national project of the creation of a pan-German racial entity ('free' of Jews, Slavs, and other 'non-Aryans') in a continental empire that would be secured by the conquest of *Lebensraum* and by German agricultural settlement in 'the East'. Recently, two scholars have suggested that the ideological and causal links between the Nazi colonization programmes and the Holocaust are 'tenuous'[9] and that any relationship between the two operations 'was not a linear one of cause and effect'.[10] However, the evidence and arguments presented in this investigation, as well as Hitler's and Himmler's own understandings, strongly suggest otherwise. As historian Isabel Heinemann rightly argues, 'The annexation of "living space" (*Lebensraum*), the idea of a "necessary Germanization" of the occupied territories, and the resettlement carried out to this end represented a driving force behind National Socialist extermination policy.' As she suggests, the 'final solution of the Jewish question' and Hitler's proposed 'ethnic reconstruction' of occupied Europe need to be seen and understood by scholars as 'intertwined processes'.[11] Within the specific context of Hitler's *Lebensraum* ambitions and Himmler's envisaged settler-colonial projects, moreover, one did, to be sure, lead to the other. In the end, the 'Final Solution' resulted from a 'confluence of roadblocks'[12] to Nazi colonial plans in 'the East'.

In the case of the Holocaust and its contexts, the new 'optics' helps us see that – contrary to the prevailing image of 'industrial genocide' – many aspects of the Holocaust are akin to earlier 'colonial genocide'. It is worth noting (and emphasizing) that the distinction I make between 'colonial genocide' and 'industrial genocide' is *not* to suggest some type of crude and arbitrary 'partitioning' of the Nazi Holocaust; it is, rather, to suggest and reassert the (settler) colonial roots, content, and context of the Nazi project in the 'Wild East' – a content and context linked, in Hitler's and Himmler's 'spatial' and 'racial' fantasies, to the 'North American precedent'. And finally, the new 'optics' also allows us to understand that the 'genocide and colonialism' nexus holds the key to recognizing the Holocaust's origins, content, and context; that the Nazi Holocaust is not a copy – but an extremely radicalized variant – of earlier 'colonial genocide'; and that 'holocaust' is not a separate category from, but the most extreme variant of, the blight on human history we call 'genocide'.

Notes

Introduction

1. Adolf Hitler, *Hitler's Table Talk, 1941–1944*, trans. Norman Cameron and R. H. Stevens, H. R. Trevor-Roper (eds), (New York: Enigma Books, 2008), 17 October 1941 and 8 August 1942, pp. 55, 469.
2. Quoted in Ian Kershaw, *Fateful Choices: Ten Decisions That Changed the World, 1940–1941* (New York: The Penguin Press, 2007), p. 387.
3. Quoted in Ian Kershaw, *Hitler 1936–1945: Nemesis* (New York: W.W. Norton, 2000), pp. 434–5.
4. Norman Rich, 'Hitler's Foreign Policy', in Gordon Martel (ed.), *The Origins of the Second World War Reconsidered: The A.J.P. Taylor Debate After Twenty-Five Years* (Boston, MA: Allen & Unwin, 1986), pp. 119–36 (p. 136).
5. Quoted in Ann Curthoys and John Docker, 'Genocide: Definitions, Questions, Settler Colonies', *Aboriginal History*, Vol. 25 (2001), pp. 1–15 (n. 50, p. 14).
6. Ward Churchill, *Struggle for the Land: Indigenous Resistance to Genocide, Ecocide and Expropriation in Contemporary North America* (Monroe, ME: Common Courage Press, 1993), p. 203.
7. Robert Cribb, 'Genocide in the Non-Western World: Implications for Holocaust Studies', in S. L. B. Jensen (ed.), *Genocide: Cases, Comparisons and Contemporary Debates* (Copenhagen: Danish Centre for Holocaust and Genocide Studies, 2003), pp. 123–40 (p. 137).
8. Robert Melson, *Revolution and Genocide: On the Origins of the Armenian Genocide and the Holocaust* (Chicago, IL: University of Chicago Press, 1992), pp. 188–9.
9. Robert Melson, 'Problems in the Comparison of the Armenian Genocide and the Holocaust: Definitions, Typologies, Theories, and Fallacies', in Larry V. Thompson (ed.), *Lessons and Legacies IV: Reflections on Religion, Justice, Sexuality, and Genocide* (Evanston, IL: Northwestern University Press, 2003), pp. 24–38 (p. 35).
10. Yehuda Bauer, 'Holocaust and Genocide: Some Comparisons', in Peter Hayes (ed.), *Lessons and Legacies: The Meaning of the Holocaust in a Changing World* (Evanston, IL: Northwestern University Press, 1991), pp. 36–46 (p. 44).
11. Robert Melson, 'Response to Professor Dadrian's Review', *Holocaust and Genocide Studies*, Vol. 8, No. 3 (1994), p. 416.
12. For the purposes of this book, the term 'patterns' refers to recurring empirical patterns of events in both the 'American West' and the 'Nazi East'; the term 'logics' refers to ways of thinking, beliefs, and attitudes (conscious and unconscious) held by political elites and 'ordinary' citizens, in both historical contexts, that influenced behaviour and decisions; and the term 'pathologies' refers to values and patterns of behaviour displayed by political elites and 'ordinary' citizens in both historical contexts.

13. The term 'out-group' is Michael Mann's. According to Mann, ethnic conflict often breaks out when a 'dominant group' seeks to rid itself of an ethnic 'out-group' from its community or from a territory that the 'dominant group' defines as its own (usually by violent means such as repression, coercion, or physical violence). See the relevant discussion in Michael Mann, *The Dark Side of Democracy: Explaining Ethnic Cleansing* (New York: Cambridge University Press, 2005), pp. 10–18.
14. Walter Nugent, 'Comparing Wests and Frontiers', in Clyde A. Milner II, Carol A. O'Connor, and Martha A. Sandweiss (eds), *The Oxford History of the American West* (New York: Oxford University Press, 1994), pp. 803–33 (p. 803).
15. Robert V. Hine and John Mack Faragher, *The American West: A New Interpretative History* (New Haven, CT: Yale University Press, 2000), p. 11.
16. Colin G. Calloway, *One Vast Winter Count: The Native American West Before Lewis and Clark* (Lincoln, NE: University of Nebraska Press, 2003), p. 2.
17. Vejas Gabriel Liulevicius, *The German Myth of the East: 1800 to the Present* (New York: Oxford University Press, 2009), p. 2.
18. Elizabeth Harvey, *Women and the Nazi East: Agents and Witnesses of Germanization* (New Haven, CT: Yale University Press, 2003), p. 20.
19. Karl Jacoby, *Shadows at Dawn: A Borderlands Massacre and the Violence of History* (New York: The Penguin Press, 2008), p. 2.
20. Ned Blackhawk, *Violence Over the Land: Indians and Empires in the Early American West* (Cambridge, MA: Harvard University Press, 2008), p. 3.
21. Brenden Rensink, 'The Sand Creek Phenomenon: The Complexity and Difficulty of Undertaking a Comparative Study of Genocide *vis-a-vis* the North American West', *Genocide Studies and Prevention*, Vol. 4, No. 1 (2009), pp. 9–27 (p. 19).
22. Liulevicius, *The German Myth of the East*, p. 7.
23. For an excellent collection of essays on how comparative history can stimulate fresh historical thinking, see Deborah Cohen and Maura O'Connor (eds), *Comparison and History: Europe in Cross-National Perspective* (New York: Routledge, 2004).
24. Given the 'general hybridity' of war and genocide, Shaw observes, the phenomenon of 'genocidal war' is 'probably the most common form of genocide and a very common form of war'. Italics are Shaw's. Martin Shaw, 'The General Hybridity of War and Genocide', *Journal of Genocide Research*, Vol. 9, No. 3 (2007), pp. 461–73 (p. 462).

Part I Continental Imperialism

1. Charles S. Maier, *Among Empires: American Ascendancy and Its Predecessors* (Cambridge, MA: Harvard University Press, 2006), pp. 7, 24–5.
2. Stephen Howe, 'Empire', in William A. Darity, Jr. (ed.), *International Encyclopedia of the Social Sciences*, 2nd ed., 9 Vols. (New York: Macmillan Reference USA, 2008), Vol. 2, pp. 574–7 (pp. 574–5).
3. Sudipta Sen, 'Imperialism', in Darity (ed.), *International Encyclopedia of the Social Sciences*, Vol. 3, pp. 586–9 (p. 586).
4. Alexander Laban Hinton, 'The Dark Side of Modernity: Toward an Anthropology of Genocide', in Alexander Laban Hinton (ed.), *Annihilating Difference: The*

Anthropology of Genocide (Berkeley, CA: University of California Press, 2002), pp. 1–40 (p. 14).

5. Patrick Wolfe, 'Land, Labor, and Difference: Elementary Structures of Race', *The American Historical Review*, Vol. 106, No. 3 (2001), pp. 866–905 (p. 894).

6. Eric D. Weitz, *A Century of Genocide: Utopias of Race and Nation* (Princeton, NJ: Princeton University Press, 2003), p. 49.

7. Audrey Smedley, *Race in North America: Origin and Evolution of a Worldview*, 2nd ed. (Boulder, CO: Westview Press, 1999 [1993]), pp. xi, 72; italics in the original.

8. Daniel Jonah Goldhagen, *Worse Than War: Genocide, Eliminationism, and the Ongoing Assault on Humanity* (New York: PublicAffairs, 2009), p. 319.

9. Hannah Arendt, *The Origins of Totalitarianism* (New York: Harcourt, Brace & World, 1966 [1951]), pp. 223–4, 232–3, 238.

1 Empire: National Projects of 'Space' and 'Race'

1. William Earl Weeks, *Building the Continental Empire: American Expansion from the Revolution to the Civil War* (Chicago, IL: Ivan R. Dee, 1996), p. ix.

2. Walter Nugent, *Habits of Empire: A History of American Expansionism* (New York: Alfred A. Knopf, 2008), p. xiii. Importantly, Nugent's history of 'American empire' (emphasizing the period 1782–1853) ties together the diplomatic and military history of the nation's territorial acquisitions with occupation, displacement, and settlement in the 'American West' (themes previously treated separately by most, if not all, historians of Early America). For a study which links Indian policy and national westward expansion, emphasizing the role of the federal government in both, see Stephen J. Rockwell, *Indian Affairs and the Administrative State in the Nineteenth Century* (New York: Cambridge University Press, 2010).

3. For an insightful collection of essays on Eastern Europe as Germany's true 'colonial' empire, see Robert L. Nelson (ed.), *Germans, Poland, and Colonial Expansion to the East: 1850 to the Present* (Basingstoke: Palgrave Macmillan, 2009).

4. Alan E. Steinweis, 'Eastern Europe and the Notion of the "Frontier" in Germany to 1945', *Yearbook of European Studies*, Vol. 13 (1999), pp. 56–69 (p. 66).

5. For a recent interpretation of the Manifest Destiny ideology, which emphasizes its strong religious component (as derived from Puritan theology), see Anders Stephanson, *Manifest Destiny: American Expansion and the Empire of Right* (New York: Hill and Wang, 1995).

6. Quoted in Stephanson, *Manifest Destiny*, p. xii.

7. Richard W. Van Alstyne, *The Rising American Empire* (New York: W. W. Norton, 1974), p. vii.

8. Bruce Lenman, *Britain's Colonial Wars, 1688–1783* (Harlow: Longman, 2001), p. 230.

9. Colin G. Calloway, *The American Revolution in Indian Country: Crisis and Diversity in Native American Communities* (New York: Cambridge University Press, 1995), p. xv.

10. Alan Taylor, 'Land and Liberty on the Post-Revolutionary Frontier', in David Thomas Konig (ed.), *Devising Liberty: Preserving and Creating Freedom in*

the New American Republic (Stanford, CA: Stanford University Press, 1995), pp. 81–108 (p. 82).

11. Calloway, *One Vast Winter Count*, p. 428.

12. Taylor, 'Land and Liberty', p. 85.

13. For a full and useful discussion of these ideologies, see Woodruff D. Smith, *The Ideological Origins of Nazi Imperialism* (New York: Oxford University Press, 1986).

14. Edgar Feuchtwanger, *Imperial Germany 1850–1918* (London: Routledge, 2001), pp. 115–16.

15. Shelley Baranowski, *Nazi Empire: German Colonialism and Imperialism from Bismarck to Hitler* (New York: Cambridge University Press, 2010), p. 45.

16. Smith, *The Ideological Origins of Nazi Imperialism*, pp. 100–1.

17. Richard Weikart, *From Darwin to Hitler: Evolutionary Ethics, Eugenics, and Racism in Germany* (New York: Palgrave Macmillan, 2004), pp. 192–4.

18. David Thomas Murphy, *The Heroic Earth: Geopolitical Thought in Weimar Germany, 1918–1933* (Kent, OH: Kent State University Press, 1997), p. 2.

19. Quoted in Steinweis, 'Eastern Europe', p. 61.

20. David Blackbourn, 'The Conquest of Nature and the Mystique of the Eastern Frontier in Nazi Germany', in Nelson (ed.), *Germans, Poland, and Colonial Expansion to the East*, pp. 141–70 (pp. 151–2).

21. Steinweis, 'Eastern Europe', pp. 57, 61. For more on the dialogue between Ratzel and Turner, see Jens-Uwe Guettel, 'From the Frontier to German South-West Africa: German Colonialism, Indians, and American Westward Expansion', *Modern Intellectual History*, Vol. 7, No. 3 (2010), pp. 523–552 (pp. 524–5, 535, 539).

22. For a brief but nonetheless helpful introduction, see Robert W. Johannsen, 'Introduction', in Sam W. Haynes and Christopher Morris (eds), *Manifest Destiny and Empire: American Antebellum Expansionism* (College Station, TX: Texas A&M University Press, 1997), pp. 3–6.

23. Hine and Faragher, *The American West*, p. 200.

24. Quoted in Ibid., pp. 199–200.

25. David M. Pletcher, 'Manifest Destiny: An Ideal or a Justification?' See www.pbs.org (accessed 28 October 2005), pp. 1–4 (p. 1).

26. Amy S. Greenberg, *Manifest Manhood and the Antebellum American Empire* (New York: Cambridge University Press, 2005), p. 22.

27. Reginald Horsman, *Race and Manifest Destiny: The Origins of American Racial Anglo-Saxonism* (Cambridge, MA: Harvard University Press, 1981), p. 3.

28. Thomas R. Hietala, *Manifest Design: Anxious Aggrandizement in Late Jacksonian America* (Ithaca, NY: Cornell University Press, 1985), p. 172. As Hietala argues (in a view which I share), while some expansionists at times may have expressed concern for non-white peoples, interpretations of American territorial expansion that stress humanitarian motives 'cannot stand up to the abundance of evidence to the contrary'. See Hietala, *Manifest Design*, pp. 132–3.

29. Horsman, *Race and Manifest Destiny*, p. 189.

30. Stephanson, *Manifest Destiny*, p. xiv.

31. R. David Edmunds, 'Native American Displacement Amid US Expansion.' See www.pbs.org (accessed 28 October 2005), pp. 1–3 (p. 1).

32. Feuchtwanger, *Imperial Germany*, p. 118.
33. Smith, *The Ideological Origins of Nazi Imperialism*, p. 91.
34. Ibid., pp. 37–8, 84–6, 90, 100–1, 108. In his classic early study, Woodruff Smith uses the term 'migrationist colonialism' (in lieu of the more recent term 'settler colonialism').
35. Sara Friedrichsmeyer, Sara Lennox, and Susan Zantop, 'Introduction', in Sara Friedrichsmeyer, Sara Lennox, and Susan Zantop (eds), *The Imperialist Imagination: German Colonialism and Its Legacy* (Ann Arbor, MI: University of Michigan Press, 1998), pp. 1–32 (p. 16).
36. Deborah Dwork and Robert Jan van Pelt, *Auschwitz, 1270 to the Present* (New Haven, CT: Yale University Press, 1996), p. 83.
37. Richard Walther Darré, 'The Farmers and the State', *Völkischer Beobachter*, 19/20 and 21 April 1931, published in two parts, an essay reproduced in *Nazi Ideology Before 1933*, introduced and translated by Barbara Miller Lane and Leila J. Rupp (Austin, TX: University of Texas Press, 1978), pp. 131–4 (p. 133); italics in the original.
38. Dwork and van Pelt, *Auschwitz*, pp. 11–12, 81–2, 255.
39. Quoted in Stephanson, *Manifest Destiny*, p. 21.
40. Quoted in Hine and Faragher, *The American West*, p. 133.
41. Ibid.
42. Quoted in Merrill D. Peterson, *Thomas Jefferson and the New Nation: A Biography* (New York: Oxford University Press, 1970), pp. 745–6.
43. Quoted in Lawrence S. Kaplan, *Thomas Jefferson: Westward the Course of Empire* (Wilmington, DE: SR Books, 1999), pp. 174, 184.
44. Adrienne Koch and William Peden (eds), *The Life and Selected Writings of Thomas Jefferson* (New York: Random House, 2004), p. 259.
45. Ibid., p. 351.
46. Quoted in Ben Kiernan, *Blood and Soil: A World History of Genocide and Extermination from Sparta to Darfur* (New Haven, CT: Yale University Press, 2007), p. 314.
47. Koch and Peden (eds), *The Life and Selected Writings of Thomas Jefferson*, pp. 297, 299.
48. David Brown, 'Jeffersonian Ideology and the Second Party System', *The Historian*, Vol. 62, No. 1 (1999), pp. 17–27 (p. 17).
49. Quoted in Walter LaFeber, 'Jefferson and American Foreign Policy', in Peter S. Onuf (ed.), *Jeffersonian Legacies* (Charlottesville, VA: University of Virginia Press, 1993), p. 376.
50. J. Jefferson Looney (ed.), *The Papers of Thomas Jefferson, Retirement Series*, 5 Vols (Princeton, NJ: Princeton University Press, 2004–2008), Vol. 1, p. 169.
51. Daniel Walker Howe, *What Hath God Wrought: The Transformation of America, 1815–1848* (New York: Oxford University Press, 2007), pp. 706–7, 852.
52. Quoted in Hine and Faragher, *The American West*, p. 200.
53. Quoted in Hietala, *Manifest Design*, p. 255.
54. Quoted in Hine and Faragher, *The American West*, p. 199.
55. Hietala, *Manifest Design*, pp. 172, 255, 261.
56. Fred Anderson and Andrew Cayton, *The Dominion of War: Empire and Liberty in North America 1500–2000* (New York: Viking Penguin, 2005), p. 111.

57. Howard Temperley and Christopher Bigsby, 'Introduction', in Howard Temperley and Christopher Bigsby (eds), *A New Introduction to American Studies* (Harlow: Pearson Longman, 2006), pp. 1–6 (p. 6).

58. Vejas Gabriel Liulevicius, *War Land on the Eastern Front: Culture, National Identity and German Occupation in World War I* (Cambridge: Cambridge University Press, 2000), p. 255.

59. Holger H. Herwig, '*Geopolitik*: Haushofer, Hitler and Lebensraum', *The Journal of Strategic Studies*, Vol. 22, No. 2/3 (1999), pp. 218–41 (pp. 226, 221).

60. In a 1940 article, in fact, Haushofer claimed that Hitler had thoroughly studied Ratzel's *Political Geography* while in Landsberg, as part of his 'education' in geopolitics. See Weikart, *From Darwin to Hitler*, p. 225.

61. Herwig, '*Geopolitik*', pp. 232, 237.

62. Liulevicius, *War Land on the Eastern Front*, pp. 254–5.

63. Richard Weikart, *Hitler's Ethic: The Nazi Pursuit of Evolutionary Progress* (New York: Palgrave Macmillan, 2009), p. 160.

64. Herwig, '*Geopolitik*', pp. 226, 237.

65. Murphy, *The Heroic Earth*, pp. viii, 248.

66. Quoted in Herwig, '*Geopolitik*', p. 233.

67. Gerhard L. Weinberg, *The Foreign Policy of Hitler's Germany: Starting World War II 1937–1939* (Atlantic Highlands, NJ: Humanities Press, 1994), p. xii.

68. Adolf Hitler, *Mein Kampf*, trans. Ralph Manheim, Mariner Books Edn (New York: Houghton Mifflin Company, 1999 [1925/27]), pp. 612, 652. Italics in the original.

69. Liulevicius, *War Land on the Eastern Front*, pp. 256–7.

70. Hitler, *Mein Kampf*, pp. 140, 390, 654, 666. Italics in the original.

71. *Hitler's Second Book: The Unpublished Sequel to Mein Kampf by Adolf Hitler*, Gerhard L. Weinberg (ed.), (New York: Enigma Books, 2003), pp. 28, 152.

72. Hitler, *Mein Kampf*, pp. 139, 286, 304, 646.

73. Ibid., p. 138.

74. Quoted in Blackbourn, 'The Conquest of Nature and the Mystique of the Eastern Frontier in Nazi Germany', p. 155.

75. David Blackbourn, *The Conquest of Nature: Water, Landscape, and the Making of Modern Germany* (New York, W. W. Norton, 2006), p. 296.

76. Quoted in Kiernan, *Blood and Soil*, p. 427.

77. Document L-221, 16 July 1941 meeting at Hitler's Headquarters in *Nazi Conspiracy and Aggression, Volume VII*, Office of United States Chief of Counsel for Prosecution of Axis Criminality (Washington, DC: United States Government Printing Office, 1946), p. 1088. English Translation of Documentary Evidence presented before the International Military Tribunal at Nuremberg, Germany.

78. Hitler, *Table Talk*, p. 24.

79. Steinweis, 'Eastern Europe', p. 56.

80. Baranowski, *Nazi Empire*, p. 142.

81. Weikart, *Hitler's Ethic*, p. 160.

82. Kershaw, *Fateful Choices*, pp. 56–7.

83. Steinweis, 'Eastern Europe', p. 56.

84. For support for this view, see Martyn Housden, *Hans Frank, Lebensraum, and the Holocaust* (Basingstoke: Palgrave Macmillan, 2003), p. viii.

85. Hitler's address to the Industry Club in Düsseldorf, 27 January 1932, reprinted in Max Domarus, *Hitler: Speeches and Proclamations 1932–1945: The Chronicle of a Dictatorship, Volumes One – Four* (Wauconda, IL: Bolchazy-Carducci, 1990 [1962]), *Volume One: The Years 1932–1934*, p. 96.
86. Baranowski, *Nazi Empire*, p. 141.
87. Domarus, *Hitler: Speeches and Proclamations, Volume Two: The Years 1935 to 1938*, p. 973.
88. *Völkischer Beobachter*, No. 326, 22 November 1937 reprinted in Domarus, *Hitler: Speeches and Proclamations, Volume Two: The Years 1935 to 1938*, pp. 977–8.
89. Hossbach Memorandum reprinted in Domarus, *Hitler: Speeches and Proclamations, Volume Two: The Years 1935 to 1938*, pp. 962–72.
90. Hitler's May Day Speech, 1 May 1939, reprinted in Domarus, *Hitler: Speeches and Proclamations, Volume Three: The Years 1939 to 1940*, pp. 1601–4.
91. Hitler's Speech at the Berlin *Sportpalast*, 18 December 1940, reprinted in Domarus, *Hitler: Speeches and Proclamations, Volume Three: The Years 1939 to 1940*, pp. 2161–71.
92. Aristotle A. Kallis, *Fascist Ideology: Territory and Expansionism in Italy and Germany, 1922–1945* (London: Routledge, 2000), pp. 43, 52, 53.
93. Mark Mazower, *Hitler's Empire: Nazi Rule in Occupied Europe* (London: Allen Lane, 2008), p. 586.
94. Hitler's Message of 29 April 1945, reprinted in Domarus, *Hitler: Speeches and Proclamations, Volume Four: The Years 1941 to 1945*, p. 3061.
95. Robert V. Remini, *Andrew Jackson and the Course of American Empire, 1767–1821* (Baltimore, MD: The Johns Hopkins University Press, 1998 [1977]), pp. 70–1.
96. Ibid., pp. 388–9.
97. Hietala, *Manifest Design*, pp. vii–viii.
98. John Grenier, *The First Way of War: American War Making on the Frontier, 1607–1814* (New York: Cambridge University Press, 2005), pp. 3, 5, 13.
99. Hietala, *Manifest Design*, pp. x, 257.
100. Peter S. Onuf and Leonard J. Sadosky, *Jeffersonian America* (Malden, MA: Wiley-Blackwell, 2002), pp. 88, 156–61.
101. Quoted in Josef Ackermann, 'Heinrich Himmler: Reichsführer–SS', in Ronald Smelser and Rainer Zitelmann (eds), *The Nazi Elite* (London: Macmillan, 1993), pp. 98–113 (p. 110).
102. Quoted in Peter Padfield, *Himmler: Reichsführer-SS* (New York: Holt, 1990), p. 37.
103. Quoted in Richard Breitman, *The Architect of Genocide: Himmler and the Final Solution* (New York: Alfred A. Knopf, 1991), p. 16.
104. Steinweis, 'Eastern Europe', p. 64.
105. Quoted in Heinz Höhne, *The Order of the Death's Head: The Story of Hitler's SS* (New York: Penguin Books, 2000 [1969]), p. 44. It is worth noting that these words could well have been written by Thomas Jefferson in reference to his yeoman farmer and the American people's strength and character.
106. Christopher R. Browning, *The Origins of the Final Solution: The Evolution of Nazi Jewish Policy, September 1939–March 1942*, with contributions by Jürgen Matthäus (Lincoln: University of Nebraska Press, 2004), pp. 223–4.

107. Omer Bartov, 'Soldiers, Nazis and War in the Third Reich', in Christian Leitz (ed.), *The Third Reich* (Oxford: Blackwell Publishers, 1999), pp. 129–50 (pp. 134, 144, 149).
108. Baranowski, *Nazi Empire*, p. 199.
109. Quoted in Höhne, *The Order of the Death's Head*, p. 294. This statement is also attributed to Himmler; see Timothy Snyder, *Bloodlands: Europe Between Hitler and Stalin* (New York: Basic Books, 2010), p. 189.
110. Shelley Baranowski, ' "Against Human Diversity as Such": *Lebensraum* and Genocide in the Third Reich', conference paper in the author's possession, pp. 1–12 (pp. 6–7).
111. Wendy Lower, *Nazi Empire-Building and the Holocaust in the Ukraine* (Chapel Hill, NC: University of North Carolina Press, 2005), p. 19.
112. Quoted in Blackbourn, *The Conquest of Nature*, p. 296.
113. Quoted in Lower, *Nazi Empire-Building*, p. 19.
114. Quoted in Mazower, *Hitler's Empire*, p. 583.

2 Racial 'Othering': 'Manufacturing Difference'

1. Smedley, *Race in North America*, p. 169.
2. See Claudia Koonz, *The Nazi Conscience* (Cambridge, MA: Harvard University Press, 2003).
3. See Jeffrey Herf, *The Jewish Enemy: Nazi Propaganda During World War II and the Holocaust* (Cambridge, MA: Harvard University Press, 2006).
4. R. Douglas Hurt, *The Indian Frontier, 1783–1846* (Albuquerque, NM: University of New Mexico Press, 2002), p. xiv.
5. Koonz, *The Nazi Conscience*, p. 16.
6. Gary B. Nash, *Red, White & Black: The Peoples of Early North America*, 2nd edn (Upper Saddle River, NJ: Prentice Hall, 2000 [1974]), pp. 51–2.
7. Daniel K. Richter, *Facing East from Indian Country: A Native History of Early America* (Cambridge, MA: Harvard University Press, 2001), p. 2; italics are Richter's.
8. Smedley, *Race in North America*, p. 80.
9. Richter, *Facing East from Indian Country*, pp. 154, 187, 212.
10. Ibid., pp. 180, 191, 203, 292–3, (n. 28).
11. For the specific prehistories, see Richard White, *The Middle Ground: Indians, Empires and Republics in the Great Lakes Region, 1650–1815* (New York: Cambridge University Press, 1991) and Kathleen DuVal, *The Native Ground: Indians and Colonists in the Heart of the American Continent* (Philadelphia, PA: University of Pennsylvania Press, 2006).
12. Richard J. Evans, *The Coming of the Third Reich* (London: Allen Lane, 2003), pp. 23–5, 27, 31, 41.
13. Saul Friedländer, *Nazi Germany and the Jews: Volume 1: The Years of Persecution, 1933–1939* (New York: HarperCollins, 1998 [1997]), p. 86.
14. Baranowski, *Nazi Empire*, pp. 100–1.
15. Oded Heilbronner, 'German or Nazi Antisemitism ?', in Dan Stone (ed.), *The Historiography of the Holocaust* (Basingstoke: Palgrave Macmillan, 2004), pp. 9–23 (pp. 18–19).

16. Oded Heilbronner, 'From Antisemitic Peripheries to Antisemitic Centres: The Place of Antisemitism in German History', *Journal of Contemporary History*, Vol. 35 (2000), pp. 559–76 (pp. 560, 562–3, 573).

17. Doris L. Bergen, *War & Genocide: A Concise History of the Holocaust* (Lanham, MD: Roman & Littlefield, 2003), pp. 6, 11–14, 19–20.

18. Renée L. Bergland, *The National Uncanny: Indian Ghosts and American Subjects* (Hanover, NH: University Press of New England, 2000), p. 40.

19. Heilbronner, 'German or Nazi Antisemitism ?', pp. 11–12.

20. Gregory D. Smithers, 'Rethinking Genocide in North America', in Donald Bloxham and A. Dirk Moses (eds), *The Oxford Handbook of Genocide Studies* (Oxford: Oxford University Press, 2010), pp. 322–41 (p. 334).

21. 'The Declaration of Independence', 4 July 1776, in Koch and Peden (eds), *The Life and Selected Writings of Thomas Jefferson*, p. 26.

22. Quoted in Anthony F. C. Wallace, *Jefferson and the Indians: The Tragic Fate of the First Americans* (Cambridge, MA: Harvard University Press, 1999), p. 55.

23. Gary B. Nash, *The Unknown American Revolution: The Unruly Birth of Democracy and the Struggle to Create America* (New York: Viking, 2005), p. 215.

24. See William R. Nester, *The Frontier War for American Independence* (Mechanicsburg, PA: Stackpole Books, 2004).

25. Calloway, *The American Revolution in Indian Country*, pp. 293, 295.

26. Nash, *Red, White & Black*, p. 290.

27. DuVal, *The Native Ground*, p. 239.

28. Calloway, *The American Revolution in Indian Country*, pp. 295–7, 301.

29. Peter Silver, *Our Savage Neighbors: How Indian War Transformed Early America* (New York: W. W. Norton, 2008), p. xxi.

30. DuVal, *The Native Ground*, p. 243.

31. Smedley, *Race in North America*, pp. 169–71, 189.

32. Weikart, *From Darwin to Hitler*, p. 7.

33. Hitler, *Mein Kampf*, p. 688.

34. Quoted in Hermann Graml, *Antisemitism in the Third Reich*, trans. Tim Kirk (Oxford, Blackwell Publishers, 1992 [1988]), p. 86.

35. Geoff Eley, 'Ordinary Germans, Nazism, and Judeocide', in Geoff Eley (ed.), *The "Goldhagen Effect": History, Memory, Nazism – Facing the German Past* (Ann Arbor, MI: University of Michigan Press), 2000, pp. 1–32 (p. 16).

36. Bergen, *War & Genocide*, pp. 17, 24, 56–60.

37. Alden T. Vaughan, *Roots of American Racism: Essays on the Colonial Experience* (New York: Oxford University Press, 1995), p. x.

38. Wolfe, 'Land, Labor, and Difference', pp. 867, 885, 894.

39. Nash, *Red, White & Black*, pp. 318–19.

40. Wolfe, 'Land, Labor, and Difference', pp. 882, 887, 890, 892.

41. Richard Drinnon, *Facing West: The Metaphysics of Indian-Hating & Empire Building* (Norman, OK: University of Oklahoma Press, 1997), pp. xi, xxvii.

42. Thomas F. Gossett, *Race: The History of an Idea in America*, new edn (New York: Oxford University Press, 1997 [1963]), p. 236.

43. Quoted in Calloway, *The American Revolution in Indian Country*, p. 295.

44. See Alfred A. Cave, 'Genocide in the Americas', in Stone (ed.), *The Historiography of Genocide*, pp. 273–95 (p. 288) and Kiernan, *Blood and Soil*, p. 349. As Jeffrey Ostler notes, many men and women who 'settled' America's

western 'frontiers' became virulent Indian haters and advocated 'extermination' of 'the savages'. See Jeffrey Ostler, *The Plains Sioux and U.S. Colonialism from Lewis and Clark to Wounded Knee* (Cambridge: Cambridge University Press, 2004), p. 15.

45. Ostler, *The Plains Sioux and U.S. Colonialism*, pp. 15, 17n5.
46. Gossett, *Race*, pp. 242–4.
47. Smedley, *Race in North America*, pp. 176, 188–9.
48. Quoted in Wallace, *Jefferson and the Indians*, pp. 15, 17.
49. Ibid., pp. 15–20.
50. Brian W. Dippie, *The Vanishing American: White Attitudes and U.S. Indian Policy* (Lawrence, KS: University Press of Kansas, 1991 [1982]), pp. xi–xii, 10–11, 86.
51. Quoted in Michael Burleigh and Wolfgang Wippermann, *The Racial State: Germany 1933–1945* (New York: Cambridge University Press, 1991), pp. 168, 170, 192.
52. Bergen, *War & Genocide*, p. 3.
53. Marion Kaplan, *Between Dignity and Despair: Jewish Life in Nazi Germany* (New York: Oxford University Press, 1998), p. 5.
54. Koonz, *The Nazi Conscience*, pp. 15–16, 166, 192–3, 256.
55. Ibid., pp. 3, 13–15, 256, 273.
56. Gretchen E. Schafft, 'Scientific Racism in Service of the Reich: German Anthropologists in the Nazi Era', in Hinton (ed.), *Annihilating Difference*, pp. 117–34 (p. 120).
57. See, for example, Götz Aly, Peter Chroust, and Christian Pross, *Cleansing the Fatherland: Nazi Medicine and Racial Hygiene*, trans. Belinda Cooper (Baltimore, MD: The Johns Hopkins University Press, 1994).
58. Omer Bartov, 'Antisemitism, the Holocaust, and Reinterpretations of National Socialism', in Michael Berenbaum and Abraham J. Peck (eds), *The Holocaust and History: The Known, the Unknown, the Disputed and the Reexamined* (Bloomington, IN: Indiana University Press, 1998), pp. 75–98 (pp. 89–90).
59. Benoit Massin, 'The "Science of Race" ', in Dieter Kuntz and Susan Bachrach (eds), *Deadly Medicine: Creating the Master Race* (Chapel Hill, NC: University of North Carolina Press, 2004), pp. 88–125 (p. 125); an exhibition and publication of the United States Holocaust Memorial Museum, Washington, DC.
60. Gisela Bock, 'Nazi Sterilization and Reproductive Policies', in Kuntz and Bachrach (eds), *Deadly Medicine*, pp. 60–87 (pp. 86–7).
61. Paul J. Weindling, *Health, Race, and German Politics Between National Unification and Nazism, 1870–1945* (Cambridge: Cambridge University Press, 1989), p. 489.
62. Sheila Faith Weiss, 'German Eugenics, 1890–1933', in Kuntz and Bachrach (eds), *Deadly Medicine*, pp. 14–39 (p. 39).
63. Weindling, *Health, Race, and German Politics*, pp. 539–40.
64. Robert Proctor, *Racial Hygiene: Medicine under the Nazis* (Cambridge, MA: Harvard University Press, 1988), pp. 7, 201.
65. Quoted in Massin, 'The "Science of Race" ', p. 89.
66. Phillippe Burrin, *Nazi Anti-Semitism: From Prejudice to the Holocaust* (New York: The New Press, 2005), pp. 51, 62, 89, 91.

67. Herf, *The Jewish Enemy*, pp. 41, 49, 273.
68. Burrin, *Nazi Anti-Semitism*, pp. 62–3.
69. Patrick Brantlinger, *Dark Vanishings: Discourse on the Extinction of Primitive Races* (Ithaca, NY: Cornell University Press, 2003), pp. 1, 47.
70. Yehuda Bauer, *Rethinking the Holocaust* (New Haven, CT: Yale University Press, 2001), p. 102. Bauer's reference is to Daniel Jonah Goldhagen, *Hitler's Willing Executioners: Ordinary Germans and the Holocaust* (New York: Alfred A. Knopf, 1996).
71. Robert V. Remini, *The Legacy of Andrew Jackson: Essays on Democracy, Indian Removal and Slavery* (Baton Rouge, LA: Louisiana State University Press, 1988), p. 71.
72. Quoted in Andrew Burstein, *The Passions of Andrew Jackson* (New York, Alfred A. Knopf, 2004 [2003]), p. 16.
73. Horsman, *Race and Manifest Destiny*, pp. 3, 203.
74. Smedley, *Race in North America*, p. 188.
75. Quoted in Horsman, *Race and Manifest Destiny*, pp. 214, 243.
76. Quoted in Drinnon, *Facing West*, p. 119.
77. Louise K. Barnett, *The Ignoble Savage: American Literary Racism, 1790–1890* (Westport, CT: Greenwood Press, 1975), pp. 96, 189.
78. Horsman, *Race and Manifest Destiny*, pp. 190–1.
79. Gossett, *Race*, p. 157.
80. George W. Stocking, Jr., *Race, Culture, and Evolution: Essays in the History of Anthropology* (Chicago, IL: University of Chicago Press, 1982 [1968]), p. 38.
81. Robert E. Bieder, *Science Encounters the Indian, 1820–1880: The Early Years of American Ethnology* (Norman, OK: University of Oklahoma Press, 1986), p. 55.
82. Quoted in Stocking, *Race, Culture, and Evolution*, p. 48.
83. Quoted in Patrick B. Sharp, *Savage Perils: Racial Frontiers and Nuclear Apocalypse in American Culture* (Norman, OK: University of Oklahoma Press, 2007), p. 29; italics are mine. Although primarily concerned with 'differences' between blacks and whites (and an outspoken advocate of slavery), Nott believed in the 'inferiority' of the Indian. According to Nott, both races degenerated in a free state: he saw blacks as reaching their optimal potential in slavery; Indians (who did not make good slaves, he opined) were doomed to 'extinction'. Bieder, *Science Encounters the Indian*, p. 93.
84. Gossett, *Race*, p. 244.
85. Horsman, *Race and Manifest Destiny*, pp. 3, 6, 116, 134.
86. Vaughn, *Roots of American Racism*, pp. 31–3.
87. Quoted in Ibid., p. 31.
88. Brantlinger, *Dark Vanishings*, pp. 5, 17–18, 37, 164–5.
89. Horsman, *Race and Manifest Destiny*, pp. 5–6.
90. Quoted in James Wilson, *The Earth Shall Weep: A History of Native America* (New York: Grove Press, 1998), p. 234.
91. Burrin, *Nazi Anti-Semitism*, pp. 1, 6, 47.
92. Bauer, *Rethinking the Holocaust*, pp. 83, 91, 97, 116–17.
93. Saul Friedländer, *Nazi Germany and the Jews: Volume II: The Years of Extermination, 1939–1945* (New York: HarperCollins, 2007), p. 4.
94. Bauer, *Rethinking the Holocaust*, pp. 83, 91, 97, 116–17.
95. Herf, *The Jewish Enemy*, pp. 1–2, 5, 12.

96. Quoted in Isabel Heinemann, 'Towards an "Ethnic Reconstruction" of Occupied Europe: SS Plans and Racial Policies', in *Jahrbuch des Italiensch-deutschen historischen Instituts in Trient*, Vol. XXVII (2001), pp. 493–517 (p. 499).

97. James M. Glass, *'Life Unworthy of Life': Racial Phobia and Mass Murder in Hitler's Germany* (New York: Basic Books, 1997), p. 5.

98. Blackbourn, *The Conquest of Nature*, pp. 254, 303.

99. Catherine Epstein, *Model Nazi: Arthur Greiser and the Occupation of Western Poland* (Oxford: Oxford University Press, 2010), p. 12.

100. John Connelly, 'Nazis and Slavs: From Racial Theory to Racist Practice', *Central European History*, Vol. 1, No. 32 (1999), pp. 1–33 (pp. 3, 12–13, 23–4).

101. Quoted in Norman Rich, *Hitler's War Aims, Volume 2: The Establishment of the New Order* (New York: Norton, 1974), p. 327.

102. David Furber and Wendy Lower, 'Colonialism and Genocide in Nazi-Occupied Poland and Ukraine', in A. Dirk Moses (ed.), *Empire, Colony, Genocide: Conquest, Occupation, and Subaltren Resistance in World History* (New York: Berghahn Book, 2008), pp. 372–400 (pp. 375–7).

103. Quoted in Blackbourn, *The Conquest of Nature*, pp. 303, 305.

104. Smedley, *Race in North America*, p. 289.

105. Barnett, *The Ignoble Savage*, p. 10.

106. Raul Hilberg, *The Destruction of the European Jews* (New York: Holmes & Meier, 1985), p. 8.

107. Burleigh and Wippermann, *The Racial State*, p. 23.

108. Enzo Traverso, *The Origins of Nazi Violence* (New York: The New Press, 2003), p. 19.

109. Smedley, *Race in North America*, p. 289.

Part II Settler Colonialism

1. David L. Brunsma, 'Colonialism', in Darity (ed.), *International Encyclopedia of the Social Sciences*, Vol. 2, pp. 11–13 (pp. 11–12).

2. Donald Bloxham, *The Final Solution: A Genocide* (New York: Oxford University Press, 2009), p. 325.

3. Caroline Elkins and Susan Pedersen, 'Introduction: Settler Colonialism: A Concept and Its Uses', in Caroline Elkins and Susan Pedersen (eds), *Settler Colonialism in the Twentieth Century* (New York: Routledge, 2005), pp. 1–20 (p. 2).

4. Adam Jones, *Genocide: A Comprehensive Introduction* (London: Routledge, 2006), p. 40.

5. Patrick Wolfe, *Settler Colonialism and the Transformation of Anthropology: The Politics and Poetics of an Ethnographic Event* (London: Cassell, 1999), pp. 1–3, 163.

6. Patrick Wolfe, 'Structure and Event: Settler Colonialism, Time and the Question of Genocide', in Moses (ed.), *Empire, Colony, Genocide*, pp. 102–32 (p. 102).

7. Goldhagen, *Worse Than War*, p. 14.

8. Jones, *Genocide*, p. 40.

9. Dominik J. Schaller and Jürgen Zimmerer, 'Settlers, Imperialism, Genocide: Seeing the Global Without Ignoring the Local – Introduction', *Journal of Genocide Research*, Vol. 10, No. 2 (2008), pp. 191–9 (p. 195).

10. David Day, *Conquest: How Societies Overwhelm Others* (New York: Oxford University Press, 2008), p. 182.

11. Schaller and Zimmerer, 'Settlers, Imperialism, Genocide', p. 196.

12. See, for example, the relevant chapters on settler colonialism in Kiernan, *Blood and Soil*.

13. Elkins and Pedersen, 'Introduction', in Elkins and Pedersen (eds), *Settler Colonialism in the Twentieth Century*, p. 1.

14. Smithers, 'Rethinking Genocide in North America', p. 330.

15. Bloxham, *The Final Solution*, p. 180.

3   Conquest and Expansion: 'Obtaining' New 'Living Space'

1. Mark S. Joy, *American Expansionism 1783–1860: A Manifest Destiny?* (London: Pearson Education Limited, 2003), p. xxv.

2. Joel H. Silbey, *Storm Over Texas: The Annexation Controversy and the Road to the Civil War* (New York: Oxford University Press, 2005), p. 96.

3. Hietala, *Manifest Design*, pp. ix, xiv, 264, 271–2.

4. Hine and Faragher, *The American West*, p. 200.

5. Gerhard L. Weinberg, *Hitler's Foreign Policy: The Road to World War II, 1933–1939* (New York: Enigma Books, 2005), p. 950. This book was originally published in two volumes as *The Foreign Policy of Hitler's Germany: I* and *Diplomatic Revolution in Europe and Starting World War II: II*.

6. Hans-Adolf Jacobsen, 'The Structure of Nazi Foreign Policy 1933–1945', in Leitz (ed.), *The Third Reich*, pp. 53–93 (p. 89).

7. Kershaw, *Hitler 1936–1945: Nemesis*, pp. 158–9, 161.

8. Smith, *The Ideological Origins of Nazi Imperialism*, pp. 255–6.

9. Kallis, *Fascist Ideology*, p. 195.

10. Karen Ordahl Kupperman, *The Jamestown Project* (Cambridge, MA: Harvard University Press, 2007), pp. 208–9.

11. Michael Leroy Oberg, *Dominion and Civility: English Imperialism and Native America, 1585–1685* (Ithaca, NY: Cornell University Press, 1999), p. 61.

12. Kupperman, *The Jamestown Project*, pp. 194–5.

13. Kiernan, *Blood and Soil*, pp. 211–12.

14. Ibid., pp. 179, 193, 197, 204.

15. Quoted in ibid., p. 212.

16. See Nicholas P. Canny, 'The Ideology of English Colonization: From Ireland to America', *William & Mary Quarterly*, Vol. 30, No. 4 (1973), pp. 575–98.

17. Ibid., pp. 575, 583, 595–6, 598.

18. Oberg, *Dominion and Civility*, pp. 2, 5–7.

19. Colin G. Calloway, *The Scratch of a Pen: 1763 and the Transformation of North America* (New York: Oxford University Press, 2006), p. 47.

20. Ibid., p. 78.

21. Oberg, *Dominion and Civility*, pp. 6, 226.

22. Grenier, *The First Way of War*, p. 52.

23. Dwork and van Pelt, *Auschwitz*, p. 11.
24. Smith, *The Ideological Origins of Nazi Imperialism*, pp. 169–71, 176–9, 187.
25. Quoted in Robert G. L. Waite, *Vanguard of Nazism: The Free Corps Movement in Postwar Germany 1918–1923* (New York: W. W. Norton, 1969 [1952]), p. 98.
26. Quoted in Liulevicius, *War Land on the Eastern Front*, pp. 238, 240.
27. Waite, *Vanguard of Nazism*, pp. 138–9, 281.
28. Liulevicius, *War Land on the Eastern Front*, p. 243.
29. Hitler, *Mein Kampf*, p. 154.
30. Waite, *Vanguard of Nazism*, pp. 262, 281.
31. Mazower, *Hitler's Empire*, pp. 180–1.
32. Jacobsen, 'The Structure of Nazi Foreign Policy 1933–1945', pp. 54–5.
33. Joyce Appleby, *Thomas Jefferson* (New York: Henry Holt, 2003), p. 64.
34. Jon Kukla, *A Wilderness So Immense: The Louisiana Purchase and the Destiny of America* (New York: Alfred A. Knopf, 2003), p. 267.
35. Charles A. Cerami, *Jefferson's Great Gamble: The Remarkable Story of Jefferson, Napoleon, and the Men Behind the Louisiana Purchase* (Naperville, IL: Sourcebooks, 2003), p. ix.
36. Anderson and Clayton, *The Dominion of War*, p. 212.
37. Gail D. MacLeitch, 'Native Americans', in Temperley and Bigsby (eds), *A New Introduction to American Studies*, pp. 98–122 (p. 105).
38. Sean Wilentz, *Andrew Jackson* (New York: Henry Holt, 2006), p. 38.
39. Quoted in Richard Kluger, *Seizing Destiny: How America Grew from Sea to Shining Sea* (New York: Alfred A. Knopf, 2007), p. 345.
40. Quoted in Thomas M. Leonard, *James K. Polk: A Clear and Unquestionable Destiny* (Wilmington, DE: Scholarly Resources, 2001), p. 193.
41. Joy, *American Expansionism*, p. 52.
42. Hine and Faragher, *The American West*, p. 200.
43. Weeks, *Building the Continental Empire*, p. 97.
44. Joy, *American Expansionism*, p. 62.
45. Weeks, *Building the Continental Empire*, p. 93.
46. Weinberg, *Hitler's Foreign Policy*, p. 632.
47. Kershaw, *Hitler 1936–1945: Nemesis*, pp. 64, 83–4.
48. Richard J. Evans, *The Third Reich in Power, 1933–1939* (London: Allen Lane, 2005), p. 663.
49. Weinberg, *Hitler's Foreign Policy*, pp. 634, 648–9.
50. Kershaw, *Hitler 1936–1945: Nemesis*, p. 125.
51. Weinberg, *Hitler's Foreign Policy*, pp. 779–80.
52. Kershaw, *Hitler 1936–1945: Nemesis*, pp. 164–5.
53. Evans, *The Third Reich in Power*, p. 664.
54. Kershaw, *Hitler 1936–1945: Nemesis*, pp. 87, 173–4.
55. Weinberg, *Hitler's Foreign Policy*, p. 778.
56. Anderson and Cayton, *The Dominion of War*, pp. x–xi, xiii.
57. Colin G. Calloway, *The Shawnees and the War for America* (New York: Viking Penguin, 2007), pp. xxiv, xxxii, xxxvi.
58. Evans, *The Third Reich in Power*, p. 705.
59. Calloway, *One Vast Winter Count*, p. 346.
60. Anderson and Cayton, *The Dominion of War*, p. xvii.
61. Gregory H. Nobles, *American Frontiers: Cultural Encounters and Continental Conquest* (New York: Hill and Wang, 1997), p. 92.

62. Ibid., p. 15.
63. Patrick Griffin, *American Leviathan: Empire, Nation, and Revolutionary Frontier* (New York: Hill and Wang, 2007), pp. 241–2, 266.
64. Joy, *American Expansionism*, p. 34.
65. Ibid.
66. Anderson and Cayton, *The Dominion of War*, p. xvii.
67. Heather Cox Richardson, *Wounded Knee: Political Parties and the Road to an American Massacre* (New York: Basic Books, 2010), p. 20.
68. H. W. Brands, *Andrew Jackson: His Life and Times* (New York: Doubleday, 2005), pp. 510, 516, 521, 544–5.
69. Quoted in Kluger, *Seizing Destiny*, p. 447.
70. Quoted in Joy, *American Expansionism*, p. 69.
71. Quoted in Weeks, *Building the Continental Empire*, pp. 120–1.
72. Silbey, *Storm Over Texas*, p. 115.
73. Richard White, *'It's Your Misfortune and None of My Own': A New History of the American West* (Norman, OK: University of Oklahoma Press, 1991), p. 79.
74. Brian DeLay, *War of a Thousand Deserts: Indian Raids and the U.S. Mexican War* (New Haven, CT: Yale University Press, 2008), pp. xvii, 290–1.
75. Paul W. Foos, *A Short, Off-Hand, Killing Affair: Soldiers and Social Conflict During the Mexican-American War* (Chapel Hill, NC: University of North Carolina Press, 2002), p. 5.
76. Calloway, *One Vast Winter Count*, pp. 21, 372–3.
77. See Bill Yenne, *Indian Wars: The Campaign for the American West* (Yardley, PA: Westholme Publishing, 2006).
78. Quoted in Evans, *The Third Reich in Power*, p. 615.
79. Quoted in Jeremy Noakes and Geoffrey Pridham (eds), *Nazism 1919–1945: Volume 3: Foreign Policy, War and Racial Extermination, A Documentary Reader* (Exeter: University of Exeter, 1988), p. 21.
80. Kershaw, *Fateful Choices*, p. 56.
81. Quoted in Rich, *Hitler's War Aims, Volume 2*, pp. 330–1. This speech, given in July 1943, as Rich notes, could just as easily have been given in July 1941 or, for that matter, in 1924.
82. Quoted in Richard Bessel, *Nazism and War* (New York: Random House, 2004), p. 70.
83. Quoted in ibid., pp. 85–6.
84. Gerhard L. Weinberg, 'Foreword', in Rolf-Dieter Müller and Gerd R. Ueberschär, *Hitler's War in the East, 1941–1945: A Critical Assessment* (New York: Berghahn Books, 2002), p. viii.
85. Peter Fritzsche, *Life and Death in the Third Reich* (Cambridge, MA: Harvard University Press, 2008), p. 221.
86. Weinberg, *Hitler's Foreign Policy*, pp. 951–2.
87. Kershaw, *Hitler 1936–1945: Nemesis*, pp. 158–9, 166, 178.
88. Quoted in Bessel, *Nazism and War*, p. 88.
89. Quoted in Alexander B. Rossino, *Hitler Strikes Poland: Blitzkrieg, Ideology, and Atrocity* (Lawrence, KS: University of Kansas Press, 2003), pp. 196–7.
90. Quoted in Alexander B. Rossino, 'Destructive Impulses: German Soldiers and the Conquest of Poland', *Holocaust and Genocide Studies*, Vol. 11, No. 3 (1997), pp. 351–65 (p. 354).
91. Quoted in Kershaw, *Fateful Choices*, p. 56.

92. Order of 13 May 1941 quoted in Bernd Boll, Hannes Heer, and Walter Manoschek, 'Prelude to a Crime: The German Army in the National Socialist State', in Hamburg Institute of Social Research (eds), *The German Army and Genocide: Crimes Against War Prisoners, Jews, and Other Civilians, 1939–1944* (New York: The New Press, 1999 [1996]), pp. 20–33 (p. 29).
93. Order of 6 June 1941 quoted in ibid., p. 30.
94. Ben Shepherd, *War in the Wild East: The German Army and Soviet Partisans* (Cambridge, MA: Harvard University Press, 2004), p. 46.
95. Quoted in Mazower, *Hitler's Empire*, p. 143.
96. Grenier, *The First Way of War*, p. 12.
97. Robert M. Citino, *The German Way of War: From the Thirty Years' War to the Third Reich* (Lawrence, KS: University Press of Kansas, 2005), p. 273.
98. Grenier, *The First Way of War*, pp. 4, 168.
99. Anderson and Cayton, *The Dominion of War*, p. 170.
100. Grenier, *The First Way of War*, pp. 10, 15, 225.
101. Foos, *A Short, Off-Hand, Killing Affair*, pp. 116, 120–1,123, 125, 127.
102. Grenier, *The First Way of War*, p. 221.
103. Yenne, *Indian Wars*, pp. 302–303, 306.
104. Grenier, *The First Way of War*, pp. ix, 1, 225.
105. Bessel, *Nazism and War*, pp. vii, xi, xv, 93.
106. Citino, *The German Way of War*, p. 273.
107. Shepherd, *War in the Wild East*, p. 225.
108. Müller and Ueberschär, *Hitler's War in the East*, p. 235.
109. Michael Geyer, 'Foreword', in Hamburg Institute of Social Research (eds), *The German Army and Genocide*, pp. 1–8 (pp. 7–8).
110. Hannes Heer, 'Russia: Three Years of Occupation, 1941–1944', in Hamburg Institute of Social Research (eds), *The German Army and Genocide*, pp. 116–71 (p. 152).
111. Quoted in ibid., p. 156.
112. Bernd Boll and Hans Safrian, 'The Sixth Army on the Way to Stalingrad, 1941–1942', in Hamburg Institute of Social Research (eds), *The German Army and Genocide*, pp. 76–115 (p. 98).
113. Blackbourn, *The Conquest of Nature*, pp. 295–7, 305.
114. Quoted in ibid., pp. 296, 305.
115. Geyer, 'Foreword', in Hamburg Institute of Social Research (eds), *The German Army and Genocide*, p. 8.

4   Colonization: 'Peopling' the Empire

1. Hine and Faragher, *The American West*, p. 159.
2. Quoted in Henry Nash Smith, *Virgin Land: The American West as Symbol and Myth* (Cambridge, MA: Harvard University Press, 1970 [1950]), p. 201.
3. Ibid., p. 133.
4. Hitler, *Table Talk*, pp. 15, 320, 353.
5. Allan Kulikoff, *From British Peasants to Colonial American Farmers* (Chapel Hill, NC: University of North Carolina Press, 2000), p. 44.
6. Alan Taylor, *American Colonies: The Settling of North America* (New York: Penguin Books, 2001), p. 118.

7. Anderson and Cayton, *The Dominion of War*, pp. 43–4.
8. Anthony Pagden, *Lords of All the World: Ideologies of Empire in Spain, Britain and France c.1500-c.1800* (New Haven, CT: Yale University Press, 1995), p. 65.
9. Taylor, *American Colonies*, p. xv.
10. Kulikoff, *From British Peasants to Colonial American Farmers*, p. 151.
11. Ibid., pp. 284–5.
12. Ibid., p. 163.
13. Taylor, *American Colonies*, p. xvi.
14. For a useful informative discussion of the Frederician project, see 'Chapter One: Conquests from Barbarism: Prussia in the Eighteenth Century', in Blackbourn, *The Conquest of Nature*, pp. 21–75.
15. Day, *Conquest*, pp. 212, 261, n. 33.
16. For a useful survey of GSWA and GEA, see Dominik J. Schaller, 'From Conquest to Genocide: Colonial Rule in German Southwest Africa and German East Africa', in Moses (ed.), *Empire, Colony, Genocide*, pp. 296–324.
17. Benjamin Madley, 'From Africa to Auschwitz: How German Southwest Africa Incubated Ideas and Methods Adopted and Developed by the Nazis in Eastern Europe', *European History Quarterly*, Vol. 35, No. 3 (2005), pp. 429–64 (p. 441).
18. Quoted in Phillip T. Rutherford, *Prelude to the Final Solution: The Nazi Program for Deporting Ethnic Poles, 1939–1941* (Lawrence, KS: University Press of Kansas, 2007), p. 30.
19. Quoted in Liulevicius, *War Land on the Eastern Front*, p. 198.
20. Ibid., n. 156, p. 193.
21. Quoted in Waite, *Vanguard of Nazism*, n. 33, p. 165.
22. Quoted in Ibid., p. 106.
23. Quoted in Liulevicius, *War Land on the Eastern Front*, p. 240.
24. Ibid., p. 241.
25. Madley, 'From Africa to Auschwitz', p. 452.
26. Liulevicius, *War Land on the Eastern Front*, p. 241.
27. Kulikoff, *From British Peasants to Colonial American Farmers*, p. 256.
28. Letter to James Madison, 27 April 1809, in Looney (ed.), *The Papers of Thomas Jefferson*, Vol. 1, p. 169.
29. White, *'It's Your Misfortune and None of My Own'*, p. 138.
30. Quoted in Smith, *Virgin Land*, pp. 10–11.
31. Anderson and Cayton, *The Dominion of War*, p. 209.
32. DeLay, *War of a Thousand Deserts*, p. 3.
33. Quoted in Hine and Faragher, *The American West*, pp. 117–18.
34. Quoted in Kulikoff, *From British Peasants to Colonial American Farmer*, pp. 125, 127.
35. Allan G. Bogue, 'An Agricultural Empire', in Milner, O'Connor and Sandweiss (eds), *The Oxford History of the American West*, pp. 275–313 (pp. 285–6).
36. White, *'It's Your Misfortune and None of my Own'*, pp. 207–8.
37. Letter to Jean Baptiste Say of 1 February 1894, in Koch and Peden (eds), *The Life and Selected Writings of Thomas Jefferson*, p. 526.
38. Nugent, *Habits of Empire*, pp. 183–4, 233–4.

39. Götz Aly, *Hitler's Beneficiaries: Plunder, Racial War, and the Nazi Welfare State* (New York: Metropolitan Books, 2006), pp. 8, 30–1.
40. Robert L. Koehl, *RKFDV: German Resettlement and Population Policy 1939–1945: A History of the Reich Commission for the Strengthening of Germandom* (Cambridge, MA: Harvard University Press, 1957), p. 230.
41. Aly, *Hitler's Beneficiaries*, p. 324.
42. Hitler, *Table Talk*, 12 May 1942, p. 353.
43. Ibid., 13 October 1941, p. 43.
44. Blackbourn, 'Conquest and Mystique', p. 158.
45. Hitler, *Table Talk*, 17 September 1941, p. 29.
46. See Shelley Baranowski, *Strength Through Joy: Consumerism and Mass Tourism in the Third Reich* (New York: Cambridge University Press, 2004).
47. Harvey, *Women and the Nazi East*, pp. 124, 154.
48. Mazower, *Hitler's Empire*, p. 192.
49. Quoted in Koehl, *RKFDV*, p. 15.
50. See illustrations Plate 6 and Plate 16 in Harvey, *Women and the Nazi East*.
51. Mazower, *Hitler's Empire*, p. 192.
52. Harvey, *Women and the Nazi East*, p. 117.
53. Baranowski, *Nazi Empire*, p. 290.
54. Ibid., p. 285.
55. Quoted in Bessel, *Nazism and War*, p. 124.
56. Götz Aly and Suzanne Heim, *Architects of Annihilation: Auschwitz and the Logic of Destruction* (London: Phoenix, 2003 [1991]), p. 282.
57. Aly, *Hitler's Beneficiaries: Plunder*, p. 31.
58. Wendy Lower, 'Hitler's "Garden of Eden" in Ukraine: Nazi Colonialism, *Volksdeutsche*, and the Holocaust, 1941–1944', in Jonathan Petropoulos and John K. Roth (eds), *Gray Zones: Ambiguity and Compromise in the Holocaust and Its Aftermath* (New York: Berghahn Books, 2005), pp. 185–204 (p. 187).
59. Quoted in Aly, *Hitler's Beneficiaries*, p. 31.
60. Hitler, *Mein Kampf*, p. 649; italics in the original.
61. Hitler, *Table Talk*, 23 September 1941 and 28 January 1942, pp. 31, 199.
62. Weikart, *Hitler's Ethic*, pp. 125, 135.
63. Kulikoff, *From British Peasants to Colonial American Farmers*, pp. 288, 292.
64. Elizabeth Harvey, 'Management and Manipulation: Nazi Settlement Planners and Ethnic German Settlers in Occupied Poland', in Elkins and Pedersen (eds), *Settler Colonialism in the Twentieth Century*, pp. 95–112 (p. 105).
65. Quoted in Walter L. Williams, 'American Imperialism and the Indians', in Frederick E. Hoxie (ed.), *Indians in American History* (Arlington Heights, IL: Harlan Davidson, 1988), pp. 231–50 (pp. 247–8).
66. Nobles, *American Frontiers*, p. 15.
67. Quoted in Neil Longley York, *Turning the World Upside Down: The War of American Independence and the Problem of Empire* (Westport, CT: Praeger, 2003), p. 153; italics are mine.
68. Wiley Sword, *President Washington's Indian War: The Struggle for the Old Northwest, 1790–1795* (Norman, OK: University of Oklahoma Press, 1985), p. xiii.
69. Quoted in Peterson, *Thomas Jefferson and the New Nation*, p. 773.
70. Calloway, *One Vast Winter Count*, p. 373.
71. Joy, *American Expansionism*, p. 5.

72. Anderson and Cayton, *The Dominion of War*, pp. 190–1.
73. Quoted in Wallace, *Jefferson and the Indians*, p. 163; italics are mine.
74. Francis Jennings, *The Creation of America: Through Revolution and Empire* (New York: Oxford University Press, 2000), p. 282.
75. Quoted in Dippie, *The Vanishing American*, p. 5.
76. Williams, 'American Imperialism and the Indians', p. 234.
77. Hurt, *The Indian Frontier*, p. xv.
78. Dorothy V. Jones, *License for Empire: Colonialism by Treaty in Early America* (Chicago: University of Chicago Press, 1982), p. 186.
79. Hurt, *The Indian Frontier*, p. 246.
80. Williams, 'American Imperialism and the Indians', p. 237.
81. Buchanan, *Jackson's Way*, pp. 37–8.
82. DuVal, *The Native Ground*, p. 227; italics are mine.
83. Hurt, *The Indian Frontier*, p. 247.
84. Quoted in Bessel, *Nazism and War*, pp. 60–1.
85. Quoted in Koehl, *RKFDV*, pp. 27, 52.
86. Anna Bramwell, *Blood and Soil: Richard Walther Darré and Hitler's 'Green Party'* (Abbotsbrook: Kensal Press, 1985), pp. 15, 118–19, 134, 147, 179, 187.
87. Mazower, *Hitler's Empire*, p. 219.
88. Liulevicius, *War Land on the Eastern Front*, pp. 252–3, 265, 272.
89. Quoted in Kiernan, *Blood and Soil*, p. 473.
90. Quoted in Rich, *Hitler's War Aims, Volume 2*, p. 330.
91. Quoted in Bessel, *Nazism and War*, pp. 123–4.
92. Speech of 6 October 1939, quoted in Mazower, *Hitler's Empire*, p. 81.
93. Speech of 16 December 1941, quoted in Noakes and Pridham, *Nazism 1919–1945*, Vol. 3, p. 358.
94. Hitler, *Table Talk*, 6 August 1942, p. 466.
95. Ibid., 11 April 1942, p. 320.
96. Ibid., 22 July 1942, pp. 443–4.
97. Quoted in Heinemann, 'Towards an "Ethnic Reconstruction" of Occupied Europe', p. 493.
98. Speech of the *Reichsführer-SS* at the SS Group Leader Meeting in Posen, 4 October 1943, Holocaust Educational and Archive Research Team, full text of the speech at www.holocaustresearchproject.org/holoprelude/posen (accessed 22 October 2008).
99. Quoted in Heinemann, 'Towards an "Ethnic Reconstruction" of Occupied Europe', p. 507.
100. Quoted in Rich, *Hitler's War Aims, Volume 2*, p. 350.
101. For a thorough overall discussion of the GPO in English, see the relevant chapter (Chapter 12, 'The "General Plan for the East" ') in Aly and Heim, *Architects of Annihilation*, pp. 253–82.
102. Quoted in Rich, *Hitler's War Aims, Volume 2*, p. 356; italics are mine.
103. Bloxham, *Final Solution*, p. 180.
104. Harvey, *Women in the Nazi East*, pp. 237–8.
105. Snyder, *Bloodlands*, p. 254.
106. Hine and Faragher, *The American West*, p. 159.
107. Nugent, *Habits of Empire*, p. 222.
108. White, *'It's Your Misfortune and None of My Own'*, p. 58.
109. Kathleen Neils Conzen, 'A Saga of Families', in Milner, O'Connor, and Sandweiss (eds), *The Oxford History of the American West*, pp. 315–57 (p. 341).

110. Nugent, *Habits of Empire*, pp. xvi, 45.
111. White, *'It's Your Misfortune and None of My Own'*, pp. 184–6.
112. Kulikoff, *From British Peasants to Colonial American Farmers*, pp. 127, 138, 148.
113. Nugent, *Habits of Empire*, pp. 15, 39.
114. Kulikoff, *From British Peasants to Colonial American Farmers*, p. 283, 288.
115. See 'Afterword' in ibid., pp. 289–92.
116. Quoted in Hine and Faragher, *The American West*, p. 199.
117. White, *'It's Your Misfortune and None of My Own'*, p. 58.
118. Hurt, *The Indian Frontier*, p. 147.
119. Hitler, *Table Talk*, 2 November 1941, p. 86.
120. Mazower, *Hitler's Empire*, pp. 146–7.
121. Hitler, *Table Talk*, 9 July 1942, p. 434.
122. Bloxham, *Final Solution*, pp. 185–6.
123. Decree of the *Führer* and Reich Chancellor for the Strengthening of the German Nationality, 7 October 1939, in Noakes and Pridham, *Nazism 1919–1945*, Vol. 3, pp. 322–3.
124. Liulevicius, *The German Myth of the East*, p. 187.
125. Koehl, *RKFDV*, pp. 101, 110.
126. Noakes and Pridham, *Nazism 1919–1945*, Vol. 3, p. 323.
127. Hitler, *Table Talk*, 17 October 1941, p. 54.
128. Koehl, *RKFDV*, pp. 147, 226.
129. Baranowski, *Nazi Empire*, p. 270.
130. Hitler, *Table Talk*, 16 July 1941.
131. Rich, *Hitler's War Aims*, Vol. 2, pp. 82–3.
132. Michael Wildt, *An Uncompromising Generation: The Nazi Leadership of the Reich Security Main Office*, trans. Tom Lampert (Madison, WI: University of Wisconsin Press, 2009), p. 440.
133. Bloxham, *Final Solution*, p. 178.
134. Ibid., p. 182.
135. Fritzsche, *Life and Death in the Third Reich*, p. 174.
136. The references here are to self-proclaimed 'frontiersman', historian, and future 26th president of the United States Theodore Roosevelt's four-volume history *The Winning of the West* (published between 1889 and 1896) and the Hollywood cinematic class 'How the West Was Won' (1962).
137. Alexander Dallin, *German Rule in Russia, 1941–1945: A Study of Occupation Policies* (New York: St Martin's Press, 1957), pp. 7, 661.
138. Koehl, *RKFDV*, p. 227.
139. Blackbourn, 'Conquest and Mystique', p. 152.
140. Mazower, *Hitler's Europe*, pp. 582–4.
141. Snyder, *Bloodlands*, p. 160.

5   'Out-Group' Policy: 'Eliminating' the 'Natives'

1. DuVal, *The Native Ground*, p. 229.
2. Reginald Horsman, *Expansion and American Indian Policy, 1783–1812* (Norman, OK: University of Oklahoma Press, 1992 [Michigan State University Press, 1967]), p. x.

3. Robert M. Utley, *The Indian Frontier of the American West 1846–1890* (Albuquerque, NM: University of New Mexico Press, 1993 [1984]), pp. 101–3.
4. Hurt, *The Indian Frontier*, pp. 244–5.
5. Wendy Lower, 'A New Ordering of Space and Race: Nazi Colonial Dreams in Zhytomyr, Ukraine, 1941–1944', *German Studies Review*, Vol. 35, No. 2 (2002), pp. 227–54 (p. 228).
6. Browning, *The Origins of the Final Solution*, p. 300.
7. For an informative discussion of these issues, see Chapter 6: 'Make This Land German for Me Again!' and Chapter 7: 'Organizing Disorder: 1941–42' in Mazower, *Hitler's Empire*, pp. 179–256.
8. Francis Paul Prucha, *The Great Father: The United States Government and the American Indians, Volumes I and II*, Unabridged Edition (Lincoln, NE: University of Nebraska Press, 1995 [1984]), pp. 62, 83.
9. Grenier, *The First Way of War*, p. 221.
10. White, *The Middle Ground*, p. 384.
11. For the details of the 'Indian wars', see Grenier, *The First Way of War*; Robert M. Utley and Wilcomb E. Washburn, *Indian Wars* (Boston, MA: Houghton Mifflin Company, 2002 [1977]); and Yenne, *Indian Wars*.
12. Robert M. Utley, 'Total War on the American Indian Frontier', in Manfred F. Boemeke, Roger Chickering, and Stig Forster (eds), *Anticipating Total War, the German and American Experiences, 1871–1914*, (Cambridge: Cambridge University Press, 1999), pp. 399–414 (pp. 401, 405, 410).
13. Utley, *The Indian Frontier*, p. 164.
14. Rossino, *Hitler Strikes Poland*, p. 234.
15. Browning, *The Origins of the Final Solution*, pp. 259, 310.
16. Rich, *Hitler's War Aims, Volume 2*, p. 354.
17. TOP SECRET Memorandum for the Record, prepared on 17 July 1941 by Martin Bormann, as re-printed in *Nazi Conspiracy and Aggression, Volume VII*, Office of United States Chief of Counsel for Prosecution of Axis Criminality (Washington, DC: United States Government Printing Office, 1946). English Translation of Documentary Evidence presented before the International Military Tribunal at Nuremberg, Germany. Translation of Document L-221, pp. 1086–93.
18. Goebbels Directive of 15 February 1943, reprinted in Noakes and Pridham (eds), *Nazism 1919–1945: Vol. 3*, pp. 309–10.
19. Rossino, *Hitler Strikes Poland*, pp. 230, 234–5.
20. Müller and Ueberschär, *Hitler's War in the East, 1941–1945*, p. 284.
21. Quoted in Rich, *Hitler's War Aims: Volume 2*, pp. 351–2, 353.
22. Shepherd, *War in the Wild East*, p. 32.
23. Utley, *The Indian Frontier*, p. 101.
24. Theda Perdue and Michael D. Green, *The Cherokee Nation and the Trail of Tears* (New York: Viking Penguin, 2007), p. 30.
25. Quoted in Appleby, *Thomas Jefferson*, pp. 108–9.
26. Wallace, *Jefferson and the Indians*, pp. 225, 338.
27. Horsman, *Expansion and American Indian Policy*, pp. vii, viii.
28. Perdue and Green, *The Cherokee Nation and the Trail of Tears*, p. 71.
29. DuVal, *The Native Ground*, p. 239.
30. Ibid., pp. 239, 241.

31. Ostler, *The Plains Sioux and U.S. Colonialism*, p. 18.
32. Friedländer, *Nazi Germany and the Jews: Volume I*, p. 168.
33. Burrin, *Nazi Anti-Semitism*, p. 52.
34. Baranowski, *Nazi Empire*, pp. 205, 208.
35. Quoted in Friedländer, *Nazi Germany and the Jews: Volume I*, p. 392.
36. Quoted in Michael Wildt, 'Before the "Final Solution"': The *Judenpolitik* of the SD, 1935–1938', *Leo Baeck Institute Yearbook*, Vol. 43 (1998), pp. 241–69 (p. 267).
37. Friedländer, *Nazi Germany and the Jews: Volume I*, pp. 204, 331.
38. Bloxham, *The Final Solution*, p. 191.
39. Baranowski, *Nazi Empire*, pp. 173, 192.
40. Fritzsche, *Life and Death in the Third Reich*, p. 167.
41. Quoted in David Cesarani, *Eichmann: His Life and Crimes* (London: William Heinemann, 2004), p. 95.
42. White, *'It's Your Misfortune and None of My Own'*, pp. 87, 89, 91.
43. Cesarani, *Eichmann*, p. 79.
44. The phrase is Patrick Wolfe's. Patrick Wolfe, 'Settler Colonialism and the Elimination of the Native', *Journal of Genocide Research*, Vol. 8, No. 4 (2006), pp. 387–409 (p. 400).
45. Prucha, *The Great Father*, p. 179; italics are mine.
46. In his unpublished writings on 'American Indians and Genocide', Raphael Lemkin rightly notes of Indian 'removal': 'There was here no question of purchasing uncultivated land and of "civilizing" the Indian. The only intent was the expulsion of the Indian to make room for whites.' Quoted in John Docker, 'Are Settler-Colonies Inherently Genocidal?: Re-Reading Lemkin', in Moses (ed.), *Empire, Colony, Genocide*, pp. 81–101 (p. 95).
47. DuVal, *The Native Ground*, p. 239.
48. *New York Times* Editorial, 'Secretary Teller's Indian Policy', 29 April 1882, reprinted in Robert Hays (ed.), *Editorializing 'the Indian Problem': The New York Times on Native Americans, 1860–1900* (Carbondale, IL: Southern Illinois University Press, 2007 [1997]), pp. 287–90 (p. 289).
49. Quoted in Dippie, *The Vanishing American*, p. 47; italics are mine.
50. Quoted in Brands, *Andrew Jackson*, p. 435.
51. Quoted in Reginald Horsman, 'The Indian Policy of an "Empire for Liberty"', in Frederick E. Hoxie, Ronald Hoffman, and Peter J. Albert (eds), *Native Americans in the Early Republic* (Charlottesville, VA: University of Virginia Press, 1999), pp. 37–61 (pp. 60–61).
52. Quoted in Dippie, *The Vanishing American*, p. 70.
53. James H. Merrell, 'American Nations, Old and New: Reflections on Indians and the Early Republic', 'Afterword', in Hoxie, Hoffman, and Albert (eds), *Native Americans and the Early Republic*, pp. 333–53 (pp. 350–3).
54. William E. Unrau, *The Rise and Fall of Indian Country, 1825–1855* (Lawrence, KS: University Press of Kansas, 2007), pp. 3, 5.
55. Indian Commissioner Luke Lea, 27 November 1850, extract from the Annual Report of the Commissioner of Indian Affairs, reprinted in Francis Paul Prucha (ed.), *Documents of United States Indian Policy* (Lincoln, NE: University of Nebraska Press, 2000 [1975]), p. 81; italics are mine.
56. Quoted in Dippie, *The Vanishing American*, p. 75.

57. Quoted in Prucha, *The Great Father*, p. 317.
58. William T. Hagan, 'The Reservation Policy: Too Little and Too Late', in Jane F. Smith and Robert M. Kvasnicka (eds), *Indian-White Relations: A Persistent Paradox* (Washington, DC: Howard University Press, 1976), pp. 157–69 (p. 161). For a broader literature that explores very different themes in relation to the reservation system, see Robert A. Trennent, Jr, *Alternative to Extinction: Federal Indian Policy and the Beginnings of the Reservation System, 1846–51* (Philadelphia, PA: Temple University, Press, 1975) on the origins of the Indian reservation system as a perceived viable and obtainable 'alternative' to Indian 'extinction'; Prucha, *The Great Father*, pp. 631–58 on Indian policies of 'civilization' and 'Americanization'; and White, *'It's Your Misfortune and None of My Own'*, pp. 91–4 on 'fraud' and 'mismanagement' on the Indian reservations.
59. Quoted in Utley, *The Indian Frontier*, p. 63.
60. Quoted in Elliott West, *The Contested Plains: Indians, Goldseekers, and the Rush to Colorado* (Lawrence, KS: University Press of Kansas, 1998), p. 283.
61. The phrase is Elliott West's; see Elliott West, *The Last Indian War: The Nez Perce Story* (New York: Oxford University Press, 2009), p. 102.
62. Hagan, 'The Reservation Policy', p. 166.
63. Quoted in Philip Weeks, *Farewell My Nation: The American Indian and the United States in the Nineteenth Century* (Wheeling, IL: Harlan Davidson, 2001 [1990]), p. 79.
64. Quoted in Aly and Heim, *Architects of Annihilation*, p. 161.
65. Quoted in Browning, *The Origins of the Final Solution*, p. 83.
66. Quoted in Friedländer, *Nazi Germany and the Jews: Volume II*, p. 81.
67. Quoted in Rossino, *Hitler Strikes Poland*, p. 90.
68. Epstein, *Model Nazi*, p. 177.
69. Quoted in Aly and Heim, *Architects of Annihilation*, p. 162.
70. Cesarani, *Eichmann*, pp, 85–6.
71. Quoted in Götz Aly, *'Final Solution': Nazi Population Policy and the Murder of the European Jews* (London: Arnold, 1999), p. 3.
72. Peter Longerich, *Holocaust* (New York: Oxford University Press, 2010), p. 163.
73. Wildt, *An Uncompromising Generation*, p. 302.
74. Browning, *The Origins of the Final Solution*, pp. 88–9.
75. Quoted in ibid., p. 103.
76. Quoted in Friedländer, *Nazi Germany and the Jews: Volume II*, p. 136.
77. Quoted in Cesarani, *Eichmann*, p. 89.
78. Aly and Heim, *Architects of Annihilation*, p. 177.
79. Wolfe, 'Settler Colonialism and the Elimination of the Native', p. 403.
80. Hitler, *Table Talk*, p. 3.
81. Wolfe, 'Settler Colonialism and the Elimination of the Native', p. 403.
82. Prucha, *The Great Father*, pp. xxvii, 61, 488.
83. Indian Commissioner Francis A. Walker on Indian policy, 1 November 1872, extract from the Annual Report of the Commissioner of Indian Affairs, reprinted in Prucha (ed.), *Documents of United States Indian Policy*, pp. 137, 139.
84. Resolutions of the Indian Peace Commission, 9 October 1868, reprinted in Prucha (ed.), *Documents of United States Indian Policy*, p. 116.

85. Blackhawk, *Violence Over the Land*, p. 215.
86. Report of the Indian Peace Commission, 7 January 1868, reprinted in Prucha (ed.), *Documents of United States Indian Policy*, pp. 105–6.
87. *New York Times* Editorial, 'Taming the Savage', 15 April 1875, reprinted in Hays, *Editorializing 'the Indian Problem'*, pp. 69–70.
88. Hays, *Editorializing 'the Indian Problem'*, p. 255.
89. On the boarding school 'experience' and its impact on Indian children, see David Wallace Adams, *Education for Extinction: American Indians and the Boarding School Experience, 1875–1928* (Lawrence, KS: University of Kansas Press, 1995) and Ward Churchill, *Kill the Indian, Save the Man: The Genocidal Impact of American Indian Residential Schools* (San Francisco, CA: City Lights Books, 2004).
90. Quoted in Utley, *The Indian Frontier*, pp. 129–30.
91. Quoted in Ostler, *The Plains Sioux and U.S. Colonialism*, p. 48.
92. Quoted in West, *The Last Indian War*, p. 105.
93. Prucha, *The Great Father*, p. xxix.
94. *New York Times* Editorial, 'The Indian Territory', 5 December 1884, reprinted in Hays, *Editorializing 'the Indian Problem'*, p. 253.
95. Utley, *The Indian Frontier*, pp. 212–13, 269.
96. Stuart Banner, *How the Indians Lost Their Land: Law and Power on the Frontier* (Cambridge, MA: Harvard University Press, 2005), pp. 228, 285, 287.
97. Ostler, *The Plains Sioux and U.S. Colonialism*, p. 8.
98. Wolfe, 'Settler Colonialism and the Elimination of the Native', p. 397.
99. Browning, *The Origins of the Final Solution*, pp. 110, 253, 258, 279.
100. Michael R. Marrus and Robert O. Paxton, 'The Nazis and the Jews in Occupied Western Europe, 1940–1944', in Francois Fuet (ed.), *Unanswered Questions: Nazi Germany and the Genocide of the Jews* (New York: Schocken, 1989), pp. 172–98 (pp. 172, 176–7, 182).
101. The phrase is Christopher Browning's. Browning, *The Origins of the Final Solution*, p. 308.
102. Ibid., pp. 352–3.
103. Wannsee Protocol, reprinted in Noakes and Pridham (eds), *Nazism, 1919–1945: Volume 3*, pp. 535–7. As Eichmann later recalled at his 1961 trial, 'various types of solutions were discussed' by the conference participants, which involved the 'killing, elimination, and annihilation' of 'eleven million Jews'. Quoted in ibid., p. 543.
104. Dieter Pohl, 'War, Occupation and the Holocaust in Poland', in Stone (ed.), *The Historiography of the Holocaust*, pp. 88–119 (p. 99).
105. Lower, *Nazi Empire-Building*, p. 10.
106. Quoted in Lower, *Nazi Empire-Building*, p. 8.
107. Mazower, *Hitler's Empire*, p. 10.
108. Baranowski, *Nazi Empire*, p. 317.
109. Robert Gellately, 'The Third Reich, the Holocaust and Visions of Serial Genocide', in Robert Gellately and Ben Kiernan (eds), *The Specter of Genocide: Mass Murder in Historical Perspective* (New York: Cambridge University Press, 2003), pp. 241–63 (p. 262).
110. Alex J. Kay, *Exploitation, Resettlement, Mass Murder: Political and Economic Planning for German Occupation Policy in the Soviet Union, 1940–1941* (New York: Berghahn Books, 2006), p. 121.

111. Connelly, 'Nazis and Slavs', p. 33.
112. Aly, *'Final Solution'*, pp. 247, 261, n. 12.
113. Burrin, *Nazi Anti-Semitism*, p. 128.
114. Heinemann, 'Towards an "Ethnic Reconstruction" of Occupied Europe', p. 517.
115. Bloxham, *The Final Solution*, p. 186.
116. Snyder, Bloodlands, pp. 186, 254, 273.
117. Aly, *'Final Solution'*, p. 256.

Part III   Frontier Genocide

1. Maier, *Among Empires*, pp. 78–9, 82, 94.
2. Malcolm Anderson, *Frontiers: Territory and State Formation in the Modern World* (Oxford: Polity Press, 1996), pp. 2–3.
3. West, *The Contested Plains*, p. xxiii.
4. Maier, *Among Empires*, pp. 82–3.
5. Valiani, Arafaat A, 'Violence', in Darity (ed.), *International Encyclopedia of the Social Sciences*, Vol. 8, pp. 622–5.
6. Maier, *Among Empires*, pp. 19–20.
7. Jones, *Genocide*, pp. 67–8.
8. Wolfe, 'Settler Colonialism and the Elimination of the Native', p. 387.
9. Dan Stone, *Histories of the Holocaust* (New York: Oxford University Press, 2010), p. 218.
10. Jones, *Genocide*, p. 48.
11. See, for instance Martin Shaw, *War and Genocide: Organized Killing in Modern Society* (Cambridge: Polity Press, 2003). Also see Shaw, 'The General Hybridity of War and Genocide', pp. 461–73.
12. Shaw, 'The General Hybridity of War and Genocide', pp. 461–2; italics are Shaw's.
13. Jones, *Genocide*, pp. 48–9.
14. Robert Melson, 'Revolution and Genocide: On the Causes of the Armenian Genocide and the Holocaust', in R. G. Hovannisian (ed.), *The Armenian Genocide: History, Politics, Ethics* (New York: St. Martin's Press, 1992), pp. 80–102 (p. 96).
15. Martin Shaw, *What is Genocide?* (Cambridge: Polity Press, 2007), p. 35.
16. Mark Levene, *Genocide in the Age of the Nation State: Volume 1: The Meaning of Genocide* (London: I.B. Tauris, 2005), p. 51.
17. Shaw, *What is Genocide?*, pp. 111–12.

6   War and Genocide: 'Cleansing' the *Lebensraum*

1. Rather than attempting to separate 'cleansing' from 'genocide', it is more helpful, in my view, to understand 'ethnic cleansing' (following Martin Shaw) as genocide's 'territorial' and 'spatial' dimension. 'Genocide', in this conceptualization, remains the overarching category and core act.
2. For two recent considerations of 'genocide' in the case of Native Americans, see Cave, 'Genocide in the Americas', in Stone (ed.), *The Historiography of Genocide*, pp. 273–95, and Jeffrey Ostler, 'The Question of Genocide in U.S.

History, 1783–1890', occasional paper (in the author's possession) given at Yale Genocide Studies Program Seminar Series, 17 November 2005. Jeffrey Ostler is currently working on a book project with the title 'The Destruction and Survival of American Indian Nations'.

3. See, for example, Smithers, 'Rethinking Genocide in North America', in Bloxham and Moses (eds), *The Oxford Handbook of Genocide*, pp. 322–41 and Brenden Rensink, 'Genocide of Native Americans: Historical Facts and Historiographical Debates', in Samuel Totten and Robert K. Hitchcock (eds), *Genocide of Indigenous Peoples* (New Brunswick, NJ: Transaction Publishers, 2011), pp. 15–36. Also see Chapter 8, 'Genocide in the United States' in Kiernan, *Blood and Soil*, pp. 310–63.

4. For two excellent recent overviews of Holocaust historiography, see Dan Stone, 'The Holocaust and Its Historiography', in Stone (ed.), *The Historiography of Genocide*, pp. 373–99 and Stone, *Histories of the Holocaust*.

5. See, for example, Weitz, *A Century of Genocide*.

6. Hinton, 'The Dark Side of Modernity', p. 29.

7. The two phrases are Ben Kiernan's; see Kiernan, *Blood and Soil*, p. 21.

8. For support for this view, see Ostler, 'The Question of Genocide in U.S. History, 1783–1890', p. 8.

9. Quoted in Kiernan, *Blood and Soil*, p. 248.

10. Ibid., p. 319.

11. Russell Thornton, *American Indian Holocaust and Survival: A Population History Since 1492* (Norman, OK: University of Oklahoma Press, 1990 [1987]), pp. xv–xvi.

12. For support of this view, see Ostler, 'The Question of Genocide in U.S. History, 1783–1890', p. 15.

13. Quoted in Prucha (ed.), *Documents of United States Indian Policy*, pp. 102–3.

14. Kiernan, *Blood and Soil*, p. 454.

15. Fritzsche, *Life and Death in the Third Reich*, p. 155.

16. Jürgen Zimmerer, 'Colonialism and the Holocaust: Towards an Archeology of Genocide', in A. Dirk Moses (ed.), *Genocide and Settler Society: Frontier Violence and Stolen Indigenous Children in Australian History* (New York: Berghahn Books, 2004), pp. 49–76 (p. 49).

17. Browning, *The Origins of the Final Solution*, p. 241.

18. Quoted in ibid., p. 429.

19. Quoted in Aly, *'Final Solution'*, pp. 1–2.

20. Quoted in Noakes and Pridham, *Nazism 1919–1945*, Vol. 3, p. 396.

21. For support for this view, see Bergen, *War & Genocide*.

22. Furber and Lower, 'Colonial Genocide in Nazi-Occupied Poland and Ukraine', p. 373.

23. Robert Gellately, 'The Third Reich, the Holocaust and Visions of Serial Genocide', in Gellately and Kiernan (eds), *The Specter of Genocide*, pp. 241–63 (p. 263).

24. Christopher R. Browning, 'The Nazi Empire', in Bloxham and Moses (eds), *The Oxford Handbook of Genocide Studies*, pp. 407–25 (pp. 407, 413). In my view, most Holocaust scholars fail to appreciate the degree to which these projects were interconnected, as well as their essentially colonial origins, context, and content.

25. Housden, *Hans Frank, Lebensraum, and the Holocaust*, pp. 128, 142, 254.

26. Jones, *Genocide*, p. 70.
27. Grenier, *The First Way of War*, pp. 41–2.
28. Cave, 'Genocide in the Americas', pp. 283–5.
29. Grenier, *The First Way of War*, p. 221.
30. Quoted in Kiernan, *Blood and Soil*, p. 375.
31. Perdue and Green, *The Cherokee Nation and the Trail of Tears*, pp. xiv–xv, 117.
32. Thornton, *American Indian Holocaust and Survival*, p. 101.
33. Quoted in Utley, *The Indian Frontier*, p. 63.
34. *New York Times* Editorial, 'The Indian Massacre', 31 December 1890, reprinted in Hays, *Editorializing 'the Indian Problem'*, pp. 227–9. The editorial, a commentary on the recent massacre at Wounded Knee, South Dakota, claimed that the reservation Indians had been 'starved into revolt'.
35. Andrew C. Isenberg, *The Destruction of the Bison: An Environmental History, 1750–1920* (Cambridge: Cambridge University Press, 2000), pp. 3, 129–30, 155. As Isenberg points out, the deliberate destruction of Indian animal resources was used in other theatres of 'pacification' operations. Kit Carson, for instance, ordered the destruction of Navajo sheep in order to force the Navajo Indians to submit to the reservation policy, and the US Army often killed Indian horses (used to hunt for food) as a military strategy. See ibid., pp. 128–9.
36. See Adams, *Education for Extinction*.
37. See Churchill, *Kill the Indian, Save the Man*.
38. See Victoria Haskins and Margaret D. Jacobs, 'Stolen Generations and Vanishing Indians: The Removal of Indigenous Children as a Weapon of War in the United States and Australia, 1870–1940', in James Marten (ed.), *Children in War: A Historical Anthology* (New York: New York University Press, 2002), pp. 227–42.
39. Quoted in Michaela Kipp, 'The Holocaust in the Letters of German Soldiers on the Eastern Front (1939–1944)', *Journal of Genocide Research*, Vol. 9, No. 4 (2007), pp. 601–15 (p. 609).
40. Quoted in Boll, Heer, and Manoschek, 'Prelude to a Crime', p. 30.
41. Quoted in ibid., p. 29.
42. Quoted in Herr, 'Russia', p. 152.
43. Quoted in Boll and Safrian, 'The Sixth Army', p. 98.
44. Quoted in Boll, Heer, and Manoschek, 'Prelude to a Crime', p. 31.
45. Shepherd, *War in the Wild East*, p. 126.
46. Bergen, *War & Genocide*, p. 162.
47. Quoted in Dwork and van Pelt, *Auschwitz*, p. 207.
48. Browning, *The Origins of the Final Solution*, p. 89.
49. Ronnie S. Landau, *The Nazi Holocaust* (Chicago, IL: Ivan R. Dee, 1994 [1992]), pp. 154–5.
50. Hilberg, *The Destruction of the European Jews*, p. 74.
51. Dwork and van Pelt, *Auschwitz*, p. 247.
52. Quoted in Isabel Heinemann, ' "Until the Last Drop of Good Blood": The Kidnapping of "Racially Valuable" Children and Nazi Racial Policy in Occupied Eastern Europe', in Moses (ed.), *Genocide and Settler Society*, pp. 244–66 (p. 255).

53. Ibid., pp. 244–5.
54. For the details, see Kiernan, *Blood and Soil*, pp. 215, 219–36.
55. Wilson, *The Earth Shall Weep*, p. 94. For details, see Alfred A. Cave, 'The 1637 Pequot War and the Question of Native American Genocide', occasional paper (in the author's possession) given at Yale Genocide Studies Program Seminar Series, 29 August 2005, pp. 1–30.
56. See Norbert Finzsch, ' "[...] Extirpate or remove that Vermine": Genocide, Biological Warfare, and Settler Imperialism in the Eighteenth and Early Nineteenth Century', *Journal of Genocide Research*, Vol. 10, No. 2 (2008), pp. 215–32.
57. Cave, 'Genocide in the Americas', p. 283.
58. See Grenier, *The First Way of War*.
59. Ibid., pp. 41, 54.
60. Ibid., pp. 202–3.
61. Cave, 'Genocide in the Americas', pp. 284–5.
62. See Blackhawk, *Violence Over the Land*.
63. Nester, *The Frontier War for American Independence*, p. 3.
64. Quoted in Nash, *The Unknown American Revolution*, p. 351.
65. For the details, see Barbara Alice Mann, *George Washington's War on Native America, 1779–1782* (Westport, CT: Praeger, 2005).
66. Cave, 'Genocide in the Americas', p. 286.
67. Quoted in Nobles, *American Frontiers*, p. 90.
68. Quoted in Calloway, *The American Revolution in Indian Country*, pp. 51, 53.
69. Ibid., p. 293.
70. See Grenier, *The First Way of War*, pp. 170–203.
71. Anthony F. C. Wallace, *The Long, Bitter Trail: Andrew Jackson and the Indians* (New York: Hill and Wang, 1993), pp. 51, 57, 63.
72. Quoted in Sean Michael O'Brien, *In Bitterness and in Tears: Andrew Jackson's Destruction of the Creeks and Seminoles* (Westport, CT: Praeger, 2003), p. 239.
73. For details, see Gary Clayton Anderson, *The Conquest of Texas: Ethnic Cleansing in the Promised Land, 1820–1875* (Norman, OK: University of Oklahoma Press, 2005).
74. For the details, see Benjamin Madley, 'American Genocide: The Northern California Indian Catastrophe, 1846–1873', (unpublished doctoral dissertation, History Department, Yale University, 2008).
75. Kiernan, *Blood and Soil*, p. 358.
76. The *San Francisco Bulletin*, 'Indian Butcheries in California', 18 June 1860, reprinted in Clifford E. Trafzer and Joel R. Hyer (eds), *"Exterminate Them": Written Accounts of the Murder, Rape, and Slavery of Native Americans During the California Gold Rush, 1848–1868* (East Lansing, MI: Michigan State University Press, 1999), p. 129.
77. *New York Times* Editorial, 'A Premium for Scalps', 23 June 1867, reprinted in Hays, *Editorializing 'the Indian Problem'*, pp. 213–14; italics in the original.
78. Ibid., pp. 5–6.
79. Jürgen Zimmerer, 'Annihilation in Africa: The "Race War" in German Southwest Africa (1904–1908) and its Significance for a Global History of Genocide', *Bulletin of the German Historical Institute*, Washington, DC, No. 37 (Fall 2005), pp. 51–7.

80. Quoted in Kiernan, *Blood and Soil*, p. 386.
81. For a discussion of this debate, see Jürgen Zimmerer, 'Colonial Genocide: The Herero and Nama War (1904–08) in German South West Africa and Its Significance', in Stone (ed.), *The Historiography of Genocide*, pp. 323–42 (pp. 334–8). On the broader debate, see Chapter 5, 'Genocide, the Holocaust, and the History of Colonialism', in Stone, *Histories of the Holocaust*, pp. 203–44.
82. Madley, 'From Africa to Auschwitz', pp. 429, 458.
83. Zimmerer, 'Annihilation in Africa', p. 53.
84. Madley, 'From Africa to Auschwitz', p. 430. Recent research suggests some further evidence of transmission (via both direct and indirect channels) of colonial ideas, practices, and policies from German South West Africa to decision-makers and policy planners in Hitler's Third Reich. See Jürgen Zimmerer, 'The Birth of *Ostland* Out of the Spirit of Colonialism: A Postcolonial Perspective on the Nazi Policy of Conquest and Extermination', *Patterns of Prejudice*, Vol. 39, No. 2 (2005), pp. 197–219 (p. 211) and Eric Weitz's project seeking causal links, 'Germans Abroad: The Herero and Armenian Genocides and the Origins of the Holocaust', Lecture at the Strassler Family Center for Holocaust and Genocide Studies, Clark University, 2 November 2005.
85. Rossino, *Hitler Strikes Poland*, p. 234.
86. See the Directive of 13 March 1941, reprinted in Noakes and Pridham (eds), *Nazism 1919–1945: Volume 3*, p. 484.
87. For a useful study of the *Einsatzgruppen*, see Richard Rhodes, *Masters of Death: The SS-Einsatzgruppen and the Invention of the Holocaust* (New York: Alfred A. Knopf, 2002).
88. Kiernan, *Blood and Soil*, p. 241.
89. See the convincing argument in Rossino, *Hitler Strikes Poland*.
90. Hilberg, *The Destruction of the European Jews*, pp. 138–9.
91. Quoted in Shepherd, *War in the Wild East*, p. 84.
92. Wendy Lower, 'From Berlin to Babi Yar: The Nazi War Against the Jews, 1941–1944', *Journal of Religion and Society*, The Kripke Center, Kripke Center Lecture, Vol. 9 (2007), pp. 1–14 (p. 11). At Babi Yar, a ravine outside of the Ukrainian capital of Kiev, 33, 711 Jewish men, women, and children were shot over the course of two days, 29–30 September 1941. At Auschwitz, a death camp in Upper Silesia, some 1,500,000 civilians (over 90 per cent of whom were Jews) were gassed in 1941–2.
93. Ian Kershaw, *Hitler, the Germans, and the Final Solution* (Jerusalem: Yad Vashem International Institute for Holocaust Research and New Haven, CT: Yale University Press, 2008), p. 373.
94. For the Jewish victims, see Father Patrick Desbois, *The Holocaust by Bullets: A Priest's Journey to Uncover the Truth Behind the Murder of 1.5 Million Jews* (New York: Palgrave Macmillan, 2008).
95. Bloxham, *The Final Solution*, p. 251.
96. Hilberg, *The Destruction of the European Jews*, p. 221.
97. Fritzsche, *Life and Death in the Third Reich*, pp. 250–1, 262.
98. Kiernan, *Blood and Soil*, p. 320.
99. *New York Times* Editorial, 'The Piegan Slaughter and Its Apologists', 10 March 1879, reprinted in Hays, *Editorializing 'the Indian Problem'*, pp. 216–17.

100. Quoted in Weeks, *Farewell My Nation*, p. 156.
101. J. P. Dunn, *Massacres of the Mountains: A History of the Indian Wars of the Far West, 1815–1875* (New York, 1886), pp. 366–7 as cited in Kernan, *Blood and Soil*, p. 362.
102. Mann, *George Washington's War on Native America*, series foreword, Bruce E. Johansen, p. xi.
103. *New York Times* Editorial, 'Our Indian Policy', 5 July 1867, reprinted in Hays, *Editorializing 'the Indian Problem'*, pp. 262–5.
104. Thornton, *American Indian Holocaust and Survival*, p. 16.
105. Ibid., pp. 48–9.
106. Kershaw, *Fateful Choices*, p. 470.
107. Michael Burleigh, 'What if Nazi Germany had defeated the Soviet Union?', in Niall Ferguson (ed.), *Virtual History: Alternatives and Counterfactuals* (New York: Basic Books, 1999 [1997]), pp. 321–47 (p. 325).
108. Kershaw, *Fateful Choices*, p. 4.
109. Mann, *The Dark Side of Democracy*, pp. 211–12, 227.
110. Ibid., p. 277.
111. Baranowski, *Nazi Empire*, p. 228.
112. For revealing and appropriately nuanced discussions of the Nazi treatment of Slavs and Jews in 'the East', see Furber and Lower, 'Colonialism and Genocide in Nazi-Occupied Poland and Ukraine' and Connelly, 'Nazis and Slavs'.
113. Herf, *The Jewish Enemy*, p. 270.
114. Jürgen Matthäus, 'Controlled Escalation: Himmler's Men in the Summer of 1941 and the Holocaust in the Occupied Soviet Territories', *Holocaust and Genocide Studies*, Vol. 21, No. 2 (2007), pp. 218–42 (p. 221).
115. Himmler's speech to SS leaders in Posen on 4 October 1943, reprinted in Noakes and Pridham (eds), *Nazism 1919-1945: Volume 3*, pp. 617–18. The date of the speech is incorrectly given by Noakes and Pridham as '4 October 1944'.
116. Kipp, 'The Holocaust in the Letters of German Soldiers', p. 604.
117. See Browning, *The Origins of the Final Solution*, n. 21, p. 516.
118. Landau, *The Nazi Holocaust*, p. 180. Civilian deaths also included some 200,000 physically and mentally disabled persons and an estimated 220,000 Roma ('Gypsies') murdered by the Nazis and their allies (mostly in 'the East').
119. Boll, Herr, and Manoschek, 'Prelude to Crime', p. 31.
120. Deborah Dwork and Robert Jan van Pelt, *Holocaust: a History* (New York: W. W. Norton, 2003 [2002]), p. 379.
121. For a useful formulation of 'genocidal occurrence', see Levene, *Genocide in the Age of the Nation State*, Vol. 1, p. 35. Levene writes, 'Genocide occurs when a state, perceiving the integrity of its agenda to be threatened by an aggregate population … seeks to remedy the situation by the systematic, *en masse* physical elimination of that aggregate, *in toto*, or until it is no longer perceived to represent a threat'.
122. Thorton, *American Indian Holocaust and Survival*, p. 90.
123. On this point, see Elazar Barkan, Elazar, 'Genocides of Indigenous Peoples: Rhetoric of Human Rights', in Gellately and Kiernan (eds), *The Specter of Genocide*, pp. 117–39 (p. 136).

124. Mazower, *Hitler's Empire*, pp. 414–15.
125. Andrew Charlesworth, 'The Topography of Genocide', in Stone (ed.), *The Historiography of the Holocaust*, pp. 247–8.

Conclusion

1. For a thought-provoking essay in defence of the methodology of counterfactual history, see Niall Ferguson, 'Virtual History: Towards a "Chaotic" Theory of the Past', in Niall Ferguson (ed.), *Virtual History*, pp. 1–90.
2. Bloxham, *The Final Solution*, pp. 245–6.
3. For support for this view, see Aly and Heim, *Architects of Annihilation*, p. 282; Bloxham, *The Final Solution*, p. 246; Burleigh, 'Nazi Europe', pp. 332–3; Dwork and vanPelt, *Holocaust*, p. 379; and Epstein, *Model Nazi*, p. 12.
4. Karl Jacoby, ' "The Broad Platform of Extermination": Nature and Violence in the Nineteenth Century North American Borderlands', *Journal of Genocide Research*, Vol. 10, No. 2 (2008), pp. 249–67 (p. 263).
5. Quoted in Williams, 'American Imperialism', pp. 247–8).
6. For an informative discussion of the issues and challenges involved in integrating the history of the North American West into the field of genocide studies, particularly in a comparative sense, see Rensink, 'The Sand Creek Phenomenon', pp. 9–27; also see Rensink, 'Genocide of Native Americans: Historical Facts and Historiographical Debates', in Totten and Hitchcock (eds), *Genocide of Indigenous Peoples*, pp. 15–36.
7. See Marcia Klotz, 'Global Visions: From the Colonial to the National Socialist World', *European Studies Journal*, Vol. 16 (1999), pp. 37–68.
8. Bloxham, *The Final Solution*, p. 178.
9. Lower, 'Hitler's "Garden of Eden" in Ukraine', pp. 185–6, 189, 198–9.
10. Valdis O. Lumans, 'A Reassessment of *Volksdeutsch* and Jews in the Volhynia-Galicia-Narew Resettlement', in Alan E. Steinweis and Daniel E. Rogers (eds), *The Impact of Nazism: New Perspectives of the Third Reich and Its Legacy* (Lincoln, NE: University of Nebraska Press, 2003), pp. 81–100 (pp. 82, 97).
11. Heinemann, 'Towards an "Ethnic Reconstruction" of Occupied Europe', pp. 494, 517. For a study which emphasizes the connections between the Nazi persecution and murder of European Jewry and the wider Nazi imperial-colonial project, see Adam Tooze, *The Wages of Destruction: The Making and Breaking of the Nazi Economy* (New York: Penguin Books, 2008 [2006]). According to Tooze, Nazi Germany's attempt to 'carve out its own imperial hinterland' by a 'great land grab in "the East"' was 'repeating what Europeans had done across the globe over the previous three centuries'. Tooze, *The Wages of Destruction*, p. xxiv.
12. The phrase is Shelley Baranowski's; see Baranowski, *Nazi Empire*, p. 297.

Bibliography

This bibliography lists all the major works (that is, books, book chapters, journal articles, occasional papers, and theses and dissertations) that were consulted for this project, including works that do not appear in the notes. To assist the reader, it is divided into three topics that correspond to the three major historiographies used in my research.

Transnational colonialism and comparative genocide studies

Anderson, Malcolm, *Frontiers: Territory and State Formation in the Modern World* (Oxford: Polity Press, 1996).

Arendt, Hannah, *The Origins of Totalitarianism* (New York: Harcourt, Brace & World, 1966 [1951]).

Baldwin, Peter, 'The *Historikerstreit* in Context', in Peter Baldwin (ed.), *Reworking the Past: Hitler, the Holocaust and the Historians' Debate* (Boston, MA: Beacon Press, 1990), pp. 3–37.

Barkan, Elazar, 'Genocides of Indigenous Peoples: Rhetoric of Human Rights', in Robert Gellately and Ben Kiernan (eds), *The Specter of Genocide: Mass Murder in Historical Perspective* (New York: Cambridge University Press, 2003), pp. 117–139.

Barta, Tony, 'Relations of Genocide: Land and Lives in the Colonization of Australia', in Isidor Walliman and Michael N. Dobkowski (eds), *Genocide in the Modern Age: Etiology and Case Studies of Mass Death* (Westport, CT: Greenwood Press, 1987), pp. 237–251.

Barta, Tony, 'Discourses of Genocide in Germany and Australia; A Linked History', *Aboriginal History*, Vol. 25 (2001), pp. 37–56.

Barta, Tony, 'Mr. Darwin's Shooters: On Natural Selection and the Naturalizing of Genocide', *Patterns of Prejudice*, 'Special Issue on Colonial Genocide', A. Dirk Moses and Dan Stone (eds), Vol. 39, No. 2 (2005), pp. 116–137.

Barta, Tony, 'Decent Disposal: Australian Historians and the Recovery of Genocide', in Dan Stone (ed.), *The Historiography of Genocide* (Basingstoke: Palgrave Macmillan, 2008), pp. 296–322.

Barta, Tony, 'With Intent to Destroy: On Colonial Intentions and Genocide Denial', Response to Guenter Lewy's contribution, 'Can There Be Genocide Without the Intent to Commit Genocide?', *Journal of Genocide Research*, Vol. 10, No. 1 (2008), pp. 111–119.

Bartov, Omer, 'Seeking the Roots of Modern Genocide: On the Macro- and Microhistory of Mass Murder', in Robert Gellately and Ben Kiernan (eds), *The Specter of Genocide: Mass Murder in Historical Perspective* (New York: Cambridge University Press, 2003), pp. 75–96.

Bauer, Yehuda, 'Holocaust and Genocide: Some Comparisons', in Peter Hayes (ed.), *Lessons and Legacies: The Meaning of the Holocaust in a Changing World* (Evanston, IL: Northwestern University Press, 1991), pp. 36–46.

250

Bauer, Yehuda, 'Comparison of Genocides', in Levon Chorbajian and George Shirinian (eds), *Studies in Contemporary Genocide* (New York: St. Martin's Press, 1999).

Bauer, Yehuda, *Rethinking the Holocaust* (New Haven, CT: Yale University Press, 2001).

Bauman, Zygmunt, *Modernity and the Holocaust* (Oxford: Blackwell, 1989).

Bloxham, Donald and A. Dirk Moses (eds), *The Oxford Handbook of Genocide Studies* (New York: Oxford University Press, 2010).

Bloxham Donald and A. Dirk Moses, 'Editor's Introduction: Changing Themes in the Study of Genocide', in Donald Bloxham and A. Dirk Moses (eds), *The Oxford Handbook of Genocide Studies* (New York: Oxford University Press, 2010), pp. 1–15.

Brantlinger, Patrick, *Dark Vanishings: Discourse on the Extinction of Primitive Races* (Ithaca, NY: Cornell University Press, 2003).

Byrd, Jodi A., ' "Living My Native Life Deadly": Red Lake, Ward Churchill, and the Discourses of Competing Genocides', *American Indian Quarterly*, Vol. 31, No. 2 (2007), pp. 310–332.

Chalk, Frank and Kurt Jonassohn, *The History and Sociology of Genocide: Analyses and Case Studies* (New Haven, CT: Yale University Press, 1990).

Charlesworth, Andrew, 'The Topography of Genocide', in Dan Stone (ed.), *The Historiography of the Holocaust* (Basingstoke: Palgrave Macmillan, 2004), pp. 216–252.

Charny, Israel W., 'Foreword' in Alan S. Rosenbaum (ed.), *Is the Holocaust Unique?: Perspectives on Comparative Genocide* (Boulder, CO: Westview Press, 2001), pp. ix–xv.

Churchill, Ward, *Struggle for the Land: Indigenous Resistance to Genocide, Ecocide and Expropriation in Contemporary North America* (Monroe, ME: Common Courage Press, 1993).

Churchill, Ward, *A Little Matter of Genocide: Holocaust and Denial in the Americas 1492 to the Present* (San Francisco, CA: City Light Books, 1997).

Clendinnen, Inga, *Reading the Holocaust* (Cambridge: Cambridge University Press, 1999).

Mark Cocker, *Rivers of Blood, Rivers of Gold: Europe's Conquest of Indigenous Peoples* (New York: Grove Press, 1998).

Cohen, Deborah and Maura O'Connor (eds), *Comparison and History: Europe in Cross-National Perspective* (New York: Routledge, 2004).

Coombes, Annie (ed.), *Rethinking Settler Colonialism: History and Memory in Australia, Canada, New Zealand and South Africa* (Manchester: Manchester University Press, 2005).

Cribb, Robert, 'Genocide in the Non-Western World: Implications for Holocaust Studies', in S. L. B. Jensen (ed.), *Genocide: Cases, Comparisons and Contemporary Debates* (Copenhagen: Danish Centre for Holocaust and Genocide Studies, 2003), pp. 123–140.

Crosby, Alfred W., *Ecological Imperialism: The Biological Expansion of Europe, 900–1900* (New York: Cambridge University Press, 2000 [1986]).

Curthoys, Ann and John Docker, 'Genocide: Definitions, Questions, Settler Colonies', *Aboriginal History*, Vol. 25 (2001), pp. 1–15.

Curthoys, Ann and John Docker, 'Genocide and Colonialism', interview, *Australian Humanities Review*, Vol. 27 (2002).

Dadrian, Vahakn N. 'The Comparative Aspects of the Armenian and Jewish Cases of Genocide: A Sociohistorical Perspective', in Alan S. Rosenbaum (ed.), *Is the Holocaust Unique?: Perspectives on Comparative Genocide* (Boulder, CO: Westview Press, 2001), pp. 133–168.

Darity, William A. Jr. (ed.), *International Encyclopedia of the Social Sciences*, 2nd ed., 9 Vols. (New York: Macmillan Reference USA, 2008).

Day, David, *Conquest: How Societies Overwhelm Others* (New York: Oxford University Press, 2008).

Docker, John, 'Are Settler-Colonies Inherently Genocidal?: Re-Reading Lemkin', in A. Dirk Moses (ed.), *Empire, Colony, Genocide: Conquest, Occupation, and Subaltern Resistance in World History* (New York: Berghahn, 2008), pp. 81–101.

Eaglestone, Robert, *The Holocaust and the Postmodern* (Oxford: Oxford University Press, 2004).

Elkins, Caroline and Susan Pedersen, 'Introduction: Settler Colonialism: A Concept and Its Uses', in Caroline Elkins and Susan Pedersen (eds), *Settler Colonialism in the Twentieth Century: Projects, Practices, Legacies* (New York: Routledge, 2005), pp. 1–20.

Fein, Helen, 'Genocide: A Sociological Perspective', *Current Sociology*, Vol. 38, No. 1 (1990), pp. 1–126.

Friedberg, Lilian, 'Dare to Compare: Americanizing the Holocaust', *American Indian Quarterly*, Vol. 24, No. 3 (2000), pp. 353–380.

Finzsch, Norbert, ' "It is scarcely possible to conceive that human beings could be so hideous and loathsome": Discourses of Genocide in Eighteenth- and Nineteenth-Century America and Australia', *Patterns of Prejudice*, Vol. 39, No. 2 (2005), pp. 97–115.

Finzsch, Norbert, ' "The aborigines [...] were never annihilated, and still they are becoming extinct": Settler Imperialism and Genocide in Eighteenth and Nineteenth-Century America and Australia', in A. Dirk Moses (ed.), *Empire, Colony, Genocide: Conquest, Occupation, and Subaltern Resistance in World History* (New York: Berghahn Books, 2008), pp. 253–270.

Finzsch, Norbert, 'If It Looks Like a Duck, If It Walks Like a Duck, If It Quacks Like a Duck', Response to Guenter Lewy's contribution, 'Can There Be Genocide Without the Intent to Commit Genocide?', *Journal of Genocide Research*, Vol. 10, No. 1 (2008), pp. 119–126.

Finzsch, Norbert, ' "[...] Extirpate or remove that Vermine": Genocide, Biological Warfare, and Settler Imperialism in the Eighteenth and Early Nineteenth Century', *Journal of Genocide Research*, Vol. 10, No. 2 (2008), pp. 215–232.

Gellately, Robert and Ben Kiernan (eds), *The Specter of Genocide: Mass Murder in Historical Perspective* (New York: Cambridge University Press, 2003).

Gerlach, Christian, 'Extremely Violent Societies: An Alternative to the Concept of Genocide', *Journal of Genocide Research*, Vol. 8, No. 4 (2006), pp. 455–471.

Goldhagen, Daniel Jonah. *Worse Than War: Genocide, Eliminationism, and the Ongoing Assault on Humanity* (New York: PublicAffairs, 2009).

Hardt, Michael and Antonio Negri, *Empire* (Cambridge, MA: Harvard University Press, 2000).

Hinton, Alexander Laban, 'The Dark Side of Modernity: Toward an Anthropology of Genocide', in Alexander Laban Hinton (ed.), *Annihilating Difference: The Anthropology of Genocide* (Berkeley, CA: University of California Press, 2002), pp. 1–40.

Howe, Stephen, *Empire: A Very Short Introduction* (Oxford: Oxford University Press, 2000).

Huttenbach, Henry R., 'From the Editor: No Comparing, No Thinking – The Unavoidable Future of Studying Genocide', *Journal of Genocide Research*, Vol. 2, No. 3 (2000), pp. 319–320.

Huttenbach, Henry R., 'From the Editor: In Search of Genocide – (Re) Focusing on the Existential', *Journal of Genocide Research*, Vol. 3, No. 1 (2001), pp. 7–9.

Huttenbach, Henry R., 'From the Editor: The Eagles and the Worms: On the Future Agenda of Genocide Studies', *Journal of Genocide Research*, Vol. 3, No. 3 (2001), pp. 345–346.

Huttenbach, Henry R., 'From the Editor: New Directions', *Journal of Genocide Research*, Vol. 7, No. 2 (2005), pp. 169–170.

Jones, Adam, *Genocide: A Comprehensive Introduction* (London: Routledge, 2006).

Kakel, Carroll P. III, 'Manifest Destiny and *Lebensraum*: Ideologies of Race and Space, Nation-Making and Genocide', Master's Dissertation, Royal Holloway, University of London, 2004.

Katz, Steven T., 'The Pequot War Reconsidered', *New England Quarterly*, Vol. LXIV, No. 2 (1991), pp. 206–224.

Katz, Steven T., 'Ideology, State Power, and Mass Murder/Genocide', in Peter Hayes (ed.), *Lessons and Legacies: The Meaning of the Holocaust in a Changing World* (Evanston, IL: Northwestern University Press, 1991), pp. 47–89.

Katz, Steven T., *The Holocaust in Historical Context, Volume 1: The Holocaust and Mass Death before the Modern Age* (New York: Oxford University Press, 1994).

Katz, Steven T., 'The Uniqueness of the Holocaust: The Historical Dimension', in Alan S. Rosenbaum (ed.), *Is the Holocaust Unique?: Perspectives on Comparative Genocide* (Boulder, CO: Westview Press, 2001), pp. 49–68.

Kiernan, Ben, *Blood and Soil: A World History of Genocide and Extermination from Sparta to Darfur* (New Haven, CT: Yale University Press, 2007).

Lemkin, Raphael, *Axis Rule in Occupied Europe: Laws of Occupation, Analysis of Government, Proposals for Redress* (Washington, D.C.: Carnegie Endowment for International Peace, 1944).

Levene, Mark, 'Is the Holocaust Simply Another Example of Genocide?', *Patterns of Prejudice*, Vol. 28, No. 2 (1994), pp. 3–26.

Levene, Mark, 'The Changing Face of Mass Murder: Massacre, Genocide and Post-Genocide', *International Social Science Journal*, Vol. 4 (2002), pp. 443–452.

Levene, Mark, *Genocide in the Age of the Nation State: Volume 1: The Meaning of Genocide* (London: I.B. Tauris, 2005).

Levene, Mark, *Genocide in the Age of the Nation State: Volume 2: The Rise of the West and the Coming of Genocide* (London: I.B. Tauris, 2005).

Lewy, Guenter, 'Were American Indians the Victims of Genocide?', *Commentary*, Vol. 118, No. 2 (1994), pp. 55–63.

Levy, Guenter, 'Can There Be Genocide Without the Intent to Commit Genocide?', *Journal of Genocide Research*, Vol. 9, No. 4 (2007), pp. 661–674.

Madley, Benjamin, 'Patterns of Frontier Genocide 1803–1910: The Aboriginal Tasmanians, the Yuki of California and the Herero of Namibia', *Journal of Genocide Research*, Vol. 6, No. 2 (2004), pp. 167–192.

Maier, Charles S., *The Unmasterable Past: History, Holocaust, and German National Identity* (Cambridge, MA: Harvard University Press, 1988).

Mann, Michael, *The Dark Side of Democracy: Explaining Ethnic Cleansing* (New York: Cambridge University Press, 2005).

Martin, Stacie E., 'Native Americans', in Dinah L. Shelton (ed.), *Encyclopedia of Genocide and Crimes Against Humanity* (Detroit, Thomson Gale, 2005), pp. 740–746.

Mazower, Mark, 'Violence and the State in the Twentieth Century', Review Essay, *The American Historical Review*, Vol. 107, No. 4 (2002), pp. 1158–1178.

McDonnell, Michael A. and A. Dirk Moses, 'Raphael Lemkin as Historian of Genocide in the Americas', in Domink J. Schaller and Jürgen Zimmerer (eds), *The Origins of Genocide: Raphael Lemkin as an Historian of Mass Violence* (New York: Routledge, 2009), pp. 57–86.

Melson, Robert, 'Provocation or Nationalism: A Critical Inquiry into the Armenian Genocide of 1915', in Richard G. Hovannisian (ed.), *The Armenian Genocide in Perspective* (New Brunswick, NJ: Transaction Books, 1986), pp. 61–84.

Melson, Robert, 'Revolution and Genocide: On the Causes of the Armenian Genocide and the Holocaust', in Richard G. Hovannisian (ed.), *The Armenian Genocide: History, Politics, Ethics* (New York: St. Martin's Press, 1992), pp. 80–102.

Melson, Robert, *Revolution and Genocide: On the Origins of the Armenian Genocide and the Holocaust* (Chicago, IL: University of Chicago Press, 1992).

Melson, Robert, 'Response to Professor Dadrian's Review', *Holocaust and Genocide Studies*, Vol. 8, No. 3 (1994), p. 416.

Melson, Robert, 'Problems in the Comparison of the Armenian Genocide and the Holocaust: Definitions, Typologies, Theories, and Fallacies', in Larry V. Thompson (ed.), *Lessons and Legacies IV: Reflections on Religion, Justice, Sexuality, and Genocide* (Evanston, IL: Northwestern University Press, 2003), pp. 24–38.

Moses, A. Dirk, 'An Antipodean Genocide?: The Origins of the Genocidal Moment in the Colonization of Australia', *Journal of Genocide Research*, Vol. 2, No. 1 (2000), pp. 89–106.

Moses, A. Dirk, 'Coming to Terms with the Past in Comparative Perspective: Germany and Australia', *Aboriginal History*, Vol. 25 (2001), pp. 91–115.

Moses, A. Dirk, 'Conceptual Blockages and Definitional Dilemmas in the "Racial Century": Genocides of Indigenous Peoples and the Holocaust', *Patterns of Prejudice*, Vol. 36, No. 4 (2002), pp. 7–36.

Moses, A. Dirk, 'The Holocaust and Genocide', in Dan Stone (ed.), *The Historiography of the Holocaust* (Basingstoke: Palgrave Macmillan, 2004), pp. 533–555.

Moses, A. Dirk, 'Genocide and Settler Society in Australian History', in A. Dirk Moses (ed.), *Genocide and Settler Society: Frontier Violence and Stolen Indigenous Children in Australian History* (New York: Berghahn Books, 2004), pp. 3–48.

Moses, A. Dirk, 'Empire, Colony, Genocide: Keywords and the Philosophy of History', in A. Dirk Moses (ed.), *Empire, Colony, Genocide: Conquest, Occupation, and Subaltern Resistance in World History* (New York: Berghahn Books, 2008), pp. 3–54.

Moses, A. Dirk, 'Moving the Genocide Debate Beyond the History Wars', *Australian Journal of Politics and History*, Vol. 54, No. 2 (2008), pp. 248–270.

Moshman, David, 'Conceptual Constraints on Thinking about Genocide', *Journal of Genocide Research*, Vol. 3, No. 3 (2001), pp. 431–450.

Moshman, David, 'Conceptions of Genocide and Perceptions of History', in Dan Stone (ed.), *The Historiography of Genocide* (Basingstoke: Palgrave Macmillan, 2008), pp. 71–92.

Palmer, Alison, 'Colonial and Modern Genocides: Explanations and Categories', *Ethnic and Racial Studies*, Vol. 21, No. 1 (1998), pp. 89–115.

Palmer, Alison, *Colonial Genocide* (Adelaide: Crawford House, 2000).

Parella, Frank, 'Lebensraum and Manifest Destiny: A Comparative Study in the Justification of Expansionism', Master's Thesis, Georgetown University, Department of Political Science, 1950, Thesis 374.

Rensink, Brenden, 'The Sand Creek Phenomenon: The Complexity and Difficulty of Undertaking a Comparative Study of Genocide *vis-a-vis* the North American West', *Genocide Studies and Prevention*, Vol. 4, No. 1 (2009), pp. 9–27.

Rensink, Brenden, 'Genocide of Native Americans: Historical Facts and Historiographical Debates', in Samuel Totten and Robert K. Hitchcock (eds), *Genocide of Indigenous Peoples* (New Brunswick, NJ: Transaction Publishers, 2011), pp. 15–36.

Rosenfeld, Gavriel D., 'The Politics of Uniqueness: Reflections on the Recent Polemical Turn in Holocaust and Genocide Scholarship', *Holocaust and Genocide Studies*, Vol. 13, No. 1 (1999), pp. 28–61.

Rothberg, Michael, *Multidirectional Memory: Remembering the Holocaust in the Age of Decolonization* (Stanford, CA: Stanford University Press, 2009).

Rubenstein, Richard L., 'Modernization and the Politics of Extermination', in Isidor Wallimann and Michael N. Dobkowski (eds), *Genocide and the Modern Age: Etiology and Case Studies of Mass Death* (Westport, CT: Greenwood Press, 1987), pp. 3–28.

Rubenstein, Richard L., 'Afterward: Genocide and Civilization', in Isidor Wallimann and Michael N. Dobkowski (eds), *Genocide and the Modern Age: Etiology and Case Studies of Mass Death* (Westport, CT: Greenwood Press, 1987), pp. 283–298.

Russell, Lynette (ed.), *Colonial Frontiers: Indigenous-European Encounters in Settler Societies* (Manchester: Manchester University Press, 2001).

Said, Edward W., *Culture and Imperialism* (New York: Alfred A. Knopf, 1993).

Scherrer, Christian P., 'Towards a Theory of Modern Genocide. Comparative Genocide Research: Definitions, Criteria, Typologies, Cases, Key Elements, Patterns and Voids', *Journal of Genocide Research*, Vol. 1, No. 1 (1999), pp. 13–23.

Schaller, Dominik J. and Jürgen Zimmerer, 'Settlers, Imperialism, Genocide: Seeing the Global Without Ignoring the Local – Introduction', *Journal of Genocide Research*, Vol. 10, No. 2 (2008), pp. 191–199.

Shaw, Martin, *War and Genocide: Organized Killing in Modern Society* (Cambridge: Polity Press, 2003).

Shaw, Martin, *What is Genocide?* (Cambridge: Polity Press, 2007).

Shaw, Martin, 'The General Hybridity of War and Genocide', *Journal of Genocide Research*, Vol. 9, No. 3 (2007), pp. 461–473.

Shelton, Dinah L. (ed.), *Encyclopedia of Genocide and Crimes Against Humanity* (Detroit, MI: Thomson Gale, 2005).

Smith, Roger W., 'Human Destructiveness and Politics: The Twentieth Century as an Age of Genocide', in Isidor Wallimann and Michael N. Dobkowski (eds), *Genocide and the Modern Age: Etiology and Case Studies of Mass Death* (Westport, CT: Greenwood Press, 1987), pp. 21–39.

Smithers, Gregory D., 'Rethinking Genocide in North America', in Donald Bloxham and A. Dirk Moses (eds), *The Oxford Handbook of Genocide Studies* (New York: Oxford University Press, 2010), pp. 322–341.

Sousa, Ashley Riley, ' "They will be hunted down like wild beasts and destroyed!'": A Comparative Study of Genocide in California and Tasmania', *Journal of Genocide Research*, Vol. 6, No. 2 (2004), pp. 193–209.

Stannard, David E., *American Holocaust: The Conquest of the New World* (New York: Oxford University Press, 1992).

Stannard, David E., 'Preface', in Ward Churchill, *A Little Matter of Genocide: Holocaust and Denial in the Americas 1492 to the Present* (San Francisco, CA: City Light Books, 1997), pp. xiii–xviii.

Stannard, David E., 'Uniqueness as Denial: The Politics of Genocide Scholarship', in Alan S. Rosenbaum (ed.), *Is the Holocaust Unique?: Perspectives on Comparative Genocide* (Boulder, CO: Westview Press, 2001), pp. 245–290.

Stannard, David E., 'Déjà Vu All Over Again', Response to Guenter Lewy's contribution 'Can There Be Genocide Without the Intent to Commit Genocide?', *Journal of Genocide Research*, Vol. 10, No. 1 (2008), pp. 127–133.

Stein, Stuart D., 'Conceptions and Terms: Templates for the Analysts of Holocausts and Genocides', *Journal of Genocide Research*, Vol. 7, No. 2 (2005), pp. 171–203.

Sterba, James P., 'Understanding Evil: American Slavery, the Holocaust and the Conquest of the American Indians', *Ethics*, Vol. 106, No. 2 (1996), pp. 424–448.

Stoler, Ann Laura, 'Tense and Tender Ties: The Politics of Comparison in North American History and (Post) Colonial Studies', *Journal of American History*, Vol. 88, No. 3 (2001), pp. 829–865.

Stone, Dan, *Constructing the Holocaust: A Study in Historiography* (London: Valentine Mitchell, 2003).

Stone, Dan, 'The Historiography of Genocide: Beyond "Uniqueness" and Ethnic Competition', *Rethinking History*, Vol. 8, No. 1 (2004), pp. 127–142.

Stone, Dan, 'Genocide as Transgression', *European Journal of Social Theory*, Vol. 7, No. 1 (2004), pp. 45–65.

Stone, Dan (ed.), *The Historiography of the Holocaust* (Basingstoke: Palgrave Macmillan, 2004).

Stone, Dan, *History, Memory and Mass Atrocity: Essays on the Holocaust and Genocide* (London: Vallentine Mitchell, 2006).

Stone, Dan (ed.), *The Historiography of Genocide* (Basingstoke: Palgrave Macmillan, 2008).

Stone, Dan, 'The Holocaust and Its Historiography', in Dan Stone (ed.), *The Historiography of Genocide* (Basingstoke: Palgrave Macmillan, 2008), pp. 373–399.

Stone, Dan, *Histories of the Holocaust* (New York: Oxford University Press, 2010).

Straus, Scott, 'Contested Meanings and Conflicting Imperatives: A Conceptual Analysis of Genocide', *Journal of Genocide Research*, Vol. 3, No. 3 (2001), pp. 349–366.

Tatz, Colin, 'Confronting Australian Genocide', *Aboriginal History*, Vol. 25 (2001), pp. 16–38.

Tatz, Colin, *With Intent to Destroy: Reflecting on Genocide* (London: Verso, 2003).

Ulrich, Volker, 'A Provocation to a New *Historikerstreit*', in Robert R. Shandley (ed.), *Unwilling Germans?:The Goldhagen Debate* (Minneapolis, MN: University of Minnesota Press, 1998), pp. 31–33.

Wallimann, Isidor and Michael N. Dobkowski (eds), *Genocide and the Modern Age: Etiology and Case Studies of Mass Death* (Syracuse, NY: Syracuse University Press, 2000 [1987]).

Weiner, Amir, 'Introduction: Landscaping the Human Garden', in Amir Weiner (ed.), *Landscaping the Human Garden: Twentieth-Century Population Management in a Comparative Framework* (Stanford, CA: Stanford University Press, 2003), pp. 1–18.

Weitz, Eric D., *A Century of Genocide: Utopias of Race and Nation* (Princeton, NJ: Princeton University Press, 2003).

White, Richard, 'Western History', in Eric Foner (ed.), *The New American History* (Philadelphia, PA: Temple University Press, 1997 [1990]), pp. 203–230.

Wolfe, Patrick, *Settler Colonialism and the Transformation of Anthropology: The Politics and Poetics of an Ethnographic Event* (London: Cassell, 1999).

Wolfe, Patrick, 'Land, Labor, and Difference: Elementary Structures of Race', *The American Historical Review*, Vol. 106, No. 3 (2001), pp. 866–905.

Wolfe, Patrick, 'Settler Colonialism and the Elimination of the Native', *Journal of Genocide Research*, Vol. 8, No. 4 (2006), pp. 387–409.

Wolfe, Patrick, 'Structure and Event: Settler Colonialism, Time and the Question of Genocide', in A. Dirk Moses (ed.), *Empire, Colony, Genocide: Conquest, Occupation, and Subaltern Resistance in World History* (New York: Berghahn Books, 2008), pp. 102–132.

Zimmerer, Jürgen, 'Colonialism and the Holocaust: Towards an Archeology of Genocide', in A. Dirk Moses (ed.), *Genocide and Settler Society: Frontier Violence and Stolen Indigenous Children in Australian History* (New York: Berghahn Books, 2004), pp. 49–76.

Zimmerer, Jürgen, 'Annihilation in Africa: The "Race War" in German South-west Africa (1904–1908) and its Significance for a Global History of Genocide', *Bulletin of the German Historical Institute, Washington, D.C.*, Vol. 37 (2005), pp. 51–57.

Zimmerer, Jürgen, 'From the Editors: Environmental Genocide? Climate Change, Mass Violence and the Question of Ideology', *Journal of Genocide Research*, Vol. 9, No. 3 (2007), pp. 349–351.

Zimmerer, Jürgen, 'Colonial Genocide: The Herero and Nama War (1904–08) in German South West Africa and Its Significance', in Dan Stone (ed.), *The Historiography of Genocide* (Basingstoke: Palgrave Macmillan, 2008), pp. 323–342.

Early America, antecedents, and 'the West'

Adams, David Wallace, *Education for Extinction: American Indians and the Boarding School Experience, 1875–1928* (Lawrence, KS: University of Kansas Press, 1995).

Adelman, Jeremy and Stephen Aron, 'From Borderlands to Borders: Empires, Nation-States, and the Peoples in Between in North American History', *The American Historical Review*, Vol. 104, No. 3 (1999), pp. 814–841.

Anderson, Fred and Andrew Cayton, *The Dominion of War: Empire and Liberty in North America 1500–2000* (New York: Viking Penguin, 2005).

Anderson, Gary Clayton, *The Conquest of Texas: Ethnic Cleansing in the Promised Land, 1820–1875* (Norman, OK: University of Oklahoma Press, 2005).

Appleby, Joyce, *Thomas Jefferson* (New York: Henry Holt, 2003).

Banner, Stuart, *How the Indians Lost Their Land: Law and Power on the Frontier* (Cambridge, MA: Harvard University Press, 2005).

Barnett, Louise K., *The Ignoble Savage: American Literary Racism, 1790–1890* (Westport, CT: Greenwood Press, 1975).

Belohlavek, John M., 'Race, Progress, and Destiny: Caleb Cushing and the Quest for American Empire', in Sam W. Haynes and Christopher Morris (eds), *Manifest Destiny and Empire: American Antebellum Expansionism* (College Station, TX: Texas A&M University Press, 1997), pp. 21–47.

Bergland, Renée L., *The National Uncanny: Indian Ghosts and American Subjects* (Hanover, NH: University Press of New England, 2000).

Berkhofer, Robert F. Jr., *The White Man's Indian: Images of the American Indian from Columbus to the Present* (New York: Vintage Books, 1978).

Bieder, Robert E., *Science Encounters the Indian, 1820–1880: The Early Years of American Ethnology* (Norman, OK: University of Oklahoma Press, 1986).

Blackhawk, Ned, *Violence Over the Land: Indians and Empires in the Early American West* (Cambridge, MA: Harvard University Press, 2006).

Bogue, Allan G., 'An Agricultural Empire', in Clyde A. Milner II, Carol A. O'Connor, and Martha A. Sandweiss (eds), *The Oxford History of the American West* (New York: Oxford University Press, 1994), pp. 275–313.

Borneman, Walter R., *Polk: The Man Who Transformed the Presidency and America* (New York: Random House, 2008).

Brands, H.W., *Andrew Jackson: His Life and Times* (New York: Doubleday, 2005).

Brown, David, 'Jeffersonian Ideology and the Second Party System', *The Historian*, Vol. 62, No. 1 (1999), pp. 17–27.

Brown, Dee, *Bury My Heart at Wounded Knee: An Indian History of the American West* (New York: Holt, Rinehart & Winston, 1970).

Brown, Kathleen M., 'Beyond the Great Debates: Gender and Race in Early America', in Louis P. Masur (ed.), *The Challenge of American History* (Baltimore, MD: The Johns Hopkins University Press, 1999), pp. 96–123.

Buchanan, John, *Jackson's Way: Andrew Jackson and the People of the Western Waters* (New York: John Wiley & Sons, 2001).

Burstein, Andrew, *The Passions of Andrew Jackson* (New York, Alfred A. Knopf, 2004 [2003]).

Butler, Anne M. and Michael J. Lansing, *The American West: A Concise History* (Malden, MA: Blackwell Publishing, 2008).

Calloway, Colin G., Review of Francis Paul Prucha's *The Great Father*, *The American Indian Quarterly*, Vol. 10, No. 2 (1986), pp. 127–131.

Calloway, Colin G., ' "We Have Always Been the Frontier": The American Revolution in Shawnee Country', *American Indian Quarterly*, Vol. 16, No. 1 (1992), pp. 39–52.

Calloway, Colin G., *The American Revolution in Indian Country: Crisis and Diversity in Native American Communities* (New York: Cambridge University Press, 1995).

Calloway, Colin G., 'The Continuing Revolution in Indian Country', in Frederick E. Hoxie, Ronald Hoffman, and Peter J. Albert (eds), *Native Americans in the Early Republic* (Charlottesville, VA: University Press of Virginia, 1999), pp. 3–33.

Calloway, Colin G., *One Vast Winter Count: The Native American West Before Lewis and Clark* (Lincoln, NE: University of Nebraska Press, 2003).

Calloway, Colin G., *The Scratch of a Pen: 1763 and the Transformation of North America* (New York: Oxford University Press, 2006).

Calloway, Colin G., *The Shawnees and the War for America* (New York: Viking Penguin, 2007).

Canny, Nicholas P., 'The Ideology of English Colonization: From Ireland to America', *William & Mary Quarterly*, Vol. 30, No. 4 (1973), pp. 575–598.

Cave, Alfred A., 'The 1637 Pequot War and the Question of Native American Genocide', occasional paper (in the author's possession) given at Yale Genocide Studies Program Seminar Series, 29 August 2005.

Cave, Alfred A., 'Genocide in the Americas', in Dan Stone (ed.), *The Historiography of Genocide* (Basingstoke: Palgrave Macmillan, 2008), pp. 273–295.

Cerami, Charles A., *Jefferson's Great Gamble: The Remarkable Story of Jefferson, Napoleon, and the Men Behind the Louisiana Purchase* (Naperville, IL: Sourcebooks, 2003).

Champagne, Duane, 'A Multidimensional Theory of Colonialism: The Native North American Experience', *Journal of American Studies of Turkey*, Vol. 3 (1996), pp. 3–14.

Churchill, Ward, *A Little Matter of Genocide: Holocaust and Denial in the Americas 1492 to the Present* (San Francisco, CA: City Lights Books, 1997).

Churchill, Ward, *Kill the Indian, Save the Man: The Genocidal Impact of American Indian Residential Schools* (San Francisco, CA: City Lights Books, 2004).

Conzen, Kathleen Neils, 'A Saga of Families', in Clyde A. Milner II, Carol A. O'Connor, and Martha A. Sandweiss (eds), *The Oxford History of the American West* (New York: Oxford University Press, 1994), pp. 315–357.

Countryman, Edward, *The American Revolution* (New York: Hill and Wang, 2003 [1985]).

DeLay, Brian, *War of a Thousand Deserts: Indian Raids and the U.S.-Mexican War* (New Haven, CT: Yale University Press, 2008).

Deloria, Philip J., *Playing Indian* (New Haven, CT: Yale University Press, 1998).

Dippie, Brian W., *The Vanishing American: White Attitudes and U.S. Indian Policy* (Lawrence, KS: University Press of Kansas, 1991 [1982]).

Dowd, Gregory Evans, *A Spirited Resistance: The North American Indian Struggle for Unity 1745–1815* (Baltimore, MD: The Johns Hopkins University Press, 1992).

Drinnon, Richard, *Facing West: The Metaphysics of Indian-Hating & Empire Building* (Norman, OK: University of Oklahoma Press, 1997).

DuVal, Kathleen, *The Native Ground: Indians and Colonists in the Heart of the American Continent* (Philadelphia, PA: University of Pennsylvania Press, 2006).

Edmunds, R. David, 'Native American Displacement Amid U.S. Expansion'. On pbs.org, pp. 1–3.

Ellis, Joseph J., *American Creation: Triumphs and Tragedies at the Founding of the Republic* (New York: Alfred A. Knopf, 2007).

Egnal, Marc, *A Mighty Empire: The Origins of the American Revolution* (Ithaca, NY: Cornell University Press, 1988).

Faragher, John Mack, ' "More Motley than Mackinaw": From Ethnic Mixing to Ethnic Cleansing on the Frontier of the Lower Missouri, 1783–1833', in Andrew R. L. Cayton and Fredrika J. Teute (eds), *Contact Points: American Frontiers from the Mohawk Valley to the Mississippi, 1750–1830* (Chapel Hill, NC: University of North Carolina Press, 1998), pp. 304–326.

Ferguson, Niall, *Colossus: The Price of America's Empire* (New York: Penguin Press, 2004).

Foos, Paul W., *A Short, Off-Hand, Killing Affair: Soldiers and Social Conflict During the Mexican-American War* (Chapel Hill, NC: University of North Carolina Press, 2002).

Francaviglia, Richard V. and Douglas W. Richmond (eds), *Dueling Eagles: Reinterpreting the U.S.-Mexican War, 1846–1848* (Fort Worth, TX: Texas Christian University Press, 2000).

Frazier, Donald Shaw (ed.), *The United States and Mexico at War: Nineteenth-Century Expansionism and Conflict* (New York: MacMillan Reference USA, 1998).

Gossett, Thomas F., *Race: The History of an Idea in America* (New York: Oxford University Press, 1997 [1963]).

Greenberg, Amy S., *Manifest Manhood and the Antebellum American Empire* (New York: Cambridge University Press, 2005).

Grenier, John, *The First Way of War: American War Making on the Frontier, 1607–1814* (New York: Cambridge University Press, 2005).

Griffin, Patrick, *American Leviathan: Empire, Nation, and Revolutionary Frontier* (New York: Hill and Wang, 2007).

Hagan, William T., 'The Reservation Policy: Too Little and Too Late', in Jane F. Smith and Robert M. Kvasnicka (eds), *Indian-White Relations: A Persistent Paradox* (Washington, D.C.: Howard University Press, 1976), pp. 157–169.

Haskins, Victoria and Margaret D. Jacobs, 'Stolen Generations and Vanishing Indians: The Removal of Indigenous Children as a Weapon of War in the United States and Australia, 1870–1940', in James Marten (ed.), *Children in War: A Historical Anthology* (New York: New York University Press, 2002), pp. 227–241.

Haynes, Sam W., 'Manifest Destiny', On pbs.org, pp. 1–4.

Haynes, Sam W., *James K. Polk and the Expansionist Impulse* (New York: Longman Publishing Group, 1997).

Haynes, Sam W. and Christopher Morris (eds), *Manifest Destiny and Empire: American Antebellum Expansionism* (College Station, TX: Texas A&M University Press, 1997).

Hays, Robert, *Editorializing 'the Indian Problem': The New York Times on Native Americans, 1860–1900* (Carbondale, IL: Southern Illinois University Press, 2007 [1997]).

Henderson, Timothy J., *A Glorious Defeat: Mexico and Its War with the United States* (New York: Hill and Wang, 2007).

Hietala, Thomas R., *Manifest Design: Anxious Aggrandizement in Late Jacksonian America* (Ithaca, NY: Cornell University Press, 1985).

Hietala, Thomas R., ' "This Splendid Juggernaut": Westward a Nation and Its People', in Sam W. Haynes and Christopher Morris (eds), *Manifest Destiny and Empire: American Antebellum Expansionism* (College Station, TX: Texas A&M University Press, 1997), pp. 48–67.

Hinderaker, Eric, *Elusive Empires: Constructing Colonialism in the Ohio Valley, 1673–1800* (New York: Cambridge University Press, 1997).

Hinderaker, Eric and Peter C. Mancall, *At the Edge of Empire: The Backcountry in British North America* (Baltimore, MD: The Johns Hopkins University Press, 2003).

Hine, Robert V. and John Mack Faragher, *The American West: A New Interpretative History* (New Haven, CT: Yale University Press, 2000).

Horsman, Reginald, *The Origins of Indian Removal 1815–1824* (East Lansing, MI: Michigan State University Press, 1970).

Horsman, Reginald, *Race and Manifest Destiny: The Origins of American Racial Anglo-Saxonism* (Cambridge, MA: Harvard University Press, 1981).

Horsman, Reginald, *Expansion and American Indian Policy, 1783–1812* (Norman, OK: University of Oklahoma Press, 1992 [Michigan State University Press, 1967]).

Horsman, Reginald, 'The Indian Policy of an "Empire for Liberty"', in Frederick, E. Hoxie, Ronald Hoffman, and Peter J. Albert (eds), *Native Americans and the Early Republic* (Charlottesville, VA: University of Virginia Press, 1999), pp. 37–61.

Howe, Daniel Walker, *What Hath God Wrought: The Transformation of America, 1815–1848* (New York: Oxford University Press, 2007).

Howe, John R., *From the Revolution Through the Age of Jackson: Innocence and Empire in the Young Republic* (Englewood Cliffs, NJ: Prentice-Hall, 1973).

Hoxie, Frederick E., *Indians in American History: An Introduction* (Arlington Heights, IL: Harlan Davidson, 1988).

Hoxie, Frederick E., Ronald Hoffman, and Peter J. Albert (eds), *Native Americans in the Early Republic* (Charlottesville, VA: University of Virginia Press, 1999).

Hoxie, Frederick E., Peter C. Mancall, and James H. Merrell (eds), *American Nations: Encounters in Indian Country, 1850 to the Present* (New York: Routledge, 2001).

Huhndorf, Shari M., *Going Native: Indians in the American Cultural Imagination* (Ithaca, NY: Cornell University Press, 2001).

Hunt, Michael H., *Ideology and U.S. Foreign Policy* (New Haven, CT: Yale University Press, 1987).

Hurt, R. Douglas, *The Indian Frontier, 1783–1846* (Albuquerque, NM: University of New Mexico Press, 2002).

Isenberg, Andrew C., *The Destruction of the Bison: An Environmental History, 1750–1920* (Cambridge: Cambridge University Press, 2000).

Jackson, Donald, *Thomas Jefferson & the Stony Mountains: Exploring the West from Monticello* (Urbana, IL: University of Illinois Press, 1981).

Jacobson, Matthew Frye, *Barbarian Virtues: The United States Encounters Foreign Peoples at Home and Abroad, 1876–1917* (New York: Hill and Wang, 2000).

Jacoby, Karl, *Shadows at Dawn: A Borderlands Massacre and the Violence of History* (New York: The Penguin Press, 2008).

Jacoby, Karl, ' "The Broad Platform of Extermination": Nature and Violence in the Nineteenth Century North American Borderlands', *Journal of Genocide Research*, Vol. 10, No. 2 (2008), pp. 249–267.

Jaimes, M. Annette, 'Introduction: Sand Creek: The Morning After', in M. Annette Jaimes (ed.), *The State of Native America: Genocide, Colonization and Resistance* (Boston, MA: South End Press, 1992), pp. 1–12.

Jennings, Francis, *The Invasion of America: Indians, Colonialism and the Cant of Conquest* (New York: W.W. Norton, 1976 [1975]).

Jennings, Francis, *The Founders of America: How Indians Discovered the Land, Pioneered It and Created Great Classical Civilizations; How They Were Plunged into the Dark Age by Invasion and Conquest, and How They Are Reviving* (New York: W.W. Norton, 1993).

Jennings, Francis, *The Creation of America: Through Revolution and Empire* (New York: Oxford University Press, 2000).

Johannsen, Robert W., 'Introduction', in Sam W. Haynes and Christopher Morris (eds), *Manifest Destiny and Empire: American Antebellum Expansionism* (College Station, TX: Texas A&M University Press, 1997), pp. 3–6.

Johannsen, Robert W., 'The Meaning of Manifest Destiny', in Sam W. Haynes and Christopher Morris (eds), *Manifest Destiny and Empire: American Antebellum Expansionism* (College Station, TX: Texas A&M University Press, 1997), pp. 7–20.

Jones, Dorothy V., *License for Empire: Colonialism by Treaty in Early America* (Chicago, IL: University of Chicago Press, 1982).

Joy, Mark S., *American Expansionism 1783–1860: A Manifest Destiny?* (London: Pearson Education Limited, 2003).

Kaplan, Amy, 'Left Alone with America: The Absence of Empire in the Study of American Culture', in Amy Kaplan and Donald E. Pease (eds), *Cultures of United States Imperialism* (Durham, NC: Duke University Press, 1993), pp. 3–21.

Kaplan, Lawrence S., *Thomas Jefferson: Westward the Course of Empire* (Wilmington, DE: SR Books, 1999).

Kluger, Richard, *Seizing Destiny: How America Grew from Sea to Shining Sea* (New York: Alfred A. Knopf, 2007).

Koch, Adrienne and William Peden (eds), *The Life and Selected Writings of Thomas Jefferson* (New York: Random House, 2004).

Krenn, Michael L. (ed.), *Race and U.S. Foreign Policy From Colonial Times Through the Age of Jackson* (New York: Garland Publishing, 1998).

Krenn, Michael L. (ed.), *Race and U.S. Foreign Policy in the Ages of Territorial and Market Expansion, 1840–1890* (New York: Garland Publishing, 1998).

Kukla, Jon, *A Wilderness So Immense: The Louisiana Purchase and the Destiny of America* (New York: Alfred A. Knopf, 2003).

Kulikoff, Allan, *From British Peasants to Colonial American Farmers* (Chapel Hill, NC: University of North Carolina Press, 2000).

Kupperman, Karen Ordahl, *The Jamestown Project* (Cambridge, MA: Harvard University Press, 2007).

LaFeber, Walter, 'Jefferson and American Foreign Policy', in Peter S. Onuf (ed.), *Jeffersonian Legacies* (Charlottesville, VA: University of Virginia Press, 1993).

Lenman, Bruce, *Britain's Colonial Wars, 1688–1783* (Harlow: Longman, 2001).

Leonard, Thomas M., *James K. Polk: A Clear and Unquestionable Destiny* (Wilmington, DE: Scholarly Resources, 2001).

Limerick, Patricia Nelson, *The Legacy of Conquest: The Unbroken Past of the American West* (New York, W.W. Norton, 1987).

Limerick, Patricia Nelson, Clyde A. Milner II, and Charles E. Rankin (eds), *Trails: Toward a New Western History* (Lawrence, KS: University Press of Kansas, 1991).

Looney, J. Jefferson (ed.), *The Papers of Thomas Jefferson, Retirement Series*, 5 Vols. (Princeton, NJ: Princeton University Press, 2004–2008).

MacLeitch, Gail D., 'Native Americans', in Howard Temperley and Christopher Bigsby (eds), *A New Introduction to American Studies* (Harlow: Pearson Longman, 2006), pp. 98–122.

Madley, Benjamin, 'American Genocide: The Northern California Indian Catastrophe, 1846–1873', PhD Dissertation, History Department, Yale University, 2009.

Maier, Charles S., *Among Empires: American Ascendancy and Its Predecessors* (Cambridge, MA: Harvard University Press, 2006).

Mann, Barbara Alice, *George Washington's War on Native America, 1779–1782* (Westport, CT: Praeger, 2005).

Marienstras, Elise, 'The Common Man's Indian: The Image of the Indian as a Promoter of National Identity in the Early National Era', in Frederick E. Hoxie, Ronald Hoffman, and Peter J. Albert (eds), *Native Americans in the Early Republic* (Charlottesville, VA: University of Virginia Press, 1999), pp. 261–296.

Marks, Paula Mitchell, *In a Barren Land: The American Indian Quest for Cultural Survival, 1607 to the Present* (New York: HarperCollins, 2002).

McCaffrey, James M., *Army of Manifest Destiny: The American Soldier in the Mexican War, 1846–1848* (New York: New York University Press, 1992).

Merk, Frederick, *Manifest Destiny and Mission in American History: A Re-Interpretation* (Cambridge, MA: Harvard University Press, 1995 [1963]).

Merrell, James H., 'American Nations, Old and New: Reflections on Indians and the Early Republic', 'Afterword', in Frederick E. Hoxie, Ronald Hoffman, and Peter J. Albert (eds), *Native Americans and the Early Republic* (Charlottesville, VA: University of Virginia Press, 1999), pp. 333–353.

Nash, Gary B., *Red, White & Black: The Peoples of Early North America* (Upper Saddle River, NJ: Prentice Hall, 2000 [1974]).

Nash, Gary B., *The Unknown American Revolution: The Unruly Birth of Democracy and the Struggle to Create America* (New York: Viking, 2005).

Nester, William R., *The Frontier War for American Independence* (Mechanicsburg, PA: Stackpole Books, 2004).

Nobles, Gregory H., *American Frontiers: Cultural Encounters and Continental Conquest* (New York: Hill and Wang, 1997).

Nugent, Walter, 'Comparing Wests and Frontiers', in Clyde A. Milner II, Carol A. O'Connor, and Martha A. Sandweiss (eds), *The Oxford History of the American West* (New York: Oxford University Press, 1994), pp. 803–833.

Nugent, Walter, *Into the West: The Story of Its People* (New York: Alfred A. Knopf, 1999).

Nugent, Walter, *Habits of Empire: A History of American Expansionism* (New York: Alfred A. Knopf, 2008).

O'Brien, Sean Michael, *In Bitterness and in Tears: Andrew Jackson's Destruction of the Creeks and Seminoles* (Westport, CT: Praeger, 2003).

Oberg, Michael Leroy, *Dominion and Civility: English Imperialism and Native America, 1585–1685* (Ithaca, NY: Cornell University Press, 1999).

Onuf, Peter S., *Jefferson's Empire: The Language of American Nationhood* (Charlottesville, VA: University of Virginia Press, 2000).

Onuf, Peter S. and Loenard J. Sadosky, *Jeffersonian America* (Malden, MA: Wiley-Blackwell, 2002).

Onuf, Peter S. and Jeffrey L. Hantman, 'Geopolitics, Science, and Culture Conflicts', in Douglass Seefeldt, Jeffrey L. Hantman, and Peter S. Onuf (eds), *Across the Continent: Jefferson, Lewis and Clark, and the Making of America* (Charlottesville, VA: University of Virginia Press, 2005), pp. 1–15.

Ostler, Jeffrey, *The Plains Sioux and U.S. Colonialism from Lewis and Clark to Wounded Knee* (Cambridge: Cambridge University Press, 2004).

Ostler, Jeffrey, 'The Question of Genocide in U.S. History, 1783–1890', occasional paper (in the author's possession) given at Yale Genocide Studies Program Seminar Series, 17 November 2005.

Ostler, Jeffrey, *The Lakota and the Black Hills: The Struggle for Sacred Ground* (New York: Viking Penguin, 2010).

Owsley, Frank Lawrence Jr. and Gene A. Smith, *Filibusterers and Expansionists: Jeffersonian Manifest Destiny, 1800–1821* (Tuscaloosa, AL: University of Alabama Press, 1997).

Pagden, Anthony, *Lords of All the World: Ideologies of Empire in Spain, Britain and France c.1500–c.1800* (New Haven, CT: Yale University Press, 1995).

Pascoe, Peggy, 'Western Women at the Cultural Crossroads', in Patricia Nelson Limerick, Clyde A. Milner II, and Charles E. Rankin (eds), *Trails: Toward a New Western History* (Lawrence, KS: University Press of Kansas, 1991), pp. 40–58.

Pearce, Roy Harvey, *Savagism and Civilization: A Study of the Indian and the American Mind* (Baltimore, MD: The Johns Hopkins University Press, 1965 [1953]).

Perdue, Theda and Michael D. Green, *The Cherokee Nation and the Trail of Tears* (New York: Penguin, 2007).

Peterson, Merrill D., *Thomas Jefferson and the New Nation: A Biography* (New York: Oxford University Press, 1970).

Pletcher, David M., 'Manifest Destiny: An Ideal or a Justification?' On pbs.org, pp. 1–4.

Prucha, Francis Paul, *The Sword of the Republic: The United States Army on the Frontier, 1783–1846* (New York: MacMillan, 1968).

Prucha, Francis Paul, *Indian Policy of the United States: Historical Essays* (Lincoln, NE: University of Nebraska Press, 1981).

Prucha, Francis Paul, *The Great Father: The United States Government and the American Indians, Volumes I and II*, Unabridged Edition (Lincoln, NE: University of Nebraska Press, 1995 [1984]).

Prucha, Francis Paul (ed.), *Documents of United States Indian Policy* (Lincoln, NE: University of Nebraska Press, 2000 [1975]).

Raphael, Ray, *Founding Myths: Stories That Hide Our Patriotic Past* (New York: The New Press, 2004).

Ratner, Lorman A., *Andrew Jackson and His Tennessee Lieutenants: A Study in Political Culture* (Westport, CT: Greenwood Press, 1997).

Remini, Robert V., *The Legacy of Andrew Jackson: Essays on Democracy, Indian Removal and Slavery* (Baton Rouge, LA: Louisiana State University Press, 1988).

Remini, Robert V., *Andrew Jackson and the Course of American Empire, 1767–1821* (Baltimore, MD: The Johns Hopkins University Press, 1998 [1977]).

Remini, Robert V., *Andrew Jackson and His Indian Wars* (New York: Viking Press, 2001).

Richardson, Heather Cox, *Wounded Knee: Political Parties and the Road to an American Massacre* (New York: Basic Books, 2010).

Richter, Daniel K., *Facing East from Indian Country: A Native History of Early America* (Cambridge, MA: Harvard University Press, 2001).

Robertson, Lindsay G., *Conquest by Law: How the Discovery of America Dispossessed Indigenous Peoples of Their Lands* (New York: Oxford University Press, 2005).

Rockwell, Stephen J., *Indian Affairs and the Administrative State in the Nineteenth Century* (New York: Cambridge University Press, 2010).

Rogin, Michael Paul, *Fathers and Children: Andrew Jackson and the Subjugation of the American Indian* (New Brunswick, NJ: Transaction Publishers, 1991 [1975]).

Satz, Ronald N., *American Indian Policy in the Jacksonian Era* (Lincoln, NE: University of Nebraska Press, 1975).

Scheckel, Susan, *The Insistence of the Indian: Race and Nationalism in Nineteenth-Century American Culture* (Princeton, NJ: Princeton University Press, 1998).

Segal, Charles M. and David Steinbeck, *Puritans, Indians and Manifest Destiny* (New York: Putnam, 1977).

Sharp, Patrick B., *Savage Perils: Racial Frontiers and Nuclear Apocalypse in American Culture* (Norman, OK: University of Oklahoma Press, 2007).

Sheehan, Bernard W., *Seeds of Extinction: Jeffersonian Philanthropy and the American Indian* (Chapel Hill, NC: University of North Carolina Press, 1973).

Shoemaker, Nancy, 'How Indians Got to be Red', *The American Historical Review*, Vol. 102, No. 3 (1997), pp. 624–644.

Silbey, Joel H., *Storm Over Texas: The Annexation Controversy and the Road to the Civil War* (New York: Oxford University Press, 2005).

Silver, Peter, *Our Savage Neighbors: How Indian War Transformed Early America* (New York: W.W. Norton, 2008).

Smedley, Audrey, *Race in North America: Origin and Evolution of a Worldview*. 2nd ed. (Boulder, CO: Westview Press, 1999 [1993]).

Smits, David D., ' "Fighting Fire with Fire": The Frontier Army's Use of Indian Scouts and Allies in the Trans-Mississippi Campaigns, 1860–1890', *American Indian Culture and Research Journal*, Vol. 22, No. 1 (1998), pp. 73–116.

Smith, F. Todd, *From Dominance to Disappearance: The Indians of Texas and the Near Southwest, 1786–1859* (Lincoln, NE: University of Nebraska Press, 2005).

Smith, Henry Nash, *Virgin Land: The American West as Symbol and Myth* (Cambridge, MA: Harvard University Press, 1970 [1950]).

Stephanson, Anders, *Manifest Destiny: American Expansion and the Empire of Right* (New York: Hill and Wang, 1995).

Stocking, George W. Jr., *Race, Culture, and Evolution: Essays in the History of Anthropology* (Chicago, IL: University of Chicago Press, 1982 [1968]).

Sword, Wiley, *President Washington's Indian War: The Struggle for the Old Northwest, 1790–1795* (Norman, OK: University of Oklahoma Press, 1985).

Takaki, Ronald, *A Different Mirror: A History of Multicultural America* (Boston: Little, Brown and Company, 1993).

Taylor, Alan, 'Land and Liberty on the Post-Revolutionary Frontier', in David Thomas Konig (ed.), *Devising Liberty: Preserving and Creating Freedom in the New American Republic* (Stanford, CA: Stanford University Press, 1995), pp. 81–108.

Taylor, Alan, *American Colonies: The Settling of North America* (New York: Penguin Books, 2001).

Temperley, Howard and Christopher Bigsby, 'Introduction', in Howard Temperley and Christopher Bigsby (eds), *A New Introduction to American Studies* (Harlow: Pearson Longman, 2006), pp. 1–6.

Thornton, Russell, *American Indian Holocaust and Survival: A Population History Since 1492* (Norman, OK; University of Oklahoma Press, 1990 [1987]).

Torgovnick, Marianna, *Gone Primitive: Savage Intellectuals, Modern Lives* (Chicago, IL: University of Chicago Press, 1990).

Trafzer, Clifford E. and Joel R. Hyer (eds), *"Exterminate Them": Written Accounts of the Murder, Rape, and Slavery of Native Americans During the California Gold Rush, 1848–1868* (East Lansing, MI: Michigan State University Press, 1999).

Trennert, Robert A. Jr., *Alternative to Extinction: Federal Indian Policy and the Beginnings of the Reservation System, 1846–51* (Philadelphia, PA: Temple University, Press, 1975).

Unrau, William E., *The Rise and Fall of Indian Country, 1825–1855* (Lawrence, KS: University Press of Kansas, 2007).

Utley, Robert M. and Wilcomb E. Washburn, *Indian Wars* (Boston, MA: Houghton Mifflin Company, 2002 [1977]).

Utley, Robert M., *Frontiersmen in Blue: The United States Army and the Indians, 1848–1865* (Lincoln, NE: University of Nebraska Press, 1981).

Utley, Robert M., *The Indian Frontier of the American West 1846–1890* (Albuquerque, NM: University of New Mexico Press, 1984).

Utley, Robert M., 'Total War on the American Indian Frontier', in Manfred F. Boemeke, Roger Chickering, and Stig Forster (eds), *Anticipating Total War, the German and American Experiences, 1871–1914*, (Cambridge: Cambridge University Press, 1999), pp. 399–414.

Van Alstyne, Richard W., *The Rising American Empire* (New York: W.W. Norton, 1974).

Vaughan, Alden T., *Roots of American Racism: Essays on the Colonial Experience* (New York: Oxford University Press, 1995).

Wallace, Anthony F. C., *The Long, Bitter Trail: Andrew Jackson and the Indians* (New York: Hill and Wang, 1993).

Wallace, Anthony F. C., *Jefferson and the Indians: The Tragic Fate of the First Americans* (Cambridge, MA: Harvard University Press, 1999).

Weeks, Philip, *Farewell My Nation: The American Indian and the United States in the Nineteenth Century* (Wheeling, IL: Harlan Davidson, 2001 [1990]).

Weeks, William Earl, *Building the Continental Empire: American Expansion from the Revolution to the Civil War* (Chicago, IL: Ivan R. Dee, 1996).

Weeks, William Earl, 'New Directions in the Study of Early American Foreign Relations', in Michael Hogan (ed.), *Paths to Power: The Historiography of the American Foreign Relations to 1941* (New York: Cambridge University Press, 2000), p. 8–43.

West, Elliott, *The Way to the West: Essays on the Central Plains* (Albuquerque, NM: University of New Mexico Press, 1995).

West, Elliott, *The Contested Plains: Indians, Goldseekers, and the Rush to Colorado* (Lawrence, KS: University Press of Kansas, 1998).

West, Elliott, 'Reconstructing Race', *Western Historical Quarterly*, Vol. 34, No. 1 (2003), pp. 7–26.

West, Elliott, *The Last Indian War: The Nez Perce Story* (New York: Oxford University Press, 2009).

White, Richard, *The Middle Ground: Indians, Empires and Republics in the Great Lakes Region, 1650–1815* (New York: Cambridge University Press, 1991).

White, Richard, *'It's Your Misfortune and None of My Own': A New History of the American West* (Norman, OK: University of Oklahoma Press, 1991).

Winders, Richard Bruce, *Crisis in the Southwest: The United States, Mexico, and the Struggle Over Texas* (Wilmington, DE: Rowman & Littlefield, 2002).

Yenne, Bill, *Indian Wars: The Campaign for the American West* (Yardley, PA: Westholme Publishing, 2006).

Widmer, Edward L., *Young America: The Flowering of Democracy in New York City* (New York: Oxford University Press, 1999).

Wilentz, Sean, *Andrew Jackson* (New York: Henry Holt, 2006).

Williams, Walter L., 'American Imperialism and the Indians', in Frederick E. Hoxie (ed.), *Indians in American History* (Arlington Heights, IL: Harlan Davidson, 1988), pp. 231–250.

Wilson, James, *The Earth Shall Weep: A History of Native America* (New York: Grove Press, 1998).

Worster, Donald, 'Beyond the Agrarian Myth', in Patricia Nelson Limerick, Clyde A. Milner II, and Charles E. Rankin (eds), *Trails: Toward a New Western* (Lawrence, KS: University Press of Kansas, 1991), pp. 3–25.

York, Neil Longley, *Turning the World Upside Down: The War of American Independence and the Problem of Empire* (Westport, CT: Praeger, 2003).

Young, Mary, 'Indian Policy in the Age of Jefferson', Review Article, *Journal of the Early Republic*, Vol. 20, No. 2 (2000), pp. 297–307.

Nazi Germany, antecedents, and 'the East'

Ackermann, Josef, 'Heinrich Himmler: *Reichsführer – SS*', in Ronald Smelser and Rainer Zitelmann (eds), *The Nazi Elite* (London: Macmillan, 1993), pp. 98–113.

Aly, Götz, Peter Chroust, and Christian Pross, *Cleansing the Fatherland: Nazi Medicine and Racial Hygiene*, trans. Belinda Cooper (Baltimore, MD: The Johns Hopkins University Press, 1994).

Aly, Götz, *'Final Solution': Nazi Population Policy and the Murder of the European Jews* (London: Arnold, 1999).

Aly, Götz and Suzanne Heim, *Architects of Annihilation: Auschwitz and the Logic of Destruction* (London: Phoenix, 2003 [1991]).

Aly, Götz, *Hitler's Beneficiaries: Plunder, Racial War, and the Nazi Welfare State* (New York: Metropolitan Books, 2006).

Bankier, David, *The Germans and the Final Solution: Public Opinion Under Nazism* (New York: Oxford University Press, 1992).

Bankier, David (ed.), *Probing the Depths of Antisemitism: German Society and the Persecution of the Jews, 1933–1944* (New York: Berghahn Books, 2000).

Baranowski, Shelley, *Strength Through Joy: Consumerism and Mass Tourism in the Third Reich* (New York: Cambridge University Press, 2004).

Baranowski, Shelley, ' "Against Human Diversity as Such": *Lebensraum* and Genocide in the Third Reich', conference paper in the author's possession, pp. 1–12.

Baranowski, Shelley, *Nazi Empire: German Colonialism and Imperialism from Bismarck to Hitler* (New York: Cambridge University Press, 2010).

Barkai, Avraham, 'Volksgemeinshaft, "Aryanization" and the Holocaust', in David Cesarani (ed.), *The Final Solution: Origins and Implementation* (New York: Routledge, 1994 [2002]), pp. 33–50.

Bartov, Omer, *The Eastern Front, 1941–1945: German Troops and the Barbarization of Warfare* (New York, St. Martin's, 1986).

Bartov, Omer, *Hitler's Army: Soldiers, Nazis and the War in the Third Reich* (Oxford: Oxford University Press, 1992).

Bartov, Omer, 'Antisemitism, the Holocaust, and Reinterpretations of National Socialism', in Michael Berenbaum and Abraham J. Peck (eds), *The Holocaust and History: The Known, the Unknown, the Disputed and the Reexamined* (Bloomington, IN: Indiana University Press, (1998), pp. 75–98.

Bartov, Omer, 'Soldiers, Nazis and War in the Third Reich', in Christian Leitz (ed.), *The Third Reich* (Oxford: Blackwell Publishers, 1999), pp. 129–150.

Bartov, Omer, *Mirrors of Destruction: War, Genocide and Modern Identity* (New York: Oxford University Press, 2000).

Bartov, Omer, 'Killing Space: The Final Solution as Population Policy', in Omer Bartov, *Germany's War and the Holocaust: Disputed Histories* (Ithaca, NY: Cornell University Press, 2003), pp. 79–98.

Bergen, Doris L., 'The *"Volksdeutschen"* of Eastern Europe, World War II, and the Holocaust: Constructed Ethnicity, Real Genocide', in *Yearbook of European Studies*, Vol. 13 (1999), pp. 70–93.

Bergen, Doris L., *War & Genocide: A Concise History of the Holocaust* (Lanham, MD: Roman & Littlefield, 2003).

Berghahn, Volker R., 'Germans and Poles, 1871–1945', in Alan E. Steinweis (ed.), *The Impact of Nazism: New Perspectives on the Third Reich and Its Legacy* (Lincoln, NE: University of Nebraska Press, 2003), pp. 15–36.

Berenbaum, Michael (ed.), *A Mosaic of Victims: Non-Jews Persecuted and Murdered by the Nazis* (New York: New York University Press, 1990).

Berkhoff, Karel C., *Harvest of Despair: Life and Death in the Ukraine Under Nazi Rule* (Cambridge, MA: Harvard University Press, 2005).

Bessel, Richard, *Nazism and War* (New York: Random House, 2004).

Blackbourn, David, *The Conquest of Nature: Water, Landscape, and the Making of Modern Germany* (New York, W.W. Norton, 2006).

Blackbourn, David, 'The Conquest of Nature and the Mystique of the Eastern Frontier in Nazi Germany', in Robert L. Nelson (ed.), *Germans, Poland, and Colonial Expansion to the East, 1850 to the Present* (Basingstoke: Palgrave Macmillan, 2009), pp. 141–170.

Bloxham, Donald, *The Final Solution: A Genocide* (New York: Oxford University Press, 2009).

Bock, Gisela, 'Nazi Sterilization and Reproductive Policies', in Dieter Kuntz and Susan Bachrach (eds), *Deadly Medicine: Creating the Master Race* (Chapel Hill, NC: University of North Carolina Press, 2004), pp. 60–87; an exhibition and publication of the United States Holocaust Memorial Museum, Washington, D.C., book distributor.

Boll, Bernd, Hannes Heer, and Walter Manoschek, 'Prelude to a Crime: The German Army in the National Socialist State', in Hamburg Institute of Social Research (eds), *The German Army and Genocide: Crimes Against War Prisoners, Jews, and Other Civilians, 1939–1944* (New York: The New Press, 1999 [1996]), pp. 20–33.

Bramwell, Anna, *Blood and Soil: Richard Walther Darré and Hitler's 'Green Party'* (Abbotsbrook: Kensal Press, 1985).

Brandon, Ray and Wendy Lower (eds), *The Shoah in Ukraine: History, Testimony, Memorialization* (Bloomington, IN: Indiana University Press, 2008).

Browning, Christopher R., *Nazi Policy, Jewish Workers, German Killers* (New York: Cambridge University Press, 2000).

Browning, Christopher R., *The Origins of the Final Solution: The Evolution of Nazi Jewish Policy, September 1939–March 1942*, with contributions by J. Matthäus (Lincoln, NE: University of Nebraska Press, 2004).

Browning, Christopher R., 'The Nazi Empire', in Donald Bloxham and A. Dirk Moses (eds), *The Oxford Handbook of Genocide Studies* (New York: Oxford University Press, 2010), pp. 407–425.

Breitman, Richard, *The Architect of Genocide: Himmler and the Final Solution* (New York: Alfred A. Knopf, 1991).

Burleigh, Michael and Wolfgang Wippermann, *The Racial State: Germany 1933–1945* (New York: Cambridge University Press, 1991).

Burleigh, Michael, *Ethics and Extermination: Reflections on Nazi Genocide* (New York: Cambridge University Press, 1997).

Burleigh, Michael, 'What If Nazi Germany Had Defeated the Soviet Union?', in Niall Ferguson (ed.), *Virtual History Alternatives and Counterfactuals* (New York: Basic Books, 1999 [1997]), pp. 321–347.

Burleigh, Michael, *The Third Reich: A New History* (London: Macmillan, 2000).

Burleigh, Michael, *Germany Turns Eastward: A Study of Ostforschung in the Third Reich* (London: Pan Macmillan, 2002 [1988]).

Burleigh, Michael, 'Nazi "Euthanasia" Programs', in Dieter Kuntz and Susan Bachrach (eds), *Deadly Medicine: Creating the Master Race* (Chapel Hill, NC: University of North Carolina Press, 2004), pp. 126–153; an exhibition and publication of the United States Holocaust Memorial Museum, Washington, D.C., book distributor.

Burrin, Philippe, *Hitler and the Jews: The Genesis of the Holocaust* (London: Edward Arnold, 1994).

Burrin, Philippe, *Nazi Anti-Semitism: From Prejudice to the Holocaust* (New York: The New Press, 2005).

Cesarani, David (ed.), *The Final Solutions: Origins and Implementation* (New York: Routledge, 1996).

Cesarani, David, *Eichmann: His Life and Crimes* (London: William Heinemann, 2004).

Childers, Thomas and Jane Caplan (eds), *Reevaluating the Third Reich* (New York: Holmes & Meier, 1993).

Citino, Robert M., *The German Way of War: From the Thirty Years' War to the Third Reich* (Lawrence, KS: University Press of Kansas, 2005).

Connelly, John, 'Nazis and Slavs: From Racial Theory to Racist Practice', *Central European History*, No. 32, Vol. 1 (1999), pp. 1–33.

Corni, Gustavo, 'Richard Walter Darré: The Blood and Soil Ideologue', in Ronald Smelser and Rainer Zitelmann (eds), *The Nazi Elite* (New York; New York University Press, 1993), pp. 18–27.

Crew, David F. (ed.), *Nazism and German Society, 1933–1945* (New York: Routledge, 1994).

Dallin, Alexander, *German Rule in Russia, 1941–1945: A Study in Occupation Policy* (London: MacMillan, 1981[1957]).

Darré, Richard Walther, 'The Farmers and the State', *Völkischer Beobachter*, 19/20 and 21 April 1931, published in two parts, an essay reproduced in *Nazi Ideology Before 1933*, intro. and trans. by Barbara Miller Lane and Leila J. Rupp (Austin, TX: University of Texas Press, 1978), pp. 131–134.

Davidowicz, Lucy, *The War Against the Jews 1933–45* (New York: Seth Press, 1986 [1975]).

Desbois, Father Patrick, *The Holocaust by Bullets: A Priest's Journey to Uncover the Truth Behind the Murder of 1.5 Million Jews* (New York: Palgrave Macmillan, 2008).

Domarus, Max, *Hitler: Speeches and Proclamations 1932–1945: The Chronicle of a Dictatorship, Volumes One – Four* (Wauconda, IL: Bolchazy-Carducci, 1990 [1962]).

Dwork, Deborah and Robert Jan van Pelt, *Auschwitz, 1270 to the Present* (New Haven, CT: Yale University Press, 1996).

Dwork, Deborah and Robert Jan van Pelt, *Holocaust: a History* (New York: W.W. Norton, 2003 [2002]).

Eley, Geoff, 'The German Right, 1860–1945: How It Changed', in Geoff Eley, *From Unification to Nazism: Reinterpreting the German Past* (Boston, MA: Allen & Unwin, 1986), pp. 231–253.

Eley, Geoff, 'Conservatives and Racial Nationalists in Germany: The Production of Fascist Potentials, 1912–1928', in Martin Blinkhorn (ed.), *Fascists and Conservatives: The Radical Right in the Establishment of Twentieth-Century Europe* (London: Unwin Hyman, 1990), pp. 50–70.

Eley, Geoff, 'Ordinary Germans, Nazism, and Judeocide', in Geoff Eley (ed.), *The "Goldhagen Effect": History, Memory, Nazism - Facing the German Past* (Ann Arbor, MI: University of Michigan Press, 2000), pp. 1–32.

Eley, Geoff, 'Empire by Land or Sea: Germany's Imperial Imaginary, 1870–1945' Birbeck- Wiener Library Lecture, 13 May 2010.

Epstein, Catherine, *Model Nazi: Arthur Greiser and the Occupation of Western Poland* (Oxford: Oxford University Press, 2010).

Evans, Richard J., *The Coming of the Third Reich* (London: Allen Lane, 2003).

Evans, Richard J., *The Third Reich in Power, 1933–1939* (London: Allen Lane, 2005).

Evans, Richard J., *The Third Reich at War* (London: Allen Lane, 2009).

Fest, Joachim C., *Hitler* (New York: Harcourt, 2002 [1974]).

Feuchtwanger, Edgar, *Imperial Germany 1850–1918* (London: Routledge, 2001).

Friedlander, Henry, *The Origins of Nazi Genocide: From Euthanasia to Final Solution* (Chapel Hill, NC: University of North Carolina Press, 1995).

Friedlander, Henry, 'From "Euthanasia" to the "Final Solution"', in Dieter Kuntz and Susan Bachrach (eds), *Deadly Medicine: Creating the Master Race* (Chapel Hill, NC: University of North Carolina Press, 2004), pp. 154–183; an exhibition and publication of the United States Holocaust Memorial Museum, Washington, D.C., book distributor.

Friedländer, Saul, 'Political Transformations During the War and Their Effect on the Jewish Question', in Herbert A. Strauss (ed.), *Hostages of Modernization: Studies in Modern Antisemitism 1870–1933/39* (New York: Walter de Gruyter, 1993), pp. 150–164.

Friedländer, Saul, *Nazi Germany and the Jews: Volume 1: The Years of Persecution, 1933–1939* (New York: HarperCollins, 1998 [1997]).

Friedländer, Saul, 'Ideology and Extermination: The Immediate Origins of the Final Solution', in Ronald Smelser (ed.), *Lessons and Legacies V: The Holocaust and Justice* (Evanston, IL: Northwestern University Press, 2002), pp. 31–48.

Friedländer, Saul, *Nazi Germany and the Jews: Volume II: The Years of Extermination, 1939–1945* (New York: HarperCollins, 2007).

Friedrichsmeyer, Sara, Sara Lennox, and Susanne Zantop, 'Introduction', in Sara Friedrichsmeyer, Sara Lennox, and Susanne Zantop (eds), *The Imperialist Imagination: German Colonialism and Its Legacy* (Ann Arbor, MI: University of Michigan Press, 1998), pp. 1–32.

Fritzsche, Peter, *Life and Death in the Third Reich* (Cambridge, MA: Harvard University Press, 2008).

Furber, David, 'Near as Far in the Colonies: The Nazi Occupation of Poland', *The International History Review*, Vol. 26, No. 3 (2004), pp. 541–579.

Furber, David and Wendy Lower, 'Colonial Genocide in Nazi-Occupied Poland and Ukraine', in A. Dirk Moses (ed.), *Empire, Colony, Genocide: Conquest,*

Occupation, and Subaltern Resistance in World History (New York: Berghahn Books, 2008), pp. 372–400.

Gellately, Robert, *The Gestapo and German Society: Enforcing Racial Policy, 1933–1945* (New York: Oxford University Press, 1990).

Gellately, Robert, *Backing Hitler: Consent and Coercion in Nazi Germany* (New York: Oxford University Press, 2001).

Gellately, Robert and Nathan Stoltzfus (eds), *Social Outsiders in Nazi Germany* (Princeton: Princeton University Press, 2001).

Gellately, Robert, 'The Third Reich, the Holocaust and Visions of Serial Genocide', in Robert Gellately and Ben Kiernan (eds), *The Specter of Genocide: Mass Murder in Historical Perspective* (New York: Cambridge University Press, 2003), pp. 241–263.

Gellately, Robert, *Lenin, Stalin, and Hitler: The Age of Social Catastrophe* (New York: Alfred A. Knopf, 2007).

Glass, James M., *'Life Unworthy of Life': Racial Phobia and Mass Murder in Hitler's Germany* (New York: Basic Books, 1997).

Goldhagen, Daniel Jonah, *Hitler's Willing Executioners: Ordinary Germans and the Holocaust* (New York: Alfred A. Knopf, 1996).

Graml, Hermann, *Antisemitism in the Third Reich*, trans. Tim Kirk (Oxford, Blackwell Publishers, 1992 [1988]).

Gregor, Neil, *How to Read Hitler* (New York: W.W. Norton, 2005).

Guettel, Jens-Uwe, 'From the Frontier to German South-West Africa: German Colonialism, Indians, and American Westward Expansion', *Modern Intellectual History*, Vol. 7, No. 3 (2010), pp. 523–552.

Hamburg Institute for Social Research (eds), *The German Army and Genocide: Crimes Against War Prisoners, Jews, and Other Civilians, 1939–1944* (New York: The New Press, 1999).

Harvey, Elizabeth, *Women and the Nazi East: Agents and Witnesses of Germanization* (New Haven, CT: Yale University Press, 2003).

Harvey, Elizabeth, 'Management and Manipulation: Nazi Settlement Planners and Ethnic German Settlers in Occupied Poland', in Caroline Elkins and Susan Pedersen (eds), *Settler Colonialism in the Twentieth Century: Projects, Practices, Legacies* (New York: Routledge, 2005), pp. 95–112.

Heer, Hannes, 'Russia: Three Years of Occupation, 1941–1944', in Hamburg Institute for Social Research (eds), *The German Army and Genocide: Crimes Against War Prisoners, Jews, and Other Civilians, 1939–1944* (New York: The New Press, 1999 [1996]), pp. 116–171.

Heer, Hannes and Klass Naumann (eds), *War of Extermination: The German Military in World War II 1941–1944* (New York: Berghahn Books, 2000).

Heilbronner, Oded, 'From Antisemitic Peripheries to Antisemitic Centres: The Place of Antisemitism in German History', *Journal of Contemporary History*, Vol. 35 (2000), pp. 559–576.

Heilbronner, Oded, 'German or Nazi Antisemitism?', in Dan Stone (ed.), *The Historiography of the Holocaust* (Basingstoke: Palgrave Macmillan, 2004), pp. 9–23.

Heinemann, Isabel, 'Towards an "Ethnic Reconstruction" of Occupied Europe: SS Plans and Racial Policies', *Jahrbuch des Italiensch-deutschen historischen Instituts in Trient*, Vol. XXVII (2001), pp. 493–517.

Heinemann, Isabel, ' "Until the Last Drop of Good Blood": The Kidnapping of "Racially Valuable" Children and Nazi Racial Policy in Occupied Eastern

Europe', in A. Dirk Moses (ed.), *Genocide and Settler Society: Frontier Violence and Stolen Indigenous Children in Australian History* (New York: Berghahn Books, 2004), pp. 244–266.

Herbert, Ulrich (ed.), *National Socialist Extermination Policies: Contemporary German Perspectives and Controversies* (New York: Berghahn Books, 2000).

Herbert, Ulrich, 'Extermination Policy: New Answers and Questions about the History of the "Holocaust" in German Historiography', in Ulrich Herbert (ed.), *National Socialist Extermination Policies: Contemporary German Perspectives and Controversies* (New York: Berghahn Books, 2000), pp. 1–52.

Herf, Jeffrey, *The Jewish Enemy: Nazi Propaganda During World War II and the Holocaust* (Cambridge, MA: Harvard University Press, 2006).

Herwig, Holger H., '*Geopolitk*: Haushofer, Hitler and Lebensraum', *The Journal of Strategic Studies*, Vol. 22, Nos. 2/3 (1999), pp. 218–241.

Hilberg, Raul, *The Destruction of the European Jews* (New York: Holmes & Meier, 1985).

Hirschfeld, Gerhard, 'Nazi Germany and Eastern Europe', in Eduard Mühle (ed.), *Germany and the European East in the Twentieth Century* (New York, Berg, 2003), pp. 67–90.

Hitler, Adolf, *Mein Kampf*, trans. Ralph Manheim, Mariner Books Edition (New York: Houghton Mifflin Company, 1999 [1925/27]).

Hitler, Adolf, *Hitler's Table Talk, 1941–1944*, trans. Norman Cameron and R.H. Stevens, H.R. Trevor-Roper (ed.), (New York: Enigma Books, 2008).

Hitler, Adolf, *Hitler's Second Book: The Unpublished Sequel to Mein Kampf by Adolf Hitler*, trans. Krista Smith, Gerhard L. Weinberg (ed.), (New York: Enigma Books, 2003).

Höhne, Heinz, *The Order of the Death's Head: The Story of Hitler's SS* (New York: Penguin Books, 2000 [1969].

Housden, Martyn, *Hans Frank, Lebensraum, and the Holocaust* (Basingstoke: Palgrave Macmillan, 2003).

International Military Tribunal Documents in *Trial of the Major War Criminals Before The International Military Tribunal, Nuremberg, 14 November 1945–1 October 1946*, published at Nuremberg, Germany, 1949, Vol. 38, Document 221-L (Exhibit USA-317), pp. 86–94.

Jäckel, Eberhard, *Hitler's World View: A Blueprint for Power* (Cambridge, MA: Harvard University Press, 1981).

Jacobsen, Hans-Adolf, 'The Structure of Nazi Foreign Policy 1933–1945', in Christian Leitz (ed.), *The Third Reich* (Oxford: Blackwell Publishers, 1999), pp. 53–93.

Johnson, Eric, *Nazi Terror: The Gestapo, Jews and Ordinary Germans* (New York: Basic Books, 1999).

Kaiser, David E., 'Hitler and the Coming of the War', in Gordon Martel (ed.), *Modern Germany Re-Considered 1870–1945* (New York: Routledge, 1992), pp. 178–196.

Kallis, Aristotle A., *Fascist Ideology: Territory and Expansionism in Italy and Germany, 1922–1945* (London: Routledge, 2000).

Kaplan, Marion, *Between Dignity and Despair: Jewish Life in Nazi Germany* (New York: Oxford University Press, 1998).

Kay, Alex J., *Exploitation, Resettlement, Mass Murder: Political and Economic Planning for German Occupation Policy in the Soviet Union, 1940–1941* (New York: Berghahn Books, 2006).

Kershaw, Ian, 'The Persecution of the Jews and German Public Opinion in the Third Reich', *Leo Baeck Institute Yearbook*, Vol. 26 (1981), pp. 261–289.

Kershaw, Ian and Moshe Lewin, *Stalinism and Nazism: Dictatorships in Comparison* (New York: Oxford University Press, 1997 [1977]).

Kershaw, Ian, *Hitler 1889–1936: Hubris* (New York: W.W. Norton, 1998).

Kershaw, Ian, *Hitler 1936–1945: Nemesis* (New York: W.W. Norton, 2000).

Kershaw, Ian, *The Nazi Dictatorship: Problems and Perspectives of Interpretation* (New York: Oxford University Press, 2001 [1991]).

Kershaw, Ian, *Fateful Choices: Ten Decisions That Changed the World, 1940–1941* (New York: The Penguin Press, 2007).

Kershaw, Ian, *Hitler, the Germans, and the Final Solution* (Jerusalem, Yad Vashem: International Institute for Holocaust Research and New Haven, CT: Yale University Press, 2008).

Kipp, Michaela, 'The Holocaust in the Letters of German Soldiers on the Eastern Front (1939–1944)', *Journal of Genocide Research*, Vol. 9, No. 4 (2007), pp. 601–615.

Kirk, Tim, *The Nazi 'New Order' and Fascist Europe* (New York: Oxford University Press, 2004).

Klotz, Marcia, 'Global Visions: From the Colonial to the National Socialist World', *European Studies Journal*, Vol. 16 (1999), pp. 37–68.

Koehl, Robert L., *RKFDV: German Resettlement and Population Policy 1939–1945: A History of the Reich Commission for the Strengthening of Germandom* (Cambridge, MA: Harvard University Press, 1957).

Koonz, Claudia, *The Nazi Conscience* (Cambridge, MA: Harvard University Press, 2003).

Kühl, Stefan, 'The Cooperation of German Racial Hygienists and American Eugenicists Before and After 1933,' in Michael Berenbaum and Abraham J. Peck (eds), *The Holocaust and History: The Known, the Unknown, the Disputed and the Reexamined* (Bloomington, IN: Indiana University Press, 1998), pp. 134–151.

Landau, Ronnie S., *The Nazi Holocaust* (Chicago, IL: Ivan R. Dee, 1994 [1992]).

Leitz, Christian (ed.), *The Third Reich* (Oxford: Blackwell Publishers, 1999).

Leitz, Christian, *Nazi Foreign Policy, 1933–1941: The Road to Global War* (New York: Routledge, 2004).

Liulevicius, Vejas Gabriel, *War Land on the Eastern Front: Culture, National Identity and German Occupation in World War I* (Cambridge: Cambridge University Press, 2000).

Liulevicius, Vejas Gabriel, 'The Languages of Occupation: Vocabularies of German Rule in Eastern Europe in the World Wars', in Robert L. Nelson (ed.), *Germans, Poland, and Colonial Expansion to the East, 1850 to the Present* (Basingstoke: Palgrave Macmillan, 2009), pp. 121–139.

Liulevicius, Vejas Gabriel, *The German Myth of the East: 1800 to the Present* (New York: Oxford University Press, 2009).

Longerich, Peter, 'From Mass Murder to the "Final Solution"', in Bernd Wegner (ed.), *From Peace to War: Germany, Soviet Russia and the World, 1939–1941* (Oxford: Oxford University Press, 1997), pp. 253–275.

Longerich, Peter, 'Policy of Destruction: Nazi Anti-Jewish Policy and the Genesis of the "Final Solution"', occasional paper delivered as the Joseph and Rebecca Meyerhoff Annual Lecture, United States Holocaust Memorial Museum, Center for Advanced Holocaust Studies, 22 April 1999, pp. 1–30.

Longerich, Peter, *Holocaust* (New York: Oxford University Press, 2010).

Lower, Wendy, 'A New Ordering of Space and Race: Nazi Colonial Dreams in Zhytomyr, Ukraine, 1941–1944', *German Studies Review*, No. 35, Vol. 2 (2002), pp. 227–254.

Lower, Wendy, *Nazi Empire-Building and the Holocaust in the Ukraine* (Chapel Hill, NC: University of North Carolina Press, 2005).

Lower, Wendy, 'Hitler's "Garden of Eden" in Ukraine: Nazi Colonialism, *Volksdeutsche*, and the Holocaust, 1941–1944', in Jonathan Petropoulos and John K. Roth (eds), *Gray Zones: Ambiguity and Compromise in the Holocaust and Its Aftermath* (New York: Berghahn Books, 2005), pp. 185–204.

Lower, Wendy, 'From Berlin to Babi Yar: The Nazi War Against the Jews, 1941–1944', *Journal of Religion and Society*, The Kripke Center, Kripke Center Lecture, Vol. 9 (2007), pp. 1–14.

Lumans, Valdis O., 'A Reassessment of *Volksdeutsch* and Jews in the Volhynia-Galicia-Narew Resettlement', in Alan E. Steinweis and Daniel E. Rogers (eds), *The Impact of Nazism: New Perspectives of the Third Reich and Its Legacy* (Lincoln, NE: University of Nebraska Press, 2003), pp. 81–100.

Madley, Benjamin, 'From Africa to Auschwitz: How German Southwest Africa Incubated Ideas and Methods Adopted and Developed by the Nazis in Eastern Europe', *European History Quarterly*, Vol. 35, No. 3 (2005), pp. 429–464.

Marrus, Michael R., *The Holocaust in History* (Hanover, NH: University of New England Press, 1987).

Marrus, Michael R. and Robert O. Paxton, 'The Nazis and the Jews in Occupied Western Europe, 1940–1944', in Francois Fuet (ed.), *Unanswered Questions: Nazi Germany and the Genocide of the Jews* (New York: Schocken, 1989), pp. 172–198.

Massin, Benoit, 'The "Science of Race"', in Dieter Kuntz and Susan Bachrach (eds), *Deadly Medicine: Creating the Master Race* (Chapel Hill, NC: University of North Carolina Press, 2004), pp. 88–125; an exhibition and publication of the United States Holocaust Memorial Museum, Washington, D.C., book distributor.

Matthäus, Jürgen, 'Controlled Escalation: Himmler's Men in the Summer of 1941 and the Holocaust in the Occupied Soviet Territories', *Holocaust and Genocide Studies*, Vol. 21, No. 2 (2007), pp. 218–242.

Mazower, Mark, *Hitler's Empire: Nazi Rule in Occupied Europe* (London: Allen Lane, 2008).

Mommsen, Hans, 'The Realization of the Unthinkable: The "Final Solution of the Jewish Question" in the Third Reich', in Gerhard Hirschfield (ed.), *The Politics of Genocide: Jews and Soviet Prisoners of War in Nazi Germany* (London: Allen & Unwin, 1986), pp. 73–92.

Müller, Rolf-Dieter and Gerd R. Ueberschär, *Hitler's War in the East, 1941–1945: A Critical Assessment* (New York: Berghahn Books, 2002).

Mulligan, Timothy P., *The Politics of Illusion and Empire: German Occupation Policy in the Soviet Union, 1942–1943* (New York: Praeger, 1988).

Murphy, David Thomas, *The Heroic Earth: Geopolitical Thought in Weimar Germany, 1918–1933* (Kent, OH: Kent State University Press, 1997).

Nelson, Robert L., 'Introduction: Colonialism in Europe?: The Case Against Salt Water', in Robert L. Nelson (ed.), *Germans, Poland, and Colonial Expansion to the East, 1850 to the Present* (Basingstoke: Palgrave Macmillan, 2009), pp. 1–9.

Niewyk, Donald L., *The Jews in Weimar Germany* (Baton Rouge, LA: Louisiana State University Press, 1980).

Noakes, Jeremy and Geoffrey Pridham (eds), *Nazism 1919–1945: Vol. 3: Foreign Policy, War and Racial Extermination, A Documentary Reader* (Exeter: University of Exeter Press, 2001 [1988]).

Noakes, Jeremy, 'Hitler and the Third Reich', in Dan Stone (ed.), *The Historiography of the Holocaust* (Basingstoke: Palgrave Macmillan, 2004), pp. 24–51.

Peukert, Detlev, *Inside Nazi Germany: Conformity, Opposition and Racism in Everyday Life* (London: Penguin, 1993).

Pohl, Dieter, 'War, Occupation and the Holocaust in Poland', in Dan Stone (ed.), *The Historiography of the Holocaust* (Basingstoke: Palgrave Macmillan, 2004), pp. 88–119.

Proctor, Robert, *Racial Hygiene: Medicine under the Nazis* (Cambridge, MA: Harvard University Press, 1988).

Rich, Norman, *Hitler's War Aims, Volume 1: Ideology, the Nazi State and the Course of Expansion* (New York: Norton, 1973).

Rich, Norman, *Hitler's War Aims, Volume 2: The Establishment of the New Order* (New York: Norton, 1974).

Rich, Norman, 'Hitler's Foreign Policy', in Gordon Martel (ed.), *The Origins of the Second World War Reconsidered: The A.J.P. Taylor Debate After Twenty-Five Years* (Boston, MA: Allen & Unwin, 1986), pp. 119–136.

Rossino, Alexander B., 'Destructive Impulses: German Soldiers and the Conquest of Poland", *Holocaust and Genocide Studies*, Vol. 11, No. 3 (1997), pp. 351–365.

Rossino, Alexander B., *Hitler Strikes Poland: Blitzkrieg, Ideology, and Atrocity* (Lawrence, KS: University of Kansas Press, 2003).

Rhodes, Richard, *Masters of Death: The SS-Einsatzgruppen and the Invention of the Holocaust* (New York: Alfred A. Knopf, 2002).

Rutherford, Phillip T., *Prelude to the Final Solution: The Nazi Program for Deporting Ethnic Poles, 1939–1941* (Lawrence, KS: University Press of Kansas, 2007).

Schafft, Gretchen, E., 'Scientific Racism in Service of the Reich: German Anthropologists in the Nazi Era', in Alexander Laban Hinton (ed.), *Annihilating Difference: The Anthropology of Genocide* (Berkeley, CA: University of California Press, 2002), pp. 117–134.

Schaller, Dominik J., 'From Conquest to Genocide: Colonial Rule in German Southwest Africa and German East Africa', in A. Dirk Moses (ed.), *Empire, Colony, Genocide: Conquest, Occupation, and Subaltern Resistance in World History* (New York: Berghahn Books, 2008), pp. 296–324.

Schulte, Theo J., *The German Army and Nazi Policies in Occupied Russia* (Oxford: Berg, 1989).

Shepherd, Ben, *War in the Wild East: The German Army and Soviet Partisans* (Cambridge, MA: Harvard University Press, 2004).

Smith, Woodruff D., *The Ideological Origins of Nazi Imperialism* (New York: Oxford University Press, 1986).

Stackelberg, Roderick, *Hitler's Germany: Origins, Interpretations, Legacies* (New York: Routledge, 1999).

Stargardt, Nicholas, *Witnesses of War: Children's Lives Under the Nazis* (London: Jonathan Cape, 2005).

Steinweis, Alan E., 'Eastern Europe and the Notion of the "Frontier" in Germany to 1945', *Yearbook of European Studies*, Vol. 13 (1999), pp. 56–69.

Stoakes, Geoffrey, *Hitler and the Conquest for World Dominion* (New York: St. Martin's Press, 1986).

Taylor, A.J.P., *The Origins of the Second World War* (London: Hamilton, 1961).

Tooze, Adam, *The Wages of Destruction: The Making and Breaking of the Nazi Economy* (New York: Penguin Books, 2008 [2006]).

Traverso, Enzo, *The Origins of Nazi Violence* (New York: The New Press, 2003).

Volkov, Shulamit, 'Antisemitism as a Cultural Code: Reflections of the History and Historiography of Antisemitism in Imperial Germany', *Yearbook of the Leo Baeck Institute*, Vol. xxiii (1978), pp. 25–46.

Waite, Robert G.L., *Vanguard of Nazism: The Free Corps Movement in Postwar Germany 1918–1923* (New York: W.W. Norton, 1969 [1952]).

Wegner, Bernd (ed.), *From Peace to War: Germany, Soviet Russia and the World, 1939–1941* (New York, Berghahn Books, 1997).

Weikart, Richard, *From Darwin to Hitler: Evolutionary Ethics, Eugenics, and Racism in Germany* (New York: Palgrave Macmillan, 2004).

Weikart, Richard. *Hitler's Ethic: The Nazi Pursuit of Evolutionary Progress* (New York: Palgrave Macmillan, 2009).

Weinberg, Gerhard L., *Germany, Hitler and World War II: Essays in Modern Germany and World History* (Cambridge: Cambridge University Press, 1995).

Weinberg, Gerhard L., *Hitler's Foreign Policy: The Road to World War II, 1933–1939* (New York: Enigma Books, 2005). Originally published, in 1970 and 1994, respectively, as *The Foreign Policy of Hitler's Germany: I. Diplomatic Revolution in Europe and II. Starting World War II.*

Weinberg, Gerhard L., *Visions of Victory: The Hopes of Eight World War II Leaders* (New York: Cambridge University Press, 2005).

Weindling, Paul J., *Health, Race, and German Politics Between National Unification and Nazism, 1870–1945* (Cambridge: Cambridge University Press, 1989).

Weiss, John, *Ideology of Death: Why the Holocaust Happened in Germany* (Chicago, IL: Ivan R. Dee, 1997).

Weiss, Sheila Faith, 'German Eugenics, 1890–1933', in Dieter Kuntz and Susan Bachrach (eds), *Deadly Medicine: Creating the Master Race* (Chapel Hill, NC: University of North Carolina Press, 2004), pp. 14–39; an exhibition and publication of the United States Holocaust Memorial Museum, Washington, D.C., book distributor.

Westermann, Edward B., *Hitler's Police Battalions: Enforcing Racial War in the East* (Lawrence, KS: University of Kansas Press, 2005).

Wildt, Michael, 'Before the "Final Solution": The *Judenpolitik* of the SD, 1935–1938', *Leo Baeck Institute Yearbook*, Vol. 43 (1998), pp. 241–269.

Wildt, Michael, 'Violence Against Jews in Germany, 1933–1939', in David Bankier (ed.), *Probing the Depths of Antisemitism: German Society and the Persecution of the Jews, 1933–1944* (New York: Berghahn Books, 2000), pp. 181–209.

Wildt, Michael, *An Uncompromising Generation: The Nazi Leadership of the Reich Security Main Office*, trans. by Tom Lampert (Madison, WI: University of Wisconsin Press, 2009).

Yahil, Leni, 'Madagascar: Phantom of a Solution for the Jewish Question', in George Mosse and Bela Vago (eds), *Jews and Non-Jews in Eastern Europe, 1918–1945* (New York: Wiley, 1974), pp. 315–334.

Zimmerer, Jürgen, 'The Birth of *Ostland* Out of the Spirit of Colonialism: A Postcolonial Perspective on the Nazi Policy of Conquest and Extermination', *Patterns of Prejudice*, Vol. 39, No. 2 (2005), pp. 197–219.

Index